W9-BJN-751

Career Planning & Development for College Students and Recent Graduates

Career Planning & Development for College Students and Recent Graduates

John E. Steele

Marilyn S. Morgan

VGM Career Horizons
a division of *NTC Publishing Group*
Lincolnwood, Illinois USA

Library of Congress Cataloging-in-Publication Data

Steele, John E.
  Career planning and development for college students and recent
graduates / John E. Steele, Marilyn S. Morgan.

    p. cm.
  Includes bibliographical references.
  ISBN 0-8442-8558-7 : $29.95. — ISBN 0-8442-8559-5 (pbk.) : $17.95
  1. Vocational guidance—United States. 2. College students-
-Employment—United States. I. Morgan, Marilyn S., 1941–
II. Title.
HF5381.S742   1990
331.7'02'0973—dc20   90-36521
                                                            CIP

Published by VGM Career Horizons, a division of NTC Publishing Group.
© 1991 by NTC Publishing Group, 4255 West Touhy Avenue,
Lincolnwood (Chicago), Illinois 60646-1975 U.S.A.
All rights reserved. No part of this book may be reproduced, stored
in a retrieval system, or transmitted in any form or by any means,
electronic, mechanical, photocopying, recording or otherwise, without
the prior permission of NTC Publishing Group.
Manufactured in the United States of America.
0 1 2 3 4 5 6 7 8 9 VP 9 8 7 6 5 4 3 2 1

Table Of Contents

v

Preface

Although this book is written primarily for students in college and for recent graduates, it is also written for those who provide these students and graduates with career advice and assistance. This group includes career counselors, faculty, parents, alumni association network advisors, and employment agencies. The approach used in this book is that of an advisor giving counsel to college students or graduates on career and job matters.

From their combined experience the authors provide an understanding of present-day practices and resources, which should be helpful in counseling students and recent graduates on employment or graduate school matters, in providing a textbook for career courses in college, and in designing services for a career center. Students should find the sequence of topics helpful in approaching, formulating, and developing their personal career planning in a logical and systematic order. Recent graduates should find this material useful since many rarely realize how important their first few years after graduation are in developing their potential and furthering their careers.

Although parents may be willing to pay all or part of college expenses, they hope their sacrifices and contributions will enable their children to become self-sufficient and productive citizens. College students are quite idealistic, but they need also to be pragmatic and realize that a job is necessary to pay the rent, obtain "creature comforts," and be able to "live the good life."

In *What Color Is Your Parachute?*, Richard N. Bolles gave new meaning to the old adage: "Give me a fish, and I will eat for today; teach me to fish, and I will eat for the rest of my life." Graduation from college does not guarantee career success. Most college graduates will change jobs seven to ten times, and change occupations two to five times. That's why this book teaches "how to fish," that is, to understand the system, learn how to explore careers, chart career patterns, find appropriate jobs or graduate schools, and progress toward a career destination.

This book emphasizes informing you of the career resources available in college to help you take charge of your career and be in control of your life. It presents the principles, practices, and procedures that have survived the test of time as experienced by professionals in the field of career planning and placement. By applying the recommendations in this book to your personal objectives, you should be able to utilize your talents more effectively and, therefore, capitalize on your investment in a college education. Failure to take time out for career planning will lead to a combination of anxiety at graduation time, job dissatisfaction, fewer financial rewards, and a great deal of frustration.

This book should help you utilize your college's career resources more effectively, take an inventory of your qualifications and interests, set a tentative career goal, chart a course and a time schedule for developing a career, obtain the appropriate job when needed, and navigate successfully to your chosen destination with dependence on skill and planning, rather than on luck. With such career planning, you will, in effect, determine your own future.

The principles and suggestions in this book result from the combined fifty years' experience of the authors in developing and teaching career planning courses, in managing career planning and placement offices at four major universities and one business college, and in business and government personnel work.

Our experiences are enhanced by additional insights from recruiters and executives in hundreds of profit-making, nonprofit, government, and educational organizations. We also utilized data from research projects, articles and books, professional association meetings, and suggestions and experiences of college faculty and administrators, and from counseling many thousands of college students and recent graduates on all aspects of career planning and job seeking.

Based on our experience, it seems most practical to organize material on career planning in four parts.

Part I—Chapters 2–5 develop the concept of exploring and utilizing all the opportunities and resources offered by a college so that you can lay a real foundation for a lifelong career.

Part II—Chapters 6–7 help you appraise your interests and talents, and explore various occupational fields to identify those careers most compatible with your qualifications and ambitions.

Part III—Chapters 8–12 cover the practical steps in designing an effective campaign to launch or change your career, or to gain admission to a graduate school.

Part IV—Chapters 13–15 concentrate on the first fifteen years after college graduation, during which time you will develop professional status and, ideally, reach your career peak years.

Appendix A presents some pragmatic and theoretical theories of career planning to help you understand the evolution of thinking on how people choose their life's work. Appendix B provides the nationally recognized standards for ethical conduct in this field for schools, employers, and students.

The authors derive their own career satisfaction from observing students who take advantage of the many opportunities for growth and development in college, and who launch their careers properly, whether into the job market or graduate school. We are always disappointed to see students who have not utilized their college possibilities, who get a degree but not an education, and who lose valuable time in finding and advancing their careers. We hope this book will enable you to use a realistic approach to career planning, thereby achieving maximum career satisfaction.

We would like to express our appreciation to the many colleagues, friends, students, graduates, and employers who contributed their experience and thoughts to this book. Special thanks should go to Robert Calvert, Jr., Herbert W. Robinson, Robert K. Weatherall, Elmer J. Roka, Domenic A. DeLeo, and Lisa Pakus for their valuable contributions. Our appreciation also goes to Mary Weisslinger and Janet Ringuest for their thoughts and the initial typing of endless revisions of this manuscript.

Marilyn S. Morgan
and
John E. Steele

Boston, MA
January 1990

chapter one

The Importance of Career Planning

I n planning for a marathon race, most participants go through an extensive training and conditioning program, plan their strategy, and periodically check their progress. The marathon winners generally are the ones who had the best preparation, strategy, and perseverance. In contrast, many students go blissfully through college with very little planning about an appropriate career or future.

This book begins by introducing you to career planning—a lifelong process that affects all aspects of living. The importance of careers—the vocational path(s) you choose to follow after graduation from college—is seldom appreciated, and rarely enters into a student's thinking before the senior year.

By stressing the significance of careers, how your job may affect others, and the importance of work, and by discussing various approaches to career planning, we hope you will develop a better understanding of why career planning is becoming more and more important. Pressures from parents, work, and day-to-day living present a series of hurdles in one's life, but proper career planning reduces problems and helps develop the ability needed to cope with changes and seize opportunities as they become available.

One of the most important benefits from career planning is the recognition that you *can* control your destiny, thus increasing

1

your self-confidence and self-direction. Career planning does not solve all problems, but it does help to approach and cope more effectively with new problems.

Why Is Career Planning Important?

What happens when you graduate from college is of great importance to five different individuals and groups.

1. You—After spending four years of your life in college, thousands of dollars, considerable energy, and countless hours of study, you naturally are interested in capitalizing on your education. Though you enter college as a teenager, you graduate as an adult and are expected to assume responsibility and make a contribution to society in the real world.

2. Parents—Along with their financial contributions and encouragement, parents hope that a college education will result in a better life for their offspring. Parents believe that a college education will provide the kind of foundation that will enable their children to cope with the challenges and changes in life, while enabling them to earn their own living.

3. Your School—One of the major purposes of a college or university is to train students to become responsible citizens and leaders in their fields. The accomplishments of alumni have a great influence on the reputation of the school, and affect its ability to attract superior students, operating funds, research grants, and quality faculty.

4. Employers—The cost of finding, hiring, and training competent workers and potential managers has ranged from $9,000 to $15,000, depending on the field of training and activity. Employers count on college graduates to research and develop new products, to create marketing strategies, to improve communications, and to provide leadership in all areas. Frequent staff turnover is not only expensive, but also frustrating in conducting operations and in planning for management succession.

5. Society—Every city and state needs capable and concerned citizens to provide civic and cultural leadership to help make that community a better place to live. College graduates are expected to take leadership in planning programs, undertaking campaigns,

raising funds, recognizing and solving problems, and other activities to improve their community.

Approach to Careers

With such importance attached to college graduates' futures, it is disappointing to observe how apathetic and procrastinating many students can be when it comes to planning their careers. Sports, campus activities, and social events naturally merit support and participation; along with studying they provide the heartbeat of college life. But such activities also provide many excuses for postponing decision making regarding career actions.

Dr. Howard Figler of the University of Texas aptly segregated students' approaches to careers into three groups:

1. *The Divine Calling*—I have known what my life's work will be ever since the age of 10 so there is no need to explore this question at all.

2. *Hang Loose*—I am keeping my options as open as possible for as long as possible because I have no ideas what life holds in store for me and I don't even want to think about it.

3. *Grocery Store Mentality*—Just tell me what's available (on the grocery shelf of work opportunities) and I will choose the one that is most attractively packaged.[1]

Figler concludes that all three of these career approaches have a common basic defect: "They permit other people to have control over *your* decision process." Our experience confirms his conclusion. Not more than ten percent of college students know definitely that they want to be lawyers, doctors, or teachers. The other ninety percent have to search, analyze, research, experiment, and otherwise try to find the careers that would be best for them.

A second problem category includes the students who are mentally lazy or afraid to make decisions. Their procrastination is based upon the hope that something good will happen if they just wait long enough. Such naiveté wastes valuable time in determining what they want to do with their lives. Thinking and planning

---

[1]Figler, Howard E. *PATH: A Career Workbook for Liberal Arts Students,* 1979. Reprinted with permission.

are hard work, but the forty years after graduation reward those students who take the time to do career planning while in college.

The third category has a veneer of rationality and is unfortunately highly contagious. This is looking into the few opportunities most easily available, and making a decision upon that basis. Too many job applicants use this approach, thereby limiting their opportunities to the twenty percent of jobs that are widely published. Career planning is hard work and requires time and attention. As Figler states: "The temptation of a job offered by a friend of the family, a classified ad, or a campus recruiter becomes ever more inviting as time grows short and you drift into pre-graduation panic."

College training provides opportunities, and a degree opens the door to many career possibilities. But it does not guarantee success. Too many graduates feel their way through several fields, virtually bumming their way from job to job, from career to career, until they hit on one more or less to their liking, or more likely, until age catches up to them and employers are no longer interested in them. Too often they end up with work in which they are unhappy, frustrated, and have no prospects for the future. With the increasing cost of a college education and the increasing competition from more and more college graduates, the importance of selecting a career and charting its development is greater than ever.

The Importance of Work

The word "career" used to be applied only to professional occupations; now it is used for all people in all walks of life. The world of work has jobs, but people have careers. Today we think of career planning as a lifelong process, not just as an activity pursued during the senior year of college. A person's work influences his or her way of life, so choice of a career actually determines who our friends will be, the attitudes and values we will develop, the geographical area where we will live, the patterns of family living we will adopt, and how our leisure time will be spent. Therefore you should give careful thought to the way you wish to spend and utilize the approximately 100,000 working hours after graduating from college. Your career confers status and dignity upon you in the field of work, among friends, in the family, and most importantly, in your own conception of yourself.

Our society tends to look down on people who are idle and it believes, like Horatio Alger, that hard work will pay off in the long run. In spite of all the negative connotations of work, there is truth to the old adage, "there is one thing worse than working, and that is not having a job." The benefits of a steady job and a satisfying career are psychologically important to everyone, along with such monetary rewards as a steady income, paid vacations, medical and unemployment insurance, discounts on products, reduced or paid tuition, and other fringe benefits.

A job provides an environment, a small world in which you have a definite identity. Many students experience an identity crisis as they try to "find themselves," not realizing that the self is not something one finds, but something one creates. As Charles A. Reich wrote in his 1970 book, *The Greening of America:* "Work and function are basic to man. They fulfill him, establish his identity, give him his place in the community. Life without function is the nightmare of Kurt Vonnegut's *Player Piano,* not the dream of humanistic experience."

Employers always want to know your work experience and what you have achieved and learned in courses, extracurricular activities, summer jobs, volunteer work, internships, and co-op experiences. Such information, plus references, will indicate your habits and attitudes, and have a great influence on the employment decision. Students who are serious about their careers will realize the importance of a positive work attitude and work record, and strive to develop attributes that will enable them to have choices of jobs and careers. Strong motivation to do a job well not only leads to even more opportunities, but also enables you to make the greatest contribution to your profession, career, personal growth and development, and society.

Career and Life Pressures

More and more students today look upon work and earning money as a means of satisfying their needs (earning a living) and helping to fulfill their dreams and aspirations, including how they wish to contribute to the rest of society. People no longer work to subsist, but are demanding self-fulfillment and challenge. In previous decades "success" was identified with the pursuit of money, which often took on a meaning far beyond its real value.

Today, students' idealism is tempered with a pragmatic concern for the environment, equality of opportunity, and the dangers of nuclear war. They refuse to become work addicts and sell their souls to employers. Their criticisms of modern business ethics and the obsession with more and more profits and less service have definite merit, as do their criticisms of short-sighted government leaders. However, much of their discontent with our society has been due to the rapid changes in the past two generations—an ever-quickening pace that affects individuals quite differently.

In his fascinating book *Future Shock*, which is about what happens to people when they are overwhelmed by change, Alvin Toffler illustrates such changes by pointing out that in transportation, it took millions of years for us to reach a speed of 100 miles per hour with the steam locomotive in the 1880s. It took only 58 years to quadruple the speed limit: by 1938 planes were traveling at 400 miles per hour. In another 20 years we were able to double the speed again, and by the 1960s rocket planes approached speeds of 4,000 miles per hour. When the first atomic bomb exploded over Japan in 1945, very few people envisioned that satellites propelled by nuclear energy would be orbiting the moon and the earth, and that people would actually land on the moon and later have a shuttle aircraft going into space and returning to earth.

These and other scientific advancements, in Toffler's words, have become a "roaring current of change, a current so powerful it overturns institutions, shifts our values, and shrivels our roots." Obviously such rapid changes have a great influence on our economy, society, perspectives, careers, and value systems. Some individuals approach change with the zest of a challenge, while others become disoriented, feel that they are on a merry-go-round, and believe that changes cause our lives to be entirely out of our control. This defeatist attitude is fostered by all the ups and downs in our economy, the layoffs and unemployment, and the manufacturing competition from other countries that have such severe repercussions in our steel, automotive, shoe, and textile industries.

Inflation is another factor contributing to the uncertainty, anxiety, and resentment of students and other members of society. When people realize that their money, life insurance, and savings are losing value because of inflation, they tend to spend as if they want to consume everything in sight. Inflation has such a terrific impact that people feel our economic system is out of control, so they naturally feel dissatisfied and insecure because they feel they have lost control over their own fate and their financial destiny.

However, our government and business leaders are well aware of the necessity for making changes in order to compete economically on an international basis. It is important for us to realize that change is the only constant thing in our lives.

Although we may personally not be able to prevent misfortunes, inflation, or the impact of technology upon our lives, we do have a broad latitude in the way we respond to such pressures. We can become dejected and give up, or we can roll with the punches and adapt to changes by being flexible and learning from our experiences. Such a positive attitude and response will enable us to become stronger for the experience, and more capable of coping with future adversities. Career planning will enable us to do the best we can with the part of our lives that we *can* control.

Parental pressures also play a role in choosing careers. Most parents have some idea of what kind of careers they would like for their children. Sometimes these ideas are very helpful; other times they are irrelevant and actually harmful to the real needs and interests and abilities of the young person. Because parents usually know the likes and dislikes, strengths and weaknesses, and preferences of their children, their opinions and advice can be very valuable in helping students choose careers.

In a very informative booklet entitled *Are You An Occupational Ignoramus?*, Newell Brown responds to parental advice:

> Parental advice should be heard with skepticism. Inevitably, it is colored by emotion; concern for your welfare; a desire to feel pride in your accomplishments and aspirations; anxiety when you seem to be on the wrong track. Further, most parents have a limited and sometimes inaccurate understanding of today's world of work, but they're not to be tuned out entirely. Much of what you are and know you inherited or learned from them. And they know a lot you don't. The trick is to be able to glean the wheat of solid, useful information from the chaff, a neat trick if you normally feel your parents are either infallible or intolerable.[2]

College career counselors report students tend to plan the most convenient and easy activities, and that the most popular form of career exploration is consultation with family and friends.

---

[2]Brown, Newell. *Are You An Occupational Ignoramus?* (a leaflet published by the College Placement Council).

You Be the Driver

Each of us is a separate and distinct human being different from each other and from our parents, with distinctive abilities, interests, and aspirations. A natural teacher may make an unhappy computer programmer, a natural forester could be a frustrated lawyer, and an engineer could feel terribly out-of-place as a sales manager. When a person does something he or she enjoys and does well, real success and fulfillment are a natural consequence. Studying the careers of persons rising to the top of their respective fields, we find that they have certain common characteristics: they found something they wanted to do, believed in doing it, set their goals, and followed the dictates of their own hearts and drives.

Look at the careers of Larry Bird and Earvin (Magic) Johnson, both of them designated as the Most Valuable Player more than once in the National Basketball Association. Each man thoroughly enjoys his work, is very good at it, but constantly seeks to improve his skills. During summers when most professional basketball players take a long vacation, these two men play basketball "for fun," to keep sharp, and to improve their skills and performance.

If you wish to control and manage your career, you must take the initiative in discovering your natural talents and interests, focus on a career field, and plan your activities to progress toward your desired goals, as illustrated in the ROADMAP THEORY in appendix A. Take charge and determine what you wish to do with your life and career.

What Is Career Planning?

Planning a career is quite different from getting a job. Taking a job involves getting work as it comes along and performing certain tasks whether for pay, as a volunteer, or for experience. Individuals take jobs, but they choose careers. A series of jobs constitutes a career.

Career planning is *not* another name for job hunting, nor is it some kind of magical solution or panacea. Rather, it is an individual activity, and a continuous process that helps you determine what you would like to do with your working life. It involves identifying your own interests and abilities, exploring options, setting goals, and implementing plans. It requires considerable thinking, work, motivation, flexibility, and decision making. Its main objective is to enable you to make economic and personal choices that will provide a satisfying, challenging, and fulfilling career. By coordinating your interests, abilities, economics, and decision making (in short, getting it all together), you begin to realize that merging all these factors develops the confidence that you *can* control your career and life instead of relinquishing them to the whims of nature.

In an interesting article Dr. Benjamin Litt emphasizes that lifework planning, which is based on the work goals we pursue, ought to be equal and compatible with our personal and social goals. Such planning should result in compatible goals, thus reducing future disappointments and frustrations, and lessening the danger that you will put all your eggs in one basket and then lose that basket.

In summary, *career/life planning puts purpose and direction into your efforts!* Just as financial planning helps you take better control of your financial assets and manage your money more successfully, so career planning enables you to control your working life by selecting the most appropriate type of work commensurate with your interests, abilities, values, and ambitions, and developing that career to fulfillment.

If a budget in financial planning is used as a straitjacket, it takes all the fun out of planning and becomes more of a curse and a source of frustration. Similarly, if a career plan is interpreted too rigidly, it causes great anxiety when milestones are not achieved—such as a promotion that does not come when expected. A financial plan requires flexibility to cope with unexpected expenses or events. A career plan is a guide and serves as a measure of progress toward life's work objectives, allowing for job or career changes due to possible layoffs, recessions, budget cuts, mergers and acquisitions, or changing career interests.

Career planning will not guarantee a job or admission to graduate school, but it will help you understand the significance and relationship of studies and jobs. Furthermore, career planning facilitates goal setting so that the short-range objectives become landmarks toward your career progress and long-range goals and ambitions.

Figure I-1. Career Decision Tree

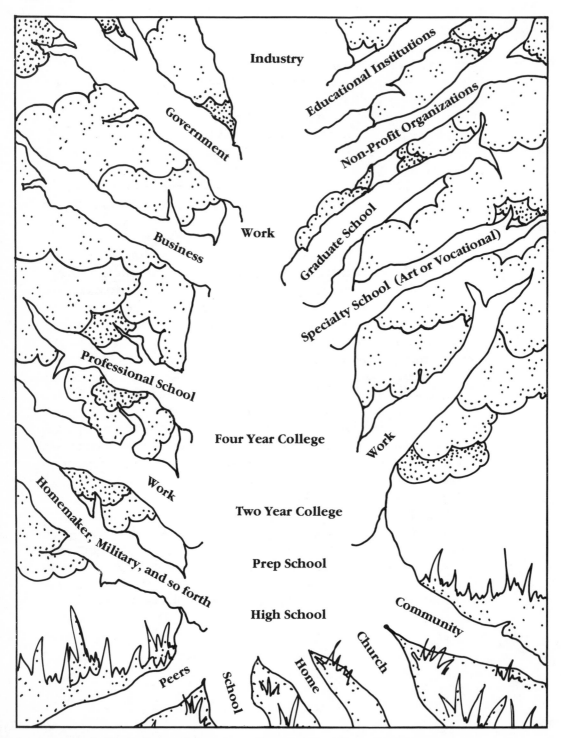

Industry

Government

Educational Institutions

Non-Profit Organizations

Graduate School

Business

Work

Specialty School (Art or Vocational)

Professional School

Four Year College

Work

Work

Homemaker, Military, and so forth

Two Year College

Prep School

Community

High School

Peers

School

Home

Church

Source: Compiled by the Boston College Career Center, 1977. Artist: Lee Lechtenberg

PART ONE

Your Career Foundation

THIS PART OF the book covers the various actions that should and can be taken during each of the four years in college, years during which you literally build a foundation for the rest of your life.

A firm foundation is just as important to a career plan as it is to a house. If you were planning to build a permanent house, you certainly would not build upon a foundation of shifting sand. It would be wise to search for a suitable site that would support the kind of building you have in mind, then get advice from family and friends, and finally consult an architect who would formulate your building plans into a blueprint. Such a procedure would enable you to engage a contractor who would then lay a solid foundation and develop your house according to your plans.

The Career Decision Tree in figure I-1 on the facing page illustrates the various levels at which alternative decisions are made. Just as a tree has roots forming its foundation, so people have their personal foundations influenced by their home, school, church, peers, and community. As children grow into adulthood, they may follow a certain accepted course for a time, similar to the trunk of a tree. At various stages in life, they make decisions as to which direction they wish to travel in; which branch of the tree is next on their progress through life.

You can decide to continue climbing the tree with more and more education, or branch off at a level determined by ambition, economics, physical ability, or other factors. Eventually, the educational trunk and its branches lead to careers in business, government, industry, educational institutions, or nonprofit organizations.

You should start thinking about careers in your freshman year, and build throughout the next three years. A career plan starts with your college education as the foundation for your life's work. Then, it launches your career upon graduation, and serves as a blueprint over the next fifteen years as you develop your career.

chapter two

Why Is College Important?

Before entering college, applicants take admissions tests such as the S.A.T. (Scholastic Aptitude Test), the A.T.S. (American Testing Service), or the A.T.P. (Admissions Testing Program). Having survived the lengthy, costly, and traumatic (for many students and parents) experience of applying to several colleges, students generally have several objectives in mind for going to college.

Although you came to college to get an education, there are others who also are interested in your college career. Let's look at your college education from the perspective of those individuals and groups to review its importance.

You, the Student

Investing four years of your life, and several thousands of dollars in obtaining a degree from a college, is warranted for several good reasons:

1. To prepare for a field of work that will result in a satisfying and fulfilling career.

2. To explore several areas of knowledge for the personal pleasure of learning, being informed, and appreciating some of the complexities of life and the world.

3. To qualify for graduate school and later life in a profession, or for specializing in a particular field of work.

4. To get credentialing, that is, a degree regardless of whether an education is obtained. To most authorities the credentialing objective leaves a lot to be desired, and is considered a waste of money and time that could have been spent in getting an education. By hoping that somehow the degree by itself will provide an entrée to a career, many students postpone thinking about careers because mental work is so much harder than physical work.

5. To succumb to parental or peer pressure because it is the thing to do, or it is a place to enjoy the last few years of being a teenager with little or no responsibility before entering the real world. Any thoughts of getting an education or preparing for your life's work are secondary.

One of the most popular statements summarizing why students go to college was made by Dr. James J. O'Connell, the former Director of Career Planning and Placement at Iona College and later at Pace University. He offered three reasons:

To broaden their intellectual horizons.
To get a better job and make more money.
To prolong the inevitable—avoid making a career choice, put off deciding on a job, avoid the draft (during wartime), etc.

One of the most succinct yet meaningful statements of what you can and should get out of college, was provided by Reverend J. Donald Monan, S. J., President of Boston College. In a talk to parents and freshman students, he articulated the goal of education and discussed these major objectives for students:

The goal of undergraduate education is to develop the "whole" person—intellectually, psychologically, morally, and physically.

To help students relate more easily to the above objective, the four parts were discussed by counselors in meetings with students.

The *intellectual* development comes primarily from the academic or formal side of college—the curriculum and academic programs; the faculty guidance and inspiration through lectures and advising; and the classrooms, laboratories, and libraries where students gain knowledge and skills.

The *psychological* development, often referred to as the *personal* development, comes from the nonclassroom experiences, the informal part of a college education. In social events sponsored by fraternities, sororities, dormitories, and clubs, and in other extracurricular activities, students develop habits, responsibility, poise, and maturity in learning how to work with others, how to plan events, participate in cultural events, and practice social amenities.

The *moral* development would come from having their ideas, ethical standards, and value system stimulated by University policies, and challenged and encouraged by peers and faculty. Throughout four years, students are exposed to different values and ethical practices. Slowly they develop their own moral standards, which will give them the courage of their convictions later in life.

The *physical* development is the easiest to comprehend since students naturally gravitate to the recreation building(s) and take an active interest in sports and other physical activities either as participants or spectators.

By budgeting your time and putting the proper emphasis on each of the above objectives, you can prepare yourself to lead a balanced life and develop as a whole person.

One of your major objectives is to obtain skills and competencies to be used in your career and life. You expect to learn *how* to learn; solve problems; research and evaluate data; present ideas or findings in essays or reports; segregate and distinguish between important and less important information; set up models and experiments and evaluate their results; record your thinking and conclusions on tests, reports, and term papers; present your ideas and thinking in class discussions and/or committee meetings; learn how to accept people as they are; and develop a sensitivity toward others in your daily living. You should also learn how to concentrate on a stated objective, and then figure out how to accomplish your goal by formulating and carrying out a program or procedure. By learning how to combine facts with reasoning and personal values, you learn to develop sound judgment.

Your College or University

In almost every statement of the purposes of an institution of higher learning, there is reference to three basic objectives: to teach, to research, and to provide services. Colleges and universities are expected to express the needs of society and also to meet the needs and desires of their students. Most educators would agree that a person's educational career and life achievements depend mainly on his or her personal commitment, dedication, and effort. The term "educators" typically refers to the administrators and faculty who formulate and implement the policies of the school.

A good summary of what educators expect of students was expressed by Dr. Henry Rosovsky, the former Dean of the Faculty of Arts and Sciences at Harvard University. He stated that "not all college graduates are educated persons, nor are all educated persons necessarily college graduates." He went on to state that the mental skills and powers of educated people have met a reasonable standard. Finally, he articulated six standards as follows:

An educated person:

1. must be able to think and write clearly and effectively . . . must be able to communicate with precision, cogency, and force.

2. should have a critical appreciation of the ways in which we gain knowledge and understanding of the universe, of society, and of ourselves.

3. cannot be provincial in the sense of being ignorant of other cultures and other times.

4. is expected to have some understanding of, and experience in, thinking about moral and ethical problems.

5. should have good manners and high esthetic and moral standards.

6. should have achieved depth in some field of knowledge, called a "concentration." In every concentration students should gain sufficient control of the data, theory, and methods to define the issues in a given problem, develop the evidence and arguments that may reasonably be advanced on the various sides of each issue, and reach conclusions based on a convincing evaluation of the evidence.[1]

---

[1]Rosovsky, Henry. "Undergraduate Education: Defining the Issues." In his Dean's Report, 1975–76.

Employers

From the viewpoint of employers, colleges should prepare students for life in a competitive and changing environment. After graduation employers will expect college graduates to know how our economic system and levels of government operate, be aware of our international relations and competition, have some definite career aspirations, and be able to apply their talents toward improving the future. As work becomes more complex because of technological advances, jobs will require a greater degree of specialized knowledge and creative skills, and employees will have to learn to cope with change. Employers depend on colleges to provide a sound foundation and the initial skills for students to begin a fulfilling and rewarding career.

After listening to countless speakers at employer's meetings, their viewpoints can be summarized by stating that education is not an end in itself. Any graduate expecting to enter the work force is going to have to continue his or her education throughout a lifetime, and be retrained or re-tooled as the years go by. Therefore, the kind of education needed is that which will open your eyes to the need for a lifetime of a study, and gives you the foundations on which your continued study can be based.

Small employers (in terms of the number of people employed) expect colleges to provide well-trained graduates who can step right into a job and help the organization. Because such organizations generally are too small to train college graduates, their viewpoint is understandable but not pragmatic.

Larger employers in all walks of life realize that colleges provide only a foundation, and that some training and development has to be given college graduates in order to bring out their potential and to utilize their skills and abilities.

Society

Various segments of our society have different but definite ideas as to the objective of a college education. Although most persons would agree that our leaders for the future in most fields will come primarily from the ranks of college graduates, there is considerable disagreement on how such leadership talent should be developed.

In the 1970s, President Nixon called for a massive reform of the nation's schools. Former Commissioner of Education for the United States Sidney P. Marland gave his views on how society can implement the necessary reforms in our educational system by stressing career education. He stated:

> A fundamental purpose of education is to prepare the young to live a productive and rewarding life . . . the main thrust of career education is to prepare all students for a successful life by increasing their options for occupational choice, by eliminating barriers—real and imagined—to attaining job skills, and by enhancing learning achievement in all subject areas and at all levels of education.[2]

A well-known psychiatrist, Dr. Walter Menninger, in a speech given before the Midwest College Placement Association, said, "Our most effective accomplishments will come from a mix of various viewpoints—no one group can solve the problems of society." Other leaders continually stress the need for the development of social, psychological, and cultural growth so that students will use their talents and skills for the betterment of society.

It is reasonable to expect that every one of you will have some future influence on various segments of society. Some emphasis on career planning should facilitate utilizing your college education for the betterment of all parties concerned. Taking advantage of the many career resources available at most colleges will definitely help you in developing your interests and talents, and in ascertaining which careers are the best for you.

---

[2]Marland, Sidney P. *Career Education.* U. S. Dept. of Health, Education, and Welfare.

chapter three

Career Resources on College Campuses

On every campus there are a number of resources that you can utilize to obtain information, advice, and other assistance for career purposes. Small colleges often combine several functions in one office or have part-time personnel available; giant universities will have full-time specialists working with only one career function. From a student's viewpoint, the following college service areas can influence your career planning.

Academic Sources

All students need help in ascertaining what courses are needed for their major, when they are offered, in what sequence, and what elective courses are available. Records of all courses taken comprise the credentials for job or graduate school purposes. The registrar maintains the official academic records.

For academic assistance, you should obviously contact your teaching faculty, members of the counseling services, the dean's office, or the administrative personnel in the respective teaching departments or school. Near the end of your junior year you should see your advisor and take an inventory of all courses taken and planned to make sure you complete all requirements for graduation during your senior year.

From a career planning viewpoint, your courses ideally should be scheduled so as to allow you the equivalent of a three- to five-hour credit course during your senior year for job searching and interviewing for graduate school or employment. If your school has a career planning course, you should take it no later than the first semester or quarter of your senior year in college.

There is a great need to clarify the relationship between the choice of a major and a career field. The major (also called a concentration) will determine the sequence of courses needed for degree requirements, but it often merely reflects personal likes and may or may not be related to your career choice. For certain fields (especially professional areas like accounting, nursing, teaching, and engineering) the major and the career goal are usually closely aligned. For nontechnical careers, a liberal arts or business background with any major will satisfy degree requirements, and provide a good foundation for a career.

You can derive the most value from your courses if there is specific information provided on the knowledge and skills that can be obtained, as well as their marketability. In most career fields, it is not the major but the individual skills that are marketable.

Graduate or Professional Schools

If you are contemplating professional education or graduate training, there are a number of places on most college campuses to obtain pertinent advice and assistance.

All college teaching departments require advanced degrees of their teaching staff. Such persons are the best local sources of information on the reputation of the graduate schools in their field. They advise on course offerings and options, fields of specialization, and which faculty should be assiduously cultivated at that graduate school.

For advice on admission to a graduate program, you may also turn to qualified personnel in the counseling services, in the chairperson's office for your major, in the career center, and often in the dean's office. They can help you ascertain which admissions tests need to be taken and when, what deadlines need to be met, and what references need to be obtained. They can also help you estimate costs and deal with other data and procedures. Their experience with a great many graduate schools will help you accomplish the paperwork required for admission, and provide encouragement when delays and rejections occur. A suggestion or inquiry by a professor or administrator for follow-up purposes has helped many students gain admission to a graduate program.

Counseling

One of the primary reasons for going to college is to grow intellectually, personally, physically, and socially. Throughout four years in college, you will acquire knowledge, skills, and a variety of interests and abilities. Experiences in classrooms, libraries, laboratories, extracurricular activities, and dormitories or fraternities and sororities will help you develop your own value system, and hone your interpersonal skills.

Practically every college and university has a counseling service staffed with full-time professionals to help you with personal problems, academic scheduling, testing, learning difficulties, and counseling for graduate schools. From a career planning viewpoint, the school's counseling service usually has the first influence on a student's career plans—often beginning with the orientation program during the freshman year. From this activity and continuing through all four years in college, the counseling service assists students in formulating their personal goals and evaluating their interests, abilities, skills, and values.

Through personal counseling and administration and interpretation of tests, counseling professionals can provide guidance on course selections and goal determination, encourage you to develop your interests through extracurricular activities, ascertain your aptitudes and abilities, learn about occupational fields, and evaluate all of these to select the most appropriate career and preparation for your life's work. Another important service of this office is giving referrals to other appropriate resources (people and places) that may help.

Another major way for you to get counseling help is to use your faculty. Professors obviously are experts in their fields, and are cognizant of the skills, interests, and abilities required to prepare for and succeed in their career areas. In working with the teaching faculty in laboratories, extracurricular activities, classrooms, and their offices, you should work hard to cultivate at least two professors who will know you well enough to give recommendations for graduate school or employment purposes. More importantly, however, they will be able to appraise your qualifications and interests for their career fields.

The career resource used most frequently by students is the informal but regular contact with fellow students. In dormitories, fraternities, and sororities there is generally access to upper classmates who usually are willing to talk with undergraduates about courses, social amenities, jobs and career resources on campus, which professors are "best" for certain courses, which extracurricular activities might be entered, and so on. The campus grapevine is an irresistible source of information, and one which can be very useful to you.

Work-Study Programs

On-campus employment provides you with opportunities to gain work in return for remuneration to help with college expenses. By working part-time on a regular basis, you can learn quite a bit about jobs in that department, cultivate a potential faculty member or administrator, and gain exposure to a field of work. Young people often complain: "Every place I go they say I need experience for the job, but no one is willing to give me a chance to get the experience." The work-study program on college campuses is an excellent way to get some experience, and most importantly, to make contacts with people who can open the door for career and employment opportunities. Because of its financial implications, the work-study program is usually administered by the financial aid office.

Values and Self-Identity

An examination of your values as they relate to self-identity is an important step toward developing your own value system (your personal moral standards), and also your self-confidence. Throughout all four years of college, you are constantly tempted and challenged through parties, activities, bull sessions, and other relationships to go along with the crowd or stand up for your own convictions. The peer pressure to conform, especially with drinking and drugs, can put great stress on your behavior, and may cause tremendous emotional turmoil for you.

From a career planning viewpoint, it is important that you have the courage of your convictions, and are confident of your own identity and values. The two major resources on a campus to help you with these issues are the counseling service and the chaplain's office. You can find these resources especially useful because they challenge your thinking and help clarify what moral standards really are important, while providing support for your value system.

Career and Job Assistance

For specific information on job openings in career or occupational fields, the career center is the official resource on a college campus. In addition to the usual occupational reference literature, this office can provide you with informational trends in various fields, starting salaries and future earnings, the immediate job outlook, counseling on a personal and group basis, workshops on career exploration and resume construction, job campaigns, letters used in a campaign, and computer assistance on self-evaluation, values determination, and resume compilation.

One of the most visible services of the career center is the campus recruiting program (discussed more fully in chapter 5) through which visiting employers and graduate schools interview and select seniors and graduate students for their organizations. This service is particularly helpful to you when seeking an entry-level job to start your career, since college recruiters do not expect students to have much experience in their fields. On small college campuses, career and employment assistance is obtained from a favorite professor, or through an office whose director has several functions, such as career advisor, financial aid, or admissions.

Life/Career Support for Women and People of Color

Some colleges have separate departments to provide assistance for women and people of color. On smaller college campuses, the office of the dean of students usually has such responsibilities. Larger schools may have a women's resource center, a minority affairs office, or similar departments that specialize in handling academic, financial, job and career, and personal problems for such students.

These offices can help students by providing books and other references on career explorations, searching out career options, discussing mutual problems or concerns with members of their own sex or group, offering workshops, and suggesting other resources and contacts that can be utilized. Although great progress has been accomplished in the past twenty years, women and students of color on campus still need more assistance in visualizing and obtaining career opportunities.

Off-Campus Employment

Many schools provide assistance to students seeking jobs for economic or experience purposes while in college. Through the financial aid office, the career center, or another department, you can utilize such a service to obtain exposure to the world of work and to a variety of career fields, while earning part of your college expenses.

Because of the high cost of a college education, practically all students have to work for part or all of their college expenses. Employment away from the campus is the most productive in terms of remuneration and work experience. Schools in metropolitan areas have a distinct advantage in having their students obtain part-time, temporary, and summer jobs to provide income and experience. Such work experience not only helps students get acquainted with the real world, but also gives them contact with a variety of workers, supervisors, functions, and organizations.

Through such work experience, you can learn the importance of good work habits, such as getting to work on time, getting along with fellow employees—even those whom you dislike—learning to follow orders, completing given tasks, and gaining a clearer understanding and appreciation of the working environment for one or more career fields. For the great majority of undergraduate students, acquiring a variety of work experiences is more important than income. Upon graduation, you will find many examples from your jobs to influence interviewers favorably when you are trying to launch your career.

Faculty/Professional Associations

Few students go through college without encountering some obstacles in their career preparation. Academic requirements are best handled by the faculty, the registrar's office (especially for items pertaining to graduation), or by designated administrators or counselors.

Professional job qualifications may include legislation or regulations specifying the requirements to become an engineer, an economist, a teacher, a nurse, a CPA, and an attorney, for example. These can best be understood by contacting the professors in that field, by writing to the pertinent professional society, and by consulting the designated administrators or counselors on the campus. On questions of discrimination regarding employment, you can obtain assistance from the office of affirmative action (if there is one at your school), from the career center, from knowledgeable faculty, and from the school's personnel office.

Potential career concerns combining academic, time, and money considerations (such as the clinical internship required of nurses and the practice teaching required of teachers), can best be handled in consultation with the appropriate faculty or administrative member in the pertinent department.

Internships

There are several types of internships that have a direct bearing on career plans: paid, unpaid, for-credit, and co-op. Each of these forms of internship carries a career connotation when compared with opportunities listed in a student employment office where jobs are obtained primarily for economic reasons. An internship enables you to gain firsthand work experience in a professional field while you are still an undergradute. It helps you test career possibilities, determine whether an occupation is really a good match for you, make contacts, and it provides you with an opportunity to directly contribute to an organization.

In **paid** internships, students usually work part-time while going to school or during vacation periods, in a capacity relevant to their career objective. Schools having a well-organized career center will generally have an internship office as part of their services. Professional staff members solicit internship opportunities to help students who need such work to earn money, and also to explore careers.

In certain areas such as public accounting, a professor may be responsible for coordinating the assignment of students who will go to CPA firms for six to eight weeks (for schools on a semester basis) or for a full three months (for schools on a quarter system). Students work full time, and get paid at a rate usually negotiated by the faculty member and the firms.

Unpaid internships are obviously more available to you since employers get free labor assistance. Such internships are usually offered through the services of the career center, but often are initiated by a faculty member on behalf of a student. Some schools call unpaid internships "externships," and often recent graduates offer students the opportunity to visit them at their place of work for a day of "job shadowing." Such volunteer work could help you explore career options, and is viewed by employers as indicative of a student who is self-motivated, dependable, reliable, eager to learn or serve, and probably a good team worker.

For credit internships involve the faculty directly. In fields like nursing and teaching, such internships have long been part of the academic requirements for graduation. In other areas such an internship could be worked out if you wish to research a certain topic for academic credit. If you can persuade a faculty member to supervise your project and then grade it (usually a term paper or a report), academic credit will be given. Some schools actively encourage students to pursue independent study and research for academic credit; prudent students will select topics pertinent to their career plans or topics of special interest to them.

Co-op internships involve employers, colleges, and students. Schools like the University of Cincinnati, University of Detroit, and Northeastern University have full-time professional staff members who solicit and cultivate job opportunities in a variety of fields so that their students can obtain hands-on experience in a real life environment while getting paid for their efforts. In other schools, a certain department may have co-op relationships with employers. For example, the communications department will assign students to internships with TV, radio, or newspaper organizations. Many co-op education programs combine five years of study and work for a bachelor's degree.

Education Outside the Classroom

One of the most significant and pragmatic career influences on any college campus involves your life outside the classroom. You can acquire the technical skills and knowledge for careers from classrooms, work in laboratories, research in libraries, and discussions with faculty members. In some fields such information and skills become obsolete within five to ten years following college, and it becomes necessary to take refresher courses or seminars to keep up with the field. In many cases, you may spend only fifteen hours a week in classrooms, so the nontechnical part of education is learned or acquired outside the classroom.

A much more pertinent career influence is obtained from the living arrangements and extracurricular activities that are so important for your personal and social development. In dormitories, fraternities, and sororities, you learn the need for rules and regulations, customs and traditions, procedures and rituals to be followed, penalties, and getting along with peers. Housing arrangements, problems, regulations, and activities usually come under the responsibility of the director of housing, the dean of students, or the vice-president for student affairs office.

Extracurricular Activities

Often termed "the fun part of college," extracurricular activities are coordinated by a student activities office, a student union, an office of student programs and resources, or by the faculty. Because of the popularity, cost, and almost universal appeal of sports, such extracurricular activities usually have a separate department in a college or university. If you participate in activities outside the classroom, you can enhance your personal and social development, and make lifelong contacts that often determine or facilitate career plans.

Most students who think they are athletes are well aware that participating and excelling in college sports programs may lead to a professional career. Unfortunately, the percentage of college students who actually develop professional careers in sports is very small, so career planning calls for alternative choices.

Skills Developed in Extracurricular Activities

Social Skills

By participating in campus activities, you can learn to work with a wide variety of people: fellow students, faculty, administrators, alumni, and community leaders or officials. Such participation helps you learn how to make and acknowledge introductions, to converse, to express your ideas, to contribute your thinking in meetings and discussions, and to close conversations. In many housing arrangements, especially fraternities and sororities, you may be exposed to a variety of social events every month, and learn from upper classmates how to dress for different occasions, acquire proper table manners, respect the privacy of roommates and others, and do your share of cleaning and other maintenance duties for the good of the house or dormitory. Your rough edges can get smoothed out, and you will learn to develop poise and self-control.

Managerial Skills

All extracurricular activities need a variety of programs and events to keep their members interested. Participation enables you to learn how committees work; why it is necessary to have rules, regulations, and procedures; how to get the necessary clearances to implement an event or a project; what safety or security steps must be taken; and how knowledge and skills are passed from seniors, to juniors, to sophomores, to freshmen. Without realizing it, you will acquire and start developing the basic managerial skills of planning, organizing, and controlling an event or program.

Planning. An important lesson to learn from activities is setting goals (long-range—for example for the school year) and objectives (short-range—for example for the particular event or program), and then determining how to implement these goals to obtain the desired results. Planning involves not only determining *what* is to be achieved, but also *when, how,* and *why* it will be achieved, including deadlines for each part of the work to be done. Planning also involves estimating expenses and obtaining necessary funds. Thus you acquire experience in budgeting. An important part of planning is figuring out how to get the necessary space, equipment, supplies, and people for the event or program desired.

Organizing skills.   These are developed when you get involved in separating and delegating tasks to be performed while implementing plans. Knowing how to separate the functions to be performed, and then selecting the right person(s) to handle the responsibilities, are valuable learning lessons.

Controlling.   This involves supervising fellow students and others involved to make sure each part of the event or project is being taken care of successfully and on time. You should learn how to organize and delegate a task rather than doing it all by yourself. When you learn how important it is to follow up on committees and individuals, you soon realize that the success of any venture depends on effective controlling skills.

Personal Skills
Participating in extracurricular activities enables you to learn the importance of getting along with peers, faculty and administrators, and visitors to the campus. Playing host to speakers helps you develop personally. Participating on committees enables you to contribute your thoughts and energies toward the stated objective. By assuming responsibility for tasks or functions to be performed, you will grow personally by gaining confidence in your own abilities and learning how to get results.

Such personal development will also help you form your own value system, since you will be exposed to the adulation given to athletes, the accolades given to scholars, and the quiet acceptance of most students who are not outstanding in any particular trait. Mingling with and participating in activities with fellow students will definitely influence your self-esteem, self-confidence, aggressiveness (or lack thereof), and moral standards. Thus you develop your own values of relative importance: what ethical conduct is most acceptable to having peace of mind, how much work and time needs to be devoted to studies and pleasure, which activities should receive the highest priority, and what degree of friendliness and trust is optimal in dealing with fellow students, faculty and administration, and others. Throughout college, you will find your conduct and ideas challenged frequently; active participation in campus activities will enable you to test the courage of your convictions and resist peer pressures.

A major part of personal development comes in the opportunity to cultivate friends, especially those with similar career interests. Friendships formulated during college can and often do last a lifetime. They are important in serving as a network of contacts during college, and even more so after graduation. The process of acquiring friends (either casual acquaintances or sincere friendships) will be especially helpful when you are seeking employment and need to utilize contacts. As alumni, you will find a network of friends particularly helpful in lining up potential job possibilities and interviews.

Friendships developed with students having similar interests pay off in another respect. By joining student clubs, employers may conclude that you have a real interest in such an activity, especially if your career interests are in education, nursing, accounting, engineering, or marketing. Such pre-professional interest on your part enables you to make contact with employers and alumni visiting the campus, and facilitates the job search for summer or career employment.

One of the most important personal skills to be developed in campus activities is that of teamwork. In sports and theater, students soon learn that not everyone can become the star or the hero. In extracurricular activities not everyone can become the president of an organization. But *all* students can develop the personal skill of teamwork. In all activities on the campus, and later in job performance, your teamwork is one of the first things noted in an evaluation by peers, coaches, and supervisors.

Leadership Skills

Every organization needs people who can organize activities, make suggestions, provide ideas, have vision, create action, and motivate others through their own commitment and enthusiasm. Campus activities give you many opportunities to test your own abilities, practice speaking before groups, make mistakes, plan agendas and run meetings, create programs or improve existing ones, get results, cooperate with others, and develop teamwork with everyone working toward stated objectives.

Leaders who earn the respect of their peers are elected to office. As officers of their respective organizations, they have more opportunities to develop their skill in budgeting time and money; in planning, organizing, and supervising events; in making reports to document the results obtained; and in contacting faculty, administration, recent graduates, and community members, As you develop your leadership skills, you will derive a great deal of satisfaction from knowing that your efforts and leadership were responsible for obtaining successful results. Your achievements will be especially recognized by employers when presenting your resumes and interviewing during the senior or graduate school year.

Communication Skills

Throughout society in all kinds of endeavors, we rely on our written and oral skills to communicate our messages to others. In various extracurricular activities on every campus, you will get many chances to develop your communication skills. You may find that you are adept at writing, and improve this skill by creating posters, programs, and advertising material for events, or by reporting for the campus newspaper. You may also take advantage of classroom requirements in writing themes, term papers, or research reports.

All campus activities give students opportunities to develop their oral communication skills. In club meetings, in committees, in pep rallies, and in bull sessions, you get ample time to express ideas, propose action, or disagree with others. You can develop the abilities to think on your feet and express yourself clearly and succinctly. During interviews for employment, oral communication is especially important. Too many students lose job offers and recognition for their accomplishments because they have not developed their ability to speak clearly, distinctly, and effectively.

All careers require a combination of both oral and written communication abilities. Throughout four years in college, you will have a golden opportunity to develop these skills, but it still requires perseverance and lots of practice.

Alumni Associations

Every college and university tries to develop and retain the loyalty of its graduates, and often calls upon its alumni for assistance in raising funds, participating in reasearch studies, lobbying before legislatures (especially for state schools), providing speakers for events on the campus, and other similar actions. From a career planning viewpoint, the alumni can be helpful to you by giving advice on jobs and careers, helping to arrange internships and externships, and providing contacts for networking purposes.

Practically all alumni associations now have information on the graduates from that college on computer databases. Depending on the school's policies and procedures, the data available on alumni could be obtained by appropriate persons. In colleges having an organized program, you can utilize the network of alumni. In the smaller colleges with an informal program, alumni can be contacted if you make the effort to cultivate the people working in the alumni office.

chapter four

Career Blueprint for College

Most colleges today have a full-time, professionally staffed office to help students with a variety of career services throughout all four years of undergraduate study and graduate school. Such a service is known by different names—career center, center for career development, career planning and placement office, or career services office—but the functions performed are very similar in all schools. (Throughout this book we will use "career center" for all such departments.) The primary objective of such offices is to help and encourage you to "know thyself," explore career alternatives, and reach decisions as to which careers are most appropriate for your combination of interests, talents, personal values, and life objectives.

You must, however, take the responsibility and initiative to utilize the career resources available, and to maximize the career progress that can be obtained during each year in college. At the University of California at San Diego, the Career Services Center uses the pyramids on the next page to advertise their message on career planning to students.

To help students develop their career plans during four years of undergraduate training, more and more schools are providing a blueprint to enable students to get the most out of their college

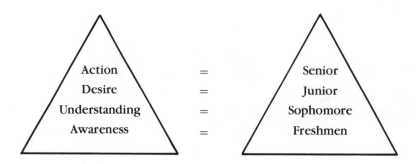

Action	=	Senior
Desire	=	Junior
Understanding	=	Sophomore
Awareness	=	Freshmen

experience. One school's program, which serves as a checklist to facilitate career planning and development, is indicated in figure 4–1.

The Freshman Year

Most students entering college lack substantial work experience, and are quite naive about the world of work. From a career planning viewpoint, you should use the first year in college to become knowledgeable with the many ways a college education provides the foundation for a career and a life. This is the time for inquiry and awareness.

Parents and counselors try to impress upon college students that their four years in higher education are really a preparation for life. To get off to a good start, you should seek the counseling of academic advisors and enroll in the core courses that begin the path toward a degree. For some fields, especially pre-medicine and pre-law, certain courses have to be taken in a specified sequence, beginning with the first semester of college. If you have a tentative area of study in mind (teaching, business, languages, engineering, agriculture, liberal arts, or sciences), the academic advisor can do a much better job of guiding you into required and helpful courses.

As a first year student, read and study the student handbook, which not only provides useful information about the school's rules and regulations, but also includes data on student clubs and organizations. These can play a key role in facilitating your personal and social development. Joining a club or activity of interest

Figure 4-1. Developing Your Career Plan and Self Development at Boston College

The following chart is issued during many career development workshops and programs at Boston College. Reviewing it may help you recall the people, activities, courses, and experiences that influenced your career decision making. Now that you are developing a career plan you can draw on the insights and achievements of your college years. The self-confidence gained from your accomplishments, and your ability to persevere, will serve you well in your career and job search.

Freshman Year (Inquiry and Awareness)

Consider college as preparation for your life.

Enroll in core courses with help of advisors.

Make a tentative selection of a major field.

Study the student guide to learn of resources available on campus.

Start your personal development (activities, internships).

Learn the academic system and utilize the bulletin and schedule of courses.

Begin to consider possible career choices.

Get to know faculty, counselors, and administrators.

Pick up bimonthly career center calendar of events.

Summer get a job—earn money—get work experience—learn to get along with people—develop maturity. **Vacation**

Sophomore Year (Assessment and Exploration)

Complete introductory courses in your prospective major field.

Self-assessment: compile interests, strengths, skills, values, and abilities; attend career center workshop and career/life planning sessions.

Utilize "DISCOVER" Career Guidance System.

Read up on fields of interest, attend career panels, get an internship.

Explore occupations: training needed, demands for jobs, and alternatives.

Make a tentative career choice.

Get to know counselors, faculty, administrators, and career advisors.

Summer get a job—earn money—develop skills and confidence—build a good work reputation. **Vacation**

Junior Year (Testing Career Decision)

Join organizations to develop leadership skills.

Utilize the career resource library.

Get a career-related internship.

Assume responsibility for making a decision on your life's work.

Consider alternative careers.

Begin to combine reality testing with values and skills assessment.

Test your qualifications for work in your possible career field(s).

Get to know faculty, counselors, administrators, and career advisors.

Take a course in career development.

Take electives in other areas.

Summer try out work in your potential field—compile inventory of interests, values, skills. **Vacation**

Senior Year (Job Search)

Complete the course requirements in your major(s).

Plan your job or graduate school campaigns.

Attend workshops on résumés, cover letters, interviews, job search techniques.

Take interviews on campus.

Discuss opportunities with faculty and counselors.

Choose the faculty and administrators you want to use for references.

Develop a timetable for your career development after graduation.

Learn how to network.

Source: *Boston College Placement Manual,* 1988–89, p. 18.

starts the process of developing friendships and contacts, and introduces you to other benefits described in chapter 3 under Extracurricular Activities.

It is vitally important to learn your school's academic system. By studying and utilizing the bulletin or catalog and also the schedule of courses, you can begin to appreciate the vast amount of knowledge that can be obtained from a variety of fields. In consulting with the academic counselor, you can learn the intricacies of scheduling and taking the most pertinent and desired courses, so that extra time can be scheduled in the senior year for job hunting. Counselors can also help in scheduling elective courses to enhance your personal development and supplement any courses pertinent to a prospective career field.

Through your meetings with the academic counselor during the first year, you can begin the all-important task of learning how to meet and get to know the members of the faculty and administration. Such a process will help you throughout the remaining years of college, and therefore influence your career after college. Developing poise and a relaxed manner when meeting and talking with your supervisors or superiors is an attribute worth cultivating.

On almost every college campus there is a newspaper published to give students, faculty, and administrators an update on current events pertinent to that school and community. If the college has a well-staffed career center, this office may also publish a calendar of career events. You should pick up a copy of the career center news not only to be aware of current career events, but also to participate in them whenever possible. During your first year, visit and get acquainted with the staff and resources in your school's career center, and periodically review the variety of internship and summer opportunities that are usually on file in this office.

Freshmen should investigate major fields by taking courses from a number of different departments, thus determining which faculty members can help with counseling and references.

After the first year in college, try to get a job that would provide you with career transferable skills. Searching for a job can be a very discouraging experience; the sooner you learn how to develop a job campaign, the easier it will be to get a job in the future. In addition to making money for tuition, living expenses, or just plain spending money, the work experience will help you gain maturity, learn how to get along with people, and start learning the ways in which an organization operates.

The Sophomore Year

The second year in college is very important for career planning. By this time the novelty and anxiety of entering college are gone, and you can seriously think of beginning your vocational inventory and looking into a variety of potential careers. Thus this year becomes a period of assessment and exploration.

In the last part of the freshman year, most colleges ask students to meet with their academic counselor to schedule the courses for the sophomore year, and to make sure the requirements for a degree will be completed on time. Once the academic scheduling is completed, you should devote some time to the process of compiling your vocational inventory. If the school has career planning workshops, be sure to participate.

A *vocational inventory* is simply a compilation and assessment of your interests, strengths, weaknesses, skills and abilities, and values. Because most students have only a limited (if any) work record, they usually need help in preparing such an inventory. Through the workshops or seminars available, you can receive the professional guidance and assistance needed to list and appraise your inventory. It is very helpful to solicit the ideas and evaluations of fellow students, faculty and administrators, parents, and former employers to obtain as accurate and complete a list as possible. Such information will be utilized in compiling credentials (mostly for teachers and nurses), and in composing resumes for employment, or for applications to graduate schools.

Some students may find it advisable to take a battery of tests and have the results evaluated and interpreted by professionals (see chapter 6). These are usually given by the counseling services office, in the tests and measurements department, or through the psychology department.

In metropolitan areas there usually are commercial and non-profit centers where testing can be obtained. Some organizations specialize in administering and interpreting certain types of tests, like the Johnson O'Connor Research Foundation, which works with aptitude tests through offices in fifteen cities. This organization tests clients for graphoria (clerical speed), ideaphoria (the free flow of ideas), foresight (comfort in setting long-term goals), inductive reasoning (problem solving and troubleshooting), analytical reasoning (organizing concepts in logical sequence), numerical ability, auditory ability, structural visualization (ability to see things in three-dimensional forms), abstract thinking, and personality. People who undergo testing pay a fee of $375 and, for an additional $35 per visit, may return at almost any point in life for further consultation.[1]

The major point to remember about tests is that they will not pinpoint a single career field or occupation for you, but they can help point toward broad areas of employment and suggest alternative career options to consider. The ideal is an occupation that makes the best use of your combined aptitudes, interests, values, skills, and abilities. To derive the most out of tests, professional assistance and interpretation is mandatory.

In some fields like teaching and nursing, the whole process of establishing credentials begins in the sophomore year. Although you have to take the initiative in analyzing and compiling your inventory, assistance and guidance can be obtained by participating in workshops run by the career center staff.

Students often have access to computerized programs like SIGI (System for Interactive Guidance and Information), DISCOVER, and CAREER NAVIGATOR to help them consider and evaluate various factors that are important in discovering their true interests and values, and which occupations would be most related to them. Such programs force you to think about your life's work, to make choices that narrow the endless career possibilities to a few relevant and practical ones, and then help in some aspects of the job search campaign.

This is a good time to cultivate or to emphasize interactions with peers, faculty, and family. These three groups can be the best resources for evaluating yourself, and for getting beneficial advice or suggestions. You should also make a special effort to get to know your fellow students, faculty, and administrators. During vacations or other visits home, family and hometown friends could be of valuable assistance in helping you compile your strengths and weaknesses as part of a vocational inventory.

While compiling your inventory, read available material on fields that might interest you. In addition to the main college library, most career centers have a career resource library. Perusing its materials will not only introduce you to occupational fields, but also help you ascertain whether you are interested in that type of work, and whether you have the training and other qualifications needed to pursue a career in that field. Individual schools

---

[1]"A Lab for Detecting Hidden Aptitudes," Sept. 19, 1985. Reprinted courtesy of *The Boston Globe*.

such as nursing and law, may have a separate library that collects and classifies material pertinent to that field, including career reference information. You should explore several occupations to see what training is needed, whether the field is in demand, and what alternative fields are worth considering.

One of the best places to start your research and reading is the *Occupational Outlook Handbook* and its special edition *Occupational Outlook for College Graduates.* This extensive research publication by the federal government's Bureau of Labor Statistics serves as a guide to career opportunities in a broad range of occupations for which a college degree is the usual background for employment. It analyzes the overall supply and demand situation for college graduates on a decade-to-decade basis, and assesses the employment outlook for college graduates. An important part of this publication is the information presented on each occupational field (see chapter 7 for details).

As recent graduates or other speakers come to the campus to report on their careers, you should attend to pick up ideas on that field, ask questions, and try to contact the speaker later to begin building up a network. As career panels are scheduled by the career or counseling services, you should attend and learn whatever career tips are given. This is also a good time to seek out internships.

Exploring alternative career fields through reading, discussions with counselors and faculty, and attendance at club or alumni panel sessions will give you a much more realistic view and appreciation of what is actually involved, and whether the qualifications and interests required in your chosen field suit you. During this year in college you should make a tentative career choice to provide some goal toward which future research and thinking can be directed.

By working closely with counselors, faculty, and other advisors, you can also explore ways of using elective credits to gain marketable skills beyond those that are acquired in your major. By spending enough time and thought in self-assessment and exploration during the second year in college, you will still have two more years to refine your career goals.

During the summer vacation between the sophomore and junior years in college, get a job to explore another type of industry or organization, and possibly another field of work. In addition to earning money, such a job would help develop skills and self-confidence, and enable you to develop a good work reputation.

The Junior Year

The third year in college has often been referred to as the best year in college. By this time students have learned the academic system, know how to study, have developed friendships, and look forward to beginning or concentrating in their major subject. Not only is this a fun year, but it is also a year of testing your career decision without the responsibility of entering the real world.

From a career planning viewpoint, there are several actions that should be taken during your junior year. The first is to analyze your attitude about career planning, and assume responsibility for making decisions on your life's work. The career resource library should be utilized fully, as well as the specialized libraries for different fields located throughout the university or college. Familiarize yourself with the services, and participate in workshops and other events arranged by your career center. Thus you can begin to combine reality testing with your values and skills assessment, and appraise your qualifications for work in your chosen career field.

If possible, obtain an internship in your preferred career field so that you can get a firsthand impression of what it's like to work in that environment, and what is necessary to perform the duties and responsibilities of jobs in that career field. The classroom environment in college does not adequately enable students to acquire the necessary knowledge of how to get along with fellow employees in the working atmosphere in their chosen career field. By your own observations and discussions with fellow employees, and by asking questions of your supervisor(s), you can obtain a realistic view of what is needed in that career field, and compare such data with your own desires and qualifications.

If you have not already done so, be sure to establish contacts with career advisors and faculty in your academic and administrative departments. They can help you evaluate and interpret various career factors such as interests, qualifications needed, where to get more information, and how to make contacts to help enter that career field. Instead of learning the hard way—through trial-and-error experiences—we recommend you take advantage of the knowledge and experience of advisors in their academic specialty. Such contacts can help you decide whether you are on the right career path, whether you should consider alternative career fields, and what courses can or should be taken in other areas to supplement your major or to give you another skill that will be needed in your chosen career field.

Because the junior year is so important in starting the advanced courses in your major, this is also the time to develop friendships with fellow students who have similar interests. By cultivating their friendship you can start building a network of contacts that can be invaluable after college. Most colleges and universities have student chapters of professional clubs or societies in each career field. By participating in such organizations' activities, you can become personally recognized by the faculty advisor, your peers, recent graduates who belong to that profession, and speakers who visit the campus to talk on some subject pertinent to that career field.

Developing College Contacts

For those occupational fields where the major courses actually start in the junior year, it is imperative for students to begin cultivating contacts that will have a great influence on their professional careers.

Faculty

Students are usually shy in approaching their professors because of fear of negative comments from fellow students. What they don't realize is that most faculty (and administrators) welcome inquiries and expressions of interest by students. One way to develop profitable relationships with professors is to ask them to elaborate on some point made in class; this can be done by stopping after class or by going to the professor's office. Not only will this approach clarify the unclear message, but it will also enable the faculty member to recognize you as an individual who is genuinely interested in the subject matter and wants to learn.

Another method is to take as many courses as possible from a professor you are "cultivating," and read or at least become acquainted with his or her published articles and books. This will show your interest and assure the professor that you value any advice and suggestions. If you need help in finding some written works, ask your librarian or go directly to the professor. If the professor has several publications, the chances are pretty good that he or she has good contacts in the professional field. If you are thinking of going on to graduate school, it is especially important to cultivate the faculty in your field.

Another method of getting acquainted with professors is to join the campus organization of their professional society, participate in its activities, and perhaps get elected to office, so you will have official reasons for visiting the faculty advisor's office. This is one of the best ways to develop a mentor who can provide new insights beyond the course work, open doors to opportunities, and serve as a reference for employment or as an informed source to discuss graduate schools and programs.

By thinking of your faculty and college administration as friends, you will find it easier to pay them a visit in their offices occasionally. But don't wait until you have a crisis. They will be more responsive to your needs if they already know who you are. Athletes know that coaches can help them develop their talents and skills and build on what they already know. Similarly, mentors can show you the best way to do things, introduce you to meaningful contacts, advise you on all levels of decisions and strategies, and help in the process of transferring knowledge and values.

Fellow Students

Without question the most used source of college contacts that are most meaningful for career purposes is that of fellow students. The friendships formed while studying, working on research projects, participating in extracurricular activities, and living in the same quarters, could be very influential in developing your career preferences, and later in developing your career.

If you commute to school, make a special effort to join activity clubs or athletics. You need opportunities to practice speaking in committees; to develop your leadership and persuasive skills; to learn how to plan, organize, and produce a program or social event; and to develop friendships that could become lifelong resources and influences on jobs, careers, and your personal life (commonly called networking).

Such organizations usually have the greatest influence on your social life, and present many opportunities for self-development, which could lead to leadership, political, and career aspirations. Daily contacts facilitate getting to know each other quite well, provide many chances for teamwork, encourage criticism and praise for your efforts, and enable you to discuss your career and other plans with someone you can confide in and in whom you trust. Comparing job opportunities, starting salaries, and other job search data becomes a popular pastime in the senior year, and can have a direct influence on your choice of a job decision to begin your career.

After graduation contacts with other recent graduates can facilitate making housing and transportation arrangements for the first job, and provide a sympathetic ear for problems. As problems develop on the job or in a career, the contacts developed with fellow students in school could be very helpful in appraising the working environment, evaluating job and career possibilities, planning a job campaign, getting referrals and assistance in the job search, and/or taking corrective action to bring the hoped-for promotions to fruition.

If your school has a career planning or development course, it would be wise to take it during the junior year. In practically all such courses, you receive a systematic approach to self-assessment, decision making, conducting a thorough job or graduate school campaign, deciding how to evaluate jobs, and in many cases, designing a career timetable to blueprint your career development after graduation.

By the end of the junior year in college, you should have a pretty good idea of your skills and abilities, and whether you are on the right career path. If still in doubt, the summer and final year remain to confirm your career choice or to change directions.

The summer between the junior and senior years in college gives you one more chance to try out a career field. In addition to earning money and gaining work experience, you should try to apply the principles of finding a job, which you learned about in the career planning or development course. During this summer job, pay particular attention to learning how to get along with fellow employees and supervisors, and try to develop a mature outlook on interpersonal relationships. It would be helpful to study the organization to learn more about its structure, its lines of authority and communication, and its informal chain of command.

Near the end of this summer period, you should compile a resume and bring it to the campus as soon as school starts for your senior year. By registering early for placement and career assistance, you can polish up the resume with the help of career advisors before the class assignments get too heavy, and before the campus recruiting program begins.

The Senior Year

The fourth year in college is obviously very critical for career planning purposes. The first important action is to make sure you satisfy all the course requirements for graduation. The next most important action is to focus on issues related to career choice. Then plan and implement your campaign for graduate school or for that first job after graduation to begin your life's work, your career.

If you did not enroll in a career planning or development course in your junior year, it would still help to do so in the first term of your senior year. In addition, make the most of all the services of your career center, including its workshops, and participate in meetings held by the department in which you are majoring, by the alumni association, or by student organizations in various career fields. Every college graduate should know how to compile a resume, write application and other letters, interview for a job, and design a job search or a graduate school campaign. These techniques are so common today that the college student who does not know how to utilize them is at a definite disadvantage. Obviously the better prepared you are, the better your chances are for getting the right job or being admitted to the graduate school of your choice.

One of the services offered by a college career center is the campus recruiting program, where employers send recruiters to the campus to interview seniors for entry-level jobs. Getting hired through this program is still the best answer to the old nemesis "we can't hire you because you do not have experience." Chapter 5 discusses this program and other services in more detail. If you do not take advantage of this opportunity to meet employers, you are missing wonderful and diversified chances to begin your career, or to compare graduate schools.

Because so many graduate schools and employers want references from applicants, you should make a special effort to develop good rapport with selected faculty and administrators. You should never use someone's name for a reference without getting permission from that person. Therefore it is important that your prospective reference gets to know you outside the classroom. You must take the initiative and make individual appointments with your desired references to seek their counsel, to discuss career plans, to obtain suggestions regarding prospective employers or graduate schools, to help evaluate offers from graduate schools or employers, and to benefit from the advisor's personal knowledge of you as an applicant.

During the job search or graduate school campaign, you should learn how to network. This phrase refers to the process of making and utilizing various contacts and sources of contacts to reach the right person, not only to make an application, but also to obtain favorable consideration for admission to graduate school or to get an interview for employment. If this subject is not covered in your school's career planning or development course, or in the workshops on careers, try your alumni association because networking is a favorite subject for alumni seminars. In larger cities you will generally find several organizations that teach you how to network to facilitate your job search or graduate school campaign.

In certain fields like teaching and nursing, it is necessary for seniors to learn the certification process and compile a credential file. Credential files are created by the cooperative efforts of the student, the faculty advisor, and career counselors, and are usually maintained in the career center. Chapters 5 and 8 have more to say about credentials.

It is advantageous for you to get to know a career advisor well enough to obtain advice and assistance on formulating the best strategy on individual aspects of a job or graduate school campaign. Such aspects include job hunting at a geographical distance, how to keep job offers or graduate school admittances pending, coping with parental pressure for getting a job by graduation day, and rejecting admittance to a graduate program or a job offer in a diplomatic way.

Assuming you have made that final decision to get a job to start your career, it would be wise to develop a preliminary timetable for your career development after graduation (see chapter 15 for details). From the notes resulting from discussions with advisors and recent graduates, your questions and answers from employers, and from your career research, you should be able to plot a timetable to set tentative goals for your progress and advancement in your chosen career field.

Graduate School

For certain career fields like law, medicine, and college teaching, graduate training beyond the baccalaureate degree is necessary. In some career fields, additional education is optional, but usually helpful. Some graduate programs prefer students who have had at least two years of work experience after finishing college; the comment most frequently heard from senior faculty members is "we want students who can contribute as well as take" from class discussions, research projects, or other graduate activities. An exception has been medical school where it has been better to try for admission immediately after graduating with a bachelor's degree. However, even this exception is being challenged as medical schools are admitting more and more applicants in their late twenties and thirties.

Positive Reasons for Considering Graduate School

Many individuals seek graduate education but cannot qualify, resulting in much frustration and many lost years. Before applying to any graduate program, you should consider the pro's and the con's. First, let's look at the positive reasons for going on to graduate study.

1. Is graduate school necessary to attain your career goals? In certain fields like scientific research, college teaching or administration, medicine, law, and consulting, advanced education is a requirement, so there is no choice but to consider graduate school.

2. Would graduate study help round out your education? If you have a personal desire to grow and be more fulfilled, then graduate study could add much more to your life. It could open more doors for job opportunities, give you more options to consider, satisfy your thirst for knowledge, and enable you to enjoy a fuller life.

3. Would it broaden your skills? Graduate courses can help you acquire or maintain technical competence not only to meet the standards (legal or professional) in the field, but also to change your career or to facilitate personal growth. In some fields graduate training is necessary to avoid technical obsolescence.

4. Would it give you an edge over your competition? As mentioned in appendix A, more and more people are going to college, and the competition often dictates graduate education. As indicated in appendix A, figure A–2, about twenty-five percent of all degrees granted are going to persons who have completed graduate work. An advanced degree does provide more potential to offer employers, and helps meet the growing competition.

5. Are you highly motivated and want responsibility quickly? Because so much of graduate education depends on the motivation of the individual, your learning and progress is much more dependent on how well you respond to the challenge of self-study. Not all people have the initiative or energy to cope with the stresses of graduate study. For those who do, graduate school can be a fasci-

nating and challenging experience, create new horizons, and provide multiple options for career purposes.

Negative Reasons for Considering Graduate School

Negative reasons for graduate study include the following.

1. To postpone a career decision or avoid employment. This usually applies to students who have not done their homework regarding the planning of their careers after graduation. Such students soon become disenchanted and alienated with graduate school, the field, and society.

2. Succumbing to pressures from peers, parents, and from the faculty. Graduate study for this reason results in mismatches and is a waste of money and two or more years of one's life; it often produces another school dropout. Going to graduate school because "it's the thing to do" does not provide the motivation to cope with its intellectual, emotional, and physical demands.

3. "I will find myself in graduate school." Graduate school demands concentration and perseverance that only those students who are committed can manage effectively. Self-motivation is a prime requisite for graduate study, with no one to coddle the students who are undirected.

4. "I got a financial assistance offer." Whether you get a fellowship, a graduate assistantship, a loan, or other type of financial assistance, this would be an incentive, but only if it is in the field you are truly interested in developing as a career. If not, any rationalization would be a poor excuse for wasting a year or two of your life. The growing complexity of all careers may cause an unwillingness to leave the relatively safe academic environment, where grades are clear marks of success or failure and constitute a certain logic and predictability, which are lacking in fields like business and politics.

5. "Graduate degree holders start out at a higher salary." This is generally true, but individuals may find themselves over-educated and underemployed in a specialized field. The cost of a graduate degree (tuition, room and board, books and supplies, and earnings you have lost by not working) may well turn out to be a speculative investment.

In summary, if you are contemplating going on to graduate school, have definite reasons for doing so. Be sure that they are reasons that fit into your plans for your life goals and aspirations. In addition, you should *really want* to go into a graduate program so you will be sufficiently motivated to spend the time and energy required.

Admission Tests for Graduate Schools

Since practically all graduate schools require your test scores as part of the application process, you should find out which tests are appropriate for your particular field of study. Among the most common tests in usage at the present time are:

LSAT (Law School Admission Test)

This consists of six 35-minute sections of multiple-choice questions and one 30-minute writing sample, and is given five times a year. It is designed to measure reading comprehension, logical reasoning using verbal and quantitative materials, and skill in the use of standard written English. This test is given at test centers in all states, Canada, Puerto Rico, and many foreign countries. The current fee is $63 for LSAT. Specific information can be obtained by contacting Law School Admission Council/Law School Admission Services, Box 2000, Newtown, PA 18940–0998.

MCAT (Medical College Admission Test)

This test lasts a full day, and is given twice a year—fall and spring. It is designed to measure an applicant's knowledge in biology, chemistry, and physics; application of specified scientific knowledge to solve related problems; and basic reasoning skills through the ability to comprehend, evaluate, and utilize information presented in narrative, tabular, and graphic formats. The fee currently is $75. Specific information can be obtained by contacting MCAT Registration, American College Testing Programs, P.O. Box 414, 2255 North Dubuque Road, Iowa City, IA 52243.

GRE (Graduate Record Examination)

This test consists of seven 30-minute sections. The general aptitude test provides a general scholastic ability at the graduate level; it is designed to measure verbal, quantitative, and analytical abilities. The subject tests are designed to measure knowledge and understanding of subject matter, that is, your mastery and comprehension of material basic to success in the field of a specific graduate major. The GRE is offered in many cities in the United States and in 106 foreign nations several times a year. The fee is currently $29 for each test in the U. S. and Puerto Rico; in other locations the fee is $39 for a single test, or $58 for both the general and one subject test. More information can be obtained by contacting Graduate Record Examinations, Educational Testing Service, P. O. Box 6000, Princeton, NJ 08541–6000.

GMAT (Graduate Management Admissions Test)

This is a four-hour test measuring general verbal and mathematical abilities that are developed over a long period and are associated with success in the first year at a graduate school of management. Specific knowledge of business subjects is *not* tested. The test is administered four times a year, and the current fee is $28 in the U. S. and its territories, and $34 for test centers elsewhere.

The quantitative section of the test measures basic mathematical skills, understanding of elementary concepts, the ability to reason quantitatively, solving quantitative problems, and interpreting graphic data. The verbal sections measure ability to understand and evaluate what is read, and to recognize basic conventions of standard written English. For additional information, contact Graduate Management Admissions Test, Educational Testing Service, CN 6103, Princeton, NJ 08541–6103.

NTE (National Teachers Examination)

Consists of a core battery, which includes 3 two-hour tests of communication skills, general knowledge, and professional knowledge. It is administered three times a year and the current fees are $35 for one core battery test, $45 for two, and $50 for all three tests if taken on the same day. Specialty area tests measure understanding of the content and methods applicable to thirty subject areas; each of these takes two hours, the fee is $40, and they are given three times a year. More information can be obtained by contacting NTE Programs, Educational Testing Service, CN 6050, Princeton, NJ 08541–6050.

TOEFL (Test of English as a Foreign Language)

The purpose of this test is to evaluate the English proficiency of people whose native language is not English. The test uses a multiple-choice format and consists of three sections. The listening comprehension section measures the ability to understand spoken English. The structure and written expression section measures the ability to recognize language that is appropriate for standard written English. The vocabulary and reading comprehension section measures the ability to understand nontechnical reading matter. The test is given at more that 1,100 test centers in 170 countries and areas, and is required by over 2,300 colleges and universities in the United States and Canada. The current fee is $27 for the International Testing Program and $35 for the Special Center Testing Program. Further information can be obtained by writing to TOEFL, CN 6151, Princeton, NJ 08541–6151.

MAT (Miller Analogies Test)
This is a high-level mental ability test that requires the solution of one hundred intellectual problems stated in the form of analogies. The items sample a number of fields such as literature, mathematics, fine arts, natural science, and social science. The test takes fifty minutes, and is offered at more than 600 test centers in the United States and Canada. Schedules and fees are determined by each center. More information is available from Psychological Corporation, 555 Academic Court, San Antonio, TX 78204–0952.

Other Tests
In addition to the above, there are several other aptitude tests for admission to graduate school programs. These include DAT (dental), OAT (optometry), PCAT (pharmacy), and VAT (veterinary) aptitude tests. Detailed information on these and other graduate admission tests can be found in reference volumes such as *Peterson's Graduate and Professional Programs*, or in *Lovejoy's College Guide*. Pamphlets and forms for most of the tests used for graduate school admission purposes are usually available in each school's career center and sometimes in the department or dean's office.

Because the fee structures change periodically, if you are contemplating going on to graduate school, get the most current pamphlet providing information on the test for admission in the field you plan to study. If unavailable on your campus, you can always write to the Educational Testing Service in Princeton, NJ 08541, and ask for the appropriate bulletin in your field of interest. Some bookstores will have publications such as the Graduate School Guide, which provides a comprehensive directory of graduate schools by regions.

If you are quite certain you need or want to go on to graduate school, you should begin maintaining the necessary academic record from the first year in college. Practically all graduate schools try to be selective, with a high scholastic average (preferably the top ten to twenty-five percent of your undergraduate class) as a primary admission requirement.

The Kaplan Test Preparation Program

Some college graduates feel a need for preparatory work to ensure making a satisfactory passing score on entrance exams for admission to a graduate school program. Just as the Berlitz Language Centers help individuals learn a specific language and customs of a certain nation, so too the Kaplan program helps prepare applicants to take one of the more common tests discussed above to improve their chances for admittance to a graduate program.

The Kaplan program typically begins with a diagnostic analysis of an applicant's strengths and weaknesses, and provides valuable tips to save time and effort. In addition to experienced instruction in classes, the Kaplan program includes test-based practice, home study material, and TEST-N-TAPE review (audio-tape reinforcement). Included in their packet of material is a review of admissions standards, recommendations, and the personal essay. In addition, the packet includes an admissions calendar and special track sheets to meet deadlines.

This organization operates in approximately forty states and provinces in the United States and Canada, and in other locations. Class sessions usually meet twice a week in the evening and on weekends, lasting about four hours. The number of classes varies with the program (for the GRE, there are nine class sessions; for the GMAT, eight). The tuition at present is $595 for the GMAT and $495 for the GRE. Interested applicants can call a toll-free number 800-KAP-TEST; write to the executive offices of the Stanley H. Kaplan Educational Center, Ltd., at 131 W. 56th Street, New York, NY 10019; or check the yellow pages for their local Kaplan center.

chapter five

Utilizing Your Career Center Services

The most logical and helpful place to start your career planning process is in your own college's career center, which is specifically designed to provide and help students and recent graduates with career services. To maximize the benefits provided by this career service, you should put in some extra effort because "you only get out of it what you put into it." Motivated students should start in the freshman year to learn of available services, and then utilize them for the remaining three years in college.

Career Services

Career Counseling

The most important service provided by the college career center is career counseling. Few college students have much knowledge of the great variety of occupational fields available, slight knowledge of their own interests and talents, and very little skill in understanding and successfully executing a systematic and effective campaign to obtain the right job to launch their career after college. Professionals in the career center can suggest a strategy to follow throughout college that will help you achieve your career goal.

The professional staff in your college career center office is student oriented, bringing its cumulative knowledge and experience to focus on each individual student's problems, while making appropriate suggestions for each step in the career planning process. In contrast, employers are job oriented, which requires sifting through many applicants to select the best candidate available for the position. Your career center staff is the most readily available source for all kinds of career and graduate school counseling, information, and resources. Students who have received career counseling generally have more self-confidence, thus making them more marketable.

Career Workshops

Because students often have similar needs, group sessions provide the maximum service to the greatest number of students. Group advising takes many forms, from informal meetings with a career counselor or professor, to organized seminars and workshops having specific agendas and assignments or exercises. The first month or two of each school term is usually devoted to group career sessions so that students can utilize the remainder of the academic year to work on the most appropriate phases of career planning at their level.

Career workshops introduce students to the career/life planning process, and also to topics such as self-assessment, resume preparation, creative job search, interviewing, letter writing, starting salaries, decision making, and related topics. Depending on student demand, special workshops are arranged for student clubs and pre-professional organizations, women and the job hunt, tips for minority students, graduate and professional school planning, researching the job market, and so on. A typical schedule of workshops conducted by the Career Center at the University of Maine, is illustrated in figure 5-1.

Some group sessions are arranged by level in college (freshmen, sophomores, juniors, seniors, and graduate). The professional staff of the career center selects topics and discusses issues of pertinent interest to students at that level. Emphasis is placed on what career action should be taken during that year in college.

Career Library

Depending on the support provided by top college administrators, the amount of career resource materials available to students

Figure 5-1. Workshop Schedules

GROUP WORKSHOPS

Career Planning and Placement Workshops are 50-minute seminars that present useful information about various career planning and placement topics. These workshops are free and will be held in the Seminar Room of the CP&P Office, Wingate Hall. Sign-ups for the workshops will be on the bulletin board in the hallway outside the Seminar Room. PLAN TO ATTEND! If you are unable to attend a particular workshop, you may schedule a time to view the videotaped workshop. Some of the workshops to be presented this year include:

• *Discovering and Marketing Your Skills*—Identification of things you do well and enjoy is essential to a successful job search. This workshop will help you identify these skills and demonstrate how to describe them in ways that maximize your chances of finding suitable employment.

• *Putting Your Best Foot Forward: Resume Writing Made Easy*—How to present your skills and qualifications in a concise, informative, and attractive manner. Material covered will include basic principles of successful résumés as well as different formats and their respective advantages and disadvantages.

• *Creative Cover Letters: How To Write Them*—Creation of the effective cover letter is the focus of this workshop. Content and proper format will be discussed.

• *Sweaty Palms: The Art of Interviewing*—Successful interviewing made easier. Topics discussed include personal skill identification, researching the employer, anticipating and preparing for employer questions, and the basic strategies of interviewing.

• *Jobs . . . Jobs . . . Jobs . . .: How To Find Them*—A discussion of strategies to identify, locate, and contact potential employers.

• *Preparing For The Second Interview*—A second interview or plant visit presents new hurdles to overcome. Veterans of second interviews will share their experiences, discussing the differences between the first and second interviews, how they prepared themselves, and what they found successful.

• *Practice Makes Perfect: Interview Rehearsals*—An opportunity for a dress rehearsal of your upcoming interview. The interview will be videotaped, allowing the participant to evaluate his/her performance with a professional staff member.

• *Understanding The Maze of Government Employment*—This workshop will help the participant learn to identify potential governmental employment opportunities as well as become familiar with application procedures.

Following is a partial 1986–87 WORKSHOP SCHEDULE

FALL WORKSHOP SCHEDULE

Tues.	9/16	Putting Your Best Foot Forward: Resume Writing Made Easy	9:30 A.M.
Wed.	9/17	Sweaty Palms: The Art of Interviewing	11:00 A.M.
Thurs.	9/18	Jobs . . . Jobs . . . Jobs . . .: How To Find Them	2:10 P.M.
Mon.	9/22	Putting Your Best Foot Forward: Resume Writing Made Easy	3:30 P.M.
Tues.	9/23	Sweaty Palms: The Art of Interviewing	2:10 P.M.
Wed.	9/24	Putting Your Best Foot Forward: Resume Writing Made Easy	10:00 A.M.
Thurs.	9/25	Putting Your Best Foot Forward: Resume Writing Made Easy	2:10 P.M.
Mon.	9/29	Sweaty Palms: The Art of Interviewing	3:30 P.M.
Wed.	10/1	Creative Cover Letters: How To Write Them	9:00 A.M.
Thurs.	10/2	Putting Your Best Foot Forward: Resume Writing Made Easy	11:00 A.M.
Wed.	10/8	Getting Work Experience: Summer Job Searching	2:10 P.M.
Thurs.	10/9	Creative Cover Letters: How To Write Them	3:30 P.M.
Mon.	10/13	Sweaty Palms: The Art of Interviewing	9:00 A.M.
Tues.	10/14	Putting Your Best Foot Forward: Resume Writing Made Easy	3:30 P.M.
Mon.	10/27	Putting Your Best Foot Forward: Resume Writing Made Easy	9:00 A.M.
Tues.	10/28	Sweaty Palms: The Art of Interviewing	11:00 A.M.
Mon.	11/3	Getting Work Experience: Summer Job Searching	9:00 A.M.
Wed.	11/5	Putting Your Best Foot Forward: Resume Writing Made Easy	3:00 P.M.
Thurs.	11/6	Creative Cover Letters: How To Write Them	11:00 A.M.
Mon.	11/10	Sweaty Palms: The Art of Interviewing	3:00 P.M.
Wed.	12/4	The Second Interview	2:00 P.M.

SPRING WORKSHOP SCHEDULE

Wed.	1/14	Getting Work Experience: Summer Job Searching	2:10 P.M.
Thurs.	1/15	Putting Your Best Foot Forward: Resume Writing Made Easy	11:00 A.M.
Mon.	1/19	Creative Cover Letters: How To Write Them	3:00 P.M.
Tues.	1/20	Sweaty Palms: The Art of Interviewing	9:30 A.M.
Wed.	1/28	Understanding The Maze of Government Employment	3:00 P.M.

Source: *Placement Manual*, 1986–1987, University of Maine, p. 5.

ranges from a few booklets or reference books to a well-organized career resource library, staffed by professional librarians. Sometimes career reference materials are kept in a separate section of the university library. There is a growing trend, however, toward centralizing such materials in the career center. Career libraries today may contain the following materials:

Occupational Information
Magazines, leaflets, and reference books on specific occupations are on hand. Major publications such as the *Encyclopedia of Careers and Vocational Guidance* provide a good starting point. Most career libraries contain booklets describing the duties and responsibilities, places to work, earnings, and education and training required, for various occupations. Most also contain a section on where additional information can be obtained.

Directories
Many directories are available to help students compile lists of prospective employers or graduate schools in their field of interest. These four- to five-inch-wide directories costing hundreds of dollars (such as *Moody's Industrials* . . . and *Standard & Poor's*) are usually found in the university's main library, while the less expensive directories listing employers in education, industry, business, hospitals, and government are in the career center's library.

Employer Files
Campus recruiting brochures as well as binders, annual reports, and other material provided by employers comprise a readily available source of information, often mistakenly referred to as "employer literature." Such reference materials provide the employer's view of working conditions, training programs, benefits, and career opportunities.

Job Binders
One of the most helpful resources is the file of current job openings. Most career centers classify the job opportunities by functional field, often separating those available through interviewing on the campus, and those where the applicant has to take the initiative in contacting the employer.

Resume and Letter Binders
Many career centers maintain examples of different kinds of resumes and letters used in job campaigns. More and more career

centers provide computer assistance to compile and produce resumes and letters.

Guides to Graduate and Professional Schools

Directories of graduate and professional schools, and copies of the entrance exams used for admission purposes to such programs, are usually maintained in career centers. In some schools the career center staff, or the members of the university's counseling services, will conduct preparation meetings and administer the tests for the graduate programs involved. Bulletins are available to notify undergraduate students which graduate and professional schools plan to recruit on campus, or wish to talk with prospective graduate students. When schools collaborate in conducting a forum in a community (for example, law schools, MBA programs, and nursing), such information is made available to undergraduate students through the career center and its library, and often through the counseling services.

Audio and Video Cassettes and Equipment

Tapes containing career information, comments made by recent graduates, and videotapes made by professional and trade associations or by employers, are available. Topics may include "Careers in Sales," for example. Other tapes supplement the workshops on various parts of the career planning process, such as taking inventory of your interests and skills, preparing resumes, preparing and conducting interviews, writing the job search letters, and preparing graduate school admission forms.

Handout Publications

The career center usually has a number of free leaflets, booklets, and magazines available for student use. In addition to the *CPC Annual, The ASCUS Annual,* and other publications listed in chapter 10, many career centers publish their own placement manual. This manual is especially useful because it gives specific information on what career services are available in the college, how the career programs operate, when deadlines occur, and other such data.

Of the thousands of publications available throughout the country, the one used most frequently by college students approaching graduation is the *CPC Annual,* copies of which are available through your school's career center. This publication of four volumes is an excellent source for researching and identifying those employers who traditionally seek entry-level college applicants.

Volume 1 provides articles by experienced professionals who offer advice on how to take stock of yourself, identify prospective employers, develop effective resumes and letters, prepare for interviews, and make the final decision. Volume 2 provides information on administrative and business positions, usually referred to as "nontechnical" positions, and is of most interest to liberal arts and business graduates. Volume 3 covers engineering, computer, and other scientific positions, usually referred to as "technical" positions. Volume 4 covers employment opportunities in the medical, nursing, and allied health professions.

There are also many magazines and professional journals that are designed specifically for certain fields or groups of students: *The ASCUS Annual* (for teachers), *The Black Collegian, New Engineer, Careers and the MBA, Nursing Job News, Engineering Horizons, College Level Opportunities with the U.S. Government, The Chronicle of Higher Education, Graduating Engineer, Journal of Career Planning and Employment, Physics Today, Chemical Engineering News, Peterson's Guide to Engineering, Science, and Computer Jobs.* In looking through such magazines, you should note not only the articles, but also which employers are advertising therein. Obviously such employers are targeting their ads for applicants who have training and interest in that particular field.

Some career centers also provide a series of informational leaflets for their students and recent graduates to supplement the other handout publications. At Boston College, for example, individual leaflets are available on topics such as "How to Research the Job Market," "8 Steps to Graduate School Study," "Resumes Made Easy," "Cover Letters and Other Letters," "Interview Tips Easily Remembered," "Guidelines for Informational Interviewing," "Alumni Career Services," "The B.C. Internship Program," and a "Directory of Services."

Computer Assistance

The three most frequently found computer-assistance programs for career guidance on college campuses today that help students assess themselves are the DISCOVER, SIGI (System of Interactive Guidance and Information), and CAREER NAVIGATOR systems. Each of these programs enables you to examine your interests, skills, and values, and forces you to evaluate and prioritize each part. This way you end up with a much greater knowledge of yourself and what you want. These systems also provide a printout of appropriate vocational options to fit the pattern of answers that you have provided on various parts of the program.

Computers provide specific career descriptions and information on graduate and professional schools. Such a service expedites selecting the schools that are most likely to have the kind of program you desire, and tells you whether financial assistance is available.

A very important use of computers is to facilitate the campus recruiting program described later in this chapter, and also the referral program for permanent, summer, temporary, and part-time employment.

Credentials

A credential file contains a student's academic and professional record. Credentials are used primarily for teachers, nurses, and administrative positions in the field of education. Some schools maintain such files indefinitely, while others limit retention to five years (because of space limitations and the fact that most of the information becomes obsolete). In some schools only the credentials of doctoral students are maintained indefinitely. In professional fields, the word "credentials" is synonymous with certification and implies that the person is qualified to practice in the profession. Credentials will not get you a job, but they can help you get consideration and possibly an interview.

The usual contents of a credential file include:

a. A registration form. Your signature on this form has been interpreted as giving your permission to mail your credentials to employers or to graduate or professional schools.

b. A resume (or multiple copies).

c. Reference letters, often called letters of recommendation.

d. Student teaching or clinic evaluations.

e. A transcript from your college.

f. Copies of transcripts from other institutions that you have attended.

You generally have to request in writing that your credentials be sent to a graduate school or employer. Such a requirement is specified in the Buckley amendment to the Federal Educational

Rights and Privacy Act. Some schools permit you to have access to everything in your credential file, while others have strict policies of providing access only to nonconfidential material. In order for a reference letter to be kept confidential, you would have to sign a waiver prior to the letter's receipt in the career center.

One of the most respected and experienced persons in the educational placement field is Anna Tackett from the University of Maryland. She provides the following pertinent advice on credentials:

> The manner in which you complete the credentials file is especially important as many times this is the first impression a prospective employer or graduate school has of you. Read and follow the instructions provided by the Placement Office; they were prepared for the purpose of assisting you. The forms should always be neatly and accurately prepared. Spelling and grammar do count; a glaring error can cause a negative reaction from readers and make them wonder about your potential as an effective teacher, or nurse, or professor.

> It is your responsibility to keep the Placement Office advised of changes in information, such as in name, address, and phone number. Many a job has been lost because no contact could be made with a student or alumnus.

> Initial filing of credentials, or placement papers, is just a beginning. As you progress in your professional life, attain additional degrees, change positions, and/or receive special recognition or honors, this information can and should be added to your file. It is an excellent idea to have your papers up-to-date in the event circumstances cause an unexpected change in your employment situation, thus necessitating a search for another position.[1]

Some schools charge a fee for duplicating and forwarding sets of credentials, others charge only for alumni. At some schools the policy provides that the first five sets of credentials will be free up to thirty days after graduation; after that time a fee will be required. If you are aspiring toward a nursing or teaching career, it is certainly to your advantage to be registered and have your credentials filed in your school's career center. Upon completion of graduate degrees, we recommend that you have a credentials file in both your undergraduate and your graduate school's career center.

---

[1]Tackett, Anna A. "Using Your Career Planning and Placement Office," 1983.

Newsletters and Bulletin Boards

These two sources are used to notify students and recent graduates of various career events scheduled throughout the year, and usually include information on various aspects of career planning. They also often announce current jobs prior to filing them in binders.

Internships, Externships, Co-op Programs

These programs, usually administered by or in conjunction with the career center, seek to integrate academic course work with practical work experience. Through all three of these programs described in chapter 3, students can investigate career choices, gain knowledge of professional fields by working with professionals, develop skills and contacts, test career choices in actual work settings, and obtain useful data to build up a resume. Other benefits include the experience of actually conducting a job search so you learn the value of setting goals, preparing resumes, going through interviews, and developing the possibility of employment after graduation. These programs help you ease the transition from the academic to the world of work, and lessen the fear of going after that first job after graduation. Externships, sometimes also called "mentor programs," give you access to a friend of the school (usually an alumnus) who could be a valuable mentor to help guide you on various career and job problems.

In addition to campus sources, another resource for internship opportunities is the *1987 Internships* book by Katherine Jobst, which includes 35,000 on-the-job training opportunities for college students and adults in twenty-four career areas, almost half of them offering some form of payment. This reference provides the name and address of the organization, the person to contact and his or her job title, the number and type of positions available, the eligibility requirements, and the application procedure with deadlines (if any).

Programs for People of Color

Universities in metropolitan centers often have collaborative programs with community groups to enhance the job and career prospects of students from different races or color. For several years a very successful consortium career fair has been conducted among Boston-area colleges, called *Career Expo.* It is designed to help students from African, Hispanic, Asian, and Native American backgrounds explore career opportunities throughout the United States with a great number of employers.

Referrals

This involves selecting candidates whose qualifications and interests seem to match the job requirements, and sending their resumes for consideration by employers. The referral system is used extensively by career centers at smaller colleges that do not have an active on-campus recruiting program. It is also heavily used in alumni placement, and by college professors or administrators to nominate candidates for a job. In addition to sending out resumes, the job-matching process is often accomplished by telephone, and some schools prepare and send to prospective employers a binder or booklet of resumes of their graduating seniors or graduate students.

Colleges having a computerized program will often provide students and recent graduates with notices of particular job openings, and also notify employers of available candidates who meet the requirements of their job opportunities. Students and recent graduates utilizing the career center's computer-referral system are generally assessed a fee, and the service is good for six months to a year.

Career Courses

More and more colleges offer career planning courses for academic credit. They last from one to four hours and generally are initiated and taught by the staff of the career center. Sometimes such a course is a joint venture and is taught by knowledgeable staff from several departments throughout the college or university. Students work on the individual steps comprising career planning and job seeking, including a systematic method of examining their interests, goals, and skills, and how they can formulate an effective job or graduate school campaign.

Alumni Career Services

Most of the college career centers aid former graduates through practically all of the services listed above. Individual career advising, referrals, job binders, and the periodic listing of available alumni that some schools send out to prospective employers are probably the career services most used by former students. Some career centers compile listings of jobs received and mail them to interested parties.

Sometimes special workshops are arranged by the career center staff in conjunction with the alumni association. A few schools have prepared booklets especially for alumni that contain information on career resources not only in their college, but also in the community. Alumni within the area can visit the career center during working hours and take advantage of almost all the services listed above. Generally speaking, most schools give a strong priority to current students for campus interviewing, but some allow recent graduates to participate if not enough students sign up for the interviews with recruiters.

Alumni Career Network

More and more colleges have developed a network among their former graduates to supplement the efforts of the career center's staff. By developing a close relationship with the alumni office and the development office for fund raising, the career center compiles a listing of hundreds of graduate volunteers representing a variety of occupational fields. The alumni agree to be a part of their college's network and help students and other graduates by providing career insights, information, and advice. They often host information seekers at their places of business, and provide job leads or other persons to contact.

Special Programs

Many career center offices work with the nearby community, with nearby colleges, and with the campus community in organizing and presenting timely programs on special topics. In Minnesota several colleges cooperate to entice employers to recruit at a host school or in a hotel, with career center staff sometimes transporting their interested students to that central location. Career days, career fairs, alumni speakers, and so forth all involve an extra service by the members of the career center. The Massachusetts Educational Recruiting Consortium (MERC), an association of thirty-three colleges and universities, sponsors an annual conference for three days at a Boston hotel to enable students in education to be interviewed for jobs.

The On-Campus Recruiting Program

The most visible and best known service of the career center at many schools is the on-campus recruiting program. This program provides the easiest and most effective means of contacting employers, and is especially useful for students seeking entry-level positions. It also is used by graduate and professional schools to recruit for their respective programs. Sometimes fall term recruiting is largely restricted to doctoral students, sometimes to other academic recruiting, and sometimes to special groups of students to fit in with the academic program in that discipline. The recruiting efforts of employers and graduate schools often resemble the rush program of fraternities and sororities; many applicants are courted, but only a few are chosen to join the organization.

History

On-campus recruiting became a vigorous and full-time function in the United States after World War II. Before that period, few colleges had a placement function wherein an interested professor or college administrator could help students or recent graduates obtain interviews with employers. The depression of 1921 caused several Eastern colleges to begin the program of assisting graduates to obtain jobs. In 1926 the first professional society for this function was formed, and was named Eastern College Personnel Officers. Membership was by invitation only, and the college members literally ran the organization (the employer members did not have a vote). All the recruiting was male-oriented and dominated by industrial organizations.

The lack of male graduates during the five-year period of World War II gave women college graduates a foothold in college recruiting. After World War II more and more employers sought to fill the deficit in potential management material by inundating campuses in search of graduates for their personnel needs. The increasing number of recruiters caused colleges to establish placement offices to arrange interviews for students with employers on a more organized basis. This increased interest in college recruiting led to the formation of professional societies, so that today in the United States we have seven regional organizations and a national society (The College Placement Council, Inc.) for most forms of college recruiting. In the teacher placement field, the national organization is called ASCUS (Association for School, College and

University Staffing), and throughout the country there are also several regional associations for this type of recruiting.

In addition to the national and regional professional groups mentioned above, close working relationships have developed with affiliate organizations, such as the National Association for Law Placement and the Employment Management Association. When the College Placement Council (CPC) was incorporated, it included the Canadian professional society UCPA (University and College Placement Association); the latter is now independent, but is considered a charter associate member of the CPC. Each of these groups provides a forum for members to discuss current problems and develop better policies and procedures, as well as providing professional services such as training, publications, data collection, research, public relations, and legislative liaison.

The Why of Campus Recruiting

Many employers find it is less expensive to have a recruiter visit the campus than to have candidates visit the organization.

From the recruiting organization's viewpoint, the campus recruiting program provides a window through which the organization sees the college or university. The courtesy, service, and personal attention extended by the career center staff and students to employers' representatives during the recruiting visit usually have a direct effect on the school's fund-raising programs, the scholarship or grant money made available to students, summer and part-time jobs, internship and cooperative job programs, speakers at campus events, research assistance and topics, athletic programs, and other aspects of a college relations program.

In addition to budget and travel considerations, employers place great emphasis on results from previous campus recruiting visits so they can determine at which schools to recruit the following year. Close cooperation between the faculty, the career center staff, and the recruiters results in a greater number of job opportunities for students and recent graduates.

Because of the cost and time required for campus visits, many employers cannot afford to spend several days on the college campus. Therefore, they may request that the career center staff send them resumes or college interview forms ahead of their recruiting date so they can identify the candidates they wish to interview while on campus. Some schools restrict the number of interviews permitted for each student, while other schools permit students to sign up for as many interviews as they can handle. You should remember that employers recruit on campus only for occupations where there is a shortage of applicants, or fields in which that employer had success recruiting at that college in previous years. Consequently, you should not make campus recruiting the sole focus of your job search.

A major retailing company interviewed 1,500 students on college campuses during a recent year, invited 220 in for visits, and extended 76 job offers. The selectivity is obvious as seen by the fact that only 14.7 percent were invited for secondary interviews, and only 5 percent were given job offers.

For those students who fully utilize the services of their school's career center, the campus recruiting program could easily be the major source of job opportunities. One of the most active career centers in the country is located at the Harvard Business School. In surveying the class of 1984, their MBA students gave the following data regarding their source of contact with employers:

Source of Contact	Percent
Placement office	47.3
Personal solicitation (from our own research)	23.7
Previous summer employer	13.3
Previous full-time employer	9.0
Other HBS referral (faculty)	1.9
Club resume book	1.2
Other sources	3.6

The campus recruiting program is an excellent source of career entry-level jobs for students in engineering, science, business, and graduate school. As indicated in figure 5-2, undergraduates in liberal arts and nursing find the campus recruiting program of less value than other sources of employment. Other academic areas—such as agriculture, home economics, social work, and evening college—find it necessary to utilize other sources of employment as well.

Students

The on-campus recruiting program gives you a relatively easy opportunity to consider careers with a variety of employers from business, industry, government, education, health care, and so

Figure 5.2. Undergraduate Contacts

Source	College of Arts and Sciences	School of Management	School of Nursing	Total Responses
Contacts through a relative or friend	30.4%	15.1%	14.0%	22.8%
Campus recruiting program	6.5	37.2	0	17.6
Newspaper ads	18.1	12.1	7.0	14.5
Direct mail to employers	11.2	6.5	40.4	12.6
Continuing with current employer	5.4	7.5	17.5	7.5
Other sources*	28.5	21.6	21.1	25.0
Totals	100.0%	100.0%	100.0%	100.0%

*Included faculty, staff, and alumni contacts, job listings at the career center, and family businesses.

Source: Boston College Career Center, survey of three academic divisions from the class of 1985.

forth. Recruiters come from many geographical locations, saving you time and money in making the initial contact. Unfortunately too many students expect this to be their sole source of job opportunities, not realizing that such recruiting often focuses primarily on positions where there is a shortage of talent available, or where there is keen competition for candidates.

Most of these interviews are scheduled at thirty-minute intervals, and are primarily used to help you determine whether you have a real interest in the employer's career opportunities or the graduate school's programs. Similarly, the employer's or graduate school's representative has a chance to select the best qualified candidates for his or her organization's needs.

If there is a very active recruiting program, too often students depend too much on this service. Failure to master the technique of planning and executing an effective employment or graduate school campaign may prove to be a handicap for future job changes. You should find out now how the campus recruiting program is administered on your campus, how the sign-up procedure works, and what restrictions (if any) there are on interviews, policies, and so forth.

Undergraduate students contemplating a graduate or professional degree can gain useful information on such programs from the variety of universities recruiting on campus, through forums in communities, by interviewing employers for summer jobs after graduation, or through employment between the first and second year of graduate school. By making a good impression on the recruiter, it is possible for you to work on a program whereby you can literally start your career training and gain some experience with an organization. After graduation, you will be ready to go full speed on your career in that organization.

The screening of candidates in the campus interview is usually followed by the secondary interview at the employer's place of business. Employers often try to fill the current year's quota of openings by April; therefore, students who wait until the last month or two before graduation will experience more difficulty in contacting prospective employers. They will also find that there are fewer opportunities available.

Procedure for Campus Interviews

As in most phases of life, a sound preparation will provide for better results. Working within your school's policies and procedures for on-campus recruiting will help save you time and embarrassment, and will ensure that you make contacts with the prospective employers or graduate schools in whom you are interested. Although each college or university will have unique policies, its procedures will generally entail the following steps, sometimes called the mechanics of scheduling campus interviews:

Registration
Requires filling out a form for the career center to serve as a master record on graduating students, filling out a campus interview form to standardize the information given to employers, or completing cards or special forms to be used for the computer program.

Participation in Workshops
Sometimes special meetings are held on campus to inform students of the specific steps to be taken in signing up for interviews. The workshops or meetings enable you to familiarize yourself with

the mechanics of interviewing, have your questions answered, and save time for both you and the career center staff. At these workshops or meetings, staff members usually hand out their college's placement manual, the procedure for sign-ups, and often a copy of the *College Placement Annual* or a copy of *ASCUS*.

Publicity on Recruiting Employers and Graduate Schools

Most career center offices issue some kind of calendar or schedule of employers and graduate schools that have made arrangements to recruit on their campus. These may be made up two to four weeks in advance, for a semester, or for the entire school year. A revised recruiting calendar may be issued weekly, or may be posted on the bulletin board; it contains a list of employers and/or graduate schools coming to visit the campus, the date(s) of the visit, required majors, positions or programs for which they will be interviewing, locations, and resume deadlines.

Researching Employers and Graduate Schools

As soon as the recruiting calendar is issued, you should visit the career center to read material forwarded by the employer or graduate school; to compare the positions, programs, and specifications sought with your own interests and qualifications; and to determine which ones might fit your interests and career aspirations.

Two roommates both majoring in marketing, approached their senior year with opposite viewpoints on interviewing. One decided he would interview every possible employer, and ended up with twenty-nine interviews on campus. He missed classes, had little time for any research, spent too much time visiting employers in several cities, and ended up with one job offer. He accepted this position, but quit within six months of employment. His roommate spent considerable time researching the employers, took seven well-selected interviews, and ended up with four excellent offers. Two years after graduation the second person was well on his way to a satisfactory career, was pleased with his selection and progress in terms of salary increases and advancements, and told us the best advice he could pass on to current graduates would be to spend time researching employers so as to interview only those that came close to having the type of career opportunities being sought. Such research pays off in getting priority interviews, which saves you considerable time in the long run and gets better results.

Preference Cards

On some campuses where schedules will not accommodate all interested students, a system of priorities is usually worked out, such as the bidding system, the company card preference system, or a selection by computer system.

The bidding system.   Each student is given a designated number of points to be used in bidding for an interview appointment—somewhat resembling an auction. The students bidding the highest number of their points get priority on scheduling interview appointments with an employer of their choice. When they run out of points, they run out of interviews on campus. This system discourages students from shopping around in their interviews, and assures the recruiter that those on the interviewing schedule have a definite interest in his or her organization.

The company card preference system.   Students are issued six to nine interview selection cards that they use to indicate the employers with whom they wish to schedule interviews on campus. On these cards, students give the priority rank of their preferences for each employer, along with the preferred times for interviews. The career center staff assigns interview appointments in the order of priority choice numbers and posts the schedules. Students confirm their appointments by initialing their scheduled times, or they discuss any conflicts or changes with the recruiting coordinator.

Computerization.   For some career center offices the tedious and time-consuming task of scheduling appointments for students is done by a computer program. Typically the student completes a form, designates the times he or she is available on the date the recruiter will visit the campus, and awaits the posting of the interviewing schedule. Appointments have to be confirmed according to the procedure set up by the college. Some schools have students complete a computer form for each employer, while others have a composite form listing in priority order the interviews desired by the student for the semester or school term. Computer selection of students for interviews has the psychological advantage of being nondiscriminatory, and generally it is considered to be a big time saver for students and the career staff.

Open vs. Closed Schedules

When an interviewing schedule is "open," any student who is interested can sign up for an interview with that employer. Although this type of schedule is preferred by students, it often leads to abuse by a few selfish students who literally hog all the schedules. Thus students who have to work part-time, or have an active extracurricular life, find that few times are available. Employers find that open schedules usually bring a lot of shoppers who are not really interested in a career with that employer, but just want to see what is offered, or wish to get some interviewing experience.

To reduce the number of recruiters to be sent to that campus, employers will insist on a "closed" schedule. This forces the career center staff to collect the resumes of all interested students, and forward either them or college interview forms to the employer about four weeks prior to the date of the campus visit. The employer reviews all of the forwarded resumes or interview forms, selects those that seem to match the job needs, and then either contacts the candidates directly or gives the names of those pre-screened to the career center staff. The staff then contacts the students who have been selected by the employer to arrange an interview appointment. This method spares the recruiter many hours dealing with shoppers, and makes it easier for students who are interested to be more certain of getting an interview appointment.

All interview appointment times are often filled with both types of schedules. If you are interested and can't get a campus interview, write immediately to the employer, enclose a resume with a letter expressing interest and an explanation as to why you did not get an appointment, and offer to come to the employer's place of business on your own time for an interview. Or, ask if the recruiter would be willing to see you after the interviews are completed at the career center.

Sign Ups

Following your school's policies and procedures, sign up for an interview at a time that does not conflict with your class schedule. Make sure you note the date, time, place, and name of the employer; if the recruiter's name is known, write it on the same record so you will not go to the wrong room or wait for another recruiter with the same employer. If your school's procedure calls for you to leave a copy of your resume or college interview form, be sure to take care of this when you sign up.

Cancellations

If you become ill or have a serious reason for not honoring an interview, you should call the scheduler in the career center as soon as possible. There are probably several students on a waiting list who would be happy to substitute at your appointed time.

No-Show Policy

Practically all schools have a policy to discourage no-shows. When students sign up for an interview, a professional commitment is made; therefore failure to honor interviews may result in a loss of recruiting and interviewing privileges. Some schools allow one no-show for any reason during the entire recruiting period. If it is impossible to cancel your appointment before the date of the interview, then you should write a letter of apology to the recruiter for not showing up for the interview, thus protecting the school's reputation and helping fellow students. Colleges view this policy very seriously, as indicated in the following statement from the University of Massachusetts:

"No-Show Policy"

The University Placement policy states that one failure to keep an appointment will ordinarily cause you to lose your interviewing privilege. If you miss an appointment with a recruiter, you must submit a letter of apology to that recruiter and to the Placement Director's Office before you may sign up for additional interviews.[2]

One final note: Do not rely too much on campus recruiting. Only a small percentage of employers and graduate schools make recruiting trips to college campuses. See chapter 10 for other job and graduate school sources.

---

[2]*Placement Manual.* University of Massachusetts, 1986.

PART TWO

Self-Exploration and Career Decision

TOO MANY PEOPLE make the mistake of thinking that the first step in getting a job or getting into a graduate program is to compile a resume. For college students, and also for other applicants, a more desirable and effective approach is first to do some thinking and research about yourself and about occupational fields.

Chapter 6, Self-Assessment, covers the first step in career planning as envisioned by career counselors who work with college students and recent graduates. Suggestions are given for compiling a personal inventory that enables you to ascertain and appreciate your strengths and weaknesses. By combining your own thinking with that of professionals, friends, and family, you are more likely to obtain a realistic appraisal of your interests, values, skills, and abilities. All this is information that is vitally important in order to make appropriate career decisions.

Chapter 7, Career Exploration and Objective, provides helpful data to enable students and recent graduates to use a step-by-step process to research occupational fields and prospective industries to decide on a career goal that will be most compatible with their talents, training, and ambitions.

These two chapters should help you to decide what options are available, what kind of work you want to do, where, and in what kind of environment. With such information, you can make a more realistic and accurate decision for a career goal.

chapter six

Self-Assessment

During his lifetime (469–399 B.C.) Socrates tried to stimulate the youth of Athens through his maxim "know thyself." This became known as the Socratic method, consisting of asking searching questions, insisting on the definition of terms, and analyzing statements and opinions in such a way as to reveal their consistency or inconsistency.

Career and life planning for the individual actually begins with the advice from Socrates' "know thyself." Students who have effectively utilized their years of college have developed the skills and abilities and characteristics sought by employers—ability to communicate orally and in writing, facility for learning, social skills and maturity, leadership potential, a sound foundation in course work, and some pertinent experience. Effective utilization of college will also develop a student's analytical ability, ambition, and self-reliance as well as self-confidence.

The principles of career planning are just as applicable when seeking admission to a graduate or professional school as they are for conducting a job campaign. Both objectives stress the development and evaluation of personal skills, interests, aptitudes, values, and goals as a basis for determining the most personally satisfying career field to enter after graduating with a bachelor's, master's, or doctoral degree.

After utilizing the knowledge and resources in chapters 4 and 5, you are ready to formulate a personal strategy for seeking admission to a graduate or professional school, or securing that first job towards your chosen career. A strategy helps you understand where you are, where you hope to be in the future, and what are your realistic chances of getting there.

By developing your own personal strategy, you assume responsibility for your actions and also make sure *you* control your career. As one of our national leaders in the college career planning and placement field, Arthur R. Eckberg of Roosevelt University, stated: "A systematic step-by-step marketing approach—objectively and innovatively pursued—will enable you to get at the roots of some nagging questions." Several important questions have to be answered in order to plan your career strategy:

1. What do you want to do?

2. Where do you want to work?

3. What is there to be done?

4. What are your goals?

What Do You Want to Do?

The best estimates obtained from college career counselors indicate that about ten percent of all students know exactly what careers they want to pursue. Usually this figure comprises the students who definitely want to become doctors, nurses, engineers, and so on. For such fields it is necessary to start career planning in freshman year because of the required sequence of courses to be taken. For the great majority of college students, especially in the liberal arts field, the typical response to the above question is "I don't know what I want to do after college."

For most students, trying to decide on one or more careers is similar to pick and shovel work—persistent effort is needed to explore various options and compare them with your interests, values, skills and abilities, and ambitions. By trial and error experience, research in libraries, and talks with knowledgeable people—plus some work experience—most of you will use a gradual process of elimination to discard from further consideration those fields of work that do not appeal to you. Sometimes your four years in college result in a desire to broaden your horizons, or to gain more specific training in certain fields by pursuing graduate study.

How to Get Started

Our experience indicates that many students procrastinate in their career planning because they do not know how to get started, or what steps to take. Sometimes they are reluctant to seek advice because they may feel vulnerable, or feel they should do something before they visit their career center. Although every college will have its own approach to career/life planning, the chart in figure 4-1 should be helpful to every student who takes a college education seriously, and wants to get the full benefit out of each year in school. Participating in a career/life planning workshop early in college should facilitate your strategy.

Too many people think a resume is the first step, whereas self-assessment is the logical first step to take. Most students need help in identifying their strengths and weaknesses, their skills and abilities, values, goals, and how they relate to potential careers. Throughout college it is advisable to compile a continuous inventory of courses you've taken and your interests and values, and periodically take time to evaluate your reactions to courses, activities, work experience, other students, and faculty. Just as good salespeople must know thoroughly the products or services they sell, so you must know your product—*yourself*! Then you will know what you *can* do and what you *like* to do.

In textbooks and workshops dealing with the topic of self-assessment, a series of exercises aimed at compiling a personal inventory of interests and qualifications *in writing* is generally included. Some people like to compare such an inventory to a balance sheet of their personal assets and liabilities. Compiling such an inventory and analysis will help you in determining or confirming your vocational objectives, and in preparing a summary of your qualifications for resume or application purposes. This should prove very helpful during interviews when you have to persuade graduate schools to admit you or employers to hire you. Preparing a self-assessment analysis helps you first to analyze your potential career options, and later to decide on the optimal match between your personal desires and your career alternatives.

Compiling a Self-Inventory

Your inventory should include the following items:

Education

In addition to listing your high school, college, and graduate (if any) school and the years attended, include your major and minor subjects, and select the courses that especially appealed to you. Be sure to reflect and determine why you enjoyed certain courses, and why you disliked others. As you go through college, your natural aptitude for certain types of courses will be evidenced by achieving higher grades and also by showing a greater interest in them. Athletes gravitate toward the sports in which they excel, and students tend to major in subjects in which they have a natural aptitude or interest.

Work Experience

In addition to compiling the usual information on starting and ending dates, job titles, employers' names and types of business, and duties and responsibilities, it would be helpful for you to analyze such work experiences to ascertain what you learned from such jobs, and what skills or values you obtained from them. Analyze all full-time, part-time, volunteer, and vacation experience.

Interests

Career counselors and employers found out a long time ago that people do better with a task or activity in which they are interested. Knowing your interests and how they pertain to the world of work will enable you to enter careers where you will get paid for doing things that you would do for fun. Hobbies and activities in college often steer you toward desirable careers. You may have to ask yourself whether you prefer to work with people, things, ideas, or symbols. The tests described later in this chapter have helped many students supplement their self-appraisal.

Skills and Abilities

Many students are confused with the terms talents, skills, and abilities. It may help to define these terms as:

Talent—your natural aptitude or inclination for doing something

Skills—something you acquire through study or practice

Ability—usually a combination of the above two, and a willingness to use them

In modern usage these three terms are used synonymously and generally are understood by all parties.

Every person should be able to decide whether he or she has analytical ability, a facility for learning languages, a skill in oral and written communications, intelligence (common sense as well as a high grade point average), ability to learn, and a natural aptitude for one's chosen career field.

Figure 6-1 summarizes many career-related skills that you can develop during your college years. This information may be helpful to those of you who don't think you have any skills. It should help you focus on and translate into your self-inventory many skills that you have been performing but have not recognized.

Personal Traits

Examine your character traits, such as your aptitude, cooperation, integrity, laziness and/or procrastination, perseverance, self-confidence, and adaptability. Are you willing to learn and work hard? Do you have patience, a tolerance for routine, and a good disposition? How well to do you work with or relate to other people? How well do you handle criticism, failure, frustration?

Leadership

Employers and graduate schools are particularly interested in persons with leadership talent, so you should carefully compile information regarding such questions as:

Do you have evidence of your ability to plan goals and programs to reach them?

Can you organize activities or programs, coordinate them, and follow them through to completion?

Can you assume responsibility and make decisions?

Do you have the ability to work with and motivate people?

Can you initiate projects and work well under pressure?

Can you teach and train people, and delegate authority and responsibility to others?

Figure 6-1. Career Skills Developed in College

Communication Skills:
Write clearly and concisely.
Speak effectively.
Use various media to present ideas.
Listen to, and really hear what others are saying.
Compile resumes, letters, and credentials.
Sell ideas and programs.

Research Skills:
Utilize library, visual aids, computers, and other sources of information.
Dig for information.
Design questionnaires, models, or experiments.
Conduct interviews to obtain facts and opinions.
Critically examine and assess the validity of data.
Synthesize information and concepts.
Study and develop a thirst for knowledge.

Objective Thinking Skills:
Identify issues and problems using logic to reach the best conclusions.
Analyze data to determine the facts objectively.
Focus (concentrate) on the current task and needs.
Assess your own talents, goals, interests, and skills.
Identify alternatives.
Develop solutions to problems.

Value Skills:
Identify personal life and work values.
Keep your work, promise, or other commitments.
Balance work, study, and recreation.
Appreciate other cultures and contributions from art, literature, and technology.

Leadership Skills:
Set an example by your own work and behavior.
Inspire and motivate others.
Budget time and energy.
Initiate ideas and actions.
Work independently.
Develop self-confidence and poise.
Develop standards for work and activities.

Management Skills:
Plan realistic goals and objectives.
Organize programs and activities.
Determine priorities and make decisions.
Establish policies, rules, regulations, and procedures.
Assume and delegate responsibility.
Identify and select people for tasks.
Supervise actions to implement plans.

Interpersonal Skills:
Get and give cooperation and support to and from others.
Understand feelings, thoughts, and actions of others.
Become a good team member.
Develop a tolerance for opposing views.
Develop networks.
Determine how much pressure or risk you can take.
Meet, converse with, and cultivate friends and faculty.
Express your views and feelings tactfully and courteously.
Skillfully conduct meetings.

Handicapped

If you have any physical limitations, be realistic in seeking careers that minimize your handicap. A deaf person would have severe limitations in a musical career. Persons with one leg would have great difficulties in most athletic careers. Although many physical handicaps can be partially compensated and minimized by prescription glasses, hearing aids, or artificial limbs, one should realize that the handicap usually gets worse with age. It would be more pragmatic to study the working environment and job requirements carefully to ascertain whether the physical handicap would be too great a deterrent for that particular career field.

Physical

Most college students are in good health—after all, they are in the best years of their lives, physically speaking. Be honest with yourself in appraising your ability to sustain a high energy level. Do you tire easily? Can you recuperate quickly? Everyone knows how important physical endurance is in athletic contests, but few students appreciate the physical requirements of some jobs, such as standing on your feet all day in retail establishments, pacing concrete floors in factories all day long, or surviving committee meetings in hot rooms with poor ventilation for a great part of the day.

Further Development

No inventory would be complete without a section listing areas in which you think you need further training, education, experience, or development. An honest inventory would include a section on your weaknesses. These items would provide the information needed to list the areas needing further development. It would be foolish to accept a job leading to a career wherein the performance requirements include traits or items that you know you are weak in.

Achievements

Your accomplishments to date could easily become the most important part of your inventory, and they also provide significant data for future resumes and application forms. In selecting your most noteworthy achievements, consider honors, awards, term papers, research projects or experiments, recognition during internships, and leadership in campus activities, and be sure to include information as to why you selected these examples. It may have been the challenge of the project; perhaps it was a wonderful learning experience or recognition; or it may have given you great satisfaction and a sense of fulfillment to perform a service for others. In the real world there is an old saying that states "your mother may be interested in your excuses, but we are interested only in results." This part of your inventory should provide you with evidence that you *can* get results.

Compare Your Inventory with Job Requirements

If you have a pretty good idea of your skills and abilities, then it would help to compare your inventory with the qualifications for certain fields of work that require four or more years of college. The Bureau of Labor Statistics in the U. S. Department of Labor has compiled a guide designed to help persons compare the types of job characteristics with their interests and skills. As illustrated by the excerpts in figure 6-2, the BLS lists and defines seventeen occupational characteristics and requirements that are matched with specific occupations.

Psychological Tests

Tests can be an important tool to help you with your self-assessment. Test results do not provide decisions, but they do provide more objective information to help you explore other career areas. The value of tests depends on two important factors: the honesty with which you give your answers, and the knowledge and experience of the counselor in interpreting the results and in recognizing the scope and limits of the test used. Most colleges look upon testing as part of their student services program, but some charge a fee just like commercial testing services.

Among the more popular tests being currently used are the following.

Strong-Campbell Interest Inventory

This is probably the most popular test given to college students and recent graduates. It attempts to reveal a pattern of likes and dislikes based on a person's perceptions developed from a variety of experiences and attitudes. The profile developed from your responses may highlight occupational areas that you might enjoy but had not considered previously. This test provides three sets of scores:

General Occupational Themes—give an overall view providing global categories based on Holland's hexagon (see details in appendix A, Other Theories). These scores are used to help the person identify the general section of the occupational world for more intensive study.

Basic Interest Scales—indicate the strength of your interest. These scores are constructed by clustering together items with high intercorrelations.

Occupational Scales—indicate how similar or dissimilar your interests are to people employed in various occupations. These scores suggest occupations where the student or recent graduate will be happy or satisfied, although the scores are not precise predictors.

Aptitude Tests

These are designed to measure your learning ability, not only for acquiring new information but also for how fast you acquire it. Aptitude tests include the following: high school students take the SAT test when they apply to college. College graduates take the GRE test when they apply to graduate school, the LSAT test when they apply to law school, and a similar admission test for other fields.

Achievement Tests

These are performance tests to measure your knowledge in a particular subject, such as mathematics and English, on college exams, or in an acquired skill such as athletics, computer science, photography, or acting.

Intelligence Tests

These measure your capacity for mastering problems, based on abstract reasoning. Although not used very often in career counseling, these tests are concerned with your rate and quality of mental activity in dealing with various levels of complex situations or problems.

Personality Tests

These measure your emotional stability, maturity, and degree of adjustment to life. In dealing with the feelings, values, and motives of individuals, they measure social poise, maturity, and interpersonal characteristics. One of the more popular personality

Figure 6-2. Matching Your Qualifications to Job Requirements

World of Work	1. Leadership/persuasion	2. Helping/instructing others	3. Problem-solving/creativity	4. Initiative	5. Work as part of a team	6. Frequent public contact	7. Manual dexterity	8. Physical stamina	9. Hazardous	10. Outdoors	11. Confined	12. Geographically concentrated	13. Part-time	14. Earnings	15. Employment growth	16. Number of new jobs, 1984-95 (in thousands)	17. Entry requirements
Natural Scientists and Mathematicians																	
Computer and Mathematical Occupations																	
Actuaries			•	•						•	•			H	H	4	H
Computer systems analysts	•	•	•	•	•							•		H	H	212	H
Mathematicians			•	•										H	M	4	H
Statisticians			•	•										H	M	4	H
Physical Scientists			•	•										H	M		H
Chemists			•	•										H	L	9	H
Geologists and geophysicists			•	•	•				•			•		H	M	7	H
Meteorologists			•	•	•									H	M	1	H
Physicists and astronomers			•	•										H	L	2	H
Life Scientists																	
Agricultural scientists			•	•										[1]	M	3	H
Biological scientists			•	•										H	M	10	H
Foresters and conservation scientists		•	•	•	•			•	•	•				H	L	2	H
Social Scientists, Social Workers, Religious Workers, and Lawyers																	
Lawyers	•	•	•	•	•	•								H	H	174	H
Social Scientists and Urban Planners																	
Economists			•	•										H	M	7	H
Psychologists		•	•	•		•								H	H	21	H
Sociologists			•	•		•								H	L	[2]	H
Urban and regional planners	•		•	•	•	•								H	L	2	H
Social and Recreation Workers																	
Social workers	•	•	•	•	•	•								M	H	75	H
Recreation workers	•	•	•	•	•	•	•	•		•			•	L	H	26	M
Religious Workers																	
Protestant ministers	•	•	•	•	•	•								L	[1]	[1]	H
Rabbis	•	•	•	•	•	•								H	[1]	[1]	H
Roman Catholic priests	•	•	•	•	•	•								L	[1]	[1]	H

Figure 6.2. *Continued*

World of Work	1. Leadership/persuasion	2. Helping/instructing others	3. Problem-solving/creativity	4. Initiative	5. Work as part of a team	6. Frequent public contact	7. Manual dexterity	8. Physical stamina	9. Hazardous	10. Outdoors	11. Confined	12. Geographically concentrated	13. Part-time	14. Earnings	15. Employment growth	16. Number of new jobs, 1984–95 (in thousands)	17. Entry requirements
Teachers, Counselors, Librarians, and Archivists																	
Kindergarten and elementary school teachers	•	•	•	•	•	•	•	•						M	H	281	H
Secondary school teachers	•	•	•	•	•	•		•						M	L	48	H
Adult and vocational education teachers	•	•	•	•	•	•	•	•					•	M	M	48	H
College and university faculty	•	•	•	•	•	•		•					•	H	L	−77	H
Counselors	•	•	•	•	•	•								M	M	29	H
Librarians	•	•	•	•	•	•		•					•	M	L	16	H
Archivists and curators			•	•	•									M	L	1	H
Health Diagnosing and Treating Practitioners																	
Chiropractors	•	•	•	•	•	•	•							H	H	9	H
Dentists	•	•	•	•	•	•	•							H	H	39	H
Optometrists	•	•	•	•	•	•	•							H	H	8	H
Physicians	•	•	•	•	•	•	•					•		H	H	109	H
Podiatrists	•	•	•	•	•	•	•							H	H	4	H
Veterinarians	•	•	•	•	•	•	•	•	•					H	H	9	H
Registered Nurses, Pharmacists, Dietitians, Therapists, and Physician Assistants																	
Dietitians and nutritionists	•	•	•	•	•	•								M	H	12	H
Occupational therapists	•	•	•	•	•	•	•	•						¹	H	8	H
Pharmacists	•	•	•	•	•	•						•		H	L	15	H
Physical therapists	•	•	•	•	•	•	•	•						M	H	25	H
Physician assistants	•	•	•	•	•	•	•							M	H	10	M
Recreational therapists	•	•	•	•	•	•	•	•		•				M	H	4	M
Registered nurses	•	•	•	•	•	•	•	•	•				•	M	H	452	M
Respiratory therapists	•	•	•	•	•	•	•							M	H	11	L
Speech pathologists and audiologists	•	•	•	•	•	•								M	M	8	H

Columns 14 and 15—Projected growth:
 L = lowest   M = middle   H = highest

¹Estimates not available.
²Less than 500.

Column 17—Entry requirements:
 L = high school or less education
 M = apprenticeship or junior college
 H = 4 or more years of college

Source: Fountain, Melvin. Excerpted from "Matching Yourself with World of Work."
Occupational Outlook Quarterly, 1986.

instruments today is the *Myers-Briggs Type Indicator* (MBTI), which measures decision-making style and indicates appropriate career settings. In career planning, an awareness of what types dominate a field and work environment should help ascertain the skills and attitudes needed to obtain satisfaction in a job.

In applying MBTI results, you can increase your self-understanding and improve interpersonal relationships. Managers can apply this type theory to develop teamwork, so groups of employees will work together more effectively. Basically, the MBTI theory facilitates communication and helps people understand their own and others' life-styles and cultures.

Some tests are administered in groups, others individually. The test scores do not give absolutes or decisions, but they do reveal clues and estimates. By discussing the interaction of your test scores with a career counselor or psychologist, you can get a better interpretation and idea of the environment in which you would work best, and which occupational fields would best utilize your combination of interests, aptitudes, skills, abilities, and long-range goals. No test results will bring together all the factors, but professional counselors can assist you in evaluating and interpreting test scores and can offer suggestions on how the various pieces (test results) might fit together. They can also offer information that may open new fields or paths for you to explore.

Utilizing test results has sometimes been compared to operations in hospitals or clinics. If you were going to have a surgical operation, you would be less interested in the instruments the surgeon used than in his or her ability to use them effectively. Since tests are tools or instruments for use in the hands of a professional, don't operate on yourself. Go to a professional to get the most effective interpretation of the test scores.

Values

Another part of your self-inventory should include your personal value system and needs, both for work and for life. A clear understanding of these will eliminate the confusion in career planning, and help bring you peace of mind in this changing world. By putting your thoughts in writing, you force yourself to make a decision on what is important to you in your work and life. It would be best to separate these two sets of values for your inventory.

Work Values

Although these will vary for different fields of work, some of the more common work values would include: interesting and challenging work, adequate pay, security of employment, ability to help or serve others, degree of independence, safe working conditions, an environment that encourages creativity and initiative, continuing education possibilities, variety of work assignments, opportunity to learn and be promoted into higher-level jobs, recognition of good and superior work performance, and other such factors.

Life Values

Most people do not work only for a paycheck, but realize that a paycheck enables them to do the things that make life worth living. Although the significance of family, friends, and health are usually on everyone's list of life values, your inventory should also consider the importance of continuing education, economics, leisure time facilities and programs, religion, social and professional organizations, politics, housing and environment, opportunities for charitable or other altruistic work, and similar factors.

To cope with peer, parental, and life pressures, every student has to formulate his or her own value system. During college you may feel that your personal career fulfillment would best be satisfied in a volunteer program like the Peace Corps or in a nonprofit organization like the American Cancer Society, but your desire to be of service to others faces tremendous pressure from peers who seek a job paying the most money. Changing values or economic circumstances may easily dictate accepting a high-paying job to pay off your college loans and build an economic nest egg before seeking a career that will really suit you.

Clarifying your values will help you understand yourself and prioritize what is really important to you. It will also have a positive effect on your research, interviews, and other efforts to discover the kind of career that will bring you the most satisfaction and fulfillment. A clear understanding of your value system will help you make moral choices when facing ethical problems as a student and later as an alumnus.

In surveying the values of 5,894 college men and 2,425 college women, three members of Harvard University summarized the results as indicated in figure 6-3.

In comparing the above averages with scores attained by Boston University and Harvard Business School students, Kotter and his

Figure 6-3. Values of College Men and Women*

Score	Average for Men	Average for Women
50		
		48 Religious
45		44 Social
	43 Economic 43 Religious	
	41 Political 41 Theoretical	
40		40 Aesthetic
	39 Social	38 Economic
		36 Political
35		35 Theoretical
	33 Aesthetic	

*Kotter et al. From *The AVL Study of Values in Self-Assessment and Career Development,* 1978.

associates found some interesting differences as depicted in figure 6-4.

Talk to People

People generally love to talk about themselves, their jobs and careers, and give advice to those who seek their wisdom and experience. To get a more complete inventory of your strong and weak points, you should supplement your self-analysis with an appraisal of your talents and weaknesses by discussing them with family members, fellow workers and students, friends, professors, and others who may know you. Robert Burns once stated, "to see ourselves as others see us." Getting the opinions and evaluations of the parties mentioned above could be a real eye-opener and provide a different perspective on your self-assessment. Professors

Figure 6-4. Study of Values *

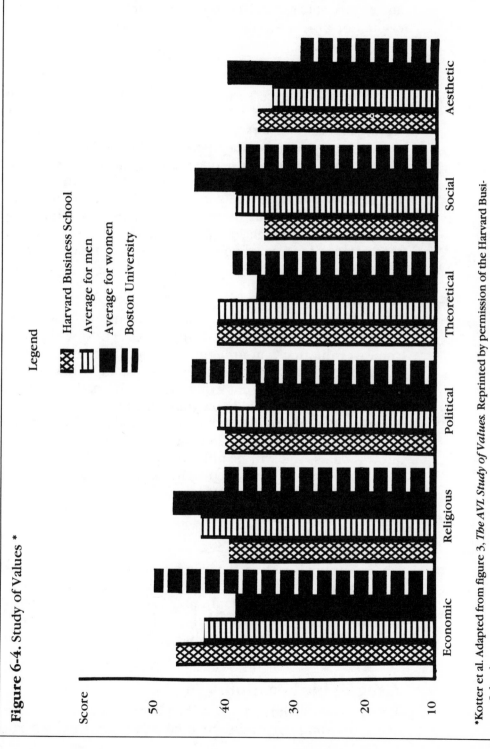

*Kotter et al. Adapted from figure 3, *The AVL Study of Values.* Reprinted by permission of the Harvard Business School.

and supervisors especially should be able to give you a desirable evaluation of your strengths and weaknesses.

Professional Assistance

Sometimes it is necessary to seek and utilize the expertise of trained professionals such as career counselors, psychologists, testing experts, and personal counselors. Such persons can review and evaluate your inventory, perhaps make changes that will add to your strong points, raise questions to clarify your values, and call your attention to logical occupational fields that could best utilize your combination of interests, skills, and goals. If such assistance does nothing more than verify your own thinking and compilation of information, you will gain self-confidence and be motivated because you know you are on the right career path.

Evaluation

Listing all the above parts of your self-inventory is a tedious task, often requiring considerable time and effort. Now the real task comes: evaluating your preferences. Some items are sure to stand out above others, and sometimes you just *know* that you prefer some traits to others. Your evaluation of each of the factors listed above will enable you to "know your product," know what you can do, what you like to do, and what you are capable of doing. By synthesizing all of the above data with the help of other people and professionals, you will be able to really "know thyself," have a much better idea of *what* you want to do, and select a vocational goal (i.e., a career) that is best for you.

Where Do You Want to Work?

The geographic location, the type of organization, and the working environment are all important factors in determining where you want to work after graduation. You also need to think about domestic employment vs. employment in another country. Consider three factors very seriously.

Geographic Location

If you have a definite desire to be near an ocean, have access to skiing or fishing, go to museums and art galleries, live where there are major league sports, attend concerts and other musical offerings, or relax in relative solitude, you can appreciate the importance of geographic location in considering potential careers. Since so many of our pleasures in life, and our opportunities for self-fulfillment, are dependent on what we do outside of working hours, it is imperative that we live in an area that has the recreational, social, religious, educational, artistic, and other facilities and organizations that meet our individual needs.

For certain types of careers, employment requires living in certain areas of the country. For example, if you are interested in advertising or investment banking, you may find it mandatory to go to New York, Chicago, San Francisco, Atlanta, Dallas, or other metropolitan centers. For careers in farming, the Midwest and the South are the logical places to locate. Careers in mining are located in the Rocky Mountain and Appalachian areas.

Since the location of the job and career is so important in determining your future for both work and life purposes, you should give careful thought to its influence. Ideally, persons should be mobile and go wherever the job and career require, but human nature does not always follow the ideal. Recent graduates who return to their college's career center often state "I love my job and my employer, but I want more out of life than just work and a paycheck."

Type and Size of Organization

Some people do best in a highly structured organization with very specific lines of authority and responsibility, while others prefer an informal, loosely knit type of organization. The type of industry will usually determine how organizations are structured, but there are variations. Producing steel obviously requires a large organization occupying many acres of property, whereas running a small bakery or retail outlet requires a small space in one location.

Another factor to be considered is the large vs. small type and size organization. Career counselors often hear students and recent graduates make comments such as: "I don't want to get lost in a big company," "I want to teach in a small, private school, not in a big, urban system," "I prefer to work in a medium-size hospital in Florida or California," or "I want to be able to use my engineering training immediately and not spend two years on the drawing board."

Some people fear a large organization because they think they have to conform and thus lose their individuality, or they believe the working environment would not be stimulating enough. Recent graduates have stated that large corporations often stifle initiative, which makes it difficult when they try to get venture capital. There are advantages in working for either size organization, as indicated in figure 6-5.

Generally speaking, it is easier to start with a large organization and move to a smaller one if things do not work out. Big organizations have more training, extensive benefit programs, and a greater number of stimulating colleagues to provide intellectual challenges.

Small companies offer a more intimate working environment, usually specialize in one product or one type of service in a single location, and often provide broader work experience, which is especially helpful to future entrepreneurs.

Because there are many paths for career success, there is no absolute best-size company or organization for all applicants. Many times a decision has to be made on the basis of "do you want to be a big fish in a small pond, or a small fish in a big pond"? In career planning, applicants should consider their options and make comparisons to facilitate making proper decisions.

A small but very important percentage of our population prefers to run their own organization. We usually refer to such individuals as *entrepreneurs*—persons who like to develop an idea into a business, and then manage the enterprise as they think it should be run. Chapter 14 contains more information on entrepreneurs, because you should definitely consider this possibility when you are researching potential careers, and take action after you have accumulated some work experience.

Working Environment

Being happy and productive in your work requires a working environment that suits you. Some people like a professional environment that is mentally challenging, such as college teaching, engineering, accounting, law, medicine, or social work. Some prefer an environment that is physically demanding, such as athletic games, geology, forestry, or physical fitness organizations. Others prefer some combination of both mental and physical attributes.

Figure 6-5. Advantages of Large and Small Employers*

Large Employer	Small Employer
More job levels, therefore greater promotional opportunities.	Person of ability may stand out sooner and more prominently.
Greater potential earnings.	May offer eventual ownership possibilities.
Starting salary often higher.	Advancement often comes faster; competition may be less.
More extensive training programs.	Quicker assumption of responsibility and more immediate assignment to a specific job.
Greater security and fringe benefits.	More opportunity to benefit from growth of the organization.
Greater financial strength to weather depressions and technological changes.	Individual may be able to give more direction to work of organization and more readily see results of his or her efforts.
Promotion from within policies enable a graduate to make careers with one employer on a lifetime basis.	More willing to hire older, experienced graduates.
More staff resources available to help solve problems as they arise.	Often greater opportunity for the independent person who works best alone.
Greater expenditures on research to ensure progress.	Work is often more varied and not as routine.
Diverse operations permit functional and geographical transfers.	Little need for geographical relocation, upsetting family life and friendships.
Often more scientific approach to management.	Policies and procedures more flexible; individual initiative may be more encouraged.
Less danger of being merged with large employer because of financial difficulties, competition of new products, or uneconomical size.	Often get better experience if you are interested in going into business yourself.
More scientific promotion policies; little danger of relatives being favored as in a family-owned business.	Easier identification with goals of employer; more apt to be known by top management.

*****Source:** Calvert, Robert Jr. and John E. Steele, *Planning Your Career*, © 1963.

Students seeking careers that require creativity—art, advertising, TV production—would be stifled in a working environment where no independence is allowed to develop ideas, where supervision is constant, or where suggestions or initiative are not encouraged.

What Is There to Be Done?

Idealism has to be tempered with realism in seeking productive and rewarding careers. If there is no demand for the products or services of your employer, you will find it very difficult to get a job and develop a career with that organization. Some years ago a popular cartoon showed a chart depicting a steady downward sales curve over a period of years. The sales manager was stating: "I cannot understand it, I know our company produces the best buggy whips in the country."

The U.S. Department of Labor compiles and publishes surveys of trends of various industries; college career offices generally have copies available for students and recent graduates, as do the campus libraries. Trade associations and professional societies make periodic surveys to estimate the future growth of jobs in their industry or field. Articles on jobs in the future are published in magazines, trade and professional journals, and newspapers.

A typical example is the article "The Economics of the Job Market" in the *CPC ANNUAL,* by John D. Shingleton, one of the country's foremost authorities on the college scene. It provides specific and current data on the demand for college graduates and accompanying salaries. Another good source is Shingleton's book *College to Career: Finding Yourself in the Job Market,* which discusses the job market, knowing what is in demand, and other data pertaining to the world of work. Interesting articles worth reading by college graduates appear frequently in magazines, newspapers, and professional journals on topics such as business and industry in the coming decade, entry-level jobs, and trends.

From researching the literature available from the above sources of information, and from talking to professors and officials in industry and government, you can begin to appreciate the variety of sources providing information on *what* is there to be done. The next chapter provides more detailed information on analyzing occupations and categories of employers.

What Are Your Goals?

Instead of wandering from job to job with no apparent accomplishment, it is far more desirable to have a long-range goal (career) and short-term objectives (jobs). Determining specific goals provides a target that enables you to put purpose and direction into your efforts. A goal determines the road on which you travel toward a destination. Breaking down the career goal into short-term job objectives will provide landmarks along the career path to help ascertain whether you are on the right road for your long-range goal.

In setting career goals you need to be realistic in selecting achievable goals, and also have a strong desire to achieve them. If you are an average basketball or baseball player in college, your long-range goal of becoming a professional athlete is not very realistic. Don't set goals just because your parents or friends think they are right for you. For example, if you do not enjoy planning, supervising, and coordinating the efforts of others, you would be very unhappy in a management position.

Sometimes a person has to do things for a short time that may be disagreeable but necessary in order to make progress toward a long-range career goal. Suppose your career goal is to become a college professor of accounting. Your short-term objectives might include two years of graduate school, then working for two or three years (depending on state requirements) to qualify for and pass the examination to become a certified public accountant. With a few years of such professional experience, you would have the minimum requirements to apply for a job teaching accounting in a college or in a university.

Generally speaking, people are more motivated when they have specific rather than general goals. Saving to buy a car will motivate you to get results quicker than just building a savings account; training for a marathon race will develop your endurance better than just running in general; planning a trip to Hawaii will get you there faster than dreaming of a vacation.

To find the right career goal, it is better to keep specific goals in mind rather than general ones. Instead of "teacher," it is better to specify "teaching social sciences in a high school." Instead of "engineer," it is better to state "civil engineer to build bridges." Instead of "business executive," specify which field of business such as "person selling consumer goods, leading to sales management." Instead of "nursing," specify your goal as "general nursing leading to a specialty in surgical nursing."

Short-term objectives will help mark your step-by-step progress on the successive jobs leading to your long-range career goal. By concentrating on the next higher level, your performance and attitudes should help you advance in much less time. Even if your objectives or goals change, if you have something specific to look forward to, it may well be all the incentive you need.

All persons have dreams, but they need focus to concentrate on what they want out of life. Whether your goal is to graduate from college, save enough money to buy a car, get tickets to a concert or sporting event, become a professional, or to get a job or graduate degree, your chances for success are enhanced if you specify your goal so that you will be willing to work and sacrifice for it, thus providing an incentive and a purpose for your efforts and actions.

Michael Adams set three goals for himself: playing basketball for a Division I college, becoming the first person in his family to graduate from college, and turning professional in the National Basketball Association. As a 5'9" guard coming out of the Bellevue Square Housing Project and Hartford Public High School, his is a great human success story. He told a college admissions counselor "give me a chance and I'll go to every class, and I'll graduate." Four years and three NCAA Final 16 appearances later, Adams received his degree in communications. At the time this book was written, Michael Adams was the point guard for the Denver Nuggets in the NBA, and established the record for three-point shots by making at least one in seventy-nine consecutive games!

Joseph Modjelewski had a dream of becoming a successful business executive. His immigrant parents spoke very little English, and had few resources to help him. By working part-time during his high school and college years, and full-time during summer vacations, Joe managed to get into a public university where he majored in business administration. From the interviews generated through the university's career center, he received three job offers and decided to join a consumer goods company. He applied himself during the sales training course, then worked hard to get his own sales territory. After two years he became a supervisor of a small unit, and after five years he progressed to the district sales manager position. Joe is well along toward his career goal of becoming an executive.

Ruth Sutin Armiger graduated from Syracuse University with a Bachelor of Fine Arts degree, and started teaching art to elementary, junior high, and high school students. Then she obtained her Master of Fine Arts degree at the Pratt Institute in New York. She continued to teach for seven years, all the while wondering if there was a better way to express her talents.

Her next career was in television, starting as a production assistant and progressing to associate producer and then production manager working on "Saturday Night Live," the "Today Show," and as producer at NBC News. Although she had "arrived" in television, she changed careers again in her 40s.

Armiger is now happily painting on a full-time basis. She displays her work publicly and sells her paintings at a profit. Her strong desire to succeed and to find a better way to express her talents, plus her perseverance, enabled her to have three different careers, all of them successful.[1]

Having answered the basic questions in this chapter, you now have some appreciation of what you *want* to do and the possible career options that would interest you. You also have some idea of *where* you want to work, and whether your long-range *goals* (your vocational career objective) will enable you to work in an industry that will grow in the future and thus provide the environment in which you can develop your plans for a worthwhile career and a satisfying life.

The next step is to research the potential careers (occupational fields) in more detail to verify your choice of a career, as well as the employers and industries that would be logical to consider in your job search. You will also need to determine whether graduate school training is necesary for your chosen career.

[1]Baum, Laurie. "The Fine Art of Job Satisfaction." In *Career Vision*, 1989.

chapter seven

Career Exploration and Objective

Assuming the typical work week is forty hours, you will work approximately 2,000 hours in one year's time (at fifty weeks of work, two weeks for vacation). If your work is boring and unrelated to what you really like, or the job doesn't utilize your interests and skills, you will be paying a high price for failing to do adequate research before entering your career.

Because of new technology, economic and political developments, and the supply of qualified workers, the job market in various occupational fields is constantly changing. Now that you have completed step one—self assessment—the second step in career planning involves an effort to research the world of work, look into various occupations, and develop career options.

By researching occupational fields, you will accumulate information about possible fields of work that complement knowledge about yourself obtained from your self-assessment. The results of this research will not only save you time in the job search, but the information you obtain should make your job-hunting or graduate school applications more effective. Thorough study of occupational data should help clarify or verify your career goal, and find out whether your field of interest is really suitable. In your letters and interviews, information from your research will demonstrate to prospective employers or graduate schools that you have explored career options, are serious about your future, and are willing to devote time and effort to becoming better informed.

The world of work can be classified in various ways. Some people like to rank various occupations by their prestige. In this system judges, doctors, scientists, and high government officials rank at the top, while janitors, garbage collectors, and bartenders, generally rank at the bottom. Another method of classifying work is by socioeconomic factors, or the degree of intelligence, education, skill required, and the income in a field. On this basis the professional and management fields are rated at the top, and the unskilled workers are rated at the bottom.

Every ten years the U.S. Census Bureau obtains information about our jobs, dividing the working world into four broad areas: white-collar workers, blue-collar workers, farm workers, and service workers. From these data you can ascertain the scope of work, comparative sizes of occupational groups, and their geographical distribution. Another government classification is the system developed for filing occupational or career materials found in the *Dictionary of Occupational Titles (D.O.T.)*, described in more detail later in this chapter.

Career exploration actually involves two different approaches: first, the overall approach, which is studying occupations (fields of work), and next, the specific approach, which is studying the prospective industries and specific employers in your chosen career field. For either approach, you would use one or more of three basic methods: the media, people, or experience.

Researching Occupational Fields

Media Research

A great deal of information is available via the media: books, magazines, pamphlets, tapes, newsletters, films, annual reports, and brochures. Throughout your college years you have been developing your research and library skills for classroom or term paper purposes. Now, use these skills to gather and evaluate occupational information pertinent to your prospective career.

Generally speaking, printed material prepared by a government agency or by professional or trade associations will be more objective than that prepared by a specific employer. College career centers, public libraries, and bookstores have a variety of printed references on occupations. In any library, you can save yourself considerable time and effort by asking the research librarian, or whoever performs this function, where you can find reference material on the career(s) you are interested in.

A good place to begin your occupational research is *The Occupational Outlook for College Graduates*. This publication:

> . . . is a guide to career opportunities in a broad range of occupations for which a college degree is, or is becoming, the usual background for employment. It contains a brief summary of the expected changes in the economy, in addition to an analysis of the overall supply and demand situations for college graduates . . . . Each occupational statement presents information on the nature of the work; places of employment; education, skills, and abilities required for entry; employment outlook; related occupations; and earnings. The statements in this publication account for about 90% of all workers in professional and related occupations, and for smaller proportions of workers in other major groups.

This publication is a condensed version of *The Occupational Outlook Handbook*, which has over 850 occupational descriptions, each containing the following information:

Nature of the Work
This section describes the major duties of workers in the occupation. It tells what workers do on the job, what tools or equipment they use, and how they perform their work. This section should help you determine whether the work done on the job is appealing.

Working Conditions
The environment (outdoor vs. indoor, noisy vs. quiet setting) and such factors as overtime, shift work, travel, hazards, and physical demands are important in considering careers that fit your interests.

Places of Employment
This section provides information on the number of workers in an occupation, and states whether they are concentrated in certain industries or geographic areas. This is important for people who have strong preferences about where they wish to live.

Training, Other Qualifications, and Advancement
This section should be read carefully because preparing for an occupation requires a considerable investment of time and money. Selecting courses considered as most useful in preparation

for the career you have in mind, finding out about certification or licensing requirements, and learning which occupations are natural stepping-stones to others will help qualify you for an occupation at a higher level and also affect your speed of advancement.

Employment Outlook

This section discusses prospective job opportunities. You can learn about the availability of jobs in the field that interests you the most, and whether that field is likely to grow, decline, or is standing still. Don't rule out a potentially rewarding career simply because the outlook is not favorable; even small or overcrowded occupations provide some jobs.

Earnings

In addition to the money, you need to know about the fringe benefits. Such things as paid vacations, health and life insurance, uniforms, discounts on purchases, sick leave, and so on will help determine the total compensation and satisfaction the job provides for your standard of living. Some parts of the country and certain industries pay higher salaries than others.

Related Occupations

This lists other occupations that require similar aptitudes, interests, education, and training.

Sources of Additional Information

There is often a wealth of career information available, at little or no cost, to provide more details about a particular occupation. These include sources such as professional and trade associations, libraries, career and counseling centers, personal contacts, and state agencies.

For a preliminary exploration of a career field, the *Occupational Outlook Handbook* or its special edition for college graduates is the best and most resourceful publication available. The primary benefit of both of these reference sources is that they enable students and recent graduates to quickly peruse many fields, and narrow their career search to those occupations that may be of most interest. The *Occupational Outlook for College Graduates* has no beginning or ending point. The table of contents provides an alphabetical list of occupational reports to help you find the occupations that match your interests.

Professional societies and trade associations usually offer free information about their field. Be wary of biased information that may give only the positive aspects of the field, exaggerate the earnings potential or the demand for workers, or omit important items. Also, if a publication is over five years old, its data may be obsolete or actually misleading. Fortunately, most of the career materials produced by professional societies and trade associations fulfill the major purpose of providing objective vocational guidance. The following examples from the *Occupational Outlook for College Graduates* illustrate professional society and trade association sources of additional career information:

Engineers
Engineers' Council for Professional Development
345 East 47th Street
New York, NY 10017

Engineering Manpower Commission of Engineers
Joint Council, 345 East 47th Street
New York, NY 10017

National Society of Professional Engineers
2029 K Street, NW
Washington, DC 20006

Society of Women Engineers
345 East 47th Street
New York, NY 10017

Societies representing the individual branches of the engineering profession are listed separately in the *Occupational Outlook* reference book. Each section provides information about careers in that particular branch.

Social Workers
National Association of Social Workers
7981 Eastern Avenue
Silver Spring, MD 20910

Information on accredited graduate and undergraduate college programs in social work is available from:

Council on Social Work Education
345 East 46th Street
New York, NY 10017

Accountants
American Institute of Certified Public Accountants
1211 Avenue of the Americas
New York, NY 10036

National Association of Accountants
919 Third Avenue
New York, NY 10022

Institute of Internal Auditors
249 Maitland Avenue
Altamonte Springs, FL 32701

For information on educational institutions offering a specialization in accounting, contact:

American Assembly of Collegiate Schools of Business
1755 Massachusetts Avenue, NW, Suite 320
Washington, DC 20036

Teaching Occupations
American Federation of Teachers
11 Dupont Circle, Fifth Floor
Washington, DC 20036

National Education Association
1201 16th Street, NW
Washington, DC 20036

Chemists
American Chemical Society
1155 16th Street, NW
Washington, DC 20036

Chemical Manufacturers Association
1825 Connecticut Avenue, NW
Washington, DC 20009

Health Services Administrators
National Health Council, Health Careers Program
1740 Broadway
New York, NY 10019

American College of Nursing Home Administrators
4560 East-West Highway
Washington, DC 20014

Association of University Programs in Health Administration
One Dupont Circle, NW
Washington, DC 20036

American College of Hospital Administration
840 North Lake Shore Drive
Chicago, IL 60611

Practically every occupational field has one or more national organizations such as those listed above. In addition, many have state societies in their profession, which often provide practical, hands-on advice and information.

The *Dictionary of Occupational Titles* (*D.O.T*), a publication of the U. S. Department of Labor first appearing in 1939, currently lists titles and descriptions for over 20,000 jobs. Because job titles can mean different things to different organizations, readers cannot rely entirely on titles to appreciate the actual content. In some organizations a "secretary" is the job title for duties involving shorthand, typing, and administrative work. In other organizations this title is given to a job entailing typing duties only. Some organizations have dignified the job of janitor by calling it a sanitary engineer. The *D.O.T.* source can help applicants get a short overview of a job, and help relate the written description to other researched material to get a more accurate portrayal of what is expected in that job.

The *D.O.T.* provides information on what is done in a great variety of jobs (typical duties and responsibilities), and helps ascertain the general qualifications for that type of work. The D.O.T. system of classifying information on jobs is very helpful to beginners and also to experienced applicants in researching occupations (career fields), in getting a better understanding of the working world, and in relating the qualifications needed in each field.

It can assist in identifying career ladders and possible skill transfers vertically within an industry, or horizontally among closely related technologies. The *D.O.T.* job definitions are coded in three parts, with nine digits as follows:

First 3 digits—identify a particular occupational group

Middle 3 digits—are the worker functions ratings of the tasks performed in the occupation

Last 3 digits—indicate the alphabetical order of titles within the six-digit code groups

The *Encyclopedia of Careers and Vocational Guidance*, edited by William E. Hopke, presents data on 650 different fields with information similar to that found in *Occupational Outlook*—nature of work, entry requirements, education and training requirements, working conditions, advancement opportunities, earnings, and sources of additional information.

Magazines, newsletters, and brochures often include excellent articles on a specific occupation. Most professional fields will have journals providing articles of current interest, including written material on jobs within that field, surveys of the supply and demand for workers in that field, salaries or other earnings data, and so forth. In a similar manner, the newsletters published by various organizations usually have job and career information of interest to people in that occupation.

Illustrative of this is a newsletter citing by Dr. Richard E. Boettcher, dean of the College of Social Work at The Ohio State University:

> There is a critical shortage of health care workers, people who work with others to help them improve their lives. By the year 2000, . . . our society will need 700,000 to 800,000 new geriatric social workers, people trained to work with the aging.[1]

Engineers can obtain excellent advice and information from periodicals like *Graduating Engineer*. Most issues contain sections on job prospects, personal development, and other articles on careers.

Annual information on the job market (figure 7-1) is printed in the *CPC Annual*, which is available in college career centers. Periodically the weekly magazines publish articles on the job market and related topics.

Every year a survey is conducted on teacher supply and demand using information from all fifty states. The results are included in *The ASCUS Annual* to provide applicants for teaching positions with the latest data regarding the potential opportunities for jobs in their field of interest (figure 7-2).

---

[1]Boettcher, Dr. Richard E. *PERI*, Jan.–Feb. 1986.

Figure 7-1. Estimated Job Demand by Field of Study in 1989–90

For Bachelor's-Degree Graduates		
Academic Major	*Estimated Number*	*Percent of Total*
More Jobs Than Candidates		
Business and Management	237,238	24.11%
Engineering	76,038	7.73%
Health Professions	64,285	6.53%
Computer and Information Sciences	41,727	4.24%
Physical Sciences	21,647	2.20%
Engineering Technologies	19,544	1.99%
Total	**460,479**	**46.80%**
Jobs Equal to Candidates Available		
Education	86,883	8.83%
Mathematics	16,243	1.65%
Protective Services	12,655	1.29%
Architecture and Environmental Design	9,084	0.92%
Communications Technologies	1,419	0.14%
Other	1,603	0.17%
Total	**127,888**	**13.00%**
More Candidates Than Jobs		
Social Sciences	93,340	9.49%
Communications	41,505	4.22%
Psychology	40,364	4.10%
Life Sciences	38,375	3.90%
Visual and Performing Arts	36,806	3.74%
Letters	35,297	3.59%
Liberal/General Studies	19,174	1.95%
Agriculture and Natural Resources	16,758	1.70%
Multi/Interdisciplinary Studies	15,639	1.59%
Home Economics/Human Ecology	15,229	1.55%
Public Affairs	13,824	1.40%
Foreign Languages	10,063	1.02%
Philosophy and Religion	6,215	0.63%
Theology	5,580	0.57%
Parks and Recreation	4,416	0.45%
Area and Ethnic Studies	3,048	0.31%
Total	**395,633**	**40.21%**
Grand Total—All Fields:	**984,000**	**100.00%**

Sources: Supply/demand ratio estimated by John D. Shingleton and L. Patrick Scheetz, Career Development and Placement Services, Michigan State University, 1989. Grand total of bachelor's-degree recipients from *Projections of Education Statistics to 1997–98*, Washington, D.C.: U.S. Department of Education, 1988, p. 63.

Figure 7-2. Relative Demand by Teaching Area 1988 Report

Based upon a Survey of Teacher Placement Officers	
Teaching fields with considerable teacher shortages . . . (5.00–4.25):	
Bilingual Education	4.35
Special Education-ED/PSA	4.33
Special Education-LD	4.26
Special Education-Multi. Handi.	4.26
Teaching fields with some teacher shortage . . . (4.24–3.45):	
Special Education-MR	4.15
Science-Physics	4.01
Mathematics	4.00
Speech Pathology/Audio.	4.00
Science-Chemistry	3.96
Special Education-Deaf	3.91
Computer Science	3.79
Special Education-Gifted	3.74
Data Processing	3.59
Language, Mod.-Spanish	3.59
Psychologist (school)	3.57
Library Science	3.56
Science-Earth	3.52
Teaching fields with balanced supply and demand . . . (3.44–2.65):	
Special-Reading	3.43
Language, Mod.-French	3.43
Science-General	3.42
Science-Biology	3.37
Language, Mod.-German	3.34
Counselor-Elementary	3.12
English	3.11
Industrial Arts	3.07
Counselor-Secondary	3.03
Social Worker (school)	3.01
Music-Instrumental	3.00
Journalism	2.91
Speech	2.91
Business	2.90
Music-Vocal	2.89
Agriculture	2.88
Elementary-Intermediate	2.72
Elementary-Primary	2.71
Driver Education	2.70
Teaching fields with some surplus of teachers ... (2.64–1.85):	
Art	2.35
Home Economics	2.26
Health Education	2.02
Social Science	2.00
Teaching field with considerable surplus of teachers . . . (1.84–1.00):	
Physical Education	1.67

5 = Greatest Demand, 1 = Least Demand

Data from the 1988 Report revealed the following:

1. Teacher placement officers continue to report improved job markets for their candidates as compared to previous years. Of the placement officers responding, 57% indicated that the job market has been better or much better for elementary teachers and 58% indicated that it has been better or much better for secondary teachers, as compared with one year earlier. Compared to four years earlier, 76% of the respondents indicated an improvement at the secondary level for their candidates.

2. Fifty-six percent of the respondents indicated that they expected the job market to be improved for this year's elementary level graduates and 51% expected improvement for secondary level candidates.

3. In the fields of bilingual education, personal and social adjustment (behavioral disorders), learning disabilities, and multiple handicapped education, there is a considerable shortage of teachers. The considerable shortage fields are all special educational areas. In thirteen fields there is some shortage of teachers.

4. In physical education there appears to be a considerable surplus of teachers. Four additional fields have some surplus of teachers.

5. Of the forty-one fields surveyed, supply and demand are approximately balanced in nineteen fields.

6. Placement officers in the Middle Atlantic and Southeast Regions (VIII and VI) indicated greater optimism for teacher opportunities while placement officers in the Northwest and Rocky Mountain Regions (I and III) indicated less optimism relative to teacher opportunities as compared to their counterparts in other regions of the country.

Generally, placement officers described opportunities for last year's graduates as the same or better than the previous year and better or much better than four years earlier. They expect the job market for this year's graduates to be better than it was for last year's graduates.

Source: *1989 ASCUS Annual.*

Since sports are a national passion in the United States, thousands of young people dream of a career as an athlete with hopes of fame and money. Although most of us look upon sports as fun or as a means of keeping physically fit, very few can actually succeed at making a livelihood at it.

One of the best articles on athletics as a career was written by Michael Stanton and appeared in the *Occupational Outlook Quarterly*. This article points out that "the total number of major league players in professional football, baseball, and basketball is only 2,261—a mere fraction of the 1,892,475 who played in high school. The odds of a high school athlete becoming a pro football, baseball, or basketball player aren't 50-50; they are 837 to 1, and even the one who makes the pros is likely to be out of sports within four years."[2]

A major benefit of researching written material first is that it enables you to become conversant with many aspects of prospective career fields, thus making it easier to further research through other methods such as people and experience. At least you will be more knowledgeable when asking questions or discussing occupations, and this knowledge will further your research in exploring occupations and trying to decide on a career objective.

In the past two decades, college students also have had access to electronic forms of media on occupations and career guidance. Some of the computer programs, such as DISCOVER, SIGI, and CAREER NAVIGATOR, provide specific information on many occupational fields, and force applicants to make decisions on career priorities. New software packages for computers are being developed constantly and coming on the market.

There is a growing number of audio and video tapes that present career information very effectively. Since "a picture is worth a thousand words," students can quickly obtain a realistic view of working conditions and job responsibilities from such audiovisual materials.

One aspect of electronic misinformation that should be recognized is the image of various occupational roles on TV, radio programs, and in films. The roles in soap operas and movies are created for entertainment, and they rarely resemble realistic jobs or careers.

Corporate brochures, annual reports, and graduate school publications contain career information of interest to anyone explor-

---

[2]Stanton, Michael. "Playing for a Living." *Occupational Outlook Quarterly*, 1987.

ing possible vocations. You can find relevant data on the industry and the company or the graduate school, specific descriptions of the various departmental functions or graduate programs, financial data, trends and plans for the future, how that firm trains and promotes college graduates, some information on salary policy and employee benefit programs, and usually a listing of the subsidiaries and locations of offices or plants. Figure 7-3 illustrates the possible careers available for college graduates in the Westvaco Corporation, as presented in this firm's recruiting brochure.

People Research

A second method for researching occupational fields is to talk with people now in that type of work. Make sure the person giving you information is actually knowledgeable in the field, and that the information you get is objectively given. For example, a college professor may be able to give you a realistic picture of what to expect in graduate school and in college teaching, but may be a poor source of information for applying the knowledge taught in college to an actual sales job. Similarly, evaluate carefully information from friends, relatives, and others who are far removed from hiring activities or do not understand the career problems facing the college student.

A salesperson may be quite loquacious and convincing in describing the glamorous aspects of his or her field of work—dealing with a varied public, filling a real need, making lots of money (usually exaggerated), being independent, and lots of travel. However, he or she might play down or ignore the negative aspects of the job—being away from family and friends for long periods, having to constantly meet higher quotas, experiencing office and production delays in fulfilling customers' orders, and having the incentives reduced whenever he or she "makes too much money."

Sometimes a person has had negative experiences in a field of work, and may have nothing good to say about it. Such a sour grapes attitude should be recognized for what it is. If a person has been in the same job for too many years, he or she has learned to "live with it" and probably has forgotten what would be of great importance to a student or a recent graduate.

Probably the person in the best position to give you advice is a recent graduate (within the past five years). He or she should be able to relate to you and remember what it was like to research

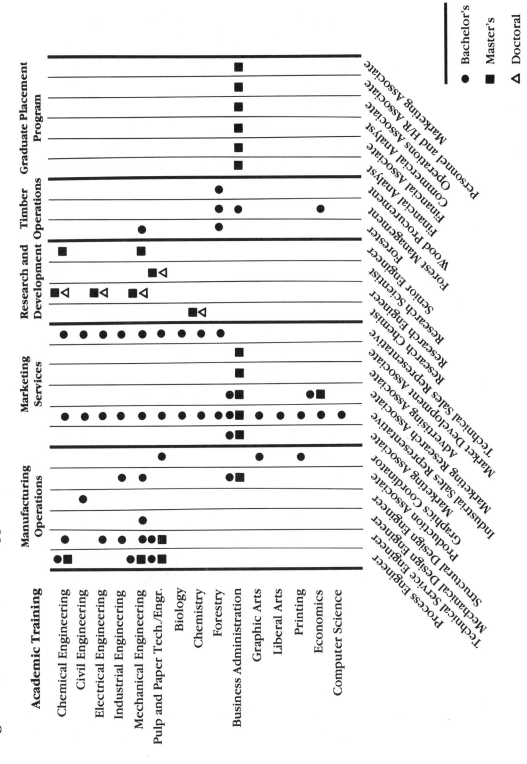

Figure 7-3. Westvaco Career Opportunities

careers and try to decide on one after graduation. The graduate will usually be able to recall starting job duties, the progression up the ladder, the challenge and satisfactions in that type of work, which college courses were most useful, and the negatives of the job field. He or she should also be able to give you straightforward answers to questions.

Students and recent graduates are often reluctant to ask executives or professional people for career advice because they think such individuals are too busy, or because they feel inadequate to discuss that career field. Most people are glad to help, sometimes because of their altruistic nature, because they remember their own formative years, or simply because they like the ego satisfaction of helping someone seeking their advice. By researching the written material available in that field, you will be able to ask pertinent questions and demonstrate a definitive interest in that business. It would also help to participate in a workshop or get help from the career center professionals on conducting informational interviews (see chapter 10).

Career conferences held on campus or in a nearby community (often called a "Career Day" if sponsored by a single college), enable you to meet with people from different occupational fields. Whether speeches are given or participants simply go to the rooms or tables set up for meeting purposes, such conferences can help you ascertain what occupations are available and what options are open to you.

Thank-You Letters
Out of courtesy and goodwill, you should write a letter to those persons who provide advice or information about career fields, thanking them for their help and informing them of what action you took. Such letters not only demonstrate your good manners, but also comprise a vital part of your strategy for an effective job or graduate school campaign. Thank-you letters should be sent to individuals who:

- counseled you on prospective employers or graduate schools, specific jobs, or on occupational fields

- provided you with information at a career or job fair

- referred you to prospective employers

- interviewed you for employment or admission to graduate or professional school

- wrote letters of reference or recommendations for you to employers or graduate schools

- gave you advice on your career plans

- showed you courtesy (secretaries, receptionists)

Because so few people take the time to write thank-you letters, that alone can easily distinguish you from other applicants. At the end of this chapter are examples of thank-you letters for five hypothetical applicants.

Experience as Research

The third basic method for researching occupations is to find work in the field because nothing beats actual work experience. By taking advantage of the internship, part-time jobs, or co-op programs available at your school, you can obtain a much more meaningful appreciation of the day-to-day tasks and responsibilities in the career field. By living in the work environment, you will get a far better insight into a career than from all the written materials you read. If your college does not have a formal internship program, you would be wise to create your own.

Whether you volunteer your services and work only for the experience, or whether you get paid for your work, you will acquire certain skills and more knowledge about your career field. Summer, part-time, co-op, internship, or volunteer work experience will provide direction in choosing more relevant and useful courses in college, give you a realistic feel for that type of career, and also add to your qualifications. Such practical experience will help you develop potentially useful contacts for your network. If you make a good impression on your supervisor, he or she may request you be hired after graduation for a permanent position.

By using all three basic methods of researching occupational fields—media research, people research, experience—you will obtain a comprehensive appreciation of the overall fields of work that might fit your needs, interests, and qualifications. You will also obtain specific information with which to judge potential employers in your chosen career field. Research often enables you to realize that you have numerous options available in starting your career.

For example, journalism and English majors interested in writing as a profession often think they have to start as copyreaders for a big city newspaper or a publishing firm. However, college graduates can learn the basics by working on company house organs, organization newsletters, annual reports, community advertisers, special interest publications, weekly newspapers, or professional journals. Then they can advance to higher positions.

Similarly, chemists and biologists do not have to limit themselves to laboratories sponsored by the government. They can also consider drug companies and cosmetics and food firms for suitable careers. If your self-assessment points to a career working with figures, you can utilize your abilities in a banking environment or you can work as an accountant, auditor, actuary, mathematician, statistician, or researcher. The possibilities are limited only by your imagination, initiative, and research perseverance.

In summary, career exploration involves two approaches: overall and specific. The overall method involves researching fields of work by studying the available material in various media, by talking to people who are knowledgeable in that field, and by working in paid or voluntary jobs to get experience. Such exploration will help you decide what are the options and which career field is most relevant for your combination of interests, abilities, values, and ambitions. The next step is to research specific employers who may have such career opportunities in their organizations.

Researching Prospective Industries and Employers

Researching fields of work will help determine your general career goal, but you must also give consideration to narrowing down the great number of possible employers. Two factors can help you focus your efforts on compiling a list of prospective employers: work environments and general types of employers within industries.

Work Environments

College graduates generally seek careers in the professional, technical, or managerial fields, typically labeled "white-collar" jobs. In our world of work, there are five major work environments: the professions, government, commercial organizations, education, and nonprofit organizations.

The Professions

The traditional professions like law, medicine, science, and college teaching, all require graduate degree training, licenses or accreditation to practice, and years of internship experience. To these traditional professions, we now add management consultants, nurses, accountants, social workers, psychologists, and others. Many professionals work for employers on a salaried basis, preferring regular hours and a steady income as compared to the fee structure and need for obtaining clients faced by independent practitioners.

Professionals operating as practitioners have all the same problems of business executives. They have to consider alternatives and make decisions on location, furniture, and equipment; hire and train staff; obtain clients; decide what price to attach for various services; collect payments; keep accurate records for tax and other purposes; worry about government regulations and laws in the field; and similar managerial decisions. They also need many of the personal attributes discussed in chapter 14 for entrepreneurs.

Government

Careers in government have three work levels—federal, state, and local (county, city, and town). The federal government is by far the largest single employer in the United States with 2.1 million employees, not counting the 840,000 in the Postal Service. Although the greatest concentration of jobs is in the Washington, D.C. area, there are also thousands of employees in regional and branch offices, and throughout the world as part of our military or State Department activities. Some agencies operate independently, but the great majority hire under the policies and procedures established by the Office of Personnel Management, formerly the U. S. Civil Service Commission.

Although most jobs are of the office variety in terms of working environment, many are outdoors, such as forestry, flood control, park maintenance, inspections in mines, and drug control. Applicants for federal employment may qualify on one of two bases: passing a competitive test, or being selected on the basis of qualifications judged by evaluating application forms and other materials. (Chapter 10 has more detailed data on federal employment.)

State government.   Most state positions are in offices, but there are jobs requiring incumbents to work out in the field, such as in fishing, law enforcement, and similar work. State offices and agencies vary in their hiring practices. Some have civil service tests, but there is little consistency among the states. Many functions performed by the federal government are also performed by state governments. Information on jobs and careers can be obtained by contacting the personnel department (some call it the human resource department) in that state.

Local governments.   The total number of jobs in the local government (counties, cities, and towns) far exceeds the number of employees in state or federal employment. This category also includes public school teachers. While some have civil service systems, many agencies on a local level hire directly. Sometimes the residency and patronage requirements and practices make it difficult for applicants to get hired.

At all levels of government, it takes longer to obtain a position compared to commercial organizations. College graduates contemplating government service have to have a lot of patience and perseverance to go through the various steps in the employment process. Although patronage does enter into the hiring picture, the top policy-making jobs obviously call for persons who are in sympathy with, and will carry out the policies of the political party in power.

Students interested in government employment can obtain examples of jobs and salaries paid to career and summer jobs by referring to the section "On the Public Payroll" in John W. Wright's book *The American Almanac of Jobs and Salaries.* The most accessible sources of information on campus regarding government jobs and starting salaries are the college career center and the faculty, if there is a department of government in your college.

Commercial Organizations

More jobs are available in the private enterprise system, or for-profit organizations, than can be found in other work environments. From the small retail "mom and pop stores" to the giant multinational corporations like General Motors and Mobil Oil, the free enterprise system in America provides services or products and employs millions. With new inventions and copyrights, additional industries are created, resulting in new firms, jobs, and careers, as evidenced by the impact of the computer industry in the past three decades.

With constant technological, economic, and political changes occurring, occupational fields and industries will also be changing. Every decade witnesses the creation of more employers and more jobs, and more complex and specialized occupational choices. The publications mentioned earlier in this chapter should help as you study broad industrial groupings and approach a complex job market. Obviously some industries and some organizations will appeal to you more than others. By researching the general categories of industries, and then researching specific employers, you can utilize this phase of career exploration to determine which organization would best fit your particular interests, goals, and qualifications. Such research also indicates where your qualifications and interests would make the most significant contribution and thus bring satisfaction in your career.

Education

Having gone through twelve to sixteen years of schooling, you are probably acquainted with the work environment in educational institutions. However, as most of your experience was accumulated in a teacher-student relationship, this does not do justice to the many other career fields within the educational industry. From a career perspective, educational occupations can be grouped into two major categories: faculty, including teaching, research, coaching, and library; and administration, including guidance and counseling, accounting, personnel, career planning, budgeting, admissions and records, engineering, and audiovisual.

The challenge of working with young people; broadening their horizons; developing their skills for study, athletics, research, and social purposes; encouraging their creativeness and utilization of talent; stimulating a thirst for knowledge; and serving as a role model are all positive reasons for contemplating a career as a faculty member. You should also explore the negative aspects of teaching or research, such as having to be a disciplinarian; having to perform the boring tasks of compiling statistics or grading papers and tests; dealing with recordkeeping, equipment, and budget frustrations; fulfilling required advisory or community duties; and dealing with the frequent lack of appreciation for your efforts by superiors, community, parents, and students.

In the administrative category are all the job classifications that appeal to people who are primarily interested in providing a service to others. There is a constant tug-of-war between providing better or additional services and obtaining the financial resources to make them possible. Positions and career fields in this category generally require people who are good with details and also have a warm sensitivity toward people's problems.

Nonprofit Organizations

This category includes professional societies, hospitals, certain types of research institutes, many types of social service organizations, art galleries, museums, labor unions, foundations, and so forth. The general work environment is to advance the frontiers of knowledge, such as in cancer or AIDS research, or to provide services to the public. Such organizations rarely recruit college graduates directly; most employees enter after accumulating experience related to the objectives of that organization. Because of the specialized nature of their goals, the career opportunities are relatively small but mostly professional in nature. The work environment is usually of two types—office and laboratory.

Office categories include jobs such as secretaries, word processors, and accountants, and also specialized positions as fund raisers, negotiators, public relations specialists, administrators, community liaison representatives, and lobbyists.

The laboratory category includes careers in research and engineering. These include the work of scientists seeking the cause and cure of human ailments, such as vaccines or drugs. Another family of occupations in this category includes engineers to design and develop medical devices and instruments; adapt computers to medical science; modernize the equipment and procedures for hospitals, clinics, and laboratories; or work with plans to build structures for such purposes.

Sometimes the occupation clearly indicates the work environment to be expected. Archeologists, mining engineers, geologists, forest rangers, and similar classifications naturally expect to work outdoors most of the time. Bacteriologists, chemists, and biologists are most commonly found in laboratories. Employees in advertising, finance, and personnel expect to work in offices. Applicants who understand the work setting or environment and what it implies or includes, will be able to better understand the jobs within that work category.

General Types of Employers within Industry

After researching the various occupational fields and getting some information on the working environment, you should then consider the kinds of industries that are most suitable for you. For this purpose, the ten major categories listed in *The Standard Industrial Classification Manual* (S.I.C.) serve as a good introduction. All researchers depend on this publication of the U. S. Office of Management and Budget to standardize the grouping of employers into various fields of endeavor.

Because there are thousands of different types of employers, it is necessary to narrow the field of prospective employers. The *S.I.C. Manual* groups all employers in the United States into ten major classifications—general categories of industries—as follows:

01 to 09   **agriculture, forestry, and fishing**
Includes all employers engaged in farming, nurseries, hunting and trapping, horticultural services, timber tracts, and fishing and fishery services.

10 to 14   **mining**
Includes mining metals, coal, crude petroleum, and natural gas, and quarrying of stone, sand, gravel, clay, gypsum, ceramic, and refractory minerals.

15 to 17   **construction**
Includes building, repairing, and improving of private and commercial structures, highways and streets, and waterworks.

20 to 39   **manufacturing**
Manufacturing is an extremely diversified classification, with twenty-one major divisions and employers, ranging in size from the gigantic petroleum refining and chemical industries down to the one-plant, small staff operation of a printer or toy manufacturer. These employers are engaged in such industries as foods, textiles and apparel, lumber, wood, paper products, and the production of machinery ranging from huge metal presses down to minute optical instruments.

40 to 49   **transportation, communications, and public utilities**
Transportation, communications, and public utilities are usually placed in one category. Transportation includes—for both freight and passengers—railroads, ships, trucks, buses, airplanes, and underground pipelines. Communications includes telephone, telegraph, radio, and television. The public utilities group contains employers engaged in electric and gas operations, water supply, sanitary services, steam companies and systems, and irrigation systems.

50 to 59   **wholesale and retail trade**
Includes distributors for industrial and consumer products—building materials, general merchandise, food, automobiles, apparel, furniture—whose outlets range from gigantic chains to small specialty shops.

60 to 67   **finance, insurance, and real estate**
Includes banks, personal and business credit institutions, investment houses, insurance companies and salespeople, and real estate brokers.

70 to 89   **services**
Major service areas are recreation—from bowling alleys to theater; health—from hospitals to medical laboratories and organizations; and education—including museums, schools, libraries, and nonprofit organizations of civic, social, and other groups. This classification also includes personal services such as photography, hairdressing, and repairs of all types, and business services such as professional accounting, employment and advertising agencies, and news syndicates.

91 to 97   **government**

The government group includes agencies of federal, state, county, municipal, and international governments. All positions compensated from public funds fall within this classification. These include civil service workers, police, firefighters, elective or appointive political officials, and teachers and administrative personnel in the public school systems from elementary schools through state universities.

99   **nonclassifiable establishments**

Because career paths vary for different industries, it is very helpful for you to select the industry which appeals to you. Furthermore, many reference sources, which are useful in researching prospective employers, are classified by function or by industry, as evidenced by the yellow pages of major telephone directories or by the standard reference sources discussed in chapter 10. Once you know your preferences on the industry, you will then be able to select those specific employers in the particular line of business to which you wish to make application. By utilizing the suggestions provided in chapter 10, you as the applicant can concentrate your energies toward a few *selected* prospective employers in the preferred industry.

Selecting a Career Objective

With the introspection gained from your self-assessment, and by studying the patterns indicated on your inventory, you can get a clearer picture of yourself and your preferred life-style, and which careers can best utilize your abilities and interests. Such thinking coupled with your research of occupational fields and industries, provides a better idea of what you want to do after graduation, and where, thus focusing your efforts toward a definitive career objective.

The key to career planning is locating the specific occupations that would best utilize your particular combination of interests, values, talents, and ambitions, and be suitable for a person with your limitations or shortcomings. The selection of a career field plays a major role in determining your future life-style, the environment in which you will be living, the type of colleagues with whom you will be working, and even the circle of friends you will be developing.

Selecting a career objective proves especially helpful in keeping your energies focused toward a goal, and in preparing resumes, writing application letters to prospective employers or graduate schools, and in answering questions during interviews.

The five chapters in part III provide the tools and techniques for searching out and getting a job to start your career, or for an intermediate move into the graduate school of your choice.

NOTE: To give readers a better perspective on the seven major items of correspondence relevant in a job campaign, or in a campaign to gain admission to a graduate school, we have included a series of examples for five hypothetical applicants throughout the entire process.

Sample letters and resumes for each step in the campaign are included in chronological order at the end of each chapter wherein that item is discussed. The seven items are:

Thank-you Letter	Follow-up Letter
The Resume	Stall Letter
Application Letter	Acceptance Letter
Rejection or Refusal Letter	

Examples of Thank-you Letters

McGregor Hall, A–23
Boston University
Boston, MA 02215

October 25, 1989

Ms. Mary J. Flynn
Director
Massachusetts State Nurses Registry, Inc.
40 Chappie Street
Boston, MA 02129

Dear Ms. Flynn:

Thank you very much for taking the time to advise me on the work of your organization, and on nursing as a career. I sincerely appreciate all the information you gave me, and feel more confident that it is a field I will really enjoy.

During my training in the School of Nursing at Boston University these past three and a half years, I have become very fond of this city. I was delighted to hear your comments on the variety and number of nursing opportunities in Boston and suburban hospitals.

Of the hospitals we discussed, I am most interested in Beth Israel, St. Elizabeth's, Brigham and Women's, and Mass. General. Preliminary research indicates that all four would have both general and surgical nursing positions, and all are located in the main part of Boston. I am trying to arrange interviews with their directors of nursing, and hope I can start my nursing career with one of these excellent hospitals.

Your encouragement, advice, and information have aided my job search. Thanks again for your help.

Very truly yours,

LaVerne Washington
LaVerne Washington

North Dormitory, R-12
State University
Laramie, WY 82071

October 18, 1989

Mr. Donald C. Rogers
Industrial Relations Dept.
Ideal Manufacturing Co.
122 West Grand Street
Detroit, MI 48221

Dear Mr. Rogers:

It was a pleasure to meet and talk with you during Career Day on our
campus. This event enabled many of our students to obtain a factual
view of careers from our own alumni.

Some of your department's problems, especially those in dealing
with your local labor union, seem both challenging and frustrating. I appreciate the candid comments and the advice you gave me regarding an industrial relations career in a manufacturing company.

In spite of the frustrations in dealing with labor unions, I think
the challenge of contributing to employee relations and motivating employees to more efficiently make products at a higher quality is worth undertaking. I believe I can help develop good working
relationships between management and workers.

Since our conversation I have been researching the companies you
suggested, and am now in the process of writing my application letters and sending my resume to them.

Thanks again for taking the time to visit the campus and give us a
pragmatic view of a career in industrial relations.

Very truly yours,

Bruce Horowitz

Bruce Horowitz
Class of '90

Mellon Hall, R–56
Indiana University
Bloomington, IN 47401

January 15, 1990

Ms. Dorothy Jones
Mathematics Department
North High School
26 Meridian Street
Columbus, OH 43211

Dear Ms. Jones:

It was very gracious of you to take time to talk with me during Christmas vacation regarding my desire to obtain a teaching job after graduation in June 1990.

Your suggestions and advice encouraged me to return to Columbus after graduation and seek an opportunity at North High School. The information you gave me on teaching loads, extracurricular expectation assignments, and the specific projects currently being worked on in your department, have stimulated my interest in becoming a part of such an active faculty.

As a result of our talk, I have discussed my career with my parents and two of my current professors, and plan to write to your principal Mr. Robert O. Forsythe this weekend.

Thank you very much for your encouragement in making my career at North High School.

Very truly yours,

Nancy R. Brennan

Nancy R. Brennan

Fairview Apts. #48
Ames, IA 50011

November 10, 1989

Dr. Robert J. Madden
Professor of Mechanical Engineering
Nathaniel Hall, R–350
Iowa State University
Ames, IA 50011

Dear Dr. Madden:

Following our talks in your office regarding my job and career plans, I took your advice by researching and writing to the Inland Steel Company.

Since they are not scheduled to recruit on our campus, I have been able to arrange a visit to their Chicago office during Christmas vacation. My interview is with Mr. D. Laurance Duvall on December 27, 1989.

The information you gave me about this company stimulated my interest, and my research indicates their management training program has many of the career factors I am seeking. Your interest in my career, and especially your cordial and cooperative discussion, are very much appreciated.

Thank you for all this assistance.

Very truly yours,

Roberto Mendes

Roberto Mendes

Simpson Hall, B–20
Rice University
Houston, TX 77251

November 1, 1989

Professor Walter J. Powers
Biology Department
Rice University
Houston, TX 77251

Dear Professor Powers:

Throughout my college career I especially enjoyed your courses in biology, but also appreciated the wise counsel you gave me regarding graduate school.

Following your advice, I have been studying the catalogs of Penn State University, Stanford University, and The Ohio State University to learn which offered the type of courses in biochemistry that would further my career.

All three of these universities are of interest to me for graduate work. I am writing to each of them for their application materials, and have applied to take the Graduate Record Examination next month.

Thank you very much for your interest in my career, and for taking the time to discuss the alternative options for a person with my background. I shall keep you informed of my progress.

Sincerely,

Susan Chin

Susan Chin

PART THREE

Your Job or Graduate School Search

THIS PART OF the book focuses on planning and implementing a campaign. It covers effective techniques and strategies needed for obtaining job offers and deciding on the right job to begin your career after graduation, or for helping you get admitted to a graduate program.

Although there are numerous books on how to get a job, few are written from the student's viewpoint. From the authors' experience in working with thousands of students and recent graduates, we approached this part of the book by visualizing the typical problems of students. A systematic step-by-step campaign is provided, which should result in the best opportunity commensurate with your interests, skills, abilities, and lifetime career aspirations.

These principles and practices can be used again and again throughout your working life, whenever you contemplate or need a change in your job or career.

Understanding the employment or application procedure of employers or graduate schools should emphasize the importance of adequate preparation for and follow-up to a job or graduate school campaign.

A graphic presentation of the step-by-step selection process for employment from an employer's viewpoint, and the actions to be taken by the college graduate, is shown in figure III-1. A similar process is used by graduate schools to select students, but they typically require prospec-

Figure III-1. Employment Procedure for Students Graduating from College

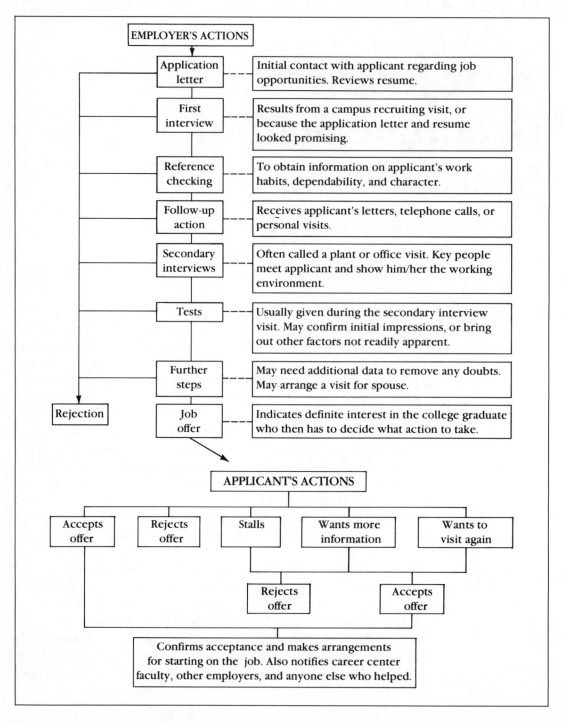

tive students to submit a transcript of their college courses and enclose reference letters before the interview.

It is important to understand and utilize the information contained in the following five chapters. By mastering job or graduate school search techniques, you will remove the fear and apprehension that most applicants face several times throughout their working lifetimes.

chapter eight

The Resume and Other Application Materials

There are several names for the documents and qualification records used to inform prospective employers of the applicant's interests and qualifications: the personal data sheet, the resume, the portfolio, the credential file, the curriculum vitae, and the application form. You will need to prepare one or more of these tools for your job search to interest employers in wanting to interview you for employment, or to gain admittance into a graduate program. Learning how to use these tools appropriately and effectively will give you a decided advantage in competition with other applicants.

The Personal Data Sheet

The personal data sheet is used by graduating students in the campus recruiting process. This one-page form is often called a registration form, a college interview form, or a placement registration form. It is designed to save you time and energy by summarizing the standard data that most employers use to consider job applicants. Either you or the career center staff duplicates this form in quantity. It serves as the first introduction to the potential employer for interviews on the campus, and serves a similar purpose in approaching graduate schools.

Periodically, professional college placement and recruiting associations throughout the country try to agree on the content of a personal data sheet. Since recruiters complain of the wide disparity of information made available to them when they recruit on college campuses, they keep hoping that all colleges and universities will someday have one standard form. In serving on regional and national committees created to design a standard form that would be universally accepted, one of our authors found that seventy-five percent of all information desired is requested by all recruiting employers. However, most employers still prefer to have their own form completed so that they know just where to look for certain types of data. Similarly, because college officials usually believe that their particular system is the best, it is very difficult, if not impossible, to get concurrence and acceptance of one standard form.

Here are some general rules to follow when filling out a personal data form.

1. Fill out the form completely and clearly; if a certain item does not pertain to you, draw a line in that space or note N/A to indicate that it is "not applicable." Otherwise you may give the impression that you overlooked that item.

2. It is best to type the information requested. Most of us do not have very good penmanship, and typing is not only neater but also more legible, making a better impression on readers.

3. Because the first impression is so important, be sure to take the time to check your grammar and spelling, while avoiding any cross-out errors.

4. Be truthful in your answers. It is easy to check the data provided, so do not ruin your chances by stretching the truth.

5. Be sure to sign and date the form.

The form developed by the College Placement Council (the national professional organization in the college career planning, recruitment, and placement field) illustrates the type of information usually requested (figure 8-1). Note its similarity to the application blank, which is discussed later.

Figure 8-1

COLLEGE/UNIVERSITY INTERVIEW FORM (Do not include information where prohibited by law.)	

☐ Regular Employment   ☐ Other Employment _____

Personal Data

Name Last First Middle Initial	Social Security No.
Present Address (Street, City, State, ZIP)	Present Phone, Area Code	U.S. Citizen ☐
Permanent Address	Perm. Phone, Area Code	Are you an alien authorized to work in the U.S.? ☐

Work Preference

Brief Statement of Job Interests and/or Description of Work Desired

Date Available for Employment	Geographical Preference	Geographical Objections

College Info.

Name and Location of Colleges Attended	Dates (Mo./Yr.) From	To	Degree Earned or Expected	Grad. Date Month	Year	Academic Major	Grade Point Average	Grade Basis
	/	/					Major Overall	A =
	/	/					Major Overall	A =

Honors, Activities and Organizations

Employment Info.

Employment and Business Experience (Include Permanent, Cooperative, Intern, Volunteer, Summer work and any prior U.S. military service.)

Work Experience (Name and Address of Employer)	Description of Work (Descriptive Title)	Hours per Week	Dates (Mo./Yr.) From	To
			/	/
			/	/
			/	/

General Info.

References: Such as faculty members who know you well and past supervisors; name, title, business address and telephone number.

Other Information: Community Activities, Hobbies, Interests, etc.

Special Info.

Federal regulations require government contractors to provide an opportunity for self identification to employment candidates who are handicapped, disabled veterans, or veterans of the Vietnam era. This information is submitted on a voluntary basis and used only in accordance with the regulation. It will not subject you to adverse treatment. If you wish to self identify, please check the box(es) which apply and sign.

☐ Handicapped Individual   ☐ Disabled Veteran   ☐ Vietnam Era Veteran   _____
(Signature)

The Resume

Of the various documents mentioned earlier, the resume is by far the most popular and widely used in a job campaign. In fact, many people lump together all forms of the applicant data and refer to them as resumes. Technically, the resume is an individually designed document summarizing personal interests and qualifications so that potential employers will become interested in the applicant. Just as a salesperson advertises the unique qualities of his or her product to generate customer interest, so do you need to compile a resume to highlight your accomplishments and make employers want to interview you.

The personal data sheet and the employer application form do not allow much flexibility in presenting your qualifications. A resume, however, provides an opportunity for you to present yourself to prospective employers as you want them to see you. The resume enables you to emphasize the strengths and "plus factors" that will sell you. You should integrate materials from your self-assessment and career exploration by compiling a resume that tailors your qualifications to the actual career alternatives available. In screening hundreds of applicants, employers may spend only half a minute scanning your resume to see if it warrants further consideration. If the information on your resume seems to fit some of the employer's job needs, you may be called for an interview.

The resume is neither an obituary nor an autobiography. It is an *inventory* and a *digest* of your background and experience, and provides a condensed history of what you have accomplished to date. Preparing a resume refreshes your memory so that you can answer interviewer's questions quickly and smoothly, and provides the material you need to create the right image. Many times it is the only document available to present your case to prospective employers, and it literally serves as your calling card, your sales promotion. Preparing a resume warrants your most careful consideration, and maximum time and effort.

Graduating seniors usually have relatively little work experience, so they must emphasize their educational achievements, extracurricular activities, internship or clinical or practice teaching experience, and whatever else may be related to their career objective. Graduate students and alumni should emphasize their accomplishments, and spotlight the results achieved that relate directly to their career or job objective.

Purpose

Resumes are not prepared to get job offers; their primary purpose is to obtain an interview. They are a vital part of your job strategy. Although applicants would prefer to talk about their interests and qualifications in an interview rather than in writing, the resume opens the door for an interview to enable you to sell yourself as the most desirable and qualified person for the job or program. Ideally a separate resume should be prepared for each specific position. However, this is not always practical, especially for students graduating from college with little work experience.

Use of Resumes

Although the number of ways you can use a resume is limited only by your imagination and initiative, you should know about and utilize some of the more common uses.

- For campus interviews, if your college does not require a standardized personal data sheet.

- For interviews off campus, resumes can provide necessary background data useful in filling out application forms, and serve you during interviews.

- For nonemployment purposes, such as applying for bank or charge account credit, providing information to facilitate introducing you as a speaker, exchanging resumes with fellow students for friendship or alumni network purposes, seeking housing, and so forth.

- For faculty or other consultations, especially if you need a reference for employment, or a recommendation to a graduate or professional school.

- To start your continuous career record or portfolio, and to refer to whenever you need to revise or update your resume.

- For networking and direct mail canvassing of the job market, to be attached to your letter of application.

- For job referrals to prospective employers, usually by your faculty members or the staff of your career center.

Although the format you use should be the one that highlights your qualifications most effectively, there are several variations possible. Select the layout and format that best represent you, and then concentrate on the mechanics of presenting your data.

Mechanics

Before you compose your resume, keep in mind the purpose of what you are about to do. Data from the self-assessment you made, as described in the previous chapters, will provide most of the information you need to compile your resume. Since you want your resume to get attention and action from employers, it would be wise first to prepare a tentative resume, have it reviewed and critiqued by a professional staff member in your career center, and then retype it in the format you desire. Have the final copy typed by a professional typist or a word processor, or have it produced by a reputable printing business.

Because first impressions are so important, pay special attention to the following mechanics:

Length
For most applicants under the age of thirty, one page is usually sufficient to present your data. Some people suffer from verbosity and don't have the skill to cull out the unimportant things in their lives and careers. Prospective employers may well assume that a resume filled with minutiae indicates the applicant is unable to differentiate important things from the irrelevant ones.

Quality of Paper
Some people save a few pennies by using cheap paper that does not reproduce well, thereby creating a negative image. Because employers often duplicate a resume and send it to several departments, use white paper, which duplicates easily. The duplicating or printing service you use can advise you about the quality of paper they have found most effective for resume purposes. Have them show you some samples.

Some applicants prefer to put their resumes on colored paper, on the theory that they will stand out among others. Some light colored paper, such as a canary yellow, off-white, or a light grey or pink will duplicate well, but you may run into trouble with other colors. One applicant used a lavender paper with purple ink to complement her personality. However, when her resume was duplicated for circulation to interested departments, it came out dingy and discolored. Unfortunately, several executives turned her down just because of the negative impression made by the duplicated copy they had received.

For most applicants, the standard 8½ " x 11" size paper should be used for resumes and letters. Social correspondence size paper or other fancy or odd shapes will not fit conveniently into file folders and drawers. The exception may be for legal applicants where 8½ " x 14" is the standard size, or for international applicants where 8" x 10" is typically used.

Appearance

A resume should be artistic, pleasing to the eye, and easy to follow. Since neatness is one way to improve a resume, be careful to proofread it for typographical errors, sentence structure, smudges, blurred letters, uniform spacing, and paragraphs and words that do not line up. Unless abbreviations are very well known and accepted, it is best to spell out the words. Abbreviations such as PHR and GPA (point hour ratio and grade point average) are standard scholastic abbreviations in different parts of the country. However, other abbreviations could be misinterpreted—AAA could stand for American Automobile Association, American Accounting Association, or American Arbitration Association, and Com could mean computer, communication, or committee.

The margins on a resume should represent a picture-frame effect. Many students have the problem of abusing the first-person pronoun, commonly referred to as "I-itis." Instead of a narrative or essay style of writing, it is better to use a telegram style.

Photographs

Career advisors today do not recommend using a photo on your resume. Too many look like passport or driving license photos, which could easily give the wrong impression of you. In states with an active Equal Employment Opportunities Commission (EEOC), a photo in applicants' files could lead to charges of discrimination on the part of the employer. Human beings often make stereotypic decisions about applicants, assuming from the photo that the person is "not sincere," "has shifty eyes and therefore cannot be trusted," "is too smug or flippant," "does not appear to be professional or businesslike," and the like. The extra cost of including a photo on your resume does not result in any additional advantage.

Phraseology

Your choice of words, and the manner in which you organize your phrases and sentences will either spoil your chances, or present a favorable view of your interests and personality. Word selection should connote your qualifications and ambitions effectively and concisely. Use easily understood words, not verbose terms such as "in articulating your esoteric cogitation, beware of platitudinous ponderosities." Your phraseology should convey a positive tone to reflecting a confident and self-assured image of yourself.

Organization

Use white space judiciously to focus the reader's eye on the important data you present. The reason we suggest a certain order of presentation is to appeal to recruiters who typically scan the resume looking for pertinent data to select prospective applicants for interviews. Therefore applicants should slant their information to appeal to the employer's interests and needs. By using well-chosen design techniques like spacing, capitalization, underlining, different size headings, and indentations, you convey the impression of orderly habits and a logical mind.

Creating Resumes on Computers

Using word processing to produce resumes has significant advantages over traditional methods of typewriting, typesetting, and offset printing. Greater flexibility and low cost are the major reasons for students who have access to computer equipment. Other advantages include:

- If you have more than one objective, you will be able to create separate resumes tailored to each objective.

- You can change and reorder sections of resumes to give more focus and support to each objective.

- The ability to produce text using different fonts and sizes allows for a more creative, effective presentation.

- The ability to alter spacing and to justify text (left, right, center) creates options for professional-looking documents.

- Each resume can be produced as an original document directly from the printing device. Any one resume can be produced as many times and as often as desired, so it is no longer necessary to order and buy more copies of a resume than are needed, or to wait for them to be produced.

There are some cautions to consider in using computers to create resumes:

- All documents should be printed letter quality. Laser printing offers the most flexibility and the best looking results. Dot-matrix printing simply does not produce results that look as good, and dot-matrix printing is more difficult to read.

- While there are software packages that have a variety of type fonts and sizes available, using several on one document is confusing and detracts from the main purpose of using a computer to create a resume. The goal is to produce a professional document, clean in its organization, pleasing to the eye, and consistent in its format.

- There are software packages on the market that guide the user through the process of creating a resume. Using these packages creates two major disadvantages. First, the actual work of deciding *what* you want on your resume, and *why*, requires careful consideration. Relying on a fill-in-the-blanks method may produce unsatisfactory results. It is better to phrase items on your resume to reflect you and your habits of expression.

  Second, using these packages usually ties the resume to one or two formats and always ties the resume to that software, as well as to that particular machine where the software is located. Computer software packages are not compatible with all computers. Using a standard word-processing software package gives access to any machine using that package—for example, a computer connected to a good printer.

Types of Resumes

Two major types of resumes are used: chronological and functional.

Chronological

The most popular type of resume, and the easiest to prepare, is the chronological, which presents biographical data in a logical sequence, in reverse chronological order. This type is preferred by the great majority of employers, agencies, and the faculty, and is generally accepted by all users. Figure 8-2 provides four models for this type of resume; most books on career planning or job seeking have other models.

Functional

This type of resume groups related skills into categories called functions, that tell prospective employers what you can do for them. It is most helpful to applicants who are results-oriented and have specific skills and achievements, who have had many jobs of short duration, who lack direct job-related experience, or who want to work in fields that are not related to their academic background. This type of resume is illustrated in figures 8-3 and 8-4.

The important point for you to remember is to compile your own resume so it will represent you and not someone whose qualifications were written by promoters or professional resume writers.

Content

There are countless numbers of books, pamphlets, manuals, and examples of resumes and how to write them in bookstores and in libraries. There is no universally accepted format or content for preparing a resume, nor any agreement on the best resume. In the opinion of the authors, the resume that enables a student or recent graduate to get an interview is the *best* resume. In general, your resume should tell employers what you have to offer; for this purpose, think of presenting your contents in sections to provide the information needed by employers.

Employer Needs	*Resume Response*
Who are you?	Identification section
What do you want to do?	Job objective section
What do you have to offer? or What can you do?	Sections on education, work experience, volunteer service, personal background, and so forth

Identification

This first section of your resume should tell who you are and help prospective employers reach you quickly. If you have a name that

Figure 8-2. Resume Models

#1 for undergraduates

YOUR NAME

School Address	(If school and home address	Permanent Address
City, State, Zip	are the same, place in this	City, State, Zip
(Area Code) Phone	area.)	(Area Code) Phone

Objective   Type of work sought.

Skills (optional)   State specific skills, abilities, and other information pertinent to the position being sought.

Education   Name and location of college/university attended
College/School of _____
   Degree in May 19xx
Concentration _____
Grade Point Average: _____ (out of 4.0) - if appropriate
Rank in class _____ .-if appropriate.
Honors: List scholarships, awards, other recognition.
Career-Related Courses or Projects.
Major Activities: (If numerous, you may wish to
            include these in a separate section.)

High School, location, year of graduation.
Major course of study.
Honors, activities, rank in class or grade average.
      (optional)

Experience   Name of present or last employer, city, and state.
Dates of employment
Job Title:
Duties, responsibilities, accomplishments.

List similar data for other employment, in reverse chronological order.

Be sure to include your volunteer and internship experiences.

Personal   Include interests, hobbies, travel, linguistic abilities, community or professional activities, and other items that may indicate your special talents or interest.

References   It is sufficient to state: Will be provided on request.

Source: PLACEMENT MANUAL, Boston College, 1988–89, p. 9.

#2 for education majors

YOUR NAME

School Address	(If school and home address	Permanent Address
City, State, Zip	are the same, place in this	City, State, Zip
(Area Code) Phone	area.)	(Area Code) Phone

Objective   (Example:) To obtain a position in the area of Elementary Education.

Education   Name and location of college/university attended
School
Date of graduation
Degree received
Major (or double major) and minor (if any)
Grade Point Average (cumulative and in major) (out of 4.0) (if appropriate)
Career-related courses

Extracurricular Activities   Name of organization and position held

Field Experience   Include your field experience, name of employer and duties.

Experience   Include your internship, volunteer, part-time and full-time work experience, name of employer, job title, and length of time worked. Include a short summary of duties or what you learned on the job.

Professional   State name of association, committees or other positions held.

Interests   Interests such as travel, sports, language proficiency, coaching, dramatics, etc.

Credentials   Available upon request

(May be 2 pages)

#3 for nursing majors

YOUR NAME

School Address City, State, Zip (Area Code) Phone	(If school and home address are the same, place in this area.)	Permanent Address City, State, Zip (Area Code) Phone

Professional Objective

(Example:) A position as a Staff Nurse in a medical-surgical unit.

Education

College/university attended
Degree received, Date of graduation
Major
Grade Point Average (out of 4.0) (if appropriate)
Honors/Academic awards

Clinical Experience

Name of employer, location and responsibilities.

Work Experience

Include your part-time and full-time work experience; name the employer, job title, and length of time worked. Include a short summary of duties or what you learned in your job.

Extracurricular Activities

Name of organization and positions held, responsibilities

Other Experience

List internship, volunteer, and other experience

Licensure

Include boards to be completed and dates

Professional Affiliations

State name of association; committee or other positions held

Interests

State interests such as travel, sports, etc.

Credentials

Will be provided on request.

(May be 2 pages)

#4 for graduate students

YOUR NAME

School Address   (If school and home address   Permanent Address
City, State, Zip   are the same, place in this   City, State, Zip
(Area Code) Phone   area.)   (Area Code) Phone

OBJECTIVE

State the type of position sought (short-range), your long-range career objective, and the type of industry or employer - if appropriate.

SUMMARY OF QUALIFICATIONS (optional)

State specific skills, degrees, licenses, years within a particular field, and other information pertinent to the position being sought. Highlight outstanding achievements.

EDUCATION

GRADUATE COLLEGE, Location
          _____ degree in May 19xx, majored in _____ ,
          minored in ____.
          Thesis or dissertation topic (if any):
          Honors:
          Activities: List organizations and describe involvement.
UNDERGRADUATE COLLEGE, degree and date received, major subject and other data.

WORK EXPERIENCE

NAME of employer, city, state, or country.
          Job Title, dates worked, or total months or years of experience.
          Duties, responsibilities, accomplishments.
          List in reverse chronological order.

PUBLICATIONS

List title, publisher, and date of publication.

PROFESSIONAL ASSOCIATIONS

Include professional and civic associations.

INTERESTS

Sports, hobbies, travel, etc.

REFERENCES

Available upon request.

Figure 8-3. Functional Resume for a College Student

MARY JANE DOE

Home Address: School Address:
2340 Longfellow Street   Hamilton Hall, R-226
El Segundo, CA 90245   State University
(213) 555-6582   San Jose, CA 94587
                                                          (408) 555-5065

CAREER OBJECTIVE

A training program with a social service or government agency, leading to a management position dealing with the public.

QUALIFICATIONS

Communication Skills
- Majored in English; minored in speech.
- Reporter for school newspaper; covered political and government news beat.
- Dormitory representative on student council.
- Member of varsity debating team.

Leadership Skills
- Elected as representative to the Junior Class Government Council.
- Editor, The Scholastic (college literary magazine).
- Student leader of orientation program for 1,500 incoming college students.

Community Skills
- Office of the Attorney General, Division of Consumer Protection Office — summer of 1988, assisted in handling consumer complaints and mediating solutions.

- United Way — summer of 1987, served as an intern observing, interviewing, and training volunteers.

- Robbins Library — three school years as weekend assistant. Filed books and magazines, helped catalogue incoming materials, served the public by providing information and assistance.

EDUCATION

B.A. degree, June 1989 from State University, San Jose, CA.
Major Subject: English. Minor Subject: Speech.
Scholarship: Upper third of class; Dean's List last two years.

PERSONAL

Interests include research, planning social and community programs, reading, League of Women Voters, and spectator sports.

REFERENCES

Will be provided upon request.

Figure 8-4. Functional Resume for a College Alumnus

JOHN DOE

Home Address:
2058 Allison Drive
Denver, CO 80260
(303) 771-3504

Business Address:
Housing Office
Denver College
Denver, CO 80205
(303) 670-5487

PROFESSIONAL OBJECTIVE

A major administrative position with a university, or in a state or federal government agency.

SUMMARY OF QUALIFICATIONS

Administrative Skills

Director of Housing — total responsibility for twelve dormitories housing 3,400 students.

Assistant Dean of Students — advised and supervised social activities for 6,500 men and women students.

Admission Director — supervised recruiting and admission program for 500 students annually for a liberal arts college.

Regional Manager, American Red Cross — directed the delivery of services in ten communities; responsible for fund raising, recruiting and training of volunteers, and program results.

Teaching Skills

Training Director, U.S. Dept. of Commerce, four years, Midwestern Region.
Assistant Professor, two years — taught U.S. and state government courses.
Lecturer, three years, part-time — taught Effective Management to executives in nonprofit agencies.

Counseling Skills

Advised college students on personal, financial, and academic problems.
Served as faculty advisor to a fraternity of eighty active students.

Community Skills

Served on Mayor's Education Committee.
Developed support and recognition of United Way as a solicitor, and by participating in recruiting, radio, and TV programs.

EDUCATION

Kansas State University, Bachelor and Master of Arts degrees.
Majored in Education; advanced training in administration.

is hard to spell or pronounce, it is advisable to spell it phonetically, in parenthesis, right after your last name. Similarly, if you prefer to be called by your nickname, you should list it as George (Bud) Stanton, or Margaret (Peggy) Anderson.

Include both your campus and your home address: the latter is especially useful to employers near the end of the school year. Recent graduates and students who are employed during business hours should also include their telephone number at work (if they can take telephone calls there). To facilitate your mail, be sure to include your zip code for both the campus and the home address. For students who commute to classes, or who work part-time, it may be desirable to note this information in this section: for example, phone: (617) 555-7041 (after 7:00 p.m.).

If you move at the end of a school term, be sure to change your resume accordingly. If some resumes are already in the hands of employers, moving will give you a good excuse to contact them again to update your phone number and address, and follow up on your previous contacts.

This section gives employers and other readers the answer to identifying you among all other applicants.

Job or Career Objective

This section on your resume summarizes for prospective employers the type of work you want to do, and the career field in which you are interested.

Some experts think it is best to omit this section on the premise that it restricts the scope and usefulness of the resume—in other words, it limits your options. For students who have superior records, such as making the top ten percent of their class; who have a very pleasing personality; who served as the president of the student chapter of their professional society; or who have similar qualifications, it may well be true that they do not need a specific job objective on their resume. Such candidates may be recruited and hired under any circumstances because some recruiters are under tremendous pressure to get the top students, and hiring such students is a definite achievement on the record of the recruiter.

As one recruiter said, "If I don't get at least three graduates who are in the top tenth of their class (for my quota of nine) this year, I'll lose my job." Unfortunately, there are recruiters who are more concerned with filling their quotas than they are in helping students to properly launch their careers. Another example of persons who advise putting no objectives on resumes are those who never

had to sort through thousands of letters and resumes from candidates, and therefore have no idea how much time is wasted on
applicants who just want a job, and have not thought out their
career plans.

Although very little research has been done on this question,
experience leads us to recommend that applicants always include
a job or career objective on their resumes. The national thinking
on this subject is presented in figure 8-5.

Figure 8-5. Employer Reaction to Resume Data

Content-Data Preferred	Should Appear	Neutral	No Need To Appear
Job objective	87%	8%	5%
Extracurricular activities	86%	13%	1%
College(s) attended other than from which earned a degree	86%	13%	1%
College grades	72%	18%	10%
Interests and hobbies	57%	37%	6%
Education prior to college	34%	41%	25%
Statements about personality, background	31%	42%	27%
Personal data (age, sex)	26%	46%	28%
The statement: references furnished upon request	17%	52%	31%
List of references	8%	47%	45%

Source: *Journal of College Placement,* fall 1979.

With over eighty-seven percent of employers indicating such
preference for a stated job objective, it is wise to consider including it. There are several positive reasons for this recommendation.

1. After four years in college, a specific objective on your resume
indicates that you have devoted considerable time and thought to
the important question of what you want to do with your ca-
reer/life. Such a statement assumes that you have assessed your
interests, skills, and ambitions, and have a definite purpose in
mind. Therefore, you have completed your "shopping around"
and are now serious in devoting your efforts toward a definite goal
in the working world.

2. This section forces you to focus your resume, so that you will be using a "rifle" versus a "shotgun" approach. The rest of the information on your resume should be designed to help you achieve your goal. If you don't know where you are going, it is almost impossible to determine which job and which career field will get you there.

3. This section on your resume gives you a competitive advantage over other applicants. Prospective employers prefer graduates who know where they are going, and have some idea of how to get there. Too many college graduates are just looking for a job.

4. A job objective saves you time. Instead of wasting your time in making trips, having interviews, and getting those "we do not have a job for a person with your qualifications" letters, you can concentrate on prospective employers who *do* have opportunities in your field of interest.

5. Faculty, college administrators, alumni, and some employers are more helpful when they know your objective; then they can zero in on that career field and relate better to your ambitions.

6. For persons with multiple career interests, a job objective section enables them to prepare several resumes designed for each of their desired interests. For example, an accounting student may well prepare one resume for public accounting, another for industrial accounting, and a third for systems management with appropriate career objective statements. A graduate student in biology could easily prepare one resume for pharmaceutical companies, and another for teaching purposes. A person interested in the distribution of goods could prepare one resume for the sales or the marketing area of manufacturing companies, and another for the retailing field.

Your career or job objective section should indicate both your short-range (job) and long-range (career) interests. In other words, where do you want to start, and where are you heading with your life? Because most students graduating from college do not have much work experience, it is usually better to specify the field or industry rather than a specific job title. (After the first job, recent graduates will be expected to apply for a specific job title or level of job.) College seniors might state:

"a career in the radio/television field," rather than "radio or TV announcer."

"personnel work leading to industrial relations," rather than "employment interviewer."

"training in retailing, leading to merchandise management," rather than "buyer" or "sales clerk."

"social work, leading to community health services," rather than "case worker."

"a career in civil engineering, specializing in the fields of environment and transportation," rather than "environmental engineer."

"a career in life sciences, with particular interest in ecology," rather than "ecologist."

"marketing trainee, leading to sales management," rather than "salesperson."

When sending resumes to prospective employers, remember that they have hundreds and sometimes thousands of resumes to peruse, and therefore should not be expected to anticipate your career objectives. It is best to use short phrases as would be used in a telegram rather than a lengthy, wordy statement of your job or career objective.

Some examples of negative job objective statements are shown in figure 8-6, while figure 8-7 illustrates the more positive and desirable ways to phrase the statements for this section of your resume. It is better to state "Professional Objective" for some fields such as nursing, teaching, and engineering. Although no one can predict where you will be in ten years, your career goal statement illustrates your ability to plan ahead, indicates you have ambition, and shows that you have given serious thought to the future.

Education
For most students graduating from college, the most important qualification they have to offer employers is their education. Therefore this section should be listed on your resume directly below your job objective statement. As working experience is accumulated, slowly the work experience becomes more important; usually by the age of 30–35 it is more effective to place the education section nearer the bottom of your resume.

Start with your highest degree level and work backwards so the most recent data will be listed first. Graduate students should list

Figure 8-6. Examples of Negative Objectives

Job Objectives:

"An interesting position that will utilize my college education effectively." (This student has done little thinking about the future or what he/she can do for the employer.)

"I like people and want a job working with them in a pleasant environment." (There are practically no jobs for hermits. This statement shows the immaturity of the student and his/her lack of knowledge of the real world.)

"My academic achievements combined with interests in government services have prepared me to explore and make contributions in a number of different areas. I want a growth-oriented position that will allow me to utilize my ability to deal with the public and to demonstrate my leadership capabilities." (Too general, too selfish, too lengthy.)

"To further develop my personal, analytical, and leadership abilities so that I can be promoted to a management position as soon as possible." (This student is not concerned with the employer's needs but wants to use the employer for his/her own needs.)

"A position with the international business division of a large company with Latin American operations, located in New England, with little travel requirements, where there is a need for an effective customer-company-employee relations representative; position must be challenging and have promotional possibilities into international management." (This statement has too many restrictions. All organizations have promotional possibilities, and they expect employees to earn them. Statement is also too lengthy.)

Career Objective:

"A management position with a reputable company doing interesting things." (College graduates should seek entry-level jobs, not management responsibilities, which come years later. Would any organization admit it is not "reputable" or is not engaged in "interesting" and necessary activities?)

Professional Objectives:

"Teacher." (Too short, does not give enough information regarding applicant's level of teaching, field(s) of subject matter, type of educational institution preferred, or location.)

"Engineer." (Which branch of the engineering profession? In which specialty within that field is this applicant interested?)

Figure 8-7. Examples of Positive Job Objectives

Job Objectives:	"Sales, preferably with a company that manufactures industrial products and has a program leading to management development."
	"A production position in a small manufacturing company, with an opportunity to work closely with and develop into management."
	"A position with an historical society or a research and educational organization leading to a career as an historian or archivist."
	"Trainee in a management development program with a major department store or chain, hoping to advance into either store management or merchandising."
	"A position in social work performing services for the elderly, preferably with a private agency."
Professional Objectives:	"A teaching position in social studies or sciences, preferably working with students in the 7th, 8th, and 9th grades. Interested in both private and public schools in the New England area."
	"Biomedical engineering work in designing and developing medical instruments and devices, preferably with a research organization or a government agency."
	"To become a registered nurse in a large community hospital, leading to a specialty in surgical nursing."
	"A laboratory assistant position with a pharmaceutical firm, working toward becoming a research chemist."
Career Objectives:	"Auditing and tax work with a major public accounting firm in the Midwest; long-range goal is to become a partner."
	"A writing position with a newspaper or a publishing firm, leading to a public relations career."
	"An accounting position with an industrial firm leading to a controller or treasurer position."
	"A position leading to a professional civil engineer, specializing in structural engineering and design."
	"To obtain a position with a federal or municipal law enforcement agency, preferably as a criminal investigator or special agent."

their doctoral or master's degrees in reverse chronological order, and include the title of their thesis or dissertation along with their concentration and any research projects that may be relative to their job/career objective. Then include the information for the college(s) from which you received your baccalaureate training.

Pertinent data include the name of the colleges attended, degrees granted and dates conferred, major and minor fields of study, scholastic record, courses of particular relevance to the position being sought, term papers or other research that might be of interest to prospective employers, extracurricular activities, and percentage of college expenses earned.

Scholastic Record

Students frequently ask "do I have to include my grade point average?" If you have a strong academic record or the position generally calls for it, include it. From the employer's viewpoint, your scholastic average indicates how well you have mastered the subject matter in your college courses, how you rate in competition with other students, and how well you persevered in your studies. Some college recruiters look upon your cumulative scholastic record like baseball managers look upon a player's batting average—someone with a 3.15 scholastic average has greater potential than someone with a 2.15 grade record, just as a batter with a .315 average is a better long-range prospect than one with a .215 record.

Students *without* a superior scholastic record may wish to present such information in a way that could be helpful. For example:

1. Analyze your grades by semester or term to see if there is anything to highlight positively. Perhaps you had difficulty adjusting to college, and your first two years were really a chore, not truly representative of your abilities. If your last two years in school resulted in better grades, it would help to show this improvement. Whether you include the first two years and compare the results with the last two years, or whether you show one school semester or term after another, indicating *the trend* could be helpful.

2. Visit your registrar's office or the dean's office to obtain their percentage breakdown of scholastic records. Based on the present or previous year's graduating class, you may be able to state: "Ranked in the upper half of my class," or possibly "Ranked in the top forty percent of my class." If you were in the lower half of your class, better not mention anything about grades.

3. Calling the employer's attention to the courses in which you did your best work could be more meaningful. One student with a very mediocre scholastic record included on his resume the three B's he achieved and the course titles in advertising. Since this field was his career objective, he received enough attention from employers' representatives to get six interviews, resulting in two very good job offers.

4. In certain fields (like accounting, and some pre-med sciences) it is necessary to state accurately how well you have done. By reflecting on the needs of the employer, you may be able to separate your best grades and spotlight the courses that are most relevant for that professional field or employer. If you were seeking a job with a public accounting firm, for instance, you could state, "My best grades and my interest were in auditing and tax courses."

If you have a superior scholastic record, obviously you should capitalize on it. There are several ways to state your achievement:

- Election to _____—the honorary scholastic society in your field (unless you prefer to include it in the "Honors and Awards" section).

- Dean's list—last two semesters, or more.

- GPA 3.2 (on a 4.0 basis). Although most colleges are on a 4.0 system with A = 4 points, B = 3 points, C = 2 points, and so on, it is best to give the reader a yardstick for measuring your grade point average.

- Ranked in top twenty percent of class (or top thirty-three percent, top ten percent, and so on). Stating your rank in percentage form is more easily understood by readers than writing "108/565," which requires some computation to become more meaningful.

- Graduated cum laude, magna cum laude, or summa cum laude. These three designations signify the top three scholastic rankings of graduates (summa being the *highest* distinction, magna indicating *great* distinction, and cum signifying *with* distinction). If these terms are used by your college, such a ranking would be helpful on your resume.

Expenses Earned

If you have earned part of your college expenses, say at least twenty-five percent, it is advantageous to give the percentage of your total expenses earned, including scholarships. Sometimes it is best to state: "Earned sixty percent of all college expenses except tuition, by working twenty hours a week while carrying a full academic load."

This is important because it shows prospective employers that you can budget your time for work and study, and that you have an appreciation of the working world and its demands for dependable employees. If the work during the summer or part-time during school is directly related to your job objective, put this information in the work experience section of your resume.

Extracurricular Activities

The fun part of college is joining and participating in activities on campus such as interest clubs, sports programs, drama and singing organizations, and student chapters of professional societies. Since such activities were performed during your college days, it is appropriate to include this information in the education section of your resume. If you had an outstanding activity record in college, you may wish to separate such data into a separate section with an appropriate heading. In other words, spotlight it.

In this section it is better to provide details regarding each activity, rather than merely listing the name of each club or organization. Start with your highest level of office and work backwards. Notice the more positive impact in the second phrasing of the following examples:

Example 1   Not this . . .

Student Government, French Club, Intramural Teams, Student United Way, Judicial Board

But this . . .

Student Government—served on finance and activities committees and helped plan budget of $300,000.

French Club—served as membership chair, planned program for annual meeting, and was selected to represent our club at a regional language society conference.

Intramural Teams—participated in several sports, and served as captain of our basketball team.

Student United Way—served as solicitor and treasurer.

Judicial Board—elected to serve on this board to hear complaints and violations of university rules, and to help decide appropriate penalties.

Example 2

Not this . . .
Resident Assistant, Orientation Program, Sports

But this . . .
Resident Assistant—responsible for administration and counseling of fifty-five students in a dormitory.
Orientation Program—co-chair of a three-day program to aid 1,200 students in the transition to college life.
Sports—participated in intramural football, basketball and hockey teams; student manager of varsity hockey.

Example 3

Not this . . .
University Choir, Student Clubs, Beta Gamma Sigma

But this . . .
University Choir—had one of the leads in a concert.
Student Clubs—participated in Marketing Club and served as membership chair in Finance Club.
Beta Gamma Sigma—elected to this honorary scholastic organization in business schools; served on Induction Committee.

Example 4

Not this . . .
Tau Beta, ASEE, Computer Club, Tutor

But this . . .
Elected to Tau Beta Pi (Engineering Scholastic Honorary Society).
Member of student chapter of American Society of Electrical Engineers (ASEE).
Project leader in Computer Club.
Served as tutor to eight freshman engineering students.

Although space may not permit doing justice to your extracurricular activities, strive for action words that show your leadership and your contributions. While being a member of a student organization is a plus on your resume, performing in a leadership capacity and getting results is much more effective. Since most college recruiters are seeking potential management material, they are interested in hiring graduates who have made significant contributions to whatever organizations they join.

Some students are much more socially oriented than others, and are sometimes labeled as "joiners." If you have a long list of activities that take most of a page, or two pages, it may be better to list the most important ones, or those that are most relevant to your job objective, and then refer the reader to a supplementary sheet or volunteer to provide additional activity information if desired. Suppose your objective is sales, you are a gregarious person, and belong to fifteen different activities on campus. You could summarize the essential data on your resume as follows:

Extracurricular Activities: advertising manager for student newspaper; sales representative for yearbook; membership chair of Marketing Club. A list of other activities can be provided upon request.

Honors and Awards

Throughout our educational system, it is customary to recognize superior performance by granting a variety of awards. Without bragging, such awards should be listed on your resume because they help you stand out among other applicants. If the award or organization is well known, an abbreviation is sufficient. For example, anyone in engineering knows that ASEE stands for American Society of Electrical Engineers. Sometimes the name of, or abbreviation for, an organization may not be known to every recruiter. In this case, it is best to spell out identifying information within parentheses:

Alpha Kappa Delta (the International Sociological Honor Society)

F.I.S.H. (Friends in Service Helping)

ALSAC (Aiding Leukemia Stricken American Children)

Beta Alpha Psi (the accounting honor society)

P.A.P. (Paraprofessional Advisement Program)

Daily Student (the university's daily newspaper)

The Stylus (a literary magazine for student writings)

The Cross and Crown (the college honor society)

Psi Chi (the national honor society in psychology)

Druids (the honorary leadership and academic fraternity for sophomore and junior men)

Sigma Theta Tau (the international honor society in nursing)

Omicron Delta Epsilon (the national honor society in economics)

Phi Alpha Theta (the international honor society in history)

Beta Gamma Sigma (the scholarship honor society in the field of commerce and business)

Tau Beta Pi (Engineering Scholastic Honorary Society)

Your professors and career counselors can help you identify the honors and awards that are most related to your career objectives. The recognition you receive through honors and awards is significant to prospective employers, so don't be reticent in presenting such information on your resumes.

Employment Experience
Graduating students typically have had only part-time, summer, or volunteer jobs. In this section you should include paid and unpaid work experience from volunteer jobs, internships, clinical experience, practice teaching, and the military (if any). Whether paid or unpaid, any experience relevant to your stated job and career objective, is significant and should be included in this section of your resume. It may be advantageous to group all volunteer and paid work experience into a separate section and label it "Relevant Experience."

If you have never held a paying position, it may be better to eliminate mention of work experience and catch the attention of employers by putting a heading for this section such as "Skills and Abilities," "Personal Qualities," "Personal Strengths," or a similar title.

If you have had many jobs of very short duration (one or two week jobs during school vacations), it may be better to group them together by function (see figures 8-3 and 8-4). If possible, note any achievements or specify what you learned in that work experience. From the examples of different types of resumes at the end of this chapter, note those that include their experiences in a more positive tone and that indicate a more meaningful relationship to the stated objective. It is important to remember to place yourself in the employer's position. Obviously the learning or practical experience you have that is directly related to your job objective and the position you are seeking, is the material that is sure to catch the eye of the reader. If you did not include the percentage of college expenses earned in the education section, then be sure to include this item in the experience section of your resume.

In using the chronological approach, be sure to list the starting and ending dates of employment. Since employers and employment agencies look for gaps in the applicant's work experience section, recent graduates and students with work experience should carefully note such dates or be prepared during the interview to explain any gaps in their employment record. As you review your work experience, try to remember how you obtained your jobs because your efforts may provide evidence of your initiative, perseverance, and resourcefulness when you respond to the interviewer's questions.

In addition to the dates of employment, this section should include the employer's name, location, job title, and a brief description of your duties and responsibilities. For part-time jobs, state how many hours per week you worked. If the employer's name brings instant recognition, it is usually advisable to start with it. Sometimes it is better to start with the job title and stress what kind of work you did on the job, rather than starting with the employer's name to indicate where you did it.

Since most students graduating from college have had little work experience, recruiters are more concerned with what skills, knowledge, or abilities they acquired on the few jobs they have had. All the more reason for learning to use action words to give a positive impression with your resume.

Highlighting Your Experience
Since job titles often do not do justice to your job, it is advisable to highlight the tasks or functions for which you were responsible. By utilizing verbs that denote action, as in figure 8-8, you can change meaningless job titles into relevant statements about your abilities, responsibilities, and accomplishments. Positive statements showing what you have done, or what you can do, make a better impression on employers. The experience section on your resume becomes more and more important as the years go by; initially it shows readers the variety of work you acquired, gives some indication of the skills and knowledge you learned on your jobs, indicates your maturity, and shows your sense of responsibility. Later this section provides a wonderful opportunity to

Figure 8-8. Action Word List
(To describe your abilities and accomplishments)

Achieved	Maintained
Adapted	Managed
Administered	Motivated
Analyzed	Negated
Conducted	Organized
Controlled	Originated
Coordinated	Participated
Created	Planned
Delegated	Produced
Designed	Proposed
Developed	Provided
Effected	Recommended
Established	Recorded
Expanded	Re-organized
Expedited	Researched
Facilitated	Revised
Founded	Scheduled
Generated	Served
Guided	Simplified
Honed	Solved
Implemented	Supervised
Improved	Trained
Increased	Utilized
Initiated	Wrote

display your leadership ability, your ability to get results, and your accomplishments.

Other Data

This section affords an opportunity to personalize your resume by listing your interests and hobbies, travels, languages spoken, publications, professional memberships and affiliations, special skills, military background (if any), professional licenses received, and certifications. Depending on the space available and the relevance to your stated job or career objective, you may wish to separate such information into separate paragraphs with appropriate headlines.

References

For most resumes it is sufficient to state "References will be provided on request." However, all applicants should have at least three references available: academic, business or professional, and character. For students graduating from college, the opinions or recommendations of your faculty and college administrators will probably be the most important. For those who had actual work experience, references will be sought from your job supervisors. Character references are occasionally helpful, but do not include politicians or clergy since these two categories always speak well of all their "constituents." Be sure to ask permission of any individual before you submit his or her name as a reference, and give all prospective references a copy of your resume. If possible, it is a good idea to personally deliver your resume at the time you request permission to use someone as a reference, thus giving that person a refresher or reminder as to which student you are, while providing an opportunity to discuss your interests, qualifications, and questions.

"To Whom It May Concern" reference letters do not carry the credibility that is associated with a confidential evaluation. However, these letters still serve a purpose, especially when professors or administrative officials are called upon to write dozens of references for their students. They save time for writers when students are trying to get into graduate or professional schools, or into fields like teaching or nursing where it is common practice to ask for credentials. Sometimes it is necessary to use such letters when applicants are changing geographical areas and need some type of reference to campaign in another locality.

Don'ts

In addition to the advice given in the mechanics section, observe the following tips in constructing your resume:

1. Don't include salary information. This topic should be discussed after there is some mutual interest, usually during the secondary interview at the employer's place of business. If it is requested, give your desired salary in your follow-up letter; for maximum flexibility, it is best to bring up the salary question near the end of the second interview.

2. Don't state your religion, race, national origin, or political affiliation on your resume. Including these items adds nothing to

your qualifications, but such information might trigger an unfavorable reaction in the mind of the reader. Although legislation prohibits discrimination, there still is a great deal of prejudice in our society. Including such data can result in rejecting your application.

3. Don't include age, height, weight, health, or marital status. Stick to the essential job requirements. For practically all college graduates, such data are not required for job performance and are irrelevant for consideration.

4. Don't list your references on the resume because they may be contacted before you have the opportunity to meet the employer and sell youself during the interview. Furthermore, you may wish to retain maximum flexibility by giving different references to different employers.

5. Don't ruin your resume by poor organization, sloppy appearance, errors in grammar or typing, poor quality paper, or by other controllable items.

6. Don't get your resume duplicated until you get it checked or reviewed by a career advisor, a professor, or a friend. This step can help you obtain valuable suggestions for improving your resume.

7. Don't get your resume duplicated by the cheapest process. You can get a relatively inexpensive but professional looking duplicating job by offset printing. Since you will use between fifty to one hundred copies of your resume, it is practical to duplicate a quantity so as to have a good inventory on hand whenever you need a copy (unless you have access to a word processor).

The Portfolio, Credentials, and Curriculum Vitae

These three terms refer to an extension of your resume—a more complex and elaborate presentation of your qualifications and accomplishments. The term "portfolio" is used more for business and industrial organizations, especially by artists, photographers, writers, advertising, and executive candidates. The term "credentials" is used more for teaching, nursing, and administrative positions in elementary and secondary schools. The term "curriculum vitae" is used more commonly in Europe, and in higher-education (college and universities) institutions.

The Portfolio

Wherever it is important to present examples of your work or performance, the portfolio is a useful additional tool for applicants. For most purposes the application (cover) letter and resume are sufficient for introductory purposes to *obtain* an interview. To make a better impression *during* the interview, applicants for certain jobs would be wise to compile and present a portfolio. Only an occasional student will use this technique during campus interviews, and less than five percent of applicants use portfolios during interviews at the employer's place of business. Because it requires a considerable amount of thought and effort, the use of a portfolio enhances the chances of the applicant during an interview.

(Note that the term "portfolio" is used for other purposes also, especially by people in the financial field when referring to the collection and variety of securities and commercial paper; and by government officials carrying documents of state. In this chapter we restrict the interpretation of "portfolio" to its career meaning and usefulness.)

Although there is no standard format for constructing a portfolio, the following sections are useful, packaged in an attractive cover:

1. Introduction—Include your name, address, and telephone number, both at school and at home. It would also be useful to prospective employers to include a statement of your job objective or field of interest.

2. Your resume—This is the one-page summary of your qualifications and interests, such as you would normally use for campus interviews or include with your application letter.

3. Education—Expand the data on your resume by providing additional information, such as a short paragraph, on the courses taken that are directly related to your stated job objective or field of interest. The content of such courses, the grade you received, and the instructor's name may all be of interest to prospective employers. Recent graduates particularly like to know the names of your professors since they may be able to tell whether you took the "easy" courses or studied under "tough" faculty.

4. Extracurricular activities—If you participated in few campus activities, it would be better to include these in the education section. An extra separate page in your portfolio would enable you

to do justice to the variety of organizations and activities on campus in which you participated, and give you an opportunity to bring out your leadership qualities.

5. Experience—For this part of your qualifications, it would be wise to have separate sections for work experience, voluntary experience, clinical or teaching or internship experience, and project experience (for those term papers and theses, and special assignments wherein you had to do original research and compile some type of report). In addition to describing what you did, bring out the scope of your responsibilities and any accomplishments, and what you learned on that particular assignment or job.

6. Personal data—The one or two lines in your resume for this topic can be expanded into separate paragraphs to list and describe other items such as your travels, languages spoken, special skills, certifications and licenses, memberships or affiliations with professional or community organizations, hobbies, and so forth. If you created a work of art, had an invention, had an article or book or poem or song published, or had another experience illustrating your talents, be sure to include such information.

7. References—Select at least three references, people whom you think will give you a good recommendation, and provide their names, addresses, job titles, phone numbers, and their places of work. It would help to identify such references under appropriate business, academic, or character headings. You should have at least two professors who actually know you well enough to comment on your ability to learn, as well as your work, attitude, personality, competence, and ability to get along with fellow students and administration officials. When using references from clinical or work experience, always try to include a reference from your immediate supervisor.

People applying for positions that emphasize skills (such as photographers, artists, and writers) should consider compiling a portfolio, which includes the identification and resume sections, and then presents examples of their work in separate categories with appropriate headings or identification. Alumni seeking executive positions could also use the first two sections, then include examples of the type of problems they faced, how they solved them, and what results they obtained. Applicants for jobs requiring creative abilities can demonstrate such talents and their own versatility by the type of composition and examples they include in their portfolios. The portfolio can be adapted in various ways to illustrate your talents or achievements, and is limited only by your imagination and willingness to put forth the time and effort to compile an interesting and informative presentation.

Credentials

Students aspiring toward teaching or nursing careers or administrative positions in academia will generally be asked to submit their credentials whenever they apply for positions in their fields. The term "credentials" has an academic connotation that is more of a testimonial, showing that a person is entitled to credit because he or she has completed the necessary required courses or training, and therefore has the right to exercise official power or practice that profession.

Curriculum Vitae

Graduate students and alumni interested in academia should learn how to utilize the curriculum vitae effectively since it is commonly requested for academic and administrative positions in higher education. Similar to the function of the portfolio in business, the curriculum vitae is a more elaborate presentation of the applicant's resume. Often called a CV, the curriculum vitae is sent along with the letter of application for faculty and administrative jobs in colleges and universities, and is used to screen out persons who do not have the qualifications specified for the position.

Since CV's are reviewed by several members of a search committee, it is important that they be organized in a professional manner, be attractive and informative, and make a favorable impression on readers. Obviously the data presented must be accurate, and should be related to the position sought. After reviewing the CV's of candidates, the search committee arranges to bring selected applicants in for interviews not only with the search committee members, but also with various faculty or administrative officials with whom the applicant would be working if hired for the position. If the geographic distance is considerable, it is often more feasible to first contact the references to obtain pertinent information on candidates before making a decision regarding which candidates should be brought in for interviews.

Although the same principles apply to curriculum vitaes as to portfolios, the contents will differ somewhat because academia stresses some factors that are more important to educational institutions. The usual introductory page provides identification data (name, campus, home and office addresses and telephone numbers), and a paragraph on your professional field of interest, and your career objective. The following separate sections or pages in a curriculum vitae could contain:

1. Educational Background. In reverse chronological order, list your earned academic degrees beginning with the degree in progress or the most recent, giving the name of the institution, dates of completion or expected completion of degrees or certificates, the grade point average, the major and minor areas of concentration, and the titles (underlined) of master's theses and doctoral dissertations.

2. Relevant Work Experience. A brief paragraph should be used to present each full-time, part-time, volunteer, temporary, clinical or practice teaching experience that is related to the type of work sought. Descriptions should include position title, department or agency or institution, complete address and phone number of the employer, dates of employment, type of employment, and name and job title of supervisor. Use active verbs in describing your job responsibilities.

3. Listing of Publications or Creations. Whether you authored, edited, or created some work, include bibliographic citations of articles, pamphlets, monographs, chapters of books, research reports, books, articles, songs, or books you reviewed for publication, and other items that have been published. Similarly, include a description of recitals, exhibits, or other public recognition of your work.

4. Papers Presented at Conferences. Give the title of your report or paper, the name of the conference, dates and location, and whether it was presented by competition, by invitation, or by consulting. Serving as a reporter, speaker, or conducting workshops also should be included in this section.

5. Professional Associations and Service. Give the names of local, state, regional, national, and international (if any) associations in which you have memberships. Be sure to include any leadership positions you have held in professional societies, such as election to office, chair or member of committees, task forces, boards, and so forth.

6. Special Awards or Honors. Include any recognition from professional honorary societies; service or commendation awards; receipt of competitive assistantships, scholarships, or fellowships; teaching or research grants and awards; and similar items.

7. Recent and Current Research. Give a description of research projects you recently conducted or that are in progress. State the type of research, its purpose, and other relevant data.

8. References and Credentials File Information. At the end of your curriculum vitae, it is a good idea to inform prospective employers where your permanent credentials file is maintained. Check with your school's career center to find out what your school's policy is regarding the length of time that such credentials files are kept for individuals. You may wish to list references in your curriculum vitae, changing them to fit your application for different positions.

The Application Form

Although employers may have your personal data sheet, resume, portfolio, or credential file, it is common practice to have an applicant fill out an application form before being hired or put on the payroll. There are several reasons for requiring applicants to fill out an application blank:

1. Many applicants do not compile a personal data sheet, a resume, a portfolio, or a credential file, so the only information available to the employer is the data on the application form.

2. A completed application form enables the employer to have greater uniformity in establishing and maintaining records; it saves staff time to be able to find needed data in the same place for each candidate.

3. Resumes and other material presented by applicants do not always include the information considered to be necessary or most important to that employer before a job offer can be made.

4. Application forms typically require candidates to sign the forms in order to verify the accuracy of the data presented. This helps avoid potential or future hiring or retention problems; no

one is served by firing employees because they were not honest in completing the application form for the employer.

At the end of this chapter is a typical application form used in college recruiting. Note how much of the data in the personal data sheet (in the first part of this chapter) are enlarged in the Sears Application Form, (figure 8-9). The important thing to remember when using any of these methods to present yourself to prospective employers, is to be accurate with your data, and present your information in an interesting and professional manner.

The resumes for our five hypothetical applicants on the pages following the sample application form illustrate various ways of presenting qualifications and interests in a resume prepared for career opportunities. Use whatever ideas may help you, but be sure to adapt them to your own needs. Copying the exact words or phrases from other resumes will create a stereotype, which does not strengthen your resume.

None of the above methods of contacting employers should be sent or given to employers without a letter of application, commonly called a cover letter. The one exception to this statement is the campus interview with a college recruiter, where initial contact typically is made by presenting your resume. Since the cover letter is one of the first of several steps involved in a job campaign, the next chapter will discuss it in more detail.

Figure 8-9. Sears, Roebuck and Co. Application for Employment

Date _____

Name   LAST _____   FIRST _____   MIDDLE _____

SEARS, ROEBUCK AND CO.
APPLICATION FOR EMPLOYMENT

SEARS IS AN EQUAL OPPORTUNITY EMPLOYER and fully subscribes to the principles of Equal Employment Opportunity. Sears has adopted an Affirmative Action Program to ensure that all applicants and employees are considered for hire, promotion and job status, without regard to race, color, religion, sex, age, national origin, handicap or status as a disabled veteran or veteran of the Vietnam Era.

NOTE: This application will be considered active for 90 days. If you have not been employed within this period and are still interested in employment at Sears, please contact the office where you applied and request that your application be reactivated.

PLEASE PRINT

Personal Data

Print Name in full _____ Social Security Number _____
(Last) (First) (Middle)

Home address _____ Telephone _____
(Street) (City) (State) (Zip Code)

Temporary Address _____ Telephone _____
(Street) (City) (State) (Zip Code)

If hired, can you furnish proof of age? ☐ YES ☐ NO   Licensed to drive car? ☐ Yes ☐ No   Is license valid in this State? ☐ Yes ☐ No
(Answer only if position for which you are applying requires driving.)

If hired, can you furnish proof you are legally entitled to work in U.S. ☐ YES ☐ NO

Have you ever been employed by Sears? ☐ Yes ☐ No   If so, when and where last employed? _____ Position _____

Former employees of Sears and certain subsidiaries may be entitled to service credit under the Pension Plan based on prior employment with Sears, Roebuck and Co., Homart Development Co., Sears Investment Management Co., Sears Roebuck Acceptance Corp., Sears, Roebuck de Puerto Rico, Inc., Sears Roebuck Overseas, Inc., Terminal Freight Handling Co., Allstate Insurance Company and their subsidiaries, Lifetime Foam Products, Pacific Installers, Sears, S.A. (Central America), Dean Witter Reynolds Organization Inc. and their subsidiaries, and Coldwell Banker and their subsidiaries.

Are any of your relatives employed by Sears? ☐ No ☐ Yes   If so, in which unit(s) are they employed? _____

Type of position desired? _____   Date available for work _____   State salary you will consider _____

Are you willing to relocate? _____   What initial location would you prefer? _____

Have you been convicted of a felony involving life or property during the past seven years?   ☐ No ☐ Yes

If yes, explain. _____

Physical Data

A PHYSICAL OR MENTAL DISABILITY WILL NOT CAUSE REJECTION IF IN SEARS MEDICAL OPINION YOU ARE ABLE TO SATISFACTORILY PERFORM IN THE POSITION FOR WHICH YOU ARE BEING CONSIDERED.

Do you have any physical condition which may limit your ability to perform the job applied for? If so, please give details. _____

_____ Do you have any Service related disability? ☐ YES ☐ NO

To protect the interests of all concerned, applicants for certain job assignments must pass a physical examination before they are hired. Alternative placement of an applicant who does not meet the physical standards of the job for which he/she was originally considered is permitted.

Education

	No. of Years	Name of School	City and State	Course or College Major	Average Grades	Did you Graduate?	Type of Degree
Senior High School							
College							
Graduate Studies							
Other— Give Type							

Military Service

Branch of Service	Service-Related Skills and Experience Applicable to Civilian Employment

Activities

Professional Organizations _____

What are your hobbies or special interests? _____

Experience

Please give a detailed account of your previous experience and training. Specify the type of work done and the type of work you would prefer to do. If more space is needed, continue on a supplementary page.

_____
_____

RECORD OF EMPLOYMENT AND REFERENCES

LIST BELOW YOUR FOUR MOST RECENT EMPLOYERS, BEGINNING WITH THE CURRENT OR MOST RECENT ONE. IF YOU HAVE HAD LESS THAN FOUR EMPLOYERS, USE THE REMAINING SPACES FOR PERSONAL REFERENCES. IF YOU WERE EMPLOYED UNDER A MAIDEN OR OTHER NAME, PLEASE ENTER THAT NAME IN THE RIGHT HAND MARGIN. IF APPLICABLE, ENTER SERVICE IN THE ARMED FORCES ON THE REVERSE SIDE.

☐ It is not satisfactory to contact my present employer.   ☐ It is satisfactory to contact my present employer.

1

NOTE: State reason for and length of inactivity between present application date and last employer.

| Nature of Employer's Business | Name of your Supervisor |

Name

Address   Tel. No.

City   State   Zip Code

What kind of work did you do?	Starting Date	Starting Pay	Date of Leaving	Pay at Leaving	Why did you leave? Give details
	Month	$	Month	$	
	Year	☐ Mo. ☐ Wk. ☐ Hr.	Year	☐ Mo. ☐ Wk. ☐ Hr.	

2

NOTE: State reason for and length of inactivity between last employer and second last employer.

| Nature of Employer's Business | Name of your Supervisor |

Name

Address   Tel. No.

City   State   Zip Code

What kind of work did you do?	Starting Date	Starting Pay	Date of Leaving	Pay at Leaving	Why did you leave? Give details
	Month	$	Month	$	
	Year	☐ Mo. ☐ Wk. ☐ Hr.	Year	☐ Mo. ☐ Wk. ☐ Hr.	

3

NOTE: State reason for and length of inactivity between second last employer and third last employer.

| Nature of Employer's Business | Name of your Supervisor |

Name

Address   Tel. No.

City   State   Zip Code

What kind of work did you do?	Starting Date	Starting Pay	Date of Leaving	Pay at Leaving	Why did you leave? Give details
	Month	$	Month	$	
	Year	☐ Mo. ☐ Wk. ☐ Hr.	Year	☐ Mo. ☐ Wk. ☐ Hr.	

4

NOTE: State reason for and length of inactivity between third last employer and fourth last employer.

| Nature of Employer's Business | Name of your Supervisor |

Name

Address   Tel. No.

City   State   Zip Code

What kind of work did you do?	Starting Date	Starting Pay	Date of Leaving	Pay at Leaving	Why did you leave? Give details
	Month	$	Month	$	
	Year	☐ Mo. ☐ Wk. ☐ Hr.	Year	☐ Mo. ☐ Wk. ☐ Hr.	

I certify that the information contained in this application is correct to the best of my knowledge and understand that any misstatement or omission of information is grounds for dismissal in accordance with Sears, Roebuck and Co. policy. I authorize the references listed above to give you any and all information concerning my previous employment and any pertinent information they may have, personal or otherwise, and release all parties from all liability for any damage that may result from furnishing same to you. In consideration of my employment, I agree to conform to the rules and regulations of Sears, Roebuck, and Co. and my employment and compensation can be terminated with or without cause and with or without notice, at any time, at the option of either the Company or myself. I understand that no unit manager or representative of Sears, Roebuck and Co. other than the President or Vice-President of the Company, has any authority to enter into any agreement for employment for any specified period of time, or to make any agreement contrary to the foregoing. In some states, the law requires that Sears have my written permission before obtaining consumer reports on me, and I hereby authorize Sears to obtain such reports.

Applicant's Signature _____

NOT TO BE FILLED OUT BY APPLICANT

Additional Information Resulting from Interview

Signature of Interviewer _____   Date _____

Date of Emp.		Job Grade	
Dept. or Div.		Compensation Arrangement	
Job Title		Manager Approving	
Job Title Code		Employe No.	

Tested		(Enter dates as required.)	· Mailed	Completed
Physical examination scheduled for		REFERENCE REQUESTS		
Physical examination form completed		CONSUMER REPORT		
		With. Tax (W-4)		
		State With. Tax		
Review Card prepared	Minor's Work Permit	Store/Pers. Rec. Card		
Tickler Card prepared	Proof of Birth	Earnings Rec.		
Timecard prepared	Training Material Given to Employe			

12025—Rev. 1/82

Examples of Resumes

LaVerne Washington

Permanent Address:
15 Stuyvesant Oval
New York, NY 10009
(212) 555-3415

School Address:
McGregor Hall, A-23
Boston University
Boston, MA 02215
(617) 555-3419

Professional Objective	General nursing in a metropolitan major hospital, leading to a career as a surgical nurse.
Education	Bachelor of Science degree, May 1990, from Boston University. Majored in Nursing.
	Dean's List: Last two semesters in school.
	Activities: Freshman Assistant Program, member of Nursing Club, served on two committees.
Nursing/Clinical Experience	Tertiary Preventive Intervention, Sept.–Dec. 1989
	New England Mt. Sinai Hospital, Stoughton, MA
	Newton Visiting Nurses Association, Norton, MA
	Aided chronically ill patients in reaching optimum functioning in all aspects of life—physical, social, financial, and nutritional. As a patient advocate, utilized both the team and the community resources.
	Advanced Clinical Nursing Practice, Sept.–Dec. 1988
	St. Elizabeth's Hospital, Boston, MA
	Rotation experience in many different units—including ICU, CCU, Dialysis, Alcoholic Rehab, Orthopedics, and Emergency Room. Training received in Nutrition Counseling and Rehabilitation Services.
	Preventive Intervention, Sept.–Dec. 1987
	Melrose–Wakefield Hospital, Melrose, MA
	Participated in prenatal classes, screenings, referrals, the Denver Developmental Screening Test, and other related activities. Developed skills in communication and crisis theory. Initial counseling of rape victims and subsequent referral.
Work Experience	Park Avenue Nursing Home, Summer 1989
	Arlington, MA
	Worked on a split–shift basis and substituted for regular staff in caring for elderly patients, helping with emotional and physical problems. Assisted in devising recreational programs.
	South Shore Hospital, Summer 1988
	Worked as nurse's aide helping take care of patients, worked in the laboratory and supply room, learned the need for keeping accurate records, ran errands, and assisted with related duties.
Interests	Reading, sports, dancing, hiking, and music.
References	Will be provided upon request.

Bruce Horowitz

After May, 1990:   North Dormitory, R-12
2135 Hunter Street   State University
Kingston, NY 07716   Laramie, WY 82071
(201) 555-1124   (307) 555-8037

OBJECTIVE   A position in personnel management or industrial re-
                        lations, with a manufacturing company.

QUALIFICATIONS   B. S. degree in Business Administration.
                        Majored in Personnel Management.
                        Four summers work experience in production.
                        Keen interest in labor relations.
                        Training in group dynamics and counseling.

EDUCATION   State University, Laramie, WY
                        School of Management, B. S. degree May 1990.
                        Major: Personnel Management Minor: Psychology
                        Related Courses: Labor Economics, Labor Relations,
                            Business Law, Collective Bargaining, Industrial
                            Psychology, Sociology, Wage and Salary Problems.

EXPERIENCE   State University, Department of Management
                            Student assistant for two years to professors
                        teaching Labor Relations and Personnel Management
                        courses, 1988–90. Graded papers, researched as-
                        signed topics, compiled bibliography of NLRB and
                        arbitrators' decisions, supervised student discus-
                        sion groups on labor–management problems.

                        Bolton Manufacturing Company, Kingston, NY
                            Production operator–summers, 1988 and 1989.
                        Operated cutting shears, drill presses, packaged
                        goods for shipment, helped arrange transportation
                        for delivery of goods, and substituted for absent em-
                        ployees on the production line.

                            Production Clerk–summer 1987.
                        Assisted in compiling production schedules, expe-
                        dited materials, and made up daily production re-
                        ports.

                            Laborer–summer 1986.
                        Worked in the production department, performing
                        physical duties as assigned.

INTERESTS   Reading, travel, automobiles, researching data on
                        labor–management relations, and sports.

COMMUNITY ACTIVITIES   Active in church affairs, Boy Scouts, local sports
                        organizations, plan to join Junior Chamber of Com-
                        merce.

REFERENCES   Will be provided upon request.

Nancy R. Brennan

2930 Maynard Avenue   Mellon Hall, R–56
Columbus, OH 43211   Indiana University
(614) 555–5316   Bloomington, IN 47401
                                                       (812) 555–4528

Professional Objective   Teacher of mathematics and/or social sciences at the
                          secondary level, in a large public school.

Education   INDIANA UNIVERSITY, BLOOMINGTON, IN
                          School of Education, A.B. degree, June 1990.
                          Major: Mathematics Minor: Social Sciences
                          Rank in Class: Upper forty percent scholastically.
                          Courses most enjoyed: Calculus, Adolescent Psychol-
                              ogy, Computer Science, and Teaching Methods.

Activities   Mathematics Club—Membership Committee, Treasurer,
                              helped get speakers for club meetings.

                          Future Teachers Club—Chairperson for field tours
                              liaison for faculty and alumni contacts, developed
                              an alumni resource list in regional schools for ad-
                              vice, research, and work purposes.

                          Dormitory Council—Vice President. Responsible for
                              planning and executing social, cultural, and commu-
                              nity events for five dormitories having approxi-
                              mately 800 students.

Field Experience   Johnson Elementary School, Indianapolis IN, one se-
                          mester, 1989.
                          Student teacher in a regular classroom setting for
                          fifth and sixth grades. Duties included lesson plan-
                          ning and presentation in the areas of mathematics, so-
                          cial studies, and science.

                          North High School, Columbus, OH, one semester, 1988.
                          Student teacher in a regular classroom setting for
                          ninth and tenth grades. Taught Algebra I and II, Plane
                          Geometry, and Computer Science I. Assisted faculty
                          advisors in Student Council and Drama Club.

                          Bloomington High School, Bloomington, IN, two morn-
                          ings a week for one semester, 1987.
                          Observed and assisted teachers in Algebra and Social
                          Studies classes for ninth grade pupils.

Work Experience   Columbus Public Library, summers 1989 and 1988, full
                          time library aide—learned the Dewey decimal system in
                          replacing books, records, and tapes in their proper
                          places; helped classify some incoming reference
                          books; assisted in related duties as assigned.

                          Private tutor, Columbus OH, summers of 1986 and 1987;
                          also part–time tutoring in Bloomington, IN. Students
                          were in the eighth and ninth grades.

References   Available on request, and in I.U. placement office.

Roberto Mendes

Home Address: Campus Address:
2441 Pleasant Street   Fairview Apts. #48
Northfield, MN 55057   Ames, IA 50011
(507) 555-4294   (515) 555-2540

CAREER OBJECTIVE

A position as a mechanical engineer with a medium-size manufacturing company,
preferably in the Midwest, with long-range plans to advance to engineering
management.

EDUCATION

B.S. degree from IOWA STATE UNIVERSITY, June 1990, in Ames, IA.
Majored in Mechanical Engineering   Minored in Electrical Engineering
Took related courses in Statistics, Computer Science, and Management.
Scholarship: 3.2 (out of 4.0). Upper thirty percent of class.

CAMPUS ACTIVITIES

Participated in intramural basketball and touch football.
Sigma Alpha Epsilon social fraternity—elected to Master Steward, Social Com-
   mittee Chairperson, and Sports Activities Chairperson.
Member of student chapter of ASEE and ASME professional societies.
Public Affairs Forum—served on Program Committee, Chairperson of Membership
   Committee, and welcomed speakers as part of duties on the Hospitality Com-
   mittee.

WORK EXPERIENCE

Superior Mfg. Co., Ames, IA, part-time, September 1989 to June 1990.
Project Assistant—worked on different projects as assigned, including production quality control, modification of a study of possible safety violations, and assisted the shift foreman as requested.

Ideal Products Corp., Iowa City, IA, summer 1989.
Engineering Assistant—worked on the design and development of power-using machines for refrigerators and air-conditioners; helped on a project to study
and solve environmental pollution problems; performed time-and-motion studies to try to expedite production on three of our products.

Allen-Bradley (a division of Rockwell International Company), Milwaukee, WI,
summer 1988.
Junior Engineer—worked on assignments with mechanical metallurgists to develop methods to work and shape metals such as forging, rolling, and drawing;
observed, studied, and used industrial computers in a communications network
to manufacture products according to inventory and shipping-time requirements.

PERSONAL DATA

Earned forty percent of college expenses; interests include solving problems; becoming an active citizen in a community; sports.

REFERENCES

Will be provided on request.

Susan Chin

2930 Maynard Avenue   Simpson Hall, B–20
Pittsburgh, PA 15220   Rice University
(412) 555–5684   Houston, TX 77251
                                             (713) 555–5763

OBJECTIVE

To obtain admission to a graduate program in biochemistry that will lead to a research position in the biotechnology field.

EDUCATION

B. S. degree from Rice University, Houston, May 1990.
Major Subject: Biology   Minor Subject: Chemistry
Scholarship: Upper ten percent of class (3.5 on a 4.0 basis)
Advanced courses taken: Immunology, Microbiology, Molecular Biology, Cell
     Biology, Biological Chemistry, Genetics.

CAMPUS AWARDS AND ACTIVITIES

Phi Beta Kappa—member of Induction Team.
Gold Key Award—for service to the university and the community.
Tutor—for two years, twenty students in basic biology and chemistry.
Mendel Club—for science and pre–medical students; Program Chairperson, Mem-
     bership Chairperson.
Student Government—Campaign Chairperson, office worker.
Phi Alpha Theta sorority—Social Chairperson, Treasurer.
Freshman Assistant Program—helped orient twenty students to university poli-
     cies, sources of information, social and cultural activities, and academic
     requirements.

WORK EXPERIENCE

Laboratory Assistant, Rice University, part–time, 1989–90.
     Worked in the Introductory Biology course supervising the running of ex-
periments, and helping students to understand and use the laboratory
equipment properly.

Nurses Aide, General Hospital in Pittsburgh, summers 1988 and 1989.
     Assisted nurses in taking care of fifteen to thirty mostly bedridden pa-
tients. Learned the need for stressing safety precautions, running errands
for medicinal supplies, disposing of contaminated clothing and bedding, serving meals, and sterilizing techniques.

Sales Clerk, Kauffman's Department Store, Pittsburgh, summer 1987.
     After training, sold merchandise in the toys and children's departments.
Learned how prices are determined, the need for accuracy in recording sales,
how to take inventory, and especially how to deal with the public and satisfy
customers.

INTERESTS AND HOBBIES

Enjoy reading articles on genetic research; tennis; swimming.

REFERENCES

Will be provided upon request; also available in the career center.

chapter nine

The Application (Cover) Letter

Even when there is an active campus recruiting program saving you time and effort in obtaining interviews for jobs, you may find it necessary to write a letter of application (often called a cover letter) to prospective employers, and to follow up with a series of letters. This chapter will discuss the most commonly used letter of application. The follow-up, stall, acceptance, and other types of letters are discussed in chapter 12.

Although many authors advocate sending a preliminary inquiry letter to ascertain whether an employer has any job openings, we believe you can save time by writing an application letter and enclosing a resume for your initial contact with prospective employers. An inquiry letter results in receiving an application blank to be filled out, or a curt "no openings at the present time" response. By providing employment interviewers with pertinent information about your interests and qualifications, personnel officers have key information useful in exploring with executives in their organization whether there is any possibility for an applicant like you.

The Importance of a Cover Letter

Application (cover) letters serve as introductory sales letters to prospective employers. A well-written letter is an effective way to present your qualifications to an employer. Such letters are read, compared, and used to screen candidates for interview consideration.

Your resume, when accompanied by a cover letter, is a sign of a serious and professional approach to job hunting. It gives employers an indication that you are sincerely interested in their organization, and that you are giving them personal attention, which is not shown by the arrival of an unaccompanied resume.

Neither a cover letter nor a resume will get you a job. Their mutual purpose is to arouse interest in you so that you will be invited for a job interview. The application letter enables you to bring out some of your personality and adds a personal flavor to your resume. Because of their limited work experience, most students and recent graduates do not realize the competition they face from hundreds or perhaps thousands of college graduates throughout the region or country.

To appreciate the problem from the employer's point of view, imagine reviewing about three hundred application letters in a typical day with a national company. Any person having the task of sorting through such a pile of mail would quickly discover the importance of organization and expression, appearance, errors in grammar or spelling, and other factors used to screen out applicants. A well-written letter warrants considerable time and effort since it represents you and your ability to communicate.

If you need help in writing such letters, study the various books on business communications that are available in libraries and in your school's career center. Utilizing the latest "know how" in writing correspondence will prevent your letters from being wordy, boring, and tedious to read. Because letters can open doors to career opportunities, it pays to rewrite them (several times if necessary) until you get the right connotation and sales appeal.

Mechanics

As with resumes, there are several tips to make your application letters more effective:

1. Each letter of application should be an original; automatically typed letters look fine and are acceptable. Duplicated letters with noticeable fill-ins are not appropriate.

2. Always keep a copy of all business correspondence. It is difficult to remember exactly what you said in a letter a month or two ago, and you will probably need to refer to a copy when further action is warranted.

3. Limit your letter to a single page with only a few paragraphs. Persons screening application letters will seldom read more than one page because time is precious and they are not interested in applicants who cannot express themselves clearly and succinctly.

4. Send only typed letters, preferably on white bond paper, the standard for business correspondence. Sometimes students are so proud of their fraternity or sorority crest that they forget the choice of stationery used may be a measure of their businesslike approach. Recent graduates should *not* use their current employer's stationery when applying for a position elsewhere.

5. To make a favorable first impression, strive for a picture-frame effect with your margins, and have the body of your letter in line with the horizontal center of the page. Business letters are usually folded in thirds and mailed in an envelope nine to ten inches long.

6. Be sure to proofread your letter for errors in spelling, grammar, and typing, or have some friend do this for you.

7. Consider the tone of your letter. It should reflect self-confidence without bragging. A positive, enthusiastic tone in an application letter invariably generates a favorable response.

8. Use the first pronoun sparingly. It's best not to start paragraphs with "I." "I-itis" reflects a lack of skill in communication and detracts from the favorable impression you hope to create with the cover letter.

9. Be sure to sign your letters and enclose your resume. Make certain your address and telephone number are plainly visible if you want to expedite making interview arrangements.

Practical Suggestions

In addition to the basic mechanics, there are several other thoughts that should help you compose more effective letters.

Who to Write to

Your letter of application should be addressed to the most appropriate contact you have made personally or throughout your research. Seniors generally find it best to write to the employer contact listed in the *CPC Annual,* to the person recommended by a faculty member, or to the college relations department of a company. For graduate school admissions, write directly to the chairperson of the department in which you wish to study. Graduate students should write to the manager of the functional department for their job objective. If you do not have the name and address of the above contacts, send your application letter and resume to the personnel department, since its responsibility is to obtain pertinent information on all prospective employees.

Graduate students and recent graduates should make a special effort to obtain the name of the person who is in charge of the department in which they hope to work. *Poor's Register of Executives* and the other references listed in chapter 10 will provide the contact for your purpose. For an especially useful reference in developing your list of contacts, applicants with experience should utilize the suggestions given in the chapter entitled, "Approaching the Hidden Job Market," in Orrin Wood's book, *Your Hidden Assets.*

There is an unwarranted myth circulating to the effect that applicants should write directly to the president of an organization. This contact is appropriate for applicants who have had policy-making and managerial experience, and are seeking executive or higher-level positions. A person must be very naive to think presidents take time to read application letters from beginners or persons with little experience. The great majority of jobs are filled when managers send a requisition to the personnel department, whose staff then advertises the openings, reviews letters and resumes, screens applicants through interviews, and refers *selected* candidates to the department sending the requisition. This is where the final hiring decision is made.

Wherever possible, address your letter to a specific person. Letters addressed to "Dear Sir" or "Dear Madam" or "To Whom

It May Concern" generally are routed, answered, and filed by some clerk or secretary. A specific name usually leads to some type of personal reply instead of a form letter response. Directing your letter to a specific job lead or possibility, or to a specific person, is often referred to as the "rifle approach." Sending your letters blindly to anyone else is called the "shotgun approach," a method that may develop some job leads, but generally is less productive. Obviously your chances for hitting a target are better with the rifle approach, which is usually more effective in time, money, and results.

Be Direct, Concise, and Specific

Employers will take faster action if they know the type of work you are seeking. Highlighting your qualifications simplifies the task of sorting out many applications, thus ensuring a more positive response.

Avoid Clichés and Empty Phrases

To impress prospective employers favorably, strive for individuality. Phrase your statements so they will reflect *you* instead of using clichés and empty phrases like the following:

"I have a broad background." (What you consider to be broad may be very narrow to employers.)

"I am well qualified for this position." (Let the employer decide this. Such presumption on your part indicates your naïveté or lack of experience.)

"I have an outstanding scholastic record." (You'd better be able to prove it. If true, your other qualifications such as extracurricular activities or other evidence of leadership qualities should also be outstanding.)

"I know I can do the job." (You don't have enough details of the job to evaluate your performance.)

"I'm willing to do anything." (Shows lack of thought and direction. The applicant has neither taken time to analyze his or her interests or qualifications, nor performed any research regarding career opportunities. This phrase is usually interpreted as "I'm just shopping around, hoping to find something interesting.")

Appeal to the Employer's Interests

Find out what the employer is seeking, then slant your letter to indicate what you have to offer—what you can do for the employer. By relating your job objective and qualifications to the employer's personnel needs, you will have more effective application letters and get more positive responses.

Time Your Letters

Mondays always bring the heaviest load of mail, and Fridays find employees trying to complete tasks before the week is over. Therefore, it is wise to send your application letters to avoid having them received on the first or last working day of the week. If responding to an ad, promptness is usually desirable because employers will fill the position with the first qualified and interested applicant.

Be Professional

A businesslike approach is preferred to a letter that is cute, gimmicky, too novel, or too unconventional. Writing to strangers about a subject that is serious and important to both of you warrants a serious and professional approach.

Check for Sales Effectiveness

A tone of modest self-confidence, correct style and mechanics, enthusiasm, and an appeal to the reader's interests will result in more effective selling of your qualifications and job or career interests.

Be Patient

You should not expect to get a one hundred percent response to your letters. Using the rifle approach, you may get interview appointments from twenty to thirty percent of your letters. Using the shotgun approach, you will do well to get around five to ten percent results, unless you have superior qualifications or write a very effective sales letter.

Content of an Application Letter

The application letter follows the basic format of business correspondence, and should reflect the personality of the writer. Although it is difficult to generalize for all applicants, it is best to compose letters of three to five paragraphs to present an attractive first impression. Figure 9-1 illustrates a format that has been effective not only for students graduating from college, but also for alumni.

First Paragraph

What you state in this introductory paragraph will determine whether the rest of your letter will be read. Put yourself in the shoes of an employer, who is faced with the task of skimming through three hundred application letters or resumes today. Unless you specify clearly the position or field you are interested in, the chances are slim that your letter will get any priority. It is helpful to state the source of your information—how did you learn about the job or employer (want ad, professor, friend, an employee on the employer's payroll, the career center, the *CPC Annual*, research). This may provide a more personal referral if the source is known to the employer, and also informs the employer about which recruiting source is effective in getting applicants for the organization.

The purpose of this paragraph is to arouse interest in and attract attention to your application by employers. Make sure the job objective information stated in your resume is the same as the one you include in the opening paragraph of your cover letter.

Second Paragraph

Every employer would like to know why you are interested in working for his or her organization, and why you are interested in your job objective. Just as athletes look for teams that want them, so do employers seek applicants who want to work for them. Your application letter should appeal to this human trait; your statements should reflect personal qualities that are not ascertainable from your resume. Without duplicating exactly what is included in your resume, highlight some achievement, courses taken, or experience that is directly related to the field or position for which you are applying.

Figure 9-1. Format for a Cover Letter

Your Street Address
City, State, Zip Code

Date

Name of Person
Job Title
Company/Organization
Street Address
City, State, Zip Code

Dear Mr./Ms. ————— :

FIRST PARAGRAPH: State the reason for writing. Name the specific position or type of work for which you are applying. Mention the resource used in finding out about the opening/company (career center, news media, friend, faculty).

SECOND PARAGRAPH: Explain why you are interested in working for that employer or in that field of work, and most importantly, what your qualifications are (academic background, work experience, personal skills). Point out achievements that relate to the field in which you are applying, without duplicating exactly what is included in your resume.

THIRD PARAGRAPH: Refer the reader to the enclosed resume or other application instrument. Indicate that your resume summarizes your qualifications and background.

CLOSING PARAGRAPH: Indicate your desire for an interview. State that you will call on a specific day to see if an interview can be arranged at this person's convenience. If you will be in their geographic vicinity on a certain day, stress the importance of setting up an interview on that day.

Sincerely,

(Be sure
to sign)

Your Name
Your Phone Number

Enclosure

Third Paragraph

To provide more detailed information about your qualifications, refer the reader to the enclosed resume, personnel data sheet, or completed application form. Point out something in this paragraph that is directly relevant to the employer's needs.

Fourth Paragraph

This is usually referred to as your closing paragraph because you have made your sales pitch, and now you need to get action. Show your self-confidence by asking for an interview in a positive, convincing manner, and by providing the telephone information needed to expedite action. Depending on your class or work schedule, you may wish to suggest possible dates or days of the week that are feasible for your visit. You can show your initiative by stating that you will call the reader on a specific day (make sure you allow enough time for your application letter and resume to be read) to see if an interview can be arranged.

For applicants who are applying to employers outside of their immediate geographic area, it is important to make some suggestion to facilitate interview arrangements. You may inquire whether one of the employer's executives will be recruiting in your area in the near future so you can meet him or her. Or let them know you plan to be in their part of the country during school vacation, perhaps to visit another company, and thus could stop in their office for an interview.

If you make telephone contacts with prospective employers, have all the pertinent data described above in front of you before you make the call. In addition, have a pen and a pad of paper handy to jot down any information that may be useful for a later interview or in a follow-up letter. For telephone interviews it is always helpful to have a written list of questions that you wish to ask the employer; this prevents uncertainty and stuttering, which may be misinterpreted by employers.

The same principles apply to students desiring admission to a graduate or professional program. The major difference is that graduate schools will usually expect you to include your Graduate Record Examination (GRE), or similar test scores, a transcript of your undergraduate courses, and letters of recommendation (reference letters). The last example of an application letter in this chapter illustrates a first step in making an application to a graduate school.

Occasionally, it is helpful to include a reference letter with your application to employers to help obtain consideration and possibly expedite your application. It is human nature to take action faster when you know the person referring or recommending the applicant. If the high school you attended has geographic or professional relevance, you may wish to include it.

Following are several examples of the application (cover) letter for each of our five hypothetical applicants. Take ideas from these and other references, but be sure to phrase your thoughts so they will sound like *you* and not a stereotyped copy of someone else's expression. Your job or graudate school search will require additional correspondence. Chapter 12 discusses other letters and provides examples to facilitate your communication with employers or graduate schools.

Examples of Application (Cover) Letters

McGregor Hall, A–23
Boston University
Boston, MA 02215

November 21, 1989

Ms. Barbara D. Graham
Director of Nursing
Beth Israel Hospital
330 Brookline Avenue
Boston, MA 02215

Dear Ms. Graham:

Upon graduation next June from the B.U. School of Nursing, I would like to start my nursing career at your hospital. For about three years I would like to work as a general nurse, and later aim for a surgical nursing career.

My interest in nursing began when I had to help my mother take care of my father after his major heart attack. This experience stimulated my interest in learning more about health and the way our bodies actually work, and I received a great deal of satisfaction in alleviating the suffering of my father.

Enclosed is my resume with more information on my background and qualifications. Among the three clinical assignments as part of my nurse's training, I enjoyed most the work in the emergency room and in primary preventive intervention. I think I could be of most service to patients in need of various health maintenance services.

Because my class and work schedule leave me little spare time, I could visit your office on a Tuesday or Thursday after 3:00 p.m. May I have an appointment for an interview to discuss a nursing career at Beth Israel?

Very truly yours,

LaVerne Washington

LaVerne Washington
Phone: 555–3419

Enc.

North Dormitory, R–12
State University
Laramie, WY 82071

October 15, 1989

Mr. Joseph J. Smith
Industrial Relations Manager
ABC Manufacturing Company
1906 North Michigan Avenue
Chicago, IL 60604

Dear Mr. Smith:

     In the current issue of the <u>CPC Annual</u> I noticed your interest in college graduates seeking a career in the field of industrial relations. Next June I will graduate with a B.S. degree in Personnel Management, and am interested in joining a manufacturing company.

     In preparing for a career in industrial relations, I did my best work in courses such as Labor Economics, Business Law, Psychology, Sociology, and Personnel Management. My work experience includes one summer as a laborer, three summers in production in a factory, and two school years as an assistant to the professors teaching Labor Relations and Personnel Management courses.

     Enclosed is a resume summarizing my qualifications. My college training and work experience stimulated a career interest in working with both management and labor. My professors told me I have a natural talent for this type of work, and my grades in these courses gave me the most satisfaction.

     During the Christmas vacation period I plan to be in Chicago. May I visit your office to talk to you about this type of career? If you decide to recruit on our campus, I will make an interview appointment through our Career Planning and Placement Office.

Sincerely,

Bruce Horowitz

Bruce Horowitz
Phone: (307) 555–8037

Enc.

Mellon Hall, R-56
Indiana University
Bloomington, IN 47401

January 21, 1990

Mr. Robert O. Forsythe
Principal
North High School
26 Meridian Street
Columbus, OH 43211

Dear Mr. Forsythe:

    Ms. Dorothy Jones from your faculty encouraged me to write you regarding a possible teaching position in North High School when I graduate from college. This June I will receive the A.B. degree from Indiana University, and would like to teach in my hometown, Columbus, Ohio.

    Since I spent my growing years in Columbus and graduated from Watterson High School, I am quite familiar with the excellent reputation of your school. In my talks with the admissions staff and the teaching faculty at Indiana University, I was pleased to learn that students who majored in mathematics at North High School did very well in this and other colleges.

    Enclosed is a resume with more information on my qualifications. You will note my practice teaching included one semester at North High School. During this time I was very happy to experience the dedication and cooperation of your teachers, and I especially enjoyed teaching the mathematics courses.

    Your school is not listed among those who plan to recruit teachers from Indiana University. During the spring vacation period in March I plan to be at my home in Columbus. May I have an appointment for an interview?

Very truly yours,

Nancy R. Brennan

Nancy R. Brennan
Phone: (812) 555-4528

Enc.

Fairview Apts. #48
Ames, IA 50011

October 1, 1989

Mr. D. Laurence Duvall
Supervisor, Personnel
Inland Steel Company
30 West Monroe Street
Chicago, IL 60603

Dear Mr. Duvall:

Since your company is not scheduled to recruit at Iowa State University this year, our Placement Director Mary Thompson suggested I write to you directly to apply for a position in your Management Training Program.

Upon graduating from Iowa State in June 1990, with a major in Mechanical Engineering and a minor in Electrical Engineering, I am interested in joining a medium-sized manufacturing company to begin working toward a career in management. In my researching of careers and employers, I was impressed with Inland's policy of giving heavy responsibility to younger people, its good relations with labor unions, and its outstanding record of leadership in civic and community affairs.

Enclosed is a resume of my qualifications. My summer and part-time work experience convinced me that I could best use my talents and satisfy my interests by working in an environment producing goods that are basic to our economy. My engineering and related courses should help in contributing to more effective production, and in enabling me to develop my long-range goal of engineering management.

If one of your recruiters or executives plans to be in a city near Ames, I could make arrangements for a personal interview. Otherwise, if you are interested in my application, I can visit Chicago during any school vacation period. May I hear from you regarding the possibility of an interview?

Very truly yours,

Roberto Mendes

Roberto Mendes
Phone: (515) 555-2540

Enc.

Simpson Hall, B-20
Rice University
Houston, TX 77251

November 17, 1989

Dr. Thomas P. Dunn
Chairman, Biology Department
The Ohio State University
McPherson Hall
Columbus, OH 43210

Dear Dr. Dunn:

My academic advisor throughout college, Dr. Walter J. Powers of our Biology Department, recommended your graduate program in biochemistry to further my career. I would like to apply for admission to your graduate school.

The undergraduate courses I've taken at Rice University have stimulated my interest in a career in the field of Biotechnology. I plan to earn a Ph.D. degree, and then specialize in research work to help find substances that will alleviate or cure cancer and other diseases.

Among the required courses in Biology and Chemistry, I especially enjoyed studying Immunology, Microbiology, Biological Chemistry, Cell Biology, and Molecular Biology. I hope to build on this foundation with the type of graduate courses your program provides.

Next month I will be taking the Graduate Record Examination, and will send you my scores. In the meantime, would you please send me whatever forms and additional material you need to consider my application for your graduate program?

Sincerely,

Susan Chin

Susan Chin

chapter ten

The Job or Graduate School Search

The job or graduate school search process can be a very discouraging and frustrating experience, deflating your ego every time an employer or graduate school rejects or ignores you. It can take months to find the right employer or school, and people who do not take the time to research their market end up in boring and unsatisfactory jobs, or in schools with poor graduate programs. This chapter is designed not only for college students but also for recent graduates, who may need to use this information again.

The key to an effective job search is to avoid a minimal campaign, which is limited to campus recruiting or the jobs in classified ads. This step in your job campaign concentrates on locating and selecting the prospective employers who best fit your objectives, interests, and requirements. As in any research endeavor, it is best to get organized and develop a systematic approach and an adequate record system.

Personal Record File

Some students like to use the 3" x 5" or 5" x 8" card system to note pertinent data on prospective employers or graduate schools, and then record on the reverse side the important information on interviews and follow-up action. For those who plan a thorough research effort, we recommend a separate 8½" x 11", three-ring binder or notebook, with data on employers or graduate schools maintained in alphabetical order. Since it is difficult to estimate the space needed for an employer or school, a flexible binder allows enough room for all the data you will want to keep. Since students are normally using notebooks, a separate notebook for all your search information, with appropriate dividers, provides a convenient and comprehensive record for your purposes. When interviews and further steps develop, it is suggested you summarize the pertinent data in your personal record book. Figure 12-4 shows a form that can easily be designed and maintained for graduate or professional schools, or for job interviews.

Thoroughness at this stage will spare you frustration and countless hours of repeating steps and looking for information that was carelessly discarded. It will also facilitate the process of comparing employers later.

The Hidden Job Market

For most occupations there are more applicants than positions available, so employers pick and choose as they please. Many employers post job openings internally before going outside the organization for applicants. Such a policy enhances morale within the organization and provides more flexibility, because it gives present employees the first chance at higher-level positions and establishes a promotion-from-within policy. Circulating job listings internally also strengthens an organization's affirmative action programs.

Sometimes it is a waste of time and money to widely publicize a job vacancy when there is a great surplus of candidates. For example, when a job in the personnel department is advertised, literally hundreds of people apply because "they love to work with people." If an internal applicant cannot be found, it is often more cost-effective to fill such jobs by word-of-mouth publicity, by recruiting at a personnel association meeting, or by assigning the opening to an employment agency, which then advertises, screens applicants, and refers the best qualified to the employer. For executive and higher professional-level jobs, a contract is made with a search firm to do the canvassing and selection.

Since most of us have faith in recommendations from friends, executives often use the informal grapevine to learn of applicants, although legally all jobs should be advertised. Graduates from the same college or graduate/professional school may be given preference and priority in hiring because "they speak the same language." For all these reasons, only twenty percent to twenty-five percent of all available jobs are advertised; therefore, a thorough job search will help you get access to the other seventy-five to eighty percent of jobs that are often referred to as being in the hidden job market.

Because there is no perfect job, it may be necessary to compromise your ideal preferences on factors such as location, employer size, salary, duties, and the realistic odds that you can get a definite job offer. Students may remember the process of applying to several colleges before making their selection, a decision that may well have been a compromise due to cost, location, and whether you were accepted for admission. Sometimes the compromise takes the form of going elsewhere to get the necessary experience. A graduating senior who wanted to teach in the Boston school system found too much competition from experienced teachers, so she had to take a job in New Hampshire for two years and finally got hired in Boston. In some fields like geology, sales, and engineering, it is often necessary to get field experience before getting a job in a preferred location.

Distributed among the ten major categories of employers listed in chapter 7 of *The Standard Industrial Classification Manual*, are thousands of employers. Applicants with college degrees have to narrow the field of opportunities to select and focus on the most logical employers having the type of jobs and careers that best fit their needs and interests. You have to do this research personally because only you know what to look for and what to avoid. As you research the various fields of work and get a better idea of the possible jobs in various industries, you will develop certain skills and knowledge that will give you the self-confidence for interviews and correspondence with employers.

Although the number of graduate or professional schools are far fewer than the number of employers, you still have to do considerable research to be able to focus on the most logical schools having programs that meet your needs. Steps to receive favorable attention and admission are very similar to the process of getting a job.

Once you complete the research to narrow the occupational fields and types of employers, further focusing is necessary. Some options to consider follow.

International Positions and Graduate Programs

Since World War II, the increasing competition among countries has generated a growing interest in international positions and careers. The process of internationalization has a ripple effect on transportation, consumer choices, advertising, companies, revenues, and especially on educational institutions training students for international careers.

Because the globalization of the economy is the most basic cause of change at this time, it "has moved the American Assembly of Collegiate Schools of Business to adopt an international content standard for accreditation. . . and is causing a resurgence in foreign language enrollments and some shift in emphasis from literature toward communication, including language courses for business purposes."[1]

Ken Curtis, former governor of Maine and U. S. Ambassador to Canada during the Carter Administration, points out: "The United States is not the world's dominant economic force any more. It's quite evident we're now part of a worldwide economy, and we're being hurt by worldwide competition which we do not understand. Our schools and colleges have a profound role in helping us understand the new global economy, other countries and governments, and developing more sensitivity."[2]

The twelve nations comprising the EEC (European Economic Community) are working toward a unified economic unit, sometimes referred to as a United States of Europe. They have set 1992 as the target date for this unification, and have taken steps to set up a Europe-wide central bank system and joint currency. When a common market is formed, barriers among the members have to be reduced, making it harder for outsiders to sell their products. Europe has already integrated the agricultural industry, effectively closing their agricultural markets to outsiders. This may happen in other areas as well.

---

[1]"New England in a World Economy," *Connection*, Winter-Spring, 1987.
[2]"Outstanding New Englander Ken Curtis: Foreign Trade Begins with Canada," *Connection*, Spring-Summer, 1987.

From the above statements, it seems clear that people with international experience will be rising to leadership positions. This is certainly true for long-range career possibilities, but you should be aware of some of the limitations and other realities of international positions.

Although the media reports news of hostage-taking and bomb threats, interest in international careers remains high. Because of the hostility toward Americans, social contacts abroad are often limited, and security measures become a way of life. Such positions do pay a premium for overseas work, but the tax and other benefits have certainly diminished recently.

There is a common misconception among college students that they can be hired and transferred immediately abroad by a company or organization. The reality is that one must usually get training and acquire experience before getting an assignment in another country.

Applicants for international positions should have language competence and aptitude, knowledge of and sensitivity to the people and customs, flexibility to adjust to other cultures, a realistic view of the health conditions and educational opportunities (especially for those with families), and a willingness to be transferred from one country to another. Some American firms rotate their overseas employees every three years, often on a contractual basis.

To prepare for federal and private business jobs overseas, students and recent graduates should consider getting special training for international careers by attending specialized programs. Such programs are offered by Tufts University's Fletcher School of Law and Diplomacy, on Packard Avenue, Medford, MA 02155; the Monterey Institute of International Studies, 425 Van Buren Street, Monterey, CA 93940; or the American Graduate School of International Management—Thunderbird Campus, Glendale, AZ 85306. You should also explore exchange programs and year abroad programs with educational institutions in other countries. More information on such programs can be obtained by contacting the National Student Exchange, 2101 Coliseum Boulevard East, Fort Wayne, IN 46805, or by talking to members of the faculty or the counseling service on your campus.

Additional information and contacts for overseas study can be obtained from the College Consortium for International Students, 866 United Nations Plaza, New York, NY 10017. Federally financed graduate-level resource centers are funded through Title VI of the Higher Education Act for the following:

East Asian Studies—at Harvard and Yale

African Studies—at Boston University and Yale

Latin American Studies—at Yale and the University of Connecticut

Middle Eastern Studies—at Harvard

International Studies—at Fletcher School of Law and Diplomacy and the University of Connecticut

At present there is only one federally designated undergraduate Canadian studies program shared by the University of Maine, the University of Vermont, and the State University of New York at Plattsburg. Such programs help students and recent graduates obtain practical knowledge and expertise for international careers.

There are several other limitations on overseas employment that you should consider if you are contemplating such a career. Many foreign countries have passed laws restricting the numbers of Americans permitted to work in their country. This legislation often limits the number of Americans to a small percentage of the total employees in an organization. In other cases, the only Americans admitted are those with skills not possessed by nationals of the country. This often limits employment of Americans to persons having experience in a specialty, such as geological exploration or sanitary engineering.

With a little research, you can find useful references for both studying and working abroad, such as this publication: *Study and Teaching Opportunities Abroad: Sources of Information About Overseas Study, Teaching, Work and Travel.* It is available for $3.00 from the U. S. Government Printing Office, Washington, DC 20402 (Stock No. 017-080-2-63-7).

If you are interested in an international academic career, the contacts listed in figure 10-1 should facilitate your job search. In addition to the above, there are several directories in almost all libraries that contain information on schools and on prospective employers. Also, consider getting some internship experience; for this purpose, *The Directory of International Internships: A World of Opportunities,* would be a useful reference. This book includes information on the sponsoring organization, the type of intern program, its objectives, the number of interns accepted, and the duration of the internship. Interested students should contact the

Figure 10-1. International Career Services For K–12 Educators

Margy Washut, Don Wood and B.J. Bryant

Each of the following universities provides varying services, such as: vacancy bulletins, recruiting fairs, referral services and international career information. For specific services, you should contact each university directly.

University of Northern Iowa Overseas Placement Center
Don Wood, Education Placement
   Director
Margy Washut, Program
   Coordinator
Career Development and
   Placement
Student Service Center
Cedar Falls, Iowa 50614
319-273-2083

Ohio State University
B.J. Bryant, Director
Educational Career Services
110 Arps Hall, 1945 N. High Street
Columbus, Ohio 43210
614-292-2741

Queen's University
Alan Travers, Placement Director
Queen's University
Faculty of Education
Kingston, Ontario K7L 3N6

Southern Illinois University International Employment Service
Frank Klein, Coordinator
University Placement Center
Carbondale, Illinois 62901
618-453-2391

Organizations and International Employment Agencies

As with the universities, each organization or agency listed here offers varying types of information or services. Contact each for specifics. (Note: some of these organizations and agencies will have registration fees and/or percentage-of-salary placement fees.)

Department of Defense Dependents' Schools
Teacher Recruitment Section
2467 Eisenhower Avenue
Alexandria, Virginia 22331
202-325-0885

Peace Corps Recruitment Office
806 Connecticut Avenue, N.W.
Washington, D.C. 20526
800-424-8580

Department of State Office of Overseas Schools
Room 234, S A 6
U.S. Department of State
Washington, D.C. 20520
703-235-9600

Association for the Advancement of International Education
Gordon Parsons, Executive
   Director
200 Norman Hall
University of Florida
Gainesville, Florida 32611
904-392-1542

RISE—Register for International Service in Education
Institute of International
   Education
800 United Nations Plaza
New York, New York 10017
212-984-5412

International School Services
Educational Staffing
P.O. Box 5910
Princeton, New Jersey 08540
609-452-0990

ECIS—European Council of International Schools
Dept. PO, 21 Lavant Street,
Petersfield
Hampshire GU32 3EL, England
Telephone: 44-730-68244

The International Educator's Institute
P.O. Box 103
West Bridgewater, Massachusetts
   02379
617-580-1880

TORC—Teachers Overseas Recruiting Conferences
Don Cermak, Director
National Teacher Placement
P.O. Box 09027
Cleveland, Ohio 44109
216-741-3771

Overseas School Services
Don Phillips
446 Louise Street
Farmville, Virginia 23901
804-392-6445

Overseas Academic Opportunities
949 East 29th Street
Second Floor
Brooklyn, New York 11210

Friends of World Teaching
P.O. Box 1049
San Diego, California 92112-1049

Source: *1989 ASCUS Annual.*

Director, Office of Overseas Study, 108 International Center, Michigan State University, East Lansing, MI 48824.

Should You Be an Entrepreneur?

Because so many college students (especially MBA's) and recent graduates fantasize about being their own boss, they should give consideration to becoming an entrepreneur. In alumni surveys, we find that the most effective time to start your own business or independent activity is after you have acquired some experience in that type of work so you will know the business, yet be young enough to take a chance and rebound if necessary. More detailed information on this subject is provided in chapter 14.

Researching Prospective Employers

In college, you develop skills in conducting research to write term papers, reports, or other assignments. Generally you begin job related research by reading to see what is available, thus funneling the mass of data into a few logical categories. It helps to follow up the research on written material by talking to people who are familiar with your field, or are considered experts in that type of work. Your written and verbal information will help you focus your energy and efforts toward a selected number of logical, prospective employers—in short, your job market.

Since each person's situation is different, it is very difficult to establish a generally accepted priority as to which resource should be utilized first. Your field of interest; the supply-and-demand situation in that field; the general U. S., regional, and international economies; and timing are all factors affecting the availability of jobs. Therefore, we suggest you begin your job or graduate school research with the available resources on the campus.

Campus Resources

Career Center

Through workshops, the campus recruiting program, and other services described in chapter 5, you can compile a selected list of prospective employers or graduate schools. When alumni or employer representatives speak on campus, you should introduce yourself to the speaker, pick up the material available, and try to get pertinent information to arrange an interview with the organization represented.

Similarly, you should capitalize on any internship/externship programs in which you may have participated. These former employers are always a possibility for developing career openings, and would give first consideration to applicants who worked there full- or part-time, summer, volunteer, or on an internship/externship basis. They would also be more likely to make referrals or give job search advice if they do not have the kind of career opportunities you are seeking.

Visits to recent graduates who volunteer to be part of your college's career network are coordinated through the career center. Some students have used these contacts during their internship and externship experiences. Others will find the data collected by their career center on the jobs held by their former students, and the listing of cooperative alumni, can be very useful in locating friendly faces in their preferred field of endeavor.

Campus Libraries

Since libraries are such a vital part of every educational system, they naturally contain a wealth of information for students and recent graduates as to sources of job information. In larger colleges and universities, it is also customary to find a library within the teaching department itself; naturally such a department library would contain reference material of particular interest to students interested in that field.

You can also find prospective employers by reading stories and advertisements in magazines in your field of interest, by utilizing the various directories, or—if you are in a hurry—by asking the reference librarian for information on your prospective field of employment. In most cases, the librarian will take the time to point out the part of the library that contains material on your subject.

There are many more directories available than the typical student needs to explore or utilize. Some of the more commonly used are sometimes referred to as basic directories, or standard reference sources.

Basic Directories

Students should start with the *Sources of Business Information,* by Edwin T. Coman, Jr. The format of this book is particularly helpful in directing you to the specific information you are seeking. It includes a list of available trade and professional directories, names and addresses of associations, and periodicals and books on subjects of business interest.

Another specific basic source is the *Public Affairs Information Service,* a publication which is a cumulative index of available information on almost every conceivable subject. Because it is so comprehensive, it is unwieldy, but the sections on industries, trade associations, and professional societies should be helpful.

Standard Reference Sources

Every library has some of the general and sometimes the specialized directories that contain a great deal of information on employers. Ask your research librarian to show you where you can find reference directories. The following detailed information will illustrate the voluminous data available in such directories.

Standard & Poor's Register of Corporations, Directors and Executives. Volume 1 contains corporate listings of over 45,000 corporations, in alphabetical order by business name, including zip codes and telephone numbers; and the names, titles, and functions of approximately 450,000 officers, directors, and other principals. Also included are descriptions of the company's products/services, the Standard Industrial Classification (SIC) codes, annual sales, number of employees, and other information.

Volume 2 contains individual listings of over 70,000 individuals serving as officers, directors, trustees, and partners.

Volume 3 contains indexes, divided into seven color-coded sections. Section 1 (green pages) has the SIC code number for the lines of business in which a company is engaged. Section 2 (pink pages) has approximately 900 different SIC codes providing a defined breakdown by a company's line of business. Section 3 (yellow pages) is the Geographical Index, which lists companies in alphabetical order by state and by major cities. Section 4 (blue pages) is the Corporation Family Index consisting of a cross-reference index, which lists subsidiaries, divisions, and affiliates in alphabetical order and links them to their parent company.

For applicants, sections 6 and 7 (both buff pages) are of definite interest because they contain new additions. Section 6 has an alphabetical listing of individuals whose names appear in the

Register for the first time, with their principal business connection and address. Section 7 has new company additions with connective companies.

Thomas Register.   Volumes 13 (A–M) and 14 (N–Z) are probably of most interest to you because they contain an alphabetical list of companies. Information on them includes addresses, phone numbers, asset ratings, company executives, locations of sales offices, distributors, plants, and service/engineering offices, products, and services.

Million Dollar Directory.   This reference includes six volumes containing 160,000 U. S. businesses with an indicated net worth of over $500,000. A separate volume, "Top 50,000 Companies..." lists those with an indicated net worth exceeding $1,850,000. Besides industrial concerns, this directory lists utilities, transportation companies, banks, trust companies, mutual and stock insurance companies, and wholesalers and retailers. It has cross-referenced volumes by geography (yellow pages), by net worth (green pages), and by industrial classification (blue pages).

Encyclopedia of Associations.   This reference is very useful as a guide to nonprofit organizations. Volume 1 contains over 20,000 organizations headquartered in the United States. Membership includes trade and professional associations, scientific and technical organizations, social welfare and public affairs organizations, religious, sports, hobby groups, and others.

Volume 2 is a Geographic and Executive Index, listing alphabetically by state and city, all the associations in volume 1. Volume 3 includes new associations and projects. Volume 4 contains over 3,200 international nonprofit member organizations based outside the United States. This volume contains the name, address, year founded, number of members, languages spoken, person to contact, purpose of the organization, publications, and the convention/meeting date.

Other directories will contain similar information. With perseverance, you can compile a list of logical and selected prospective employers who are in the line of business, the location, and the size that appeals to you.

Specific Directories
Most major libraries will also have function-oriented directories to help you. Sometimes these are found only in the departmental

library of a college. A small sample of such reference sources would include:

American Electronics Association Directory

Fine Arts Market Place

The Official Museum Directory

New England Directory for Computer Professionals

Literary Marketplace-The Directory of American Book Publishers

Directory of Public School Systems in the U.S.

Handbook of Private Schools

ISS Directory of Overseas Schools

Biological Sciences-A Directory of Information Resources in the United States

Arco's Complete Guide to U.S. Civil Service Jobs

Medical & Health Information Directory

Nurses Job Guide Directory

National Directory of Mental Health

The Social Work Yellow Pages-A Directory of 1000 Social Work Employers

Third World Resource Directory: A Guide to Organizations and Publications

Directory of Halfway Houses and Community Residences for the Mentally Ill

International Jobs: Where They Are, How to Get Them

Non-Legal Careers: Opportunities for Lawyers

Hotel and Motel Red Book

Summer Theatre Directory

Directory of Women in Business

Social Sciences: A Directory of Information Resources in the United States

Directory of Career Resources for Women

Networking: People Connecting with People, Linking Ideas and Resources

Worldwide Chamber of Commerce Directory

Standard & Poor's Stock Reports

Researching published materials will provide you with knowledge to help you act like a professional. In addition to gaining pertinent information, such research will help you adopt the attitude that you already are in the profession, show how serious you are about your future work, and save you time in the long run because you can focus your informational or job interviews on questions that were not or cannot be answered readily in print. Now is the time to send your application (cover) letter along with your resume, since you have a definite target in sight.

Student Organizations

On every campus, students who have a similar interest will generally have an activity organization. These take the form of purely social clubs, a club composed of students majoring in the same field, a service organization, or a student branch of the national professional society in a particular field.

Most meetings of student organizations usually involve a business session and a speaker. This provides a wonderful opportunity to cultivate friends and contacts among fellow students, and with the faculty advisor. A brief conversation after a speech will enable you to make contact with the speaker (usually an employer in that field), and could lead to an interview on the campus or at the speaker's place of business.

One of the easiest and most profitable ways to develop contacts is to join and participate in the student chapter of the professional society in your field. In addition to making and cultivating personal contacts, such membership enables you to attend the professional conferences and local meetings, receive their journal, correspond with members, and learn how to act as a professional.

To save time and maximize the number of job opportunities, students can organize cooperative ventures to do the research necessary to uncover the potential in their common-interest job market. One such example included the Harvard Business School MBA students who were specifically interested in working for small business organizations. They formed the Small Business

Club, allocated parts of the country according to the geographical preferences of their members, and had each member canvas the assigned territory to uncover job possibilities. Such canvassing was done during the summer vacation and during the Thanksgiving, Christmas, and semester breaks.

As job leads were developed, pertinent job information was put on a standard form developed by the club members, and classified by field of interest and geography. By pooling such information, each student had access to a great many more opportunities than he or she could research individually, and had a further advantage of discussing the prospective job and employer with interested fellow students.

Many student organizations have found that arranging a tour for half of a day, or possibly an entire day, with some employer nearby, facilitates future contacts by club members who are interested in employment with that employer. These provide firsthand information on the working environment, help to obtain written materials handed out to students on the tour, and offer contacts with executives, all of which are useful later for job or career interviews or information.

Faculty and Administrative Staff

Students often overlook one of the most accessible and knowledgeable sources of job and employer information—the faculty members and administrative staff in their academic department and school or college. These individuals frequently receive telephone calls or letters regarding job vacancies and often post such notices on bulletin boards or maintain an information file of job possibilities. Your instructors and counselors are not only interested in you, but would be glad to help you if they knew your vocational plans and the kind of job you want. Give them a chance to help you. Take a copy of your resume with you when you make an appointment to discuss your job interests and campaign with them, and ask them for job referrals, resources, or prospective employers to contact.

Alumni Association

If your school's career center does not have an alumni career network, you can still capitalize on the experience and contacts of former graduates by utilizing the knowledge and records of your college's alumni association office. Go to that office and ask for their computer breakdown of alumni in your field who are located where you wish to settle.

Noncampus Resources

In addition to the sources of job information and contacts on the campus, you can utilize a great many sources in the community and elsewhere. No one source will turn up job possibilities for all applicants, but a systematic effort to research the following sources will provide a number of prospects for consideration, and enable you to apply for that seventy-five to eighty percent of jobs that are not advertised.

Friends and Relatives

The most useful noncampus source for applicants is the experience and contacts of your own family, relatives, friends, and acquaintances—a sometimes overlooked resource. After all, these people would have a greater personal interest in you and would be more inclined to help you if they could. In talking to them, you may learn of some approaches to entering the field, and probably learn more about what the job or career actually entails. Although you may be reluctant to bother your friends, they are the people most likely to surprise you with their positive response and provide you with the best referrals. Through their work and social relationships, they may hear of possible job opportunities, but they must know that you want their help, so ask for it. Then keep all of them informed of your job status periodically so they will not assume you have found something and are no longer seeking a job.

Employment Agencies

These organizations provide a marketplace to help applicants and employers find each other, similar to the function performed by the New York Stock Exchange in the investment field. Such a service is provided by two basic types of agencies: state employment offices, and commercial employment offices.

State Employment Agencies

Every state has a number of public employment and training offices, usually located in its major cities. As orders for job vacancies are received from employers, the staff in these offices tries to match an applicant's qualifications and interests with the employer's job description and specifications of qualifications desired. They then refer the most suitable candidates to the employing organization. Since these offices are supported by our taxes, there is no fee to either the applicant or the employer. These offices are often a good source of information for local, regional, and national trends; job market changes; and specific job opportunities.

Commercial (Private) Employment Agencies

These agencies perform a similar function to the state employment agencies, but operate for a fee. Some states require the employer to pay the agency fee; it is wise for applicants to verify this before signing a registration form or a similar document. Otherwise, be prepared to pay a fee ranging from five to fifteen percent of the first year's annual salary in case the employer does not pay the agency's fee.

Private agencies often specialize in certain fields of placement, and are readily found in the yellow pages of telephone directories under "Employment" or "Personnel" headings. In general, specialized agencies rarely help undergraduates who lack experience or technical training, but agencies do provide a much needed brokerage function primarily for people with prior work experience or with training in a technical field or industry. For such candidates and for applicants seeking teaching or nursing positions in a community with which they are unfamiliar, registering with a commercial agency can save time and effort in exploring the job market.

If you are interested in utilizing this source of job possibilities, you should register with two or three agencies simultaneously because many of them forget you if no results are forthcoming after three or four referrals. It is best to avoid registering on Mondays and Tuesdays because job seekers responding to classified ads in the Sunday papers flood the offices on these days.

Here are two additional suggestions for seeking assistance from private employment agencies: First check to see if the agency is one of the nearly 2,000 members of the National Association of Personnel Consultants, the professional organization in this field. "NAPC had adopted rigid standards of ethical practice that all members have agreed...to conduct their business in a legal, ethical, and self-regulated manner that honestly serves the dual consumers (employers and job-seeking candidates) of private personnel consulting firms." (from the NAPC booklet)

The second suggestion is to ask whether the person in the agency is a CPC, a certified personnel consultant. This designation following an individual's name "indicates a personal declaration of his or her competence, and the attainment of excellence. It means such persons have mastered a body of knowledge, been tested, and have earned the right to be recognized as a professional in the personnel consulting field."

Community Sources

In every town and city there are a number of sources that can be utilized by all job seekers to discover job openings. In addition to the alumni, library, and professional societies mentioned in the previous section, the following sources can lead to specific employers and job openings:

Yellow Pages of the Telephone Directory

This source is especially good if you wish to make a local job campaign, or need to develop long-distance contacts. Telephone books for major cities throughout the country are maintained in local telephone company offices, in many community libraries, and in some college and career center libraries and offices. The functional breakdown in the yellow pages provides a quick picture of all the possible employers in that field within that community. You should call to get the nature of their business, find out who is in charge of the kind of work you are seeking, and get that person's name and job title.

Trade Associations

These are usually located in the larger cities, often with one office for an entire region—for example, an Atlanta office for all of the Southeast. They sponsor trade shows, conventions, and job fairs for their particular industry. Attending such gatherings will not only provide you with up-to-date knowledge of the latest activities (or products or services) in that industry, but also offer a wonderful opportunity to meet industry representatives and arrange job interviews with member organizations.

One student wanted to enter the real estate field in Fort Wayne, Indiana, but he had no contacts in that city. By writing to the trade association listed in the Fort Wayne yellow page directory, he not only received a listing of their membership, but also an offer to include a notice in their *Newsletter* if he would provide a summary of his interests and qualifications. With the help of his career counselor, he composed a "Position Wanted" ad and sent it to the trade association office. The notice appeared in the next issue of their *Newsletter* and resulted in nine replies. The student followed up and got six interviews and three job offers.

State and Local Chambers of Commerce

These organizations sometimes make available a directory of their members, usually for a relatively small price. They include major local or state employers, alphabetically and by classification. In addition to the name, address, telephone number, and chief products or services, the listing often includes the total number of persons employed.

In a number of cities throughout the country, the Chamber of Commerce initiates, sponsors, and conducts job fairs in a local hotel or facility. These are usually held during the Christmas vacation or between-semester breaks for college students from that area, or for those wishing to work in that area after graduation. The purpose is to give local employers the first opportunity to consider such applicants (before many students start their job campaigns and look elsewhere). Sometimes this activity is reversed when several colleges get together in one geographical area and have their graduating students interviewed by interested employers at one central location. Employers will conduct an open house similar to the job fair when they need a great number of applicants.

Nonprofit Organizations

In some communities, especially larger cities, you can get job search assistance by going to the local YMCA or YWCA, Women's Center, or similar organizations. In Boston, for example, the Women's Job Counseling Center (WJCC) started as a special service for women, then expanded to where they now service both men and women. This organization works with persons who want to make a career change, resolve job problems, or need group support during the job search. WJCC works with local employment agencies, both profit and nonprofit, maintains a wide variety of job listings and contacts, and provides counseling and testing for career/life planning.

Personal Visits
One of the most satisfying methods of researching prospective employers is to make a personal visit to that employer's place of business. We get the clearest impression of an organization through our personal experiences. Perhaps you know an employee (or several) in an organization with whom you can discuss "what it's like on the inside," and whether the information obtained is worth following up to develop a job possibility. When employees refer you to their employer, you have an excellent chance to obtain an employment interview.

If you have a preferred employer in mind, it may be advisable to first contact the competitors so you can find out what kinds of questions are asked in that field, and make your mistakes where a job interview is not at stake. For example, suppose you really wanted to work for Sears, Roebuck and Company. It would be good strategy to first contact and interview three or four other national retail chains. Interviewing the competitors will not only prepare you for the questions you can expect from Sears, but will also enlarge your knowledge of the retailing industry and may intensify your interest in a career with Sears or with one of Sears' competitors.

Newspapers and Magazines
These publications generally list job vacancies in their "Help-Wanted" or "Career Opportunities" sections. Along with such specific job notices, you should get in the habit of reviewing the business or financial pages to learn what is happening to employers in your area. If an organization is laying off 1,000 employees, this will certainly affect your chances for employment. If an organization is going to set up a branch office, build a new plant, or open a new store, such news should enhance your job chances. Articles of this nature can have an influence on the job market, and they indicate possible changes that all college graduates should be aware of.

Practically all fields have a newsletter or a journal to help their members keep abreast of changes, new research, and topics of interest, and many contain job openings or jobs wanted in that occupational field.

Job advertisements.   These ads by employers, commonly referred to as classified ads, are basically of two types: open and blind. Open ads present a summary of the job titles, expected duties and responsibilities, qualifications desired, and the name of the organization with its telephone number or address. Thus you can do some research about the organization before applying either by correspondence, in person, or by telephone.

In blind ads, you have to apply to a box number because the name of the employer is not given. Such ads are placed for various reasons. For popular positions there may be too many applicants, causing a burden in trying to acknowledge each response, or disrupting the schedule of the personnel department. Sometimes blind ads are inserted by employment agencies (or executive search firms for executive positions) that wish to build up their files of applicants, or have to protect the privacy of their clients. Occasionally an organization may "go fishing"—a term used to indicate the practice of testing the job market to see what talent may be available, thus determining what level of recruiting effort should be made to fill its positions.

Occasionally an organization will place a blind ad to ascertain whether any current employees are interested in leaving. This is done more in higher-level and technical positions where the issue of confidentiality on research, patents, financial plans, and future products may be of utmost importance. The problem of pirating information and taking it to a future employer is a never-ending one. Recent graduates should keep this possibility in mind when they are considering responding to a blind ad.

Responding to ads.   A frequent mistake made by applicants is their failure to respond to all of the requirements in the ad. Employers usually run ads because they have a problem or a need and are seeking assistance to solve the problem or fill the need. It is necessary to study the ad thoroughly to determine what the employer is looking for, and then prepare a tailor-made response. After the usually introductory paragraph of your letter of application, you may wish to adapt the following analysis and comparison for the employer's benefit:

The Job Requirements in the Ad		My Qualifications
Education:	College degree	A.B. degree from ABC College.
Experience:	One year in sales, marketing, or similar work.	Three summers, plus eighteen months part-time sales experience.

Travel:	Requires twenty-five percent of time.	Enjoy traveling; have my own car.
Personality:	Must be pleasing and meet people easily.	Have been told I have a pleasant and pleasing personality.
Interest:	In a retailing career.	Majored in marketing; worked in a department store.
Salary:	Your requirement?	Open—am more interested in an opportunity and let my performance determine my pay.

Always follow the instructions in the ad completely, and enclose a resume with your letter. Do not try to use gimmicks; best results are obtained by a businesslike, professional approach. In your closing paragraph, be sure to ask for an interview so that you can discuss your mutual interests in more detail.

Subscribing to newspapers.   One of the best ways to research a community and its potential job market is to subscribe to its daily or weekly newspaper. Over time you can get a feel for the kind of life you could expect in that community, what kind of jobs are advertised, and what kind of economy it has (i.e., is it a one-industry town, or is it a diversified city with multiple industrial and service industries?). Such a subscription is especially helpful if you are considering moving quite a distance and are not familiar with the employment opportunities in that area.

Situation wanted ads.   Occasionally your unique talents and goals may warrant placing your own ad in a newspaper or magazine. Because these ads are expensive and read by employers only during a tight labor market or when the latter are seeking hard-to-find applicants, such efforts are often not very productive. Graduating students seldom have enough experience to utilize this source; recent graduates with several years of career experience may find it helpful.

To get results from your own ad, you need to start with a specific job title or field, then include a concise statement of your major accomplishments in that type of work, summarize your years of experience, and finally state how you can be contacted. Placing your ad in the right media is very important. The trade association or professional field's journals are usually most productive. If you are interested in the publishing field, obviously you should advertise your availability in *Publisher's Weekly*. Similarly, finance candidates will find the *Wall Street Journal* most helpful, and applicants for college-level jobs should use the *Chronicle of Higher Education.*

Government Employment

Local, state, and federal government agencies all have numerous job and career opportunities. Information on government agencies can be obtained from your school's career center, from Civil Service Commissions in principal cities, and by contacting organizations in the blue pages of the telephone directory.

A useful reference containing annotated listings of sources on public service careers is the *Fourth of July Resource Guide for the Promotion of Careers in Public, Community, and International Service.* This publication is available from MAPA, 3041 Elm Drive, Allentown, PA 18103.

Federal Employment

The Office of Personnel Management (OPM), formerly known as the Civil Service Commission, is trying to streamline its recruiting and employment procedures. Under the leadership of Fran Lopes, its Director of Recruiting, OPM is placing strong emphasis on college relations and recruiting. Ms. Lopes stated that over 75,000 college students were hired in 1986 in every occupation imaginable. She stressed that OPM now has five regional offices: Atlanta, Chicago, Dallas, Philadelphia, and San Francisco, as well as the Washington Area Service Center for the metropolitan area. These offices will continue their contacts with colleges in their own regions of the country.

The OPM regional offices provide colleges with newsletters to describe their programs and initiatives, and with vacancy listings that identify the actual jobs available at that time for which a college graduate might apply. OPM will remain responsible for national examinations or national announcements.

You should note that the well-known PACE (Professional and Administrative Career Exam) and FSEE (Federal Service Entrance Exam) are no longer used. Positions in the "competitive service" are now tested for individual qualifications. Plans are being made for testing in six occupational groupings; the proposed title for the nationwide exam is Administrative Careers for America. Positions in the "excepted service" are the responsibility of the agency in which they occur; applicants for these are listed only in that agency's file.

Figure 10-2. Office of Personnel Management Federal Job Information/Testing Offices

Contact the Federal Job Information/Testing Office which is nearest the location where you would like to work for information on job opportunities in that area and the forms needed to apply.

ALABAMA
Huntsville:
Southerland Building
806 Governors Dr., S.W., 35801
(205) 544-5802

ALASKA
Anchorage:
Federal Building
701 C St., Box 22, 99513
(907) 271-5821

ARIZONA
Phoenix:
U.S. Postal Service
Building, Room 120
522 N. Central Ave., 85004
(602) 261-4736

ARKANSAS
Little Rock:
Federal Bldg., Room 3421
700 W. Capitol Ave., 72201
(501) 378-5842

CALIFORNIA
Los Angeles:
Linder Building, 3rd Floor
845 S. Figueroa, 90017
(213) 894-3360

Sacramento:
1029 J St., 2nd Floor, 95814
(916) 551-1464

San Diego:
Federal Building, Rm. 459
880 Front St., 92188
(619) 575-6165

San Francisco:
211 Main St., Second Floor, Room 235, 94105
(415) 974-9725

COLORADO
Denver:
P.O. Box 25167, 80225
(303) 236-4160
Located at: 12345 W. Alameda Pkwy., Lakewood, CO

For job information (24 hrs. a day) in the following States dial:
Montana: (303) 236-4162
Utah: (303) 236-4165
Wyoming: (303) 236-4166

For forms and local supplements dial:
(303) 236-4159

CONNECTICUT
Hartford:
Federal Building, Rm. 613
450 Main St., 06103
(203) 240-3263

DELAWARE
(See Philadelphia, PA listing)

DISTRICT OF COLUMBIA
Metro Area:
1900 E St., N.W., Rm. 1416
(202) 653-8468

FLORIDA
Orlando:
Federal Building and U.S. Courthouse
80 N. Hughey Ave., Rm. 229
(305) 648-6148

GEORGIA
Atlanta: Richard B. Russell
Federal Bldg., Rm. 960
75 Spring St., S.W. 30303
(404) 331-4315

GUAM
Agana:
Pacific Daily News Building
238 O'Hara St., Rm. 902, 96910
011-671-472-7451

HAWAII/OVERSEAS
Honolulu (and other Hawaiian Islands):
Federal Building, Rm. 5316
300 Ala Moana Blvd., 96850
(808) 541-2791
(808) 541-2784—Overseas Jobs

IDAHO
(See Washington listing)

ILLINOIS
Chicago:
175 W. Jackson Blvd., Rm. 519, 60604
(312) 353-6192

INDIANA
Indianapolis:
Minton-Capehart Federal Building
575 N. Pennsylvania St., 46204
(317) 269-7161

IOWA
(See Kansas City, MO listing)

KANSAS
Wichita:
One-Twenty Building, Rm. 101
120 S. Market St., 67202
(316) 269-6106
In Johnson, Leavenworth and Wyandotte Counties dial
(816) 374-5702

KENTUCKY
(See Ohio listing)

LOUISIANA
New Orleans:
1515 Poydras St.
Suite 608 70112
(504) 589-2764

MAINE
(See New Hampshire listing)

MARYLAND
Baltimore:
Garmatz Federal Building
101 W. Lombard Street, 21202
(303) 962-3822

MASSACHUSETTS
Boston:
Boston Federal Office Building
10 Causeway St., 02222
(617) 565-5900

MICHIGAN
Detroit:
477 Michigan Ave., Rm. 565, 48226
(313) 226-6950

MINNESOTA
Twin Cities:
Federal Building
Ft. Snelling, Twin Cities, 55111
(612) 725-3430

MISSOURI
Kansas City:
Federal Building, Rm. 134
601 E. 12th St., 64106
(816) 374-5702

St. Louis:
Old Post Office, Rm. 400
815 Olive St., 63101
(314) 425-4285

MONTANA
(See Colorado listing)

NEBRASKA
(See Kansas listing)

NEVADA
(See Sacramento, CA listing)

NEW HAMPSHIRE
Portsmouth:
Thomas J. McIntyre Fed. Bldg., Rm. 104
80 Daniel Street, 03801
(603) 431-7115

NEW JERSEY
Newark:
Peter W. Rodino, Jr., Federal Building
970 Broad Street, 07102
(201) 645-3673
In Camden, dial (215) 597-7440

NEW MEXICO
Albuquerque:
Federal Building
421 Gold Avenue., S.W., 87102
(505) 766-5583
In Dona Ana, Otero and El Paso Counties, dial (505) 766-1893

NEW YORK
New York City:
Jacob K. Javits Federal Building
26 Federal Plaza, 10278
(212) 264-0422

Syracuse:
James N. Hanley Federal Building
100 S. Clinton St., 13260
(315) 423-5660

NORTH CAROLINA
Raleigh:
Federal Building, 310 New Bern Ave.
P.O. Box 25069, 27611 (mailing address)
(919) 856-4361

NORTH DAKOTA
(See Minnesota listing)

OHIO
Dayton:
Federal Building
200 W. 2nd St., 45402
(513) 225-2720

OKLAHOMA
Oklahoma City:
(Mail or phone only)
200 N.W. Fifth St., 2nd Floor, 73102
(405) 231-4948

Figure 10-2. *(Continued)*

OREGON Portland: Federal Building, Rm. 376 1220 S.W. Third St., 97204 (503) 221-3141 **PENNSYLVANIA** Harrisburg: Federal Building, Rm. 168 P.O. Box 761, 17108 (717) 782-4494 Philadelphia: Wm. J. Green, Jr. Federal Building 600 Arch St., Rm. 1416, 19106 (215) 597-7440 Pittsburgh: Federal Building 1000 Liberty Ave., Rm. 119, 15222 (412) 644-2755	**PUERTO RICO** San Juan: Federico Degetau Federal Building Carlos E. Chardon St. Hato Rey, P.R. 00918 (809) 753-4209 **RHODE ISLAND** Providence: John O. Pastore Federal Building, Rm. 310, Kennedy Plaza, 02903 (401) 528-5251 **SOUTH DAKOTA** (See Minnesota listing) **TENNESSEE** Memphis: 200 Jefferson Avenue, Suite 1312, 38103-2335 (901) 521-3956	**TEXAS** Dallas: (Mail or phone only) Rm. 6B17, 1100 Commerce St., 75242 (214) 767-8035 Houston: (Mail only—recording) (713) 226-2375 San Antonio: (Mail or phone only) 643 E. Durango Blvd., 78206 (512) 229-6611 or 6600 **UTAH** (See Colorado listing) **VERMONT** (See New Hampshire listing) **VIRGINIA** Norfolk: Federal Building, Rm. 220 200 Granby Mall, 23510-1886 (804) 441-3355	**WASHINGTON** Seattle: Federal Building 915 Second Ave., 98174 (206) 442-4365 **WEST VIRGINIA** (See Ohio listing) **WISCONSIN** Residents in Counties of Grant, Iowa, Lafayette, Dane, Green, Rock, Jefferson, Walworth, Waukesha, Racine, Kenosha and Milwaukee should dial (312) 353-6189 for job information. All other Wisconsin residents should refer to the Minnesota listing for Federal Job Information in their area. **WYOMING** (See Colorado listing)

Application Procedure

College students and recent graduates should first contact the Federal Job Information Center (see figure 10-2) or State Employment Security Office in their area to find out what positions are available. Applications are accepted only for specific positions. The Federal Job Information Center can then provide you with pertinent information, including the appropriate application forms, such as the Standard Form 171, and other needed application materials.

Written Examinations

The Federal Job Information Center will advise you whether a written examination is required for the position for which you are applying. If so, the processing time for a test takes from four to eight weeks, depending on the position and the office that is processing the application. Applications that are incomplete in any way will obviously delay the processing of your application.

After your application has been processed, you will receive a "Notice of Rating" through the mail. If found eligible, your name is placed on a list (sometimes called a register) and is ranked according to your scores. By law, agency hiring officials may choose from among the top three applicants referred to them for a particular job, and if a veteran is included in the top three, he or she must be selected.

Excepted Positions

Policy-making positions and jobs requiring a close and confidential working relationship with someone in a policy-making position are excepted from written examinations, as are positions where Congress ruled that it is impractical to examine for such positions. For such jobs, the rating is made on the basis of the experience, education, and training described in the application. For excepted positions, applicants will receive a letter acknowledging the receipt of their application, and their names are added to a list without a numerical rating. Qualifications are compared with requirements of particular jobs, and names are referred to an agency for selection of the person they wish to hire.

Intern Program

Students scheduled to receive a graduate degree, or who have a graduate degree, are eligible to be selected as a Presidential Management Intern, a two-year program to attract to the federal service outstanding individuals who have an interest in a public service career. Applicants must be nominated for this program by their dean or the chairperson of their graduate academic program by December 1 of each year. Final selections are based on recommendations, along with interviews and an evaluation of writing samples.

Cooperative Education Program

This is a planned and progressive program through which many federal agencies offer students alternately full-time work experience with school semesters or quarters, or part-time work positions with parallel periods of study. The co-op program is designed to be a partnership between students, their schools, and the federal agency for which they will be working. Major co-op occupations include professional and technical, administrative and office support, and trade and craft. Interested students should work through their school's cooperative education coordinator or contact the cooperative education program manager in the personnel office at the federal agency of their choice.

Other Federal Jobs

Since OPM does not supply forms or information on jobs in agencies outside the competitive civil service, applicants should contact such organizations directly at the addresses given below.

U.S. Government Organizations

Defense Intelligence Agency
Civilian Personnel Operations Division
Pentagon
Washington, DC 20301

Federal Bureau of Investigation
10th Street and Pennsylvania Avenue NW
Washington, DC 20535

Federal Reserve System, Board of Governors
20th Street and Constitution Avenue NW
Washington, DC 20551

General Accounting Office
Room 4650
441 G Street NW
Washington, DC 20548

International Development Cooperation
   Agency
320 21st Street NW
Washington, DC 20523

National Security Agency
Fort Meade, MD 20775

U.S. Nuclear Regulatory Commission
Division of Organization of Personnel
Personnel Resources and Employment
   Programs Branch
Washington, DC 20555

Postal Rate Commission
Administrative Office, Room 500
2000 L Street NW
Washington, DC 20268

U.S. Postal Service
(Contact your local postmaster)

Tennessee Valley Authority
Division of Personnel
Chief, Employment Branch
Knoxville, TN 37902

United States Mission to the United Nations
799 United Nations Plaza
New York, NY 10017

Veterans Administration, Department of
   Medicine and Surgery
Employment Inquiries should be sent
to VA Medical Centers Nationwide.
(Seeking especially physicians, dentists,
nurses, nurse anesthetists, physicians'
assistants, podiatrists, optometrists, and
expanded-function dental auxiliaries.
Also seeking licensed practical/
vocational nurses, physical therapists,
and certified/registered respiratory
therapists.

Judicial Branch of the Government
(except the Administrative Office
of the United States Courts and the
United States Customs Court). Apply
to the individual office with the job
you are interested in.

Legislative Branch of the Government
(includes Senators' offices,
Representatives' offices, the Library of
Congress, and the Capitol, but not the
Government Printing Office). Apply to
the individual office with the job you are
interested in.

Starting Salaries

Most college graduates start at a grade five or seven level position, within the ten-step General Schedule Pay Chart. As of January 1989, grade five ranges from $15,738 to $20,463. Grade seven ranges from $19,493 to $25,343. The exact starting pay depends on the applicant's qualifications and also on the scarcity of candidates for that position. In the competitive service the job levels go from GS-01 to GS-16. Most career centers have copies of the annual salaries in the ten steps within each grade level.

Public International Organizations
The United States holds membership in several international organizations that are not part of the U. S. government, and OPM cannot supply information or application forms for them. Applicants seeking information on employment with international public organizations should contact them directly; telephone directories in major cities will have their addresses. Many international organizations of a public nature have their headquarters in New York City or in Washington, D.C.

The White House Fellowships
In October 1964, President Lyndon B. Johnson announced the establishment of the White House Fellowships program, whose objective is to draw individuals of exceptionally high promise to Washington for one year of personal involvement in the process of government.

This program is a highly competitive opportunity to participate in, and learn about the federal government from a unique perspective. For one year, the eleven to eighteen persons selected as White House Fellows are full-time Schedule A employees of the federal government, working in the Executive Office of the President or an executive branch agency.

The work assignment provides the Fellow with the opportunity to observe closely the process of public policy development and to come away with a sense of having participated in the governmental process as well as having made an actual contribution to the business of government. Assignments vary with the particular talents and interests of the Fellow, and depend greatly on what needs to be done.

By the end of the year, most Fellows will have written speeches, attended conferences, supervised staff work, reviewed or helped draft proposed legislation, answered Congressional inquiries, chaired meetings, drafted reports, conducted briefings, and spearheaded one or more projects. In addition to an intensive work experience, Fellows get a broader insight into government through interaction with one another and with the nation's leaders.

If you are interested in this coveted public service opportunity, write to the President's Commission on White House Fellowships, 712 Jackson Place NW, Washington, DC 20503, at least one year ahead of time. This is necessary because of the lengthy process for selecting applicants, as indicated in figure 10-3.

State and Local Governments

Many state, city, and county government agencies have employment procedures and policies similar to the federal government, but there is much more latitude in hiring. Applicants for such positions are advised to contact the appropriate personnel department or division in that agency, (listed in the blue pages of metropolitan telephone directories). Ask your nearest research librarian to direct you to the publications listing the names, job titles, addresses, and phone numbers for key officials in local and state government agencies.

Executive Search Firms

Because this source is generally misunderstood by college students and recent graduates, misconceptions need to be cleared up. First of all, such firms do not generally work with college students because they specialize in finding executives and professionals who have the appropriate years of experience and proven records of accomplishment. Minimum qualifications to utilize this source generally include five years of experience for those with graduate degrees, and ten years for candidates with undergraduate degrees.

Search firms work on a contract basis, with the fee paid by the employer. The majority of positions handled by such firms have a salary of $50,000 per year and over. Since the jobs are usually confidential and require a lot of digging to uncover prospective candidates (who are often found in competing organizations), executive search firms are interested neither in receiving resumes or seeing hundreds of applicants, nor in counseling applicants who drop in their offices. Such firms are sometimes referred to as headhunters, since their business is to ferret out potential candidates wherever they may be. The best way to utilize this source is to have contacts refer your name to an executive search firm, or to develop your career so that your reputation for leadership and accomplishments will become renowned throughout your field. Then these firms will come looking for you.

Figure 10-3. White House Fellowship Applications

Calendar of Selection Process

December 1   Application deadline. In no case will applications postmarked later than December 1 be accepted.

Approximately January 31   Applicants notified by mail whether or not they have been selected as regional finalists. Those selected will be advised of the date and location of their regional interviews.

February-March   Regional finalists interviewed by selection panels in the following 11 cities in the United States: Atlanta, Boston, Chicago, Dallas, Denver, New York, Philadelphia, San Francisco, Seattle, St. Louis, Washington, D.C. Every effort is made to assign regional finalists to the panel located closest to their homes; but, since the Commission seeks to maintain an equal distribution of regional finalists among the panels, this is not always possible. **Travel expenses incident to regional interviews are paid by the regional finalists.** Regional interviews are one or two days long.

Approximately April 15   Regional finalists notified by mail whether or not they have been selected as national finalists. The U.S. Office of Personnel Management will begin full-field background investigations of the national finalists.

May 19–22   National finalists interviewed over a three-day period at a location near Washington, D.C., by members of the President's Commission on White House Fellowships. These dates are tentative.

The week of May 23   Presidential announcement of the White House Fellows. Notification will be by mail.

June 19–24   White House Fellows are interviewed in Washington, D.C., by various Executive Branch agencies. All newly appointed Fellows must be in Washington for the entire interview period. Some Fellows may have to stay longer, or return to Washington later for additional interviews. Based on these interviews, the Director of the Commission determines the assignments of the Fellows.

September 1 to August 31   Inclusive dates of the Fellowship year.

Miscellaneous Sources

In addition to the sources listed in both the campus and non-campus sections, you can find other sources through your own ingenuity and perseverance. Be alert to possible job leads by noticing bulletin boards wherever you go—in schools, community centers, businesses, places of worship, and other organizations. For example, one student went to her insurance company to discuss her policy, and noticed a job opening posted on the bulletin board. After concluding her insurance business, she stopped in the personnel office, discussed the job that was posted, applied for it, and eventually got it.

Other sources can lead to prospective jobs. Don't overlook the contacts you can develop through the bank where you maintain your account, through businesses where you trade, through members and officials of civic and social organizations, through your recreational partners and colleagues, and through your hobby or support groups.

When seeking job contacts, you should not limit your search for prospective employers to any single source, list, or directory. It would be wise to try as many of these and other sources as time and energy permit. Since each individual's job search is unique, the timing—which is always critical when seeking jobs—varies with each of these sources. The important thing to remember is to use all sources of jobs of interest to you, study them carefully, plan your strategy, and schedule your contact with the selected employers. Use your imagination and initiative to uncover the maximum sources of job and employer information!

Networking and the Informational Interview

Although it is relatively easy to discover many sources of employers in various industries, the real problem is how to utilize these sources. This chapter would not be complete without providing more information on building up a network, and then arranging a series of informational interviews.

Networking

This can be one of your best job-hunting techniques because it is human nature to talk about jobs and other people. However, you need a system for meeting people and making friends so they will be able to provide you with contacts or connections to facilitate your job search. People who know you personally are more likely to provide information about a potential employer that you'd never find any other way. Throughout history we have had "old boy" networks to help members get job leads and climb career ladders, but women's networks did not take shape until the 1970s.

The first step in developing a network system is to map out a strategy for building a strong linkage of contacts who can offer career guidance and suggest or make job and/or employer referrals. The best way to create personal contacts is to be a joiner for professional and for personal reasons, and to get involved with individuals who have similar interests in school, social, community, and work relationships. Your strategy should be to develop friendships over a long period of time to enhance your life and provide contacts whenever you are in need of job or career assistance. Through them you will get introduced to people who are in a position to answer your career or job-related questions, and thus gain that person's "insider" information.

We all have heard the expression, "It's getting to be such a small world, you can't go anywhere without meeting someone you know." Some people generate personal acquaintances and referrals naturally, while others have to do it more systematically and consciously. By showing interest and concern in other people's problems, and trying to understand them, you help them and eventually they will help you. There is a certain therapy involved in talking to friends and acquaintances about jobs, graduate schools, and careers, especially when your ego is suffering because you have been getting turndowns from interviews. So, don't underestimate your contacts; some of them may have very influential relationships with key people.

During the year before graduation, seniors and graduate students will have a greater interest in applying the principles of networking. A second step in developing a network system is to keep in touch with others who are searching for a job; they may learn or know of jobs that may be helpful to you, and you may know of jobs that would be helpful to them. Most graduating students receive more than one job offer; and since they end up accepting only one offer, perhaps the offers they rejected may be of interest to others. It is always helpful for students to discuss offers and contacts with fellow students, and to compare the advantages and disadvantages of careers and jobs with peers and faculty. This way they get a better perspective on the job they should accept.

The third step in developing your network technique is to ask every person you contact for three referrals—a system perfected by salespeople long ago. Typically, you would ask for the names and employers of persons who would be familiar with, or actively engaged in, the type of work you are seeking. You can then contact such a person by telephone or by letter and personalize your approach by stating: "Mr./Ms. _____ suggested you are a very knowledgeable person in the field of _____ , and that you might be willing to advise me on a very important career problem. May I have ten to fifteen minutes of your time to get your thoughts on this matter?"

Students have an excellent reason for this approach by indicating they are working on a research project related to their prospective careers. Most supervisors and executives are willing to give advice to students *if* they do not have to take a lot of time, and *if* they are approached in a courteous and businesslike manner.

Recent graduates with several years of experience can obtain many practical and effective suggestions for networking by referring to chapter 8 in Orrin G. Wood's book, *Your Hidden Assets*.

The main thing to keep in mind about networking is that these contacts are not usually in a position to give you a job, but they are often in touch with persons who can. The people in your network can give you information and advice, and often open doors for you—doors that can lead to specific job opportunities. As you compile network possibilities, you will find it advantageous to take informational interviews, which follow logically your previous research efforts.

Informational Interviews

These interviews are part of your basic employment strategy. They can be obtained through personal referral—by contacts such as recent graduates, friends, and faculty; written requests; telephone calls; or by walking into an employer's place of business. Of these methods, the referral by your contact person is usually the most productive method of scheduling an appointment. It is human nature to respond more favorably when we know the person who refers a student or applicant.

The major objective is to get information about your prospective career that may lead to job interviews. A secondary objective is to verify, add to, or make you question your thinking about the career you are contemplating. Although informational interviewing does not result in job offers, it does facilitate the chances of getting an employment interview, and it is much less formal than a job interview. One of the country's leaders in the college career planning and placement field, Dr. C. Randall Powell of Indiana University, refers to this process as "infosearch interviewing," and lists its advantages as follows:

> Infosearch has some major advantages over job interviewing. If you were job interviewing, you probably would not get an audience. Job interviewing is a pressure-generating situation for both parties.
>
> Infosearch takes the heat off of both parties. You each have a greater chance of being yourselves . . . Infosearch permits both of you to create and leave a positive impression of each other . . . Infosearch costs you and the other party nothing but time.[3]

To get the best results from informational interviewing, you should do some planning so that you will give the impression of being well organized and not wanting to waste the other person's time. Do not take a resume along for these interviews—such action will be construed as a subterfuge for a job interview. It is better to send a resume later when you have completed your informational interviews. For these interviews, it is wise to write down your questions and allow space to note pertinent data as stated by your network contact. In preparing for such interviews, be sure to:

- Remember that you are gathering information on which to base some career decisions, and not applying for a job.

- State the purpose of your visit (i.e., seeking information), and how you obtained the person's name.

- Plan a manageable agenda—do not wear out your welcome. Let the interview roam freely, but within the allotted time.

- Prepare a number of open-ended questions, and be prepared to take the lead in the conversation.

- Recognize that everyone has his or her own attitudes, biases, and feelings, which must be evaluated.

- Ask for the names of two or three other individuals who might be able to help you.

Because the first five minutes will determine how much time your network contact is willing to give you, start with questions that are basic to your career fields. For example:

---

[3]Powell, Randall C. *Career Planning Today*, 1990.

• What are the entry-level jobs in this field/organization? What career paths are generally available?

• What are the major responsibilities?

• What skills, education, and experience are needed to enter this field?

• What steps would you recommend that I take in order to enter this field?

Recent graduates with experience who are researching for a specific job are advised to find out why the position is open. If the previous incumbent left the organization or department for another job, find out where that person is now employed, and arrange to talk with him or her to ascertain the reasons for leaving. In one instance, an applicant from the Midwest interviewed and received an offer from a firm in New York City. He located the former employee, took him out to lunch, and learned the reason he left the job was the manager's constantly looking over his shoulder, nitpicking on details, criticizing every action, and generally not allowing any freedom of thought or creativity. Since this applicant liked his independence and did his best creative work in a more congenial atmosphere, he rejected the job offer in spite of the fact that it paid two and one-half times his present salary.

Since the person whom you are interviewing will naturally ask you a few questions, you should have some idea of your own interests, abilities, location preference, skills, and career objectives prior to the interview. Obviously you also should develop additional questions to fit your particular experience level, should the interview go beyond the planned ten to fifteen minutes. Depending on the interest and willingness of the interviewer to talk, you can ask some of the following related questions:

What do you do as a _____ ?

• How do you spend a typical day/week?

• What kinds of problems do you deal with?

• What kinds of decisions do you make?

• What are your major responsibilities?

• What do you find most/least satisfying about your job?

Tell me about this career field.

- What are the positive/negative aspects of working in this field?

- What are typical entry-level jobs?

- Is there a definite career path in this field? Can you describe it?

- How did you enter the field, and what has your career path been?

- What are the "hot issues" in this field?

What is it like to work in this organization?

- How does your job fit into the organization/department?

- What are the toughest challenges you face in this organization?

- What is the "corporate culture" here? Is it very informal, formal, do people work autonomously, does everyone come in early, stay late?

Can you give me advice on how to break into this field?

- Could someone with my background obtain a position in this field?

- What skills, education, and experience are required?

- Can you suggest anyone else whom I could contact for additional information?

- What are the professional journals in this field that I should read?

- In which professional associations do you participate? Can nonmembers attend meetings?

- If I wanted to apply for a job, who should I contact in this organization?

In addition to the general questions above you should develop questions to fit your particular needs and experience level.

In concluding your interview, close on a positive note by thanking the person for his or her time and information, and for giving you such an enjoyable and enlightening learning experience. Then take time to reflect on what you learned from each interview and how this will further your career plans.

Be sure to send a thank-you letter to the person you interviewed; if he or she showed interest in your career, it is advisable to periodically keep such contacts informed of your progress. Such letters reflect your knowledge of desirable business practice and prompt follow-through. Examples of thank-you letters are provided at the end of chapter 7. In addition to expressing your appreciation, such letters can add to or correct some statements or impressions, and confirm your understanding of the things you talked about. It is also a good idea to thank the secretary and/or receptionist just so they will remember you favorably. Such action on your part indicates that you have one of the most sought-after skills in the world today—knowing how to treat people courteously and well.

Your network contacts will disappear if you do not nurture them. After the informational interview, you should thank any persons you spoke with and send them the results of any project or suggestion discussed during the interview, inform them what steps you have taken to apply the advice you received, or merely express your appreciation and state that you will be in touch when further action is indicated. Later on you may wish to send out a feeler letter along with your progress report by stating, "If you hear of job possibilities, I am enclosing my resume and would appreciate hearing from you."

Your off-campus research network contacts and informational interviews should help you eliminate those employers who do not meet your criteria for personal and job satisfaction. Your research efforts, networking, and informational interviews will come alive and allow you to test your knowledge and assumptions in the marketplace. They will also help you do a better job of matching your self-assessment with the actual job environment.

Having focused your search and determined the most logical prospective employers for your career desires, you are now ready to make contact for the job interviews.

Researching Graduate Schools

If your career goals require or make graduate school desirable, then follow the same pattern for researching prospective universities as you would for researching prospective employers. Assuming you have made a self-assessment and formulated your immediate and long-range goals, the following steps can be fruitful in researching the most logical graduate schools for application purposes.

1. Discuss your plans with faculty in your chosen field, and your academic advisors. They should be in the best position to know you and recommend the best fit for your continued education.

2. Talk with the professionals in your career center. Their contacts with graduate school recruiters and the resources in their office should provide pertinent information for your consideration. If this office has computerized services, you will have access to equipment and information that will enable you to survey potential schools very quickly.

3. Utilize graduate school catalogs and directories in the career center, in local libraries, and in various academic offices on the campus. Perusing reference materials can help you make the right decisions and ascertain the application steps to be taken for admission purposes. Typical general references include: *The Peterson's Guide to Graduate Study, The Pre-Law Handbook, Guide to Graduate Study in Management*, and *Graduate Programs and Admissions Manual*.

Most bookstores, career centers, and counseling services offices will have publications to help you identify degree programs offered by various graduate schools. They also provide specific information on admission procedures, tests required, available financial aid, part-time and full-time course offerings, tuition costs, and similar data.

4. Participate in school and community forums to talk with representatives of law, nursing, business, engineering, or other graduate programs. Such informal meetings give you a chance to get specific answers to your questions, as well as other pertinent information that will help you reach a decision.

5. Throughout all four undergraduate years, attend the seminars or meetings where speakers may be discussing graduate school admission requirements and problems. If the speaker is an alumnus of your school, you can obtain both job and graduate school information.

6. Look for special references on the graduate program that is of interest to you. For example, an authoritative reference on MBA programs is *The Official Guide to MBA Programs*, which provides

pertinent chapters on graduate management education; the GMA program—contents, requirements, options; choosing a school; and so forth, for 520 schools of management in the United States and in the world. For law schools, a useful reference is *The Official Guide to U. S. Law Schools: Pre-Law Handbook.*

7. Utilize whatever network you have. Some of your fellow students are sure to have similar career goals and problems in researching graduate schools. By comparing notes and experiences all of you will benefit from your mutual efforts and accumulated knowledge.

Despite all your diligent planning and efforts, you should be prepared to compromise because your final decision could well be dictated by your ability to meet admission requirements, location, and financial restrictions. Such limitations further endorse the need to have more than one preference before reaching a final decision.

Having focused your search and determined the most logical graduate schools for your career goals, you are now ready to formally apply for admission. Re-read all the application instructions carefully, then fill out the requested forms and gather whatever else is required. This might well include a four-page application form, a transcript of your undergraduate record, three faculty or other references, your test scores, and possibly some written essays. Be sure to forward every item specified in the admission procedures.

Upon Completion of a Graduate Degree

The principles of a job search upon the completion of a graduate or professional degree are the same as enumerated earlier in this chapter. You have to take the initiative in utilizing contacts, in researching directories, in capitalizing on the networks developed, and in being alert to other sources of positions in your field.

Any major library will have useful references even for very specialized fields. For example, one of our five hypothetical applicants, Susan Chin, planned to go on for her Ph.D. degree in biotechnology, and then specialize in research work to help find substances that will alleviate cancer and other diseases. One of her most useful job search references would be the *Research Centers Directory,* (Gale Research Co.). This reference is a guide to approximately 9,200 university and other nonprofit research organizations established on a permanent basis.

This two-volume publication has fifteen continuing research programs in Life Sciences, Physical Sciences and Engineering, Private and Public Policy and Affairs, Social and Cultural Studies, and Multidisciplinary Programs. Under "Life Sciences," Ms. Chin would find the section on Biological Sciences and Ecology to contain the kind of information she needs for job application purposes: the name of the organization, address, phone number, when founded, person in charge, a description of the type of research activities and fields, governance, and publications and services.

By researching specific industries and specific employers or graduate schools, you can intelligently apply directly to a small, well-chosen list of logical, prospective employers or graduate schools, and make a good impression so you will be invited for an interview.

chapter eleven

The Interview

If you are conscientious and have diligently completed the steps previously described, then you are ready for the climax of your job campaign, the interview. Employment interviews are opportunities for employers and applicants to explore their mutual interest and purposes. During the interview, three important factors will become apparent. First, from the employer's viewpoint, the interview brings out information that is not readily obtainable from a resume or letter, such as personality, appearance, and attitudes. Second, from the applicant's viewpoint, the interview provides additional information regarding the job, advancement possibilities, and insight into the employer's philosophy and objectives. And third is that which psychologists refer to as "rapport," or "a meeting of minds." During the interview, are the applicant and the interviewer on the same wavelength so that they agree and understand each other's statements and questions?

Although it is far from an exact science, the interview is the most commonly used selection device. In spite of all myths regarding shifty eyes, weak jaws, and so on, as being reasons for rejecting applicants, employers recognize the frailties of human nature with individual biases and prejudices, and now try to train their interviewers to objectively evaluate applicants' qualifications and interests. More and more employers realize that you do not have to be "at least six feet tall or a male to be a good salesperson."

The task of hiring a college graduate is a challenging one. Even the resume and the interview do not provide sufficient facts to confidently make a decision to hire an applicant. Interviewers know that they have to ask probing questions, yet present a relaxed and friendly manner.

Because students know the importance of the interview, their anxieties often interfere with their attempt to make a good impression. Every career library has numerous references on this subject filled with suggestions to help you overcome the fear of employment interviews. It is natural to be nervous for an interview.

Employers

People often ask: "Why do employers recruit on college campuses?" The answer is very similar to the often-quoted experience of Willie Sutton, the notorious bank robber. When asked "Willie, why do you rob so many banks?" he replied, "because that's where the money's at." Employers have found they have to go where the talent is—at colleges—if they hope to attract top talent.

In his article, "Why College Recruiting?," Donn L. Dennis offers four major reasons given by employers for recruiting directly on campuses:

1. To add new blood, which will allow for expansion and turnover in the managerial/professional work force.

2. To get individuals who are bright, well-educated, and capable of being trained in fairly short order.

3. Because colleges are a primary source of planned staff revitalization.

4. Because hiring experienced workers usually involves an "unlearning process to shed their ideas and previous ways of doing things so they will fit into the organization."

The value of recruiting on college campuses for employers is illustrated by figure 11-1.

Figure 11-1. Sources of New College Hires

	Percentage of New Hires
On-campus interviewing	42.2
Write-ins	10.2
Responses from want ads	8.5
Job listings with placement offices	7.7
Referrals from current employees	5.5
Walk-ins	4.4
Cooperative education programs	3.7
Internship programs	3.6
High-demand major programs	3.5
Summer employment	2.9
Part-time employment	2.4
Minority career programs	1.8
Referrals from campus organizations	1.7
Unsolicited referrals from placement	1.4
Women's career programs	0.5
Total	100

Source: Recruiting Trends 1986–87, Placement Services, Michigan State University.

What Recruiters Look for

It is important to note that recruiters are not alike. Young recruiters, recently graduated and trying to make their mark in their organizations, tend to put undue emphasis on candidates who have top scholastic records, a pleasing personality, and handle themselves well during the interview. Executives who recruit at graduate schools and sometimes for undergraduates tend to look for evidence of good judgment and the ability to think clearly, evidence of achievement and leadership, drive, ability to plan and organize, and persons with character; in short, students with convictions, honesty, and loyalty.

In recent studies on the cost effectiveness of college recruiting, the median cost-per-hire ranges from $9,000 to $15,000. Since most graduates recruited on campus are hired for exempt positions—jobs that are professional or managerial in nature and therefore not subject to overtime compensation as defined by the Fair Labor Standards Act—they are usually paid on a monthly rather than hourly basis. The expense cost figure in studies made includes advertising, recruiters' and candidates' travel, referral bonuses, agency/search firm fees, relocation costs, and the recruiters' salaries and benefits.

Most recruiters on campus have a certain image of their organizations in mind, the requirements of the jobs to be filled, and the type of person best qualified. Their selection is based on what they think are the student's chances to succeed in their organizations, as well as that student's potential in five or ten years. To ascertain students' desires, one major oil company instructs its campus recruiters to explore the following during the interview:

What does the student want to do?

Where does the student want to do it?

Can he or she do it?

In periodic studies made by Dr. Frank S. Endicott (a pioneer in the career planning and placement field best known for his research and leadership, now Emeritus Placement Director of Northwestern University), regarding what employers in different industries look for as they consider college graduates for jobs, he concludes that personal qualities are of the greatest importance. His studies indicate two types of personal qualities: the first is the ability to get along with people and work well with others. This includes poise, confidence, self-expression, and appearance. The second relates to motivation and goals, with such factors as clearly defined objectives, enthusiasm, drive, and a keen interest in one's work.

In his studies, Dr. Endicott found that achievement is the next most important quality, breaking down into two types: scholastic record and extracurricular activities. Many students ask career counselors "why so much emphasis on grades by recruiters?" Since practically all undergraduate colleges and universities are on a four-point system (A = 4, B = 3, C = 2, D = 1), the cumulative grade point average is an index as to how well you have mastered the subject matter in competition with your fellow students. Recruiters rely on grades as a major record of your intellectual achievement and feel that a student with a 3.15 average has better potential than one with a 2.55 average.

The other type of achievement readily identifiable by recruiters is that of extracurricular activities. What you do outside of the classroom not only indicates your real interests, but also helps in personal self-development. Working and competing with fellow students provide ample opportunities to assume leadership roles and develop your ability to work with others. You should join activities and clubs in which you have a definite interest, and where you can and will take an active participative role. We remember the case of one student who proudly displayed one and three-fourths pages, typed single spaced, listing all her activities. What appeared to be a magnificent activities record turned out to be an albatross when recruiters asked her such questions as "To what offices in these activities were you elected? What kinds of programs did you initiate? What other achievements or results were due to your efforts?" Since her list was entirely as a member only, she obviously did not take advantage of the opportunity to discover, exercise, and develop her talents for leadership purposes.

Dr. Endicott concludes that employers are seeking a combination of personal qualities that indicate potential for leadership, and technical competence on the job. Our experience corroborates his conclusions. Although the figures vary somewhat from year to year, we have found over a twenty-year period that the best undergraduate students (top ten percent scholastically, leaders in campus activities, and fine personalities), technical students (engineers and scientists), and MBAs average one job offer for every three campus interviews. Most seniors average one job offer for every five or six interviews, and poor students were lucky to get one job offer for every eight to ten interviews. During recessions, employers reduce their needs, upgrade their selection standards, and give fewer job offers; in fact, many cancel their campus recruiting trips entirely, or reduce the number of schools at which they recruit.

Basic Principles for the Interviewee

For all interviews, an understanding of the most common factors facing you will generally eliminate nervousness and anxieties. Whether our economy is on the upswing or the downswing, jobs usually go to those who know how to handle themselves in employment interviews. Here are a few basic principles to keep in mind:

1. Look upon the interview as an opportunity to explore the career possibilities with that employer.

2. Interviewers have jobs to fill and hope you can fill their needs; they are not interested in embarrassing applicants. It's best to just be yourself—don't try to be something you aren't.

3. The interviewers are just as anxious as you are to ascertain whether there is mutual interest in pursuing employment possibilities. They want to know whether you have something to offer and whether you will fit into their organization.

4. To make a favorable impression on interviewers, you should know what you want, and what you have to offer employers.

5. Confidence and poise are developed by preparation, proper appearance (dress), and practice. To convey your confidence and interest, you should maintain eye contact, good posture, and enthusiasm.

6. Arrive for your interview appointment fifteen minutes early, properly dressed to make a good impression. Bring along extra copies of your resume, credentials, or college interview form—you may end up talking to two different interviewers from the same employer, who may be representing different locations or divisions. Early arrival enables you to find out which building and which room number has been scheduled for your interview appointment. Also, you never know when the recruiter may be running ahead of schedule.

7. Most interviewers follow the question and answer formula. Your ability to ask relevant questions and to respond quickly, positively, and intelligently is of utmost importance in judging your career plans, enthusiasm, and general image.

8. The interview may well influence the rest of your life. Its long-term significance warrants giving serious thought to your goals, interests, and efforts to ascertain the long-range implications of your interviews.

Interviewing at Employers' Offices

Although campus recruiting is a convenient method of meeting employers, a great many students find it necessary to contact employers directly and make their own arrangements for interviews at the employer's place of business. The same principles of interviewing apply, but there is much more emphasis on filling a job immediately instead of discussing potential careers. Whereas campus interviewing takes months, and often requires trips (usually at the employer's expense) to different cities, students who contact employers directly find a shorter time frame, with more pressure to make a decision quickly should a job be offered.

This method is used by graduating students after the campus recruiting program is completed, where there is little recruiting on their campus, when no offers result from campus interviews, when personal problems prevent initiating a job campaign until after graduation (work, studies, or family require a student's total hours), by students who want to take a long vacation after graduation before seeking employment, and by students who want a specific location and are not interested in relocating to other parts of the country.

Many employers prefer having you contact them directly. Such initiative not only indicates interest on your part, but also saves the employer time and money. For jobs where there are many applicants, this practice is certainly much more economical for the employer. To illustrate, a manufacturing company was looking for a personnel assistant recently. The company received 127 responses to its one-time ad, screened the resumes so that twenty applicants were interviewed, had six finalists interviewed by a committee of nine, and finally hired one person. Statistically, we find that campus interviews are far more productive from your viewpoint, but direct solicitation is favored by many employers.

Three Parts to Interviews

Because so many students are naive or inexperienced about the world of work, career counselors spend much of their time advising them individually and through workshops as to the best way to make a positive impression on the interviewer. Usually such advice is separated into three categories: before the interview, during the interview, and after the interview.

Before the Interview

The old adage "forewarned is forearmed," summarizes the advantage of being prepared for interviews, either on the campus or at the employer's place of business. Preparation is at least half of the battle, and should circumvent many problems.

Research the Organization and the Job or Graduate Program

If you are interested enough to accept an interview, you should make the effort to learn enough about the prospective employer or school to be able to ask intelligent questions. Minimum required knowledge would be a familiarity with the service, products, or programs of the organization, and some knowledge of the position or program for which you are applying. Lack of research will lead to a quick rejection, such as happened to the student who glibly stated, "I've always admired Marathon's leadership in the oil business," when he was interviewing for a position with the Marathon Paper Company.

You should start your research efforts by utilizing all the facilities, services, and personnel at your school. The various libraries at a university all have some material in your field of interest, which will be helpful in learning about employers in that line of work. By reviewing the previous chapter, you also can find many additional ways to learn of prospective employers. It is always appropriate to ask questions of persons who may help. Such research will pay off when interviewers ask you, "What do you know about our organization? About this field of work? About this industry?"

Review Your Personal Inventory

Most students find it profitable to review for an examination; the same principle applies in preparing for an interview. Refresh your memory, select the particular strengths and skills you have, and relate them to the position for which you are applying. Develop a statement of your interests and skills as they pertain to that position. Such preparation will be especially important when you are asked "Why are you interested in this position?"

Take Care of the Mechanics

Be sure to note the date, site, and time of your interview appointment, and try to get the name and title of the interviewer. Bring two or three extra copies of your resume (in case of multiple interviews, or to assist in filling out application blanks at the employer's place of business). For some fields like advertising, art, and photography, it is very helpful to compile a portfolio of your work and bring it to interviews. Plan to arrive at least five minutes early for campus interviews, and fifteen minutes early when going to an employer's office. Check to see if you have a pen and pencil in good working order, and take a note pad with you. For interviews off-campus, it may help to make a dry run to the employer's location to make sure you will get to the right place on time for the interview.

Appearance

Dress professionally, in conservative good taste. Your personal appearance is very important in determining what kind of first impression you make. Human beings are greatly influenced by the attire and carriage of individuals, and subconsciously formulate a "like/dislike" decision when meeting people. Just as a tuxedo would be out of place at a cookout, so would informal attire be out of place for job or career interviews. Look in a mirror to check your appearance and your grooming; if acceptable, it will help you relax and concentrate on items that are important during the interview.

Practice for Your Interview

Whether on the stage, on the athletic field, in surgery, or in an interview, it is wise and usually necessary to practice going through the motions and reciting the words in the proper sequence to get the desired results. A great many students need to practice a firm handshake and the art of making and acknowledging introductions. Some students can benefit from practicing how to enter and how to leave a room, as well as sitting down and standing up gracefully.

If your school has a career center, you should attend any interview workshops and, if possible, have a simulated interview on videotape. This is an excellent method of finding out how you look to others, plus getting the benefit of a critique from the staff members. If videotaping is not available, students should practice among themselves. Any three students can get together, utilize the triangle principle, draw up a list of anticipated questions, and take turns role playing, as depicted in figure 11-2.

It is best to practice with students who have a common interest and are serious about this exercise. You will be amazed to discover how much you learn in a thirty-minute practice interview. By taking turns at each role, each student can get useful suggestions about mannerisms, body language, nonverbal impressions, answers to questions, enthusiasm, sincerity, and overall impression. Such practice also generates self-confidence, an important factor in making a favorable impression. A word of caution: Although practice makes perfect, you have to be careful to avoid delivering programmed responses like a robot. Instead of memorizing word-for-word responses, it is better to organize your key points regard-

Figure 11-2. Role-Playing Triangle for Practice Interviews

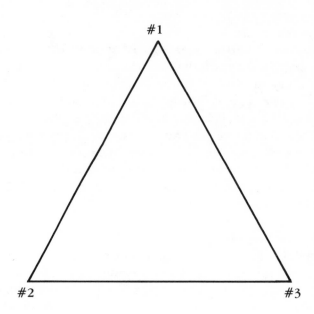

#1—Employer. This student impersonates the recruiter or interviewer.

#2—Applicant. This student plays the role of a senior seeking employment or admission to graduate school.

#3—Critic. This student has responsibility for timing the duration of the interview, observing the applicant's physical behavior and mannerisms, and noting the relevance of answers and how they are delivered.

ing your interests, skills, and other qualifications, and then be yourself in responding. One of the best ways to prepare for an interview is to put yourself in the recruiter's shoes and ask yourself, "if I were the recruiter, what would I like to know about this student?"

Be sure to practice how to respond to questions concerning your weaknesses, and how to convert such weaknesses into assets. For example:

Question: "Do you always pitch into an assignment and get it done ahead of time?"

Answer: "Sometimes I put things off until near the deadline. However, I never turned in a term paper or a major assignment that was late. My instructors and supervisors told me my work was thorough, accurate, and on time. The supervisor on last summer's job asked me to return after graduating this June."

Result: Recruiters will commend your answer as being frank and honest, and give you credit for responsibility, accuracy, and performing satisfactorily in class or on the job.

Question: "What is the major criticism fellow students have of you—your most important weakness?"

Answer: "Probably my impatience. I am always annoyed and impatient with people who come late to meetings, who cannot get their assignment done on time, and who always make excuses."

Result: Your weakness turns out to be an asset because employers want people who are prompt, have dependable habits, and set a good example for others.

Develop Several Questions To Ask the Interviewer
However, avoid asking about the salary during the first interview. Students often make the mistake of waiting for the interviewer to ask questions for them to answer. It is well to remember that the interview is a fifty-fifty proposition, just as important to you as it is to the interviewer. If your research has not answered questions regarding the job duties, responsibilities, environment, or the employer's services or products, you can easily start with questions pertaining to the job and the organization.

Different fields will elicit different questions because of students' interests. For example, nurses are interested in work schedules and work load, hospital size and reputation, degree of personal privacy, prevention of AIDS and other communicable disease programs, degree of autonomy, and congruency with lifestyle. Teachers are interested in the type of student body, teaching load, quality of laboratory resources and library, tenure requirements, and expectations for nonteaching work. Business students are interested in the type of work, opportunities for advancement, the structure of training programs, organization goals and policies, how performance is evaluated, and travel required. Engineers are interested in the type of technical assignments, how much time is spent on the drawing board, how modern and up-to-date is the equipment, what research projects are being investigated, the degree of independence and responsibility, and flexibility vs. specialization. Liberal arts graduates typically want to know how their knowledge and education can be utilized in an organization, what kind of training is available, is there educational assistance or encouragement for graduate work, what is the challenge of the job, what is the reputation of the organization, what is the quality of services performed, and what promotional possibilities exist.

Obviously all graduating students are interested in such factors as interesting work, a decent salary, fringe benefits, vertical and horizontal advancement possibilities, and working conditions. And one of the more recent trends includes questions dealing with the alternative career paths available for employment promotions. From the above suggestions, you should be able to develop several questions to ask the interviewer.

Learn the Routine of an Interview

This way you will manage your time effectively. Fear of the unknown brings anxiety, nervousness, and frustration. If you do not have any idea what is about to happen during the interview, you can get very uptight and will be unable to relax and present your natural personality. Career counselors advise students to attend workshops, participate in practice interviews, ask friends who have had interviews what they were like, and do some role playing. Although all interviewers have their own style, many employers train their campus recruiters to follow a definite pattern to be sure to obtain sufficient data to determine whether the organization has a job that might match the student's interests. The College Placement Council's pamphlet entitled "The Campus Interview—Are You Ready?" divides the typical interview into four sections:

> To a large extent, the personality and philosophy of the recruiter influence the course the interview will take. Nevertheless, while each recruiter and interview will be somewhat different, the typical interview can be broken down into four sections: (1) the introductory stage, (2) a review of your background and interests, (3) a discussion of the employer's opportunities and how you fit in, and (4) the conclusion during which points are clarified and the recruiter explains how and when the next contact will be made, if there is to be one.

Some employers have specific guidelines for their college recruiters, breaking down the usual thirty-minute interview into the following time intervals:

Minutes	Recruiter's Actions
3	Review resume, establish rapport with a friendly introduction and small talk.
10–12	Obtain applicant's objectives, interests, and background.
5–10	Discuss his/her organization and the job opportunities available.
3–10	Clarify data or answer student's questions.
2	Close interview. Note impression or preliminary evaluation of applicant.

During the Interview

In most personnel offices an interview can take from five minutes to an hour. For campus interviews, schedules are typically set up on a thirty-minute basis from 9:00 a.m. to 5:00 p.m. Most recruiters like to have about five minutes after each interview to write down their impressions of the applicant, so you really have only twenty-five minutes to get the desired information and "sell" yourself to the recruiter. The interview has often been compared to a sales presentation, whose essential components are described as:

a. Belief in the product

b. Knowledge of the product

c. Knowledge of the consumer

Before giving a speech before an audience, and before an interview, most people are a little (or very) nervous. This is very natural and nothing to worry about. In fact, some nervousness often starts the adrenaline flowing, which helps the individual keep alert and be more responsive. Before important athletic contests or games, and before operatic or speech presentations, participants generally have a coach attempt to get them psyched up. Every interview provides a major challenge, and applicants should get psyched up to develop their self-confidence to handle the assignment.

The Introductory Stage

Most recruiters start by introducing themselves and inviting students to sit down. You should acknowledge the introduction and greeting with a smile and say, "Glad to meet you, Mr. (or Ms.) Jones." Then use a firm handshake, but don't try to prove how strong your grip is by crushing the recruiter's hand. Don't be so naive as to call him by his first name if he introduces himself as Bill Jones. Some recruiters are very adept at establishing rapport to relax the student, while others find this stage difficult. It is important to remember that the recruiter is evaluating you the minute you walk into the interview room. The way you shake hands, your appearance, the way you sit, and your conversation all play a part in the impression you make. From here it is best to take your cues from the interviewer, responding to questions thoroughly yet succinctly instead of giving just a "yes" or "no" answer. Be careful to have a dialogue with the interviewer and not talk too much.

Your Background

After the introduction, some recruiters will want to know you better and ascertain your interests, objectives, background, and the qualifications not evident from your resume or application form. In this stage, questions are of the why, where, and when type and are designed to measure your ability to express yourself clearly and logically; get some idea of your self-confidence; learn something about your attitudes and values; ascertain whether you are well-adjusted, ambitious, and a self-starter; and determine how well you have prepared yourself for your chosen career.

The Mechanics During an Interview

Qualifications are often overlooked because of mistakes made or lack of attention to the little things that collectively help form a favorable impression. Therefore, you are reminded to maintain good posture and be careful of negative body language—i.e., your facial expressions, gestures, the way you sit, nervous hand movements (like tapping or drumming fingers), fidgeting, annoying mannerisms, and looking out the window. It is always helpful to look directly at the interviewer, and maintain eye contact. Let the interviewer take the initiative at least during the first half of the interview, and be sure to show interest and enthusiasm.

When speaking, use a conversational tone and modulate your voice appropriately. It is best to avoid such topics as religion and politics. However, if discussion does arise on such subjects, have the courage to state your convictions with evidence to support your views. Be sure to speak distinctly without using slang such as "you know," "yeah," "like," and other words or phrases that are common on the campus but leave a negative impression on recruiters and interviewers. Throughout all interviews, be frank and sincere, courteous and cooperative, and try to appear poised and relaxed to enhance your professional image. You should always accentuate the positive since strong points impress employers favorably.

Typical Questions Asked by Recruiters

Every book on career planning or on seeking a job will have a good selection of the kind of questions asked during an interview. Figure 11-3 lists many of these; study them and prepare your replies just as you would if you had the exam questions ahead of time. In addition to the questions in figure 11-3, there are some questions that are particularly difficult for college students. The following

Figure 11-3. Questions Frequently Asked by Interviewers

1. Why did you choose this college? Your major?

2. Which courses did you like the most? Dislike? Why?

3. Tell me about your interests and extracurricular activities. Did you hold any leadership positions?

4. How did you finance your college education?

5. What are your plans, if any, for graduate study?

6. What did you learn or gain from your summer or part-time work experiences?

7. What are your major strengths? Your weaknesses?

8. Describe your own personality.

9. Give me some examples of your innovative ability; of your ability to get results.

10. What have been your most satisfying experiences? Which have been most disappointing?

11. What motivates you to put forth your greatest effort?

12. What are your major accomplishments to date?

13. How did you obtain your previous jobs?

14. How do you feel that you will be successful in your field?

15. Are you willing to move to a location where we need you? What is your preference?

16. In what ways do you think you can make a contribution to your field?

17. What starting salary do you expect to get?

18. What kind of boss do you prefer?

19. What are the disadvantages in your chosen field?

20. Give me three references, one each from your academic, work, and personal experiences.

may provide an understanding of what interviewers expect in your answers for such sticklers:

"Tell me about yourself."   Do not narrate your autobiography, but do give the interviewer a summary of your early home environment, such as the size of your hometown and school; why you came to your college or university; and why you chose your major subject or field of work.

"What do you want to do, and why?" Because there are over 20,000 separate jobs in our economy, which appear in the *Dictionary of Occupational Titles,* and over 850 occupations described in the *Occupational Outlook Handbook,* no interviewer will take the time to guess what you want to do. It is up to you to define the area of work you wish to discuss in a thirty-minute interview. In campus recruiting you are expected to know your field of work (for example, retailing, not whether you want to be a buyer, salesperson, or manager; personnel, not trainer, job analyst, employment interviewer, or labor relations specialist), and why you are interested in it.

"What is your philosophy of the field you are interested in?" Recruiters want to know about your values in life and in your career, what is important to you, and how you expect to apply these values to contribute to your field of work.

"Why are you interested in our organization?" Sometimes this is stated as, "Why are you interested in working for us?" Your research should have shown whether this organization has the kind of work, environment and products or services that may provide the kind of career you are seeking. Your responses will enable recruiters to visualize whether their organization may have the type of opportunity you are seeking.

"What are the three most important characteristics necessary for success in your chosen field?" Your answer will tell the recruiter whether you have given this any thought, whether your thoughts are logical and practical, and whether you know what you are talking about. This question gives you an excellent opportunity to demonstrate how thoroughly you have thought out your career plans, and gives you a chance to demonstrate how you possess the needed characteristics.

"What do you want to be doing five or ten years from now?" Sometimes this question takes the form of, "What are your long-range career goals?" Interviewers know that no one can predict accurately where he or she will be in future years, but this question is a favorite because it helps to ascertain your ambition, your ability to plan ahead, and helps determine the soundness of your thinking.

"How do you expect to achieve your job and career objectives?"
Employers want to know whether you are acquainted with the
various job levels in your field, how long you expect to stay at each
level, and whether your thoughts are realistic and feasible. If you
have done your research and plotted your career timetable, you
can easily bring out what you hope to learn and do on each job
level, describe what you think is the next promotional job level,
and how long it will take you to reach it.

"Why should we hire you?" This is one of the most difficult
questions for students to answer. Interviewers are more interested
in how you answer, rather that what you answer because they
know most students do not have enough experience to provide a
good answer. This type of question gives you a chance to put the
final touch on your presentation by summarizing your interests
and qualifications, and relating them to the employer's requirements. We suggest you repeat the key points brought out by the
recruiter regarding the job and qualifications desired, then succinctly match them with your goals, training, and/or experience.
An effective closing will definitely help get an invitation to visit
the employer, or an offer for employment.

Occasionally students encounter recruiters who use a stress
interview wherein they attempt to unnerve you and see how you
react to such a challenge. Sometimes these techniques are used by
new interviewers to cover up their inexperience. Usually, though,
such recruiters want to see how well you can think on your feet,
how well you react to stressful questions when the answers are not
rehearsed and the questions are not anticipated, and whether you
would be a good candidate for a job that has a lot of pressure.

Once in a while the campus recruiter does this to make the
process a little more exciting. By the time he or she interviews
students from 9:00 a.m. to 5:00 p.m. every day at ten different
schools for three weeks, all students tend to look alike and have
well-coached answers, so the job becomes repetitive and boring.
By varying the approach with unanticipated questions, it becomes
easier to pick out the students for further consideration. Usually
such questions take the form of a problem: "What would you do,
or how would you handle (an emergency, a problem, an improvement)?" Remember that your answer is not as important as the
manner in which you respond to the question. If you can't think
up a good solution, you can always fall back on this general type
of answer. "First I would define the problem. Then I would gather
all the facts. Next I would consider various alternative solutions.

And finally, I would make my decision to handle this emergency or solve the problem."

Employer's Story

By this time, the recruiter has some idea of your interests and qualifications, and tries to visualize where you would fit into the organization. Typically the recruiter describes several topics of interest to you, and then tries to do a selling job on the organization if he or she is interested in you.

Since the campus interview is just the first step in selecting applicants, the recruiter generally describes the next step in the application process. Depending on organization policy, length of time before graduation, and mutual interest, the interviewer may suggest a visit to the employer's place of business, give you an assignment or an application blank, or indicate that you will receive some kind of communication within a few weeks. After each interview, the recruiter completes his or her impressions of you, as illustrated in figure 11-4.

After your mutual questions have been discussed, the interviewer brings the interview to a close.

Closing the Interview

Be alert for cues near the end of your interview. The recruiter's comments will enable you to appraise the impression you made, should clarify what the next step or action will be, and determine who is to take the next step in your contact with this employer. Be ready to give the recruiter two or three dates when you can visit the organization for further interviews. It is always a good practice to express thanks to the interviewer, and make a graceful exit.

After the Interview

As you are leaving, be sure to thank the receptionist, the secretary, or the person who introduced you. This courteous gesture has helped many applicants because interviewers often ask their employees for their reactions to the applicant's manners and first impressions. When interviewing at the employer's place of business, this step is especially important. Then find a place out of eyesight of the recruiter or interviewer, sit down, and do the following:

1. Jot down or verify the full name and job title of the interviewer for future follow-up contacts.

Figure 11-4. Example of a Rating Sheet for Campus Interviews

Name of Applicant _____ Phone Number _____ College _____

Degree _____ Major Field _____ Date of Graduation _____ Applying for (job) _____

Factors to Consider	Outstanding	Above Average	Satisfactory	Marginal
APPEARANCE Pleasing first impression, grooming, dress, manners, neatness.				
PERSONALITY Friendliness, poise, sense of humor, self-confidence, forcefulness.				
COMMUNICATION ABILITY Verbal delivery, grammar, animation, vocabulary, clarity in expressing ideas and thoughts.				
MATURITY Self-control, stability, realistic career plans and goals, judgment, self-reliance.				
INTELLECTUAL QUALITIES Academic record, response to questions, alertness, quick to understand, creativity.				
LEADERSHIP Initiative, energy level, drive, interest, enthusiasm, officer in campus organizations.				
OVERALL EVALUATION Goals, ambition, long-range potential.				

Result:

____ Invite

____ Possible

____ Reject

Name of Interviewer _____   Date _____

2. Review and evaluate your interview, and note:

- Questions with which you experienced difficulty. Be sure to discuss these with a career advisor or professor.

- Pertinent information about the organization, the job, and the career field, which you did not know previously, but wish to retain.

- Pertinent data on your control record (see figure 12-1 in the next chapter).

3. If interested in the position and the organization, send a follow-up letter (discussed in chapter 12) to show your interest, and to beat the competition. This should be done within a day or two if the interview was at the employer's place of business, and within a week to ten days after the campus interview or after a graduate school interview.

Figure 11-5. Reminders for Campus Interviews

- Study your college's policies and procedures.

- Read the bulletin boards and other publicity, preferably every day. Additional recruiters are usually added throughout the year.

- Research the employers and graduate schools, and select those that seem to fit your needs.

- Sign up for interviews with the selected employers or graduate schools.

- Prepare for each interview.

- Dress properly for each interview.

- Be on time and at the right location for each interview.

- Carry extra resumes with you for all interviews.

- Telephone or visit the scheduler if you need to cancel; be sure you have a good reason for doing so.

- Keep in touch and discuss any problems with the scheduler and career advisor.

- After the interview, follow up within ten days by writing a letter to those recruiters in whose organizations or schools you are interested.

- When you accept a position or admittance to a graduate program, notify all persons who helped you—the recruiter, faculty, career advisors, friends, and so forth.

4. Don't sit around waiting for a job offer or admission to a graduate program. Review and take action on the steps described in chapter 12.

One final note: Do not rely too much on campus recruiting. Only a small percentage of employers and graduate schools make recruiting trips to college campuses. (See chapter 10 for other sources.)

chapter twelve

Follow-Up and Decision-Making Processes

Too many applicants think that the interview is the final step in the selection process, so they sit back and wait for the employer's decision. They forget there is tremendous competition for jobs, and that job hunting becomes a numbers game. As an example, in a recent year the Eastman Kodak Company interviewed 6,800 students on 280 different campuses, and ended up hiring 268 (3.94 percent). Competition comes from fellow students at your own school, from graduating students from other colleges, and from recent graduates from all colleges throughout the country. The same competition faces seniors applying to graduate schools.

Even if you have an exemplary scholastic record, a fine extracurricular record, a wonderful attitude, and perseverance, you are certain to get rejected far more times than you will be offered a job or be admitted to a graduate program. Rejection is an inevitable experience for every applicant, but it has the potential to be a source of personal and career growth. This is the reason why career counselors advise sending out between fifty to one hundred resumes to prospective employers, to obtain interviews with ten to twenty employers or several graduate schools, and to follow up on every interview in which you are interested. Effective follow up will enable you to close the sale by getting a job offer from the employer, or getting admitted to a graduate program.

In interviews for graduate school, it helps to see the facilities and equipment available, get specific information on courses and thesis requirements, meet some of the faculty in your proposed field of study, and get a feel for the amount of cooperation and financial aid you can expect to get from that department.

In recruiting college graduates, it is very common to require more than one interview. If the initial interview is on the college campus, it is customary to invite the selected candidates for a secondary interview at the employer's place of business, often referred to as a plant or office visit. Job offers are very seldom made to students on the basis of the campus interview. Understanding what to expect during such a visit should help you prepare a list of questions and other items for discussion.

The Secondary (Employment) Interview

Getting to the Interview

When you receive an invitation to visit an employer, you should respond promptly, suggesting dates for such a visit, and asking any questions for which you need an answer pertaining to the trip (hotel accommodations, mode of travel, and time of appointments). If you are no longer interested in that employer, it is common courtesy to decline the invitation. A rejection on your part could easily help a fellow student get an invitation and further consideration by that employer.

If no travel instructions are given, we suggest using the most practical method. If the distance justifies travel by air, it is better to fly coach class. If you travel by first class, prospective employers may think you are too rich for their blood and not cost conscious, thus hurting your chances for employment and advancement.

Before leaving the campus, be sure to take with you the name, job title, organization, address, and telephone number of persons who could be contacted for reference purposes. Be prepared to give prospective employers such information during the secondary interview. Even if your instructions for graduate school application did not require references, take reference information with you when you visit the school. Letters of recommendation are usually an integral part of the application procedure for admission to graduate programs.

During the Interview

Upon arrival at the employer's place of business, you are usually asked to report to the personnel office. Although the recruiter you met on the campus may not be there, you can obtain the schedule of interviews or other plans for the day. Typically, you can expect three to seven interviews, possibly a tour of the facility, some employment tests, and lunch with an alumnus from your school or with an employee from the department where you would be working.

Three basic areas should be considered and carefully observed by students during secondary interviews:

Type of Work

Are the duties and responsibilities of the job suitable for your talents and interests? Be sure to get a firsthand impression of the day-to-day assignments, talk to the current employees if possible, find out the negative aspects of the job, and ask questions to learn what advancement is possible from the starting job.

Supervisor

To whom would you be reporting each day? What kind of person is he or she? Can you learn from and respect this supervisor? Are your personalities compatible? Does the supervisor consider college graduates to be a threat to his or her own position? Because the evaluation of the supervisor will be crucial to your employment and later advancement, make sure you can get along with, and respect, him or her.

Environment

The atmosphere in which you would be working is important to your personal satisfaction and happiness. Does the organization encourage questions and suggestions? What is the morale situation in the department where you will be assigned? Do fellow employees seem to be the kind who are tolerant of the mistakes typically made by newcomers? What is the attitude of co-workers? Would they be helpful in your efforts to learn the job, or do they seem to resent your employment? Comments have come back to career counselors that some supervisors grumble, "It took me ten (maybe twenty) years to get where I am, and now I'm supposed to teach this college graduate all I know so she could become my supervisor?"

Some words of caution are appropriate for students going on a visit to employers for the secondary interview. Do not ask too many questions regarding salary or benefit details, or schedule too many visits in a tight sequence. If the visit is out of town, ask the employer's representative to make hotel reservations for you (many employers maintain hotel suites to accommodate visitors). If married, you are better off making the trip alone; if a strong mutual interest is established and your spouse wants a look at the area, a second trip may be arranged. Be sure to take along extra cash and credit cards for unexpected expenses, and a pocket notebook to record all expenses incurred.

The Salary Question

If nothing is said about the starting salary, you could bring it up at the end of the day when the inevitable question, "do you have any further questions?" arises. This is the most appropriate time to work in your concern regarding money. Before leaving the campus for secondary interviews, you should visit the career center and look over the survey results on starting salaries. A nationwide report on starting salary averages is available to college career centers by the College Placement Council, the national professional organization specializing in college recruitment and placement (see figure 12-1). Talks with your career counselors and faculty will also give you some basis for what to expect in starting salaries for your particular field of interest.

The Department of Labor makes annual surveys of salaries on a regional basis for a number of major fields and occupations. The ASCUS organization makes annual surveys in the teaching fields, as indicated in figure 12-2. In addition to the above published sources of salary data, you can often obtain pertinent data from professional societies in your field of interest, from fellow students, from recent graduates, and directly from employers.

As a general rule, students with a high scholastic average and a strong leadership record in extracurricular activities may be offered somewhat higher salaries. Such a record indicates to employers that the student has a greater potential for advancement, hopefully up to executive levels in ten or fifiteen years. Such students are recruited heavily and receive the greatest number of job offers.

Fringe benefits such as paid vacations, life and health insurance, flexible hours of work, financial incentive programs, and assistance toward graduate courses, are usually described in detail in the employer's personnel handbook. Although very desirable, fringe benefits are not the most important factor to consider when accepting your first job offer after graduation. Practically all employers of college graduates now have a satisfactory package of fringe benefits.

Conduct

It is a good idea to take along several copies of your resume to save time when you get that repetitious "tell me about yourself" question from interviewers. By handing them a copy of your resume, you can state, "I've summarized most of the information on this resume, and will be glad to answer any other questions you may have." Since interviewers often ask the same questions, and each of them will be evaluating you, it is important that you not show any boredom or frustration in a meeting. Although it is boring to give the same information over and over, try to keep an enthusiastic attitude and show interest throughout the day. If the luncheon is informal and you are talking to a recent graduate or nonsupervisor, you will probably have the best opportunity to ask, "what is it really like working here?" Don't relax completely because the luncheon itself may be used to judge your social poise and behavior. As you talk to future co-workers, note their reactions to their boss and others to ascertain the morale in that department.

Feedback

At the end of your scheduled interviews, you should check with the personnel department (or the college recruiter who arranged your visit) to get some feedback on the impressions received from those who interviewed you, and to give your impressions of the day's activities. Do not expect to get a job offer at this time because most employers like to complete all their visits with the selected college students before deciding which should be given a job offer. It usually takes about two to four weeks to get some word from the employer as to the results of your visit.

Figure 12-1. Average Yearly Salary Offers

Bachelor's Degree Candidates (Data Combined for Men and Women)							
By Curriculum For All Types of Employers	**Number of Offers** July 1989	**Average $ Offer** July 1989	September 1988	**Percent Change in $ Offers from September 1988**	**Percentiles** 90th	50th	10th
Business							
Accounting	5,444	$25,290	$24,000	5.4%	$29,000	$25,500	$21,000
Business Administration (incl. Management Science)	1,411	22,274	21,456	3.8	28,000	21,996	16,800
Distribution Management . .	82	24,447	N/A	N/A	28,500	24,600	19,800
Economics & Finance (incl. Banking)	2,160	24,649	N/A	N/A	30,000	25,000	18,500
Hotel/Restaurant Management	124	19,859	20,124	−1.3	23,000	19,500	17,500
Human Resources (incl. Labor Relations)	136	23,035	20,316	13.4	28,800	22,125	18,000
Management Information Systems	514	26,861	24,864	8.0	31,000	27,000	23,000
Marketing/Marketing Management (incl. Research)	1,605	22,523	N/A	N/A	27,300	22,500	18,000
Real Estate	20	23,571	N/A	N/A	32,000	22,000	18,000
Communications							
Advertising	75	19,367	19,380	−0.1	24,000	19,000	15,000
Communications	298	20,761	20,220	2.7	27,000	20,900	15,000
Journalism	119	19,595	18,372	6.7	26,400	19,000	14,000
Telecommunications/ Broadcasting	54	19,239	N/A	N/A	25,500	19,474	13,000
Education							
Elementary Education	383	18,578	N/A	N/A	23,000	19,000	13,084
Pre-Elementary Education .	10	16,203	N/A	N/A	*	*	*
Physical Education	35	19,309	N/A	N/A	24,700	18,785	14,200
Special Education	88	19,879	N/A	N/A	24,500	19,000	17,000
Home Economics							
Human Ecology	24	18,655	N/A	N/A	24,180	18,150	13,632
Textiles & Clothing	98	19,944	N/A	N/A	25,000	19,500	17,000
Merchandising Management	50	19,458	N/A	N/A	22,200	19,000	16,500
Humanities & Social Sciences							
Foreign Languages	55	20,666	N/A	N/A	26,000	20,000	16,000
Letters	189	20,348	20,664	−1.5	26,500	20,000	15,000
Visual & Performing Arts . .	77	18,099	N/A	N/A	24,000	17,136	12,456
Humanities–Other	111	23,010	N/A	N/A	30,000	22,000	17,000
Criminal Justice	64	20,521	19,512	5.2	28,000	19,750	12,584
History	86	21,275	22,848	−6.9	26,400	21,250	14,700
Political Science/ Government	190	22,116	N/A	N/A	30,000	22,000	15,700
Psychology	229	19,061	20,592	−7.4	27,000	18,000	12,480
Sociology	86	19,021	N/A	N/A	25,000	18,500	14,000
Social Sciences–Other	96	20,205	N/A	N/A	29,500	19,650	14,000
Engineering							
Aerospace & Aeronautical	433	29,424	28,176	4.4	31,600	29,700	26,640
Agricultural	29	25,984	25,020	3.9	30,600	27,500	19,000
Architectural	31	25,871	N/A	N/A	28,080	26,300	24,960

Continued . . .

Figure 12-1. *cont.*

By Curriculum For All Types of Employers	Number of Offers July 1989	Average $ Offer		Percent Change in $ Offers from September 1988	Percentiles		
		July 1989	September 1988		90th	50th	10th
Continued . . .							
Bioengineering &							
Biomedical	26	$28,135	$28,272	−0.5%	$32,500	$29,000	$24,300
Chemical	1,760	32,949	30,996	6.3	34,800	33,000	31,200
Civil	1,085	26,735	25,596	4.5	32,000	26,400	22,880
Computer	471	30,413	N/A	N/A	33,500	31,000	26,000
Electrical	3,279	30,661	N/A	N/A	33,500	31,008	27,000
Industrial	746	29,812	28,476	4.7	32,580	30,000	26,000
Mechanical	3,037	30,539	29,388	3.9	33,280	30,900	27,500
Metallurgical	257	30,708	29,448	4.3	33,000	30,900	28,200
Mining	32	26,840	N/A	N/A	31,000	28,900	21,000
Nuclear	53	31,281	28,740	8.8	33,000	31,500	29,000
Petroleum	117	32,987	32,016	3.0	36,600	34,800	25,752
Textile	46	26,633	N/A	N/A	31,500	25,500	24,000
Engineering Technology . .	389	28,310	27,396	3.3	33,000	28,300	22,000
Industrial Technology	84	26,652	N/A	N/A	29,400	27,492	23,000
Agriculture & Natural Resources							
Agribusiness	49	23,177	N/A	N/A	30,000	23,000	17,000
Animal Sciences	23	19,381	N/A	N/A	22,500	19,992	15,200
Plant Sciences	9	20,031	N/A	N/A	*	*	*
Natural Resources	13	21,622	19,932	*	*	*	*
Other Agricultural Sciences	68	21,656	N/A	N/A	26,000	22,050	15,500
Computer Sciences							
Computer Science	1,215	28,557	N/A	N/A	32,500	29,000	23,040
Computer Programming . . .	118	28,711	N/A	N/A	33,800	30,000	20,100
Information Sciences & Systems	344	26,853	N/A	N/A	31,500	27,000	23,000
Systems Analysis	25	29,176	N/A	N/A	31,500	30,000	25,000
Health Sciences							
Allied Health	81	24,496	22,536	8.7	30,000	25,000	18,400
Health Sciences	34	20,911	N/A	N/A	28,900	18,500	15,000
Nursing	223	24,789	23,652	4.8	30,000	24,000	19,200
[1]Pharmacy	110	35,173	34,356	2.4	41,000	37,000	27,664
Sciences							
Actuarial	32	30,244	N/A	N/A	33,000	30,000	28,000
Architectural & Environmental Design . .	32	23,763	N/A	N/A	28,000	24,200	18,000
Biological	69	20,998	20,364	3.1	29,200	20,500	14,067
Chemistry	133	26,698	26,004	2.7	33,120	28,000	18,000
Geological	19	23,724	N/A	N/A	*	*	*
Mathematics (incl. Statistics)	245	26,789	N/A	N/A	32,004	27,500	18,710
Physics	51	28,296	27,816	1.7	32,011	30,000	20,500
Other Physical & Earth Sciences	15	22,829	21,216	*	*	*	*
	28,696						

N/A—No historic data available.
*Not computed for fewer than 20 offers.
[1]Pharmacy is a 5-year degree program.

Source: *CPC Salary Survey*/ July 1989.

Figure 12-2. Average Salary Reports for Teachers

		Special Education		Elementary/Secondary	
		Bachelor's	Master's	Bachelor's	Master's
Region 1	1986–1987	15,896	18,701	15,870	20,146
Northwest	1987–1988	16,462	18,899	16,669	18,559
	1988–1989	16,725	19,600	16,794	19,584
Region 2	1986–1987	17,744	19,837	18,254	18,946
West	1987–1988	21,032	22,538	20,397	21,403
	1988–1989	20,573	23,179	20,909	21,218
Region 3	1986–1987	18264	19,913	17,646	19,462
Rocky Mountain	1987–1988	17,492	19,425	17,434	19,046
	1988–1989	17,962	22,560	18,129	21,468
Region 4	1986–1987	15,838	17,475	15,476	17,207
Great Plains/	1987–1988	17,546	19,426	16,898	18,988
Midwest	1988–1989	17,723	20,345	17,523	20,013
Region 5	1986–1987	17,050	18,297	16,662	17,816
South Central	1987–1988	17,353	18,496	16,991	18,114
	1988–1989	17,927	19,339	17,817	19,123
Region 6	1986–1987	20,941	19,638	16,273	19,747
Southeast	1987–1988	17,855	19,313	17,648	19,029
	1988–1989	18,730	20,763	18,382	20,286
Region 7	1986–1987	16,163	17,238	15,913	17,047
Great Lakes	1987–1988	17,123	20,048	16,483	19,464
	1988–1989	17,837	20,550	17,659	20,463
Region 8	1986–1987	18,250	20,900	18,250	20,800
Middle Atlantic	1987–1988	19,225	21,331	18,338	20,531
	1988–1989	20,152	22,515	19,625	22,321
Region 9	1986–1987	16,500	19,000	15,632	18,250
Northeast	1987–1988	18,436	20,410	17,725	20,515
	1988–1989	18,911	20,508	18,052	20,044
Alaska	1986–1987	27,500	31,500	27,500	31,500
	1987–1988	26,000	31,000	26,000	31,000
	1988–1989	30,000	40,000	30,000	40,000
Hawaii	1986–1987	16,500	17,100	16,500	17,100
	1987–1988	N/A	N/A	N/A	N/A
	1988–1989	N/A	N/A	N/A	N/A

Source: Akin, James N. "Teacher Supply and Demand in the United States," 1989 Report. In *ASCUS Research Report.*

Travel Expenses

If the visit is out of town so that more than nominal expenses have been incurred, you should inquire of the last person you interview as to that employer's policy and procedure on reimbursement. Some employers refund expenses at the end of your visit, while others ask that you submit an expense statement or fill out their expense voucher. Be sure to save all of your travel tickets and other expense receipts because most employers will request them. Figure 12-3 illustrates the commonly accepted practices regarding reimbursement of student expenses for employer visits.

When you plan a trip to visit several employers, you should prorate your expenses. If you have difficulty doing this, ask advice from the employers you visit, since they have had a lot more experience with prorating than you have. It is unethical to pad your expenses, and the grapevine among employers could easily jeopardize your employment chances and your reputation.

Follow Up

To enhance your chances of getting job offers or admission to graduate school, follow up on all organizations in which you are interested until you get a definite rejection, offer, or admission. Because there will be multiple letters, interviews, and telephone calls, you can keep better control and manage the progress of your campaign with each employer or graduate school by devising a simple but effective record. Figure 12-4 gives an example of a record form for interviews that will enable you to see at a glance just where you are with each prospective employer or graduate school, and what follow-up action may be needed for your next step. Add these to your personal record book.

We do not recommend following up on every interview, which incurs needless postage expense, and wastes a great deal of time. If you had twelve interviews, the chances are that you will be interested in only three or four of the employers or graduate schools. It is more effective to concentrate on prospects of special interest. Depending on your record and field of interest, you can expect a ratio of one offer for every four interviews. Where the supply of candidates is scarce (in engineering, mathematics, and nursing, for example), you might expect two or three offers for every five interviews.

Figure 12-3. Reimbursement of Travel Expenses

Because reimbursement policies vary, it may take from two to four weeks for some employers, while others will reimburse you the day of your visit. Therefore, you should take along sufficient funds or credit cards to finance the trips for secondary interviews. Graduate schools rarely reimburse expenses.

Receipts. Practically all employers require airplane or train receipts, along with the hotel bill, before reimbursement is made.

Transportation. Save your plane or train ticket stubs; if you travel by car, record your mileage (beginning and end of trip) and ask the employer what the policy is for mileage allowance.

Meals. Any meals connected with the trip should include the tax and tip, and should be listed on a daily basis. Geographic location will influence the cost, so use common sense in reporting the meal costs. Employers usually pick up the luncheon expenses during your visit.

Local Transportation. Include the cost of taxis, buses, subways, suburban trains, and airport limousine service.

Baggage. Include the tips normally given to porters for checking your baggage at airports, at hotels, or other travel centers.

General Information. From daily travel experience, most employers know the cost of travel expenses, so any fudging on your report will generally result in rejecting your application. If you visit more than one employer on the same trip, you are expected to prorate your expenses among them. You may need to photocopy hotel bills or plane tickets to attach them to the expense reports you send to employers.

Nonreimbursable Expenses. Do not expect to get paid for the following types of expenses:

1. Personal expenses, such as cigarettes, magazines, Gray Line tours, and entertainment.
2. Valet expenses, unless special circumstances require such service, such as when the employer asks you to stay for additional days, or there is an emergency in travel.
3. Excessive tips, over fifteen to eighteen percent on meals or to bellhops and porters.
4. Travel insurance.
5. Interest on loans taken to make the trip.
6. Personal phone calls, except in connection with the scheduled trip (changing plane schedules).
7. Hotel or motel stopovers en route, except as may be required by the transportation schedule.
8. Expenses for spouse, unless the employer invited the spouse and authorized such expenses.

Submitting Your Expenses. Be sure to itemize your expenditures and include all your receipts with your follow-up letter to obtain reimbursement, while reminding the employer of your continued interest.

Figure 12-4. Personal Record for Interviews

Name of Employer or Graduate School	First Interview		Follow-Up Action			Secondary Interview		Employer Action			My Action		
	Date	Time	Letter	Phone Call	Personal Visit	Date	Time	Delay	Rejection	Job Offer	Acknow-ledged	Rejected	Accepted
AT & T	1/22	2:00						2/28	1/30				
May Co.	1/24	10:00	1/29	2/11		2/25	10:00			3/20	3/24	4/2	
General Electric	1/28	2:00	2/7			2/19	9:00	3/5	3/26				
Texas Instruments	2/10	9:00	2/19						3/14				
Ford Motor Co.	2/4	3:30		2/27		3/8	2:00	3/17	3/28				
General Mills	2/18	2:30	2/26	3/18	•			3/24	3/27				
Macy's	2/20	11:00							3/20				
Hallmark Cards	3/4	9:30	3/14	4/2		3/20	9:30	3/27		4/10	4/12		4/30
Polaroid Corp.	3/6	4:00	3/10	3/20	3/27	4/4	1:30	4/12		4/15	4/18	4/30	
Carnation Co.	3/12	10:30							3/26				
Proctor & Gamble	3/17	3:00		3/22		3/28	10:00		4/10				
Bank of Chicago	3/18	11:30							3/26				
Johnson & Johnson	3/26	1:30	4/2			4/8	9:00	4/11		4/22	4/25	4/30	
U. of Texas	3/27	4:30	4/7						4/29				

Methods for Following Up on Interviews

By Letter

The first method of following up is by letter, probably the best way to provide additional evidence of your interest. If the initial interview is for a job and is held at the employer's place of business, such a letter should be sent within two days to reaffirm your interest in the job as well as the employer. If the initial interview was on the college campus, we suggest waiting seven to ten days because many recruiters travel a week at a time to different schools and would not get to see your letter because it ended up in a file.

Recruiters from graduate schools usually take even longer to get caught up on the paperwork from their recruiting trip. A slight delay in following up can work to your advantage by indicating that you have given more thought to the information received during the interview, have concluded that the job or graduate program does coincide with your career plans, and therefore are reminding the employer or school of your continued interest in that organization. Sometimes it helps to enclose a letter of recommendation with your follow-up letter to stimulate or renew the employer's or graduate school's interest in your application. At the end of this chapter are examples of follow-up letters for our five hypothetical applicants. To remind the prospective employer or graduate school of your continued interest, you can borrow ideas from these examples or adapt the format used for a follow-up letter in figure 12-5.

By Telephone

If you don't receive a response to your follow-up letter in a reasonable time, then try a second method by telephoning the recruiter to remind him or her of your continued interest. Have your copy of the follow-up letter in hand to facilitate your telephone conversation. Thus the employer or graduate school recruiter will have your application, the interview notes, and your follow-up letter, to be reinforced by the interest expressed in your telephone conversation. Do not call collect unless the recruiter specifically gave you instructions to do so.

Figure 12-5. Format for a Follow-up Letter

Your Address
City, State, Zip Code

Date

Name of Person
Job Title
Name of Organization
Address
City, State, Zip Code

Dear Mr./Ms. _____:

First Paragraph: Thank the interviewer for the consideration and courtesy extended to you. Remind him or her of the position for which you were interviewed, and the date and place of the interview.

Second Paragraph: Reaffirm your interest in the position and organization. Mention anything you have done since the interview that demonstrates
your interest in that position or program (for example, additional research on
the employer or position or program, or conversations with recent graduates or
local representatives).

Third Paragraph: If expenses are to be reimbursed, attach an itemized
statement and include your stubs from plane or other transportation. Submit
any information you wish to add to your application, such as references requested, evidence of your writing ability, and so forth.

Fourth Paragraph: Reiterate your interest in this opportunity, express willingness to provide additional data, and suggest your availability
for other interviews.

Sincerely,

(Be sure
to sign)

Your Name
Phone Number

By Personal Visit

If the employer or graduate school is located within reasonable travel distance, you might pay a personal visit to follow up on your application. During school vacations, or when visiting other employers or schools in that area, you might enhance your chances by stopping in to see the employer and stating, "I happened to be in this area so I thought I'd check up on the status of my application and remind you of my continued interest in your job and organization."

Other Follow-Up Methods

Occasionally it is desirable to use infrequently used methods, such as sending a telegram or cablegram (if overseas). Such an unusual approach is sure to be noticed, will affirm your interest, and generally catch the eye of the recruiter. Another method that should be used sparingly is to have a friend within the organization or one of your faculty members inquire for you and, perhaps, put in a good word on your behalf.

Value of Following Up

From the employer's viewpoint, it is often very difficult to select from several very well-qualified applicants. When there are too many equally qualified applicants, it is very common to give further consideration to the applicants who express the most interest. If no word has been received after the initial interview, it is natural to suppose that the applicant is only mildly interested and is awaiting a better opportunity. By following up persistently, you reassure the employer or graduate school that you are definitely interested in the opportunity, and thus help to differentiate your application from the stack and beat out the competition.

To appreciate the perseverance required to beat your competition, study figure 12-6 to learn how many steps are often necessary before an employer is able to fill job openings.

To avoid becoming a nuisance, vary your follow-up methods, and be sensitive to timing. Take your cues from the hints or statements given to you by the recruiter. If you don't have cues, use a ten-day to two-week interval between your follow-up methods.

Figure 12-6. Job Applicant Selection Process

Step 1. Placed an ad in the campus newspaper for three management trainees.

Step 2. Received 96 resumes from students.

Step 3. Rejected 46 because of "no apparent interest in banking, or no letter bringing out additional reasons for considering them."

Step 4. Sorted the remaining 50 into three piles:
1st choice (to be interviewed)—22
2nd choice (to be interviewed if necessary)—20
3rd choice (maybe, depends on above two choices)—8

Step 5. Telephoned first 22 (the bank and the campus were in the same city) and made appointments for interviews with the bank's recruiters.

Step 6. Of the 22, ten were considered "employable"; rejections were sent to the other 12.

Step 7. Of the ten "desirables," rejected two after reference checking, and had two refuse to take tests administered by the bank.

Step 8. Sent offers to the three top prospects; sent "continuing interest" letters to the other three.

Step 9. Within the month received one acceptance and two rejections from the students to whom job offers were extended.

Step 10. Sent job offer letters to the other three top prospects.

Step 11. In a short time, received one more acceptance and two rejections from the applicants.

Step 12. Reviewed the 20 resumes of the applicants in the number two pile, and invited five to come in for interviews.

Step 13. Secretary mentioned the persistent follow-up of one of the candidates in the number three group—the file revealed this student had written two letters and made one phone call expressing her interest in this bank. Invited her for an interview.

Step 14. Interviewed all six students; rejected three.

Step 15. Reference checks and test results indicated all three were qualified. Wrote stall letters, expressing interest in applicants, but delaying until one stood out among the three.

Step 16. Only one follow-up letter was received—from the applicant originally placed in group number three.

Step 17. Extended job offer to the applicant who had expressed the most interest by writing the follow-up letter.

Step 18. Student accepted the job offer. Wrote rejection letters to the other applicants.

If your perseverance still results in a rejection, there is still one last possibility. Just as in professional sports, employers don't always get the persons they consider to be the number one candidates, and finally go to their second choice. Some athletes have to use the free agent route to get a chance to demonstrate their ability and end up on the team. In a similar fashion students who get rejected could inquire two to four weeks before graduation to ascertain whether the employer with whom they wanted to start their career actually did hire enough graduates from that class. If not, state that you are still interested and would be willing to come to the employer's place of business at your own expense to have another interview. In general, try to persuade the employer to hire you. For graduate school you may not get a decision on admission until late August or early September, and patience is required.

It is always a good idea to analyze each interview, evaluate your strong and weak points, and learn from each interviewing experience. Similarly, you should conduct a postmortem after each rejection to try to determine the reasons for it. Then concentrate on the areas needing improvement. This will help you focus more clearly on your job search.

An area needing improvement by most students is that of correspondence. In searching for a job, it is important to write clearly and concisely, saying exactly what you mean in as few words as possible. Choose the appropriate language and level of detail when writing about technical information, and choose different terminology when writing to people with no technical background.

Improving Your Correspondence

If it is too late to take a business writing course in your school, then follow these simple rules to improve your correspondence when seeking employment:

1. Organize your thoughts by first preparing an outline arranging the items in a systematic, logical order. This will help you rearrange the points you wish to make so that you are satisfied with the flow of ideas.

2. Be natural. It is best to write the way you talk. Too many students are verbose and stuffy on paper; they should heed the good advice, "don't use a twenty-five-cent word where a ten-cent word will do."

3. Use short paragraphs. A few sentences with correct punctuation will make your meaning much easier to grasp. Long and extensive paragraphs are much more difficult to digest, and scare away many readers.

4. Appearance. First impressions are always important. Therefore, pay particular attention to spacing, margins, headings (if any), and other items that will affect the impression made on readers. For employment purposes, it is best to use plain, white, 8 1/2" x 11" paper since that is considered most appropriate and is most used in this country.

5. Proofread your work. Errors in punctuation, grammar, typing, and spelling obviously detract from the favorable impression you wish to create in your correspondence. You may need to rewrite certain sentences, or change some phrases or words to give your writing more punch or clarity.

6. Check for tone. By reading out loud you can test your writing for unnatural, showy, or unclear phrases or sentences. Better yet, have a friend or a counselor read your letters to see whether your tone is apologetic, too brash, or distasteful in any way. Letters should reflect your self-confidence and poise, and have a positive tone.

Decision Making

All of the material in this part of the book is aimed at getting job offers, or admittance to graduate schools. You do not really face making a decision until you actually receive one or more job offers, or get accepted at more than one graduate or professional school. Since graduate school is another stepping-stone toward your career, choosing a school and the job decision will obviously influence your career direction and your life-style, and undoubtedly affect your long-range plans for success in your chosen field.

If you have followed the advice in making a job or graduate school campaign, by this time you should have several job offers or admittances to consider. The following suggestions should help you handle several offers.

1. Always acknowledge offers immediately in writing. Although you are not expected to make a decision as soon as you receive it, the employer or graduate school would appreciate

knowing that its offer or admittance has been received, and that you are still interested.

2. If no time limit has been specified for an answer, give some idea as to when you expect to make a decision. A letter acknowledging the offer could state: "I have two more visits to make for secondary interviews in the next two weeks, and should be able to reach a decision in about three weeks." For graduate schools you can state: "I expect to hear from two additional schools within three weeks, and will then be able to notify you of my decision."

3. If you have lost interest in that employer or graduate school, it is common courtesy to notify them to withdraw your application. This will give one of your fellow students a chance for an offer or admittance.

4. If the offer you received is your second or third choice, you can use it to your advantage by calling or writing to your number one choice and telling them that you are getting pressure from a very desirable offer, but you would prefer to join their organization. Then inquire as to the status of your application. A little competition always helps to expedite action. If employers or admissions officers are on the fence regarding applications, often they can be moved to action when they know someone else wants you.

5. In all such matters it is a good policy to show consideration for the other person by keeping in touch with the employer or graduate school while you are deliberating. But always notify them promptly when you have reached a decision.

The Stall Letter

College seniors and graduate student applicants often receive job offers and admission to graduate programs requesting a definite answer before they are ready to decide. All such offers should be promptly acknowledged, but sometimes it is necessary to include information to stall action. Mr. William F. Trask, director of the Office of Graduate and Career Plans at Worcester Polytechnic Institute, recommends:

"These letters are written to postpone any definite action, and are considered as interim letters toward keeping the prospective position or admission open for your consideration and possible acceptance.

    a. The first paragraph should refer to the preceding action calling for this letter, such as an offer, telegram, or telephone call.

    b. State you are definitely interested in the position or graduate program, but you:

       1. Will need time (indicate how much) to reach a decision.

       2. Would like further information on the enclosed questions or items.

       3. Have reasons why you cannot accept immediately.

    c. Always give the employer or graduate school some idea of when you can give a definite answer."

As with other letters, always keep a copy for your future reference. Also, keep all the correspondence you receive in a systematic order to facilitate future action. Several examples of stall letters are included at the end of this chapter.

Because of the tremendous influence your decision will have on your future life-style and on your career, you may need more than your gut feeling to reach a decision. The advice of Dr. Lee S. Dreyfus, former president of the Sentry Insurance Company, is worth serious thought: "The first job is a dangerous time for it controls the lives of eighty to ninety percent of all people, and the more one gets locked in, the more one is afraid to take risks." Getting accepted into a graduate program sometimes postpones the necessity for making a job decision.

Reaching a Decision

There are a number of ways to reach a decision, and several decision-making theories are taught in colleges. Scientists have an elaborate ten-step process to make decisions. The consequences of errors made in decisions involving nuclear energy, new drugs, and so forth, are too horrendous to contemplate. For a simple formula on decision making that students can readily comprehend and apply, we suggest the following:

Step 1 – Define the problem.

Step 2 – Get the facts.

Step 3 – What are the alternatives?

Step 4 – Which is the best recommendation?

Factors to Consider in Making Decisions

To properly evaluate all the facts and alternatives, you need a more systematic approach to reach the right decision. You should contemplate the various factors that are important to you in terms of your career, your desired life-style, and your value system. From the following factors, which thousands of students have used in reaching a decision, you can formulate your own yardstick to objectively evaluate offers.

For Job Decisions

Nature or Type of Work
The duties and the degree of responsibility in any job should be explored in detail not only to judge whether you can do the job, but also to ascertain whether you would be happy doing it. If you are the type of person who is seeking a challenge, would this job offer you sufficient opportunity to use your creativity and your resourcefulness? Some people have a yearning for travel, while others shun it. Would you enjoy this type of work, or is it necessary to slave at this job in order to qualify for interesting work later?

Supervision
Is your personality compatible with that of your future boss? What type of training can you expect—on-the-job, a formal course, shifting from department to department, or learned entirely on your own from trial-and-error experience? Can you expect strong leadership from your boss? Does he or she give the impression of being in control, or of constantly putting out fires? As near as you can tell, are your values similar to those of your future boss? Having a similar set of values with your first boss is very important to help you identify with your prospective employer. Just as children often seek affection and authority from their parents, employees seek appreciation of their work and expect to learn the lines of authority from their boss.

Environment
What kind of working conditions can you expect? Working in a steelmill or mine contrasts greatly with an office or store environment. Is shift work involved? Do you have to be on your feet all day, or would you share a desk with several other trainees? In your talks with employees, what kind of complaints did they have, and

what kind of morale did you find? Is the working environment conducive to freedom for self-expression? Are ideas and suggestions sought, or does the environment call for robotlike compliance with long-established procedures?

Opportunities

Does the employer encourage further education and provide assistance to obtain it? What is the organization's promotion and advancement policy—both vertically and horizontally? Were the present supervisors and executives promoted from the ranks? Does one department dominate the promotions to higher levels, like the Engineering, Marketing, or Accounting Division? How does the organization provide for the personal development of the individual employee? Is there active or passive encouragement to take courses, attend seminars, discuss job and professional matters with management, join professional associations, and initiate improvements?

Employer and Industry

What is the reputation of this employer as far as being a good place to work? Is it reputed to be a stable organization offering security to employees, and in the forefront for research and innovative practices? What kind of contribution does it make to society? Is the size of the organization suitable for your interests? Is there enough flexibility within the organization and within its industry to cope with economic and other changes? Are its personnel policies considered to be fair and equitable? What is the future growth potential for the company and the industry?

Compensation

What is the starting salary, and how does it compare to other offers? How does the benefits package compare with other offers? What financial incentives are available, and what kind of taxes should be considered?

Location

Is housing available, and what is the cost? Is the climate conducive to your health? Are the transportation facilities adequate, or do you have a long commute? Are the community, cultural, educational, athletic, and religious offerings commensurate with your personal desires? How does the cost of living compare with other locations? What recreational facilities are available—theater, skiing, boating, tennis, museums?

Cost of Living

Although starting salary figures appear to be easier to compare than the subjective factors in this and the following two sections, a more realistic comparison should include attention to the cost of living factor in different parts of the country. The American Chamber of Commerce Researchers Association's (ACCRA) Cost of Living Index is based on price data collected for 252 urban areas of all sizes throughout the country (figure 12-7).

If we use the ACCRA index figures, a salary offer of $20,000 in Denver would be the equivalent in purchasing power of $19,000 in Indianapolis, and of $29,544 in Boston, as illustrated below.

		Ratio	Offer	Ratio	Equivalent
Indianapolis Denver	$\dfrac{97.6}{103.1}$ =	.95	$20,000 x	.95 =	$19,000
Boston Denver	$\dfrac{152.3}{103.1}$ =	1.4772	$20,000 x	1.4772 =	$29,544

Unless you make a job comparison chart as in figure 12-8, and compare the cost of living figures (figure 12-7) in the cities from which you received offers, you can easily be swayed by a starting salary that is nominally higher than others. Therefore it is important to remember that salaries are just *one* of the factors to consider, and that the best decision depends on *all* factors being considered.

For Graduate or Professional School Decisions

In evaluating admissions to graduate programs, you should consider a special set of factors before choosing a school.

Reputation

Foremost probably would be the reputation of the department in the field you wish to study, and next the reputation of the faculty and the graduate school itself.

Financial Aid

Because of the ever-increasing cost of college, those of you contemplating graduate or professional programs would undoubtedly want to learn what financial assistance is available—tuition relief, part-time work, grants, a graduate assistantship, paid internships, and so forth.

Figure 12-7. ACCRA Cost of Living Index in Urban Areas with Central Cities over 500,000 Population/Fourth Quarter 1987

	All Items	Grocery Items	Housing	Utilities	Trans- portation	Health Care	Miscellaneous Goods and Services
Boston, MA	152.3	113.0	261.3	131.6	110.0	162.2	118.2
New York, NY	150.9	117.3	231.1	185.5	115.1	139.7	116.6
Philadelphia, PA	124.8	112.2	131.7	162.7	109.7	139.2	116.3
San Diego, CA	124.3	104.5	183.9	76.8	121.1	127.4	109.7
Chicago, IL*	120.6	103.6	155.6	124.4	115.2	118.2	106.2
San Jose, CA	118.0	92.7	186.5	63.0	111.9	128.7	102.4
Phoenix, AZ	106.6	101.4	109.8	94.3	102.4	128.2	108.7
Baltimore, MD	105.5	101.5	104.6	103.5	107.8	109.7	107.2
Denver, CO	103.1	92.9	119.0	89.8	112.4	109.2	96.8
Columbus, OH	102.0	95.0	106.5	107.3	104.5	100.0	100.0
Dallas, TX	102.0	102.6	101.7	106.4	101.1	113.5	97.8
Houston, TX	101.6	105.0	79.6	114.5	108.8	101.9	107.9
Jacksonville, FL	99.0	91.4	99.6	95.9	96.2	102.0	104.6
Indianapolis, IN	97.6	98.3	97.7	97.6	109.1	93.3	93.2
Memphis, TN	97.3	99.5	94.9	90.5	101.2	97.1	98.7
San Antonio, TX	96.8	101.9	89.6	101.1	101.1	95.7	96.1
New Orleans, LA	96.3	98.3	89.8	115.4	97.7	96.1	92.5

*Chicago data are averages of Naperville IL and Schamburg IL.

Please note the following cautions:

(1) The ACCRA Index is a measure of relative differences in costs for a *midmanagement* standard of living, and may not be generalizable to other living standards or to the population as a whole. As a rough rule of thumb, a husband-wife midmanagement household will have an annual income about twice the average household income for the area in which they live.

(2) The ACCRA Index measures differences in the costs of consumer goods and services, and therefore excludes tax differences. This consideration can be particularly important when moving from low- to high-tax areas.

(3) A relatively small difference between urban areas may not indicate correctly even the *direction* of the difference.

Source: American Chamber of Commerce Researchers Association.

Location

If you think you would like to settle in a certain part of the country, it would be wise to seek admittance to a graduate school in that area. By the time you spend two or more years in that area, you have a head start in contacts, knowledge of employment, and options. Because state laws differ, it is especially helpful for law students to study in the state where they expect to practice the legal profession.

Other Factors

These would include the time at which courses are offered, especially if you plan part-time graduate work, and whether credits for graduate courses taken at other institutions could be transferred.

The unwritten law of "publish or perish" makes faculty members vitally interested in research and writing. Tenure, success, and salary depend on writing and publishing, and they affect the ability to attract grants and contracts. By developing excellent faculty relationships, graduate school students can obtain sound advice, moral support (especially on theses), and grants, and they can work on articles co-authored with their faculty members.

In many fields, faculty mentors have consulting contracts and are often in positions to hire graduate students to work on specific projects. For teaching or research jobs in colleges and universities, the personal referral and recommendation by a professor or dean is practically a requirement for any applicant. The greatest benefit to graduate students from faculty mentors is probably the opportunity to learn so much more about the field through informal discussions, and to receive personal attention in furthering their learning and experience.

For Teaching or Administrative Positions in Education Decisions

The same principles of selection may be applied in other fields to help make the right decision. For example, if you were considering a teaching career, factors to be considered would include:

The Type of Educational Institution

Is the school public or private, urban or rural, general or technical (vocational)? What kind of support is given by the community?

The Type and Size of the Student Body

What is the background of the students—blue collar, professional, white collar, or foreign? Some people prefer to group the students according to higher, middle, or lower economic levels. What is the typical class size?

Curriculum

What are the typical courses offered and their sequence in your discipline? Are textbooks and supplementary materials adequate, and do you have freedom to choose? What is the availability of audiovisual materials and equipment for classroom use? What projects or changes are being contemplated? Are parents and other community members involved in the school programs?

Faculty
What is the size of the faculty in the school and in your department? What number of new teachers and administrators are hired each year? What are the interests and expertise of present faculty? Why is this position available (enrollment increase, retirement, resignation)?

Personnel Policies
What policies exist on vacations, sick leave, medical insurance, and substitutions? What is a normal teaching load? Is a graduate degree encouraged and reimbursed? How much community work is expected? What is the evaluation and promotion policy? Are contracts on a nine-, ten-, or twelve-month basis? How supportive is the school's administration?

Location
In what kind of community is the school located? Is housing available and reasonable? What kind of recreational and cultural facilities are there? Is transportation readily available or is there a long commute? Is parking a problem? What would it cost for housing, transportation, and other costs of living?

Requirements of the Institution
Are advanced degrees required? Does the school have faculty tenure? What is the availability of summer employment? Are teachers required or expected to work in extracurricular activities or nonteaching work after school hours or on weekends? Is there a religious requirement (if the school is denominational)? Is there extra pay for extracurricular responsibilities?

Personal Desires
What is the starting salary, potential for future increases, and the fringe benefit package? How extensive are the school's library facilities and contents as well as laboratory facilities and equipment? Are a school nurse and guidance service available?

Because of the high cost of living, more and more families require two paychecks to meet expenses. This creates changing roles for couples, creates new job problems for students, and requires applicants to carefully define their options.

Married couples have additional factors to consider. In two-career couples, which career should get priority at graduation time? What spouse-assistance programs are available? If children are involved, what childcare facilities are available, and what school arrangements are possible? Does either the job offer or admittance to graduate school include flexible benefits on working hours, insurance, and tuition to make the move more attractive? The pull-out article in *Ms.* magazine in the November 1987 edition has a very informative survey entitled "20 Corporations That Listen to Women," listing the various benefit programs available in these twenty well-known national companies.

You may find it helpful to make up a chart to facilitate comparisons among the offers received. Some prefer a weighted-factor approach for their job comparison, such as is used by engineers and business students. For most students a simple ranking of pertinent factors helps evaluate the offers more objectively. Figure 12-8 illustrates such a device and how it can be used to help you make the right decision. On a scale of one to ten, rank each factor you consider important, then compare the totals. If the totals for two or three offers are relatively close, then obviously subjective factors must enter into the evaluation.

In utilizing an evaluation chart of any kind, try to avoid the halo effect of allowing a generally favorable or unfavorable reaction to an organization, to affect individual ratings. In our counseling, we find that students tend to overrate the importance of starting salary. Our experience indicates that job interest and satisfaction are much more important for career planning purposes. Sometimes a personal factor is so important that it overshadows all other factors. A senior with several job offers came to the career center to report his decision. Knowing how active this student was in his Lutheran Church group, the career counselor asked him how close was the nearest church to his prospective place of employment. When the student said, "about forty miles," he wrinkled his brow and said, "maybe I'd better give this some more thought." He then declined the offer (which had the highest salary of all offers received), and accepted one that enabled him to participate more readily in church activities.

No yardstick to compare job offers or admittance to graduate programs will be as accurate as the one you develop to fit your personal values, needs, and career goals.

Figure 12-8. Job Factor Comparison Chart

Instructions: Rate each part of a factor separately for each offer, with zero being the lowest and ten the highest number of points. Then add the points for each part to get a subtotal of that factor. Add all subtotals to get the grand total to facilitate the comparison of offers.

Factors	Company A	Company B	Government Agency	Nonprofit Agency	Company C
1. NATURE OF WORK					
Duties and responsibilities	8	7	10	7	6
Challenge	7	7	4	5	10
Travel	3	0	0	0	5
Interest in job	10	9	8	7	9
Subtotal	28	23	22	19	30
2. SUPERVISION					
Personalities	7	9	6	6	10
Training	5	7	4	3	8
Similar values	7	7	6	8	7
Subtotal	19	23	16	17	25
3. ENVIRONMENT					
Working conditions	8	8	7	5	8
Morale of staff	9	10	6	6	10
Freedom (independence)	8	8	6	9	9
Subtotal	25	26	19	20	27
4. OPPORTUNITIES					
Further education	5	9	4	4	8
Advancement	9	9	8	7	9
Personal development	10	10	8	6	10
Subtotal	24	28	20	17	27
5. EMPLOYER AND INDUSTRY					
Reputation	9	8	9	7	10
Security	10	6	10	9	7
Contribution to society	8	7	5	10	8
Personnel policies	10	0	8	8	9
Growth possibilities	8	6	5	5	9
Subtotal	45	37	37	39	43
6. COMPENSATION					
Starting salary	8	10	5	5	9
Benefit package	9	8	10	8	7
Taxes	6	5	8	8	8
Subtotal	23	23	23	21	24
7. LOCATION					
Housing (cost and availability)	7	8	6	6	8
Climate	*	*	*	*	*
Transportation	8	9	7	7	8
Subtotal	15	17	13	13	16
8. OTHER FACTORS					
Subtotal	—	—	—	—	—
GRAND TOTAL	179	177	150	146	192

*Not important to me

Closing Actions

Once you have made your decision to accept a job offer or graduate admittance, there are several important steps to take to close out your job or graduate school campaign.

1. Acceptance letters. State your acceptance *in writing* to the graduate school or to the employer, repeating the details of the offer. Because so many details are given orally in person or over the telephone, it is better to provide some evidence in writing just in case something goes wrong or is misunderstood. You can never anticipate the resignation or transfer of the person who made the oral commitment. Too many students have been embittered when they report for work and find no one in the organization has any evidence that they have been hired. Similarly for graduate schools, the financial aid you expect may never materialize because no one has obligated the university by putting such an understanding in writing. Examples of acceptance letters for our five hypothetical applicants are given at the end of this chapter.

2. Report your decision to your career center, your faculty advisor, and others. These sources often use such information to help future students and to plan improvements in their respective programs. Knowing which graduate and professional schools attract their students, and learning what jobs are taken by graduating seniors obviously assist counselors on the college campus.

Sometimes students are reluctant to divulge their starting salaries, yet they expect to benefit from such information from their campus contacts. Since the basic source of information on salaries comes from the actual offers and acceptances, sharing such data with campus sources provides an important service to others. If employers know that students from your school know the starting salaries in different career fields, they are less likely to make noncompetitive offers, which may end up giving them a negative reputation.

3. Rejection or refusal letters. If you decide to reject an offer, write a short letter of thanks using professional courtesy and expressing your appreciation for the job offer, and for the employer's interest in you. If possible, state the reason(s) why you are rejecting the job offer. However, do not state that the reason is more money. This indicates you were really not serious in applying for a career opportunity with that particular employer, or a particular program with that graduate school, but were merely

shopping around for the highest dollar or taking the course of least resistance.

A primary reason for writing a good rejection letter is that many college graduates find their initial selection turned out to be not a good one, and they often wish they had accepted another offer. By declining a job offer or graduate school admission courteously, you can keep the door open and always reapply at some future date. If your rejection was handled professionally and graciously, most employers and graduate schools will reconsider and give you another chance. Furthermore, a polite rejection may help one of your fellow students obtain an offer or acceptance since the employer or graduate school may have been delaying action on another student's application until they heard from you. At the end of this chapter are several methods of refusing or rejecting job offers or admission to graduate or professional schools.

4. Write to those persons who served as your references, who referred you to employers, and who provided information about career fields, thanking them for their help and informing them of your decision.

5. Organize all your papers by company, agency, or school and put them in a large envelope. Then write an appropriate heading for identification purposes, and file it until you are again in the market for a job. At that time, a review will help you streamline your next job campaign.

6. If possible take a vacation before starting on your career's first job. If you have to move to another city, there are sure to be delays caused by moving or in locating suitable housing at a price you can afford. You should start your career or graduate program feeling fresh and well rested and ready to take off at a very rapid pace.

Legal and Ethical Considerations

While in some career fields (sports, the theater, and teaching), hiring is done on a contractual basis, for most jobs accepted by graduating seniors there is no written contract. However, the employment is commonly understood as having the same effect as a contract, because it has the three basic elements of a legal contract. Therefore, you should understand that in accepting employment your word and reputation are as binding as a legally signed document. Although some contracts are very involved and explicitly state the terms of employment, the three basic components for our purposes consist of an offer, an acceptance, and some type of consideration.

The *offer* seems to be easily understood, but too many students assume they receive an offer when the employer is merely stating an interest in the applicant. Oral or written statements to the effect that, "you certainly have the qualifications we are seeking," *do not* constitute a job offer! Be sure that the employer gives you a *written* offer, and that you use the term "offer" when accepting a position.

An *acceptance* means you are willing to take the job with the terms stated. To avoid any misunderstanding by the employer, be sure to state "I *accept* your *offer* for *(job title)* or *(graduate assistant)*."

Consideration refers to something of value, usually a salary figure for jobs and tuition remission or other comparable items of value for admission to a graduate program.

If you accept a position offered with appropriate consideration, you are legally and ethically bound to accept it. Although the employer can force you to take it, very few employers will sue you because most graduates do not have many financial resources, and employers may feel a suit in court would hurt their image and future recruiting. Although an individual may not be sued when reneging on an offer, you should keep in mind that it could hurt your professional reputation within the industry and on the campus. It also can hurt the image of your school so that future students will suffer.

If the employer reneges on a job offer, you should first notify your school's career planning and placement office to help spread the word to other students and faculty, and to discuss remedial possibilities. In an excellent article on this subject, entitled "When an Employer Says Yes . . . and Then Says No," Rochelle K. Kaplan advises that "state rules on employment-at-will and revocation of job offers vary," and that "each court seems to develop its own standards for interpreting oral and written statements made during the employment relationship." Unless liability is clearly established (such as relocation expenses), it is difficult to get courts to judge an employer's responsibility for the loss of job offers.

From a career advisor's viewpoint, a few options are available. A suggestion to the employer who reneged on a job offer could result in a month's salary to the student so affected. If moving or other relocation expenses (such as rental deposits or leasing payments on housing) have been incurred, the employer could be persuaded to reimburse the graduate involved. Sometimes another opening or a position in a different department could be offered to the graduating student. In any event, it pays to make the school's career staff and the faculty advisor aware of such employer actions, not only for your benefit but also for the benefit of future students.

From an ethical viewpoint, it is always distressing to school officials to learn from employers that some of their students were cheating on expense accounts when going for subsequent interviews. At one major nationally known university in the Midwest, three students were dismissed from school three weeks before graduation because they falsified their expense statements. When graduating students succumb to the temptation to make a fast buck at the employer's expense, they do not think of the damage they do to their own and the college's reputation, and of how much harder it will be in the future for graduates from their college. If you are uncertain as to whether a certain expense is a legitimate part of your trip, ask the employer directly.

When considering which offer to accept, do not be in a big hurry. It is better to weigh all factors deliberately, so that you can sincerely commit yourself to the job and employer or graduate school once you have made your decision. Career counselors know of too many cases where a better offer comes in after a student has already accepted a job; such a dilemma causes traumatic reactions, and tempts a student to take unethical action. If you renege on a job offer, you cause considerable embarrassment to the school, faculty, college administrators, fellow students, and alumni. All of these parties are subjected to snide remarks, possible cancellation of recruiting visits to their campus, adverse results on promotions for graduates from that college, and loss of professional reputations. Some colleges cancel further career assistance to students or recent graduates who renege on job offers or acceptances to graduate programs.

Other Suggestions

Correspondence and other communications with employers or graduate schools constitute an important part of any job search or graduate school campaign. As further questions develop, be sure to first express your continued interest in the job offer or acceptance to graduate school, then go on with your questions regarding housing assistance, employment assistance available for your spouse (if you have one), choice of locations, whether you can change the date of arrival, and so forth.

In all your contacts by correspondence, telephone calls, and personal visits, it is important to remember that procrastination makes a poor impression, and that each method of contact reflects your personality and judgment. Strive to develop your skills in writing good and effective letters, in making and answering telephone calls promptly, and in meeting people. Get help if you need it, but make sure your letters, resumes, telephone conversations, and personal visits (interviews) reflect you and your abilities, and that all contacts are consistent with your own style.

Following up with employers or graduate and professional schools will definitely enhance your chances to obtain a job offer or gain admittance for graduate work. Therefore, pursue all applications with perseverance until you receive a definite job offer or graduate admittance. Then make a careful comparison before deciding to accept, stall, or reject the offer or the graduate school admission. Closing out your file in the career center and notifying all the parties who assisted you, will wrap up your successful entry into the working world or into the graduate or professional school of your choice.

Examples of Follow-up Letters

McGregor Hall, A–23
Boston University
Boston, MA 02215

January 12, 1990

Ms. Barbara D. Graham
Director of Nursing
Beth Israel Hospital
330 Brookline Avenue
Boston, MA 02215

Dear Ms. Graham:

You were very kind to allow me to come to your office for an interview during our school break for the Christmas season. I was pleased to learn of your training program and the flexibility of scheduling workdays.

From the information obtained during my visit on December 28, 1989, I am definitely interested in the possibility of a nursing career at Beth Israel. I especially liked the way you rotate your nurses among the various departments during the first year of employment.

Because I enjoyed my clinical nursing practice experience while at St. Elizabeth's, I believe I can fit into your program easily. My previous supervisors told me I have a gentle and caring touch with patients. To apply my nursing skills to alleviate the suffering of others would bring me great satisfaction.

Please call me at 555–3419 if you need any more information to consider my application. I hope to hear from you in the near future.

Very truly yours,

LaVerne Washington

LaVerne Washington

North Dormitory, R-12
State University
Laramie, WY 82071

January 7, 1990

Mr. Joseph J. Smith
Industrial Relations Manager
ABC Manufacturing Company
1906 North Michigan Avenue
Chicago, IL 60604

Dear Mr. Smith:

Thank you for the opportunity to interview for a possible job in your department after I graduate this coming May. I enjoyed my visit to your office on December 28, and the chance to meet several key workers in your Industrial
Relations Department.

Since returning to the campus after our Christmas break, I have discussed my
visit to your company with the two professors for whom I am working part-time.
Each one borrowed and read the Newsletter and the Employee Magazine that you
gave me during our interview. I was pleased to have them state your company
seems to have an enlightened view in dealing with employees and in encouraging
them to develop their talents.

As soon as time permits, I will contact the alumnus you suggested, Thomas A.
Madison, to learn more about your production processes and how your first-time
supervisors are trained to deal with the workers on the production line.

I am definitely interested in joining your staff. The experience in the fac-
tory of Bolton Manufacturing Company gave me a firsthand view of production
workers' attitudes and grievances, and the work with my professors gave me a
''third party'' view of both the labor and the management viewpoints. I believe my talents and interests could best be utilized in persuading both labor
and management personnel that they have mutual interests and goals.

Do you need any additional information to consider my application? I can be
available for additional interviews during our spring vacation period March
13-17, and shall look forward to hearing from you.

Very truly yours,

Bruce Horowitz

Bruce Horowitz

Mellon Hall, R-56
Indiana University
Bloomington, IN 47401

March 22, 1990

Mr. Robert O. Forsythe
Principal
North High School
26 Meridian Street
Columbus, OH 43211

Dear Mr. Forsythe:

Thank you for the interview in your office on March 15, 1990. You may recall we discussed a possible vacancy for a teaching position in your Mathematics Department.

My visit to your school supplemented the information received from your Ms. Dorothy Jones. The opportunity to meet and talk with two of your teachers, and see the equipment and facilities available to teachers, was very impressive. The additions since my practice teaching semester should facilitate the teaching and laboratory assignments.

Although I can teach the elementary course in Computer Science and the Plane Geometry course, I am more comfortable teaching the Algebra courses. The extracurricular assignments you expect from your faculty seem reasonable to me; in fact, I would enjoy the opportunity to work with students outside of the classroom.

Regarding the certification problem, my college advisor assured me that an Indiana license to teach will readily be accepted in Ohio. I should know definitely whether Indiana has approved my certification by the end of April.

I am definitely interested in joining your faculty, and will provide any other information you need to consider my qualifications. Enclosed is a copy of all the courses taken at Indiana University to date; a transcript could be sent to you after graduation.

Very truly yours,

Nancy R. Brennan

Nancy R. Brennan

Enc.

Fairview Apts. #48
Ames, IA 50011

January 7, 1990

Mr. D. Laurence Duvall
Supervisor, Personnel
Inland Steel Company
30 West Monroe Street
Chicago, IL 60603

Dear Mr. Duvall:

It was a pleasure to visit your Chicago office and talk to you regarding your company's Management Training Program on December 27, 1989. This visit further stimulated my interest in joining your company.

After our interview I had a chance to talk to an Iowa State alumnus who completed your Management Training Program three years ago. I also spoke with Professor Jones in our Mechanical Engineering Department, and Professor Smith in our Electrical Engineering Department. Their comments and advice added to my favorable impression of your company's training and advancement opportunities.

I liked the rotational assignments during training to enable recent college graduates to get an overall view of various departments and the work therein, before starting their professional development. I was also impressed at the number of executives who mentioned Inland's desire to be a good corporate citizen by contributing to community and national affairs.

Enclosed is my statement for reimbursement of travel, hotel, and other expenses, along with receipts. I appreciate your offer to have me visit your Chicago office at your expense.

Do you need any additional information to consider my application? If not, what is the next step to help me become a member of your company's Management Training Program?

Very truly yours,

Roberto Mendes

Roberto Mendes

Enc.

Simpson Hall, B–20
Rice University
Houston, TX 77251

February 4, 1990

Professor Thomas P. Dunn
Chairman, Biology Department
The Ohio State University
McPherson Hall
Columbus, OH 43210

Dear Professor Dunn:

Per your instructions, I am enclosing my application form for admission to your graduate program, along with three faculty recommendations and my transcript of grades for three and a half years of undergraduate courses to date.

In addition, I am enclosing my scores on the Graduate Record Examination, and also my personal resume. As soon as the grades are available for the current semester, I will be glad to forward them to you.

Last month I had the pleasure of talking with Professor Miller from your Chemistry Department while he was visiting a mutual friend in Houston. His advice on the biochemistry possibilities at Ohio State further stimulated my interest in joining your graduate program.

During the week of March 14–18, our spring break, I will be visiting my cousin in Dayton. Would it be possible to see you or your representative during that week? Please call me at (713) 555–5763 or write to me at the above address if a visit to your department is feasible.

Sincerely,

Susan Chin

Susan Chin

Enc.

Examples of Stall Letters

McGregor Hall, A–23
Boston University
Boston, MA 02215

March 21, 1990

Ms. Barbara D. Graham
Director of Nursing
Beth Israel Hospital
330 Brookline Avenue
Boston, MA 02215

Dear Ms. Graham:

Thank you for the offer to join your nursing staff following my graduation from Boston University in May. Your letter was welcome news indeed, and made my school vacation much more enjoyable.

I am definately interested in your offer, but need more time to make a decision. Following my initial interview at three other Boston hospitals, I have secondary interviews scheduled during the last two weeks of this month, and the first week of April.

Between April 10–15 I should be able to make a definite decision on which job offer to accept. In the meantime I would appreciate receiving information about your benefit package for employees, and some idea as to the career path from general nursing to surgical nursing.

Your interest and consideration is appreciated, and I look forward to receiving the above information to make the right decision.

Very truly yours,

LaVerne Washington

LaVerne Washington

North Dormitory, R–12
State University
Laramie, WY 82071

March 19, 1990

Mr. Joseph J. Smith
Industrial Relations Manager
ABC Manufacturing Company
1906 North Michigan Avenue
Chicago, IL 60604

Dear Mr. Smith:

Thank you for your letter of March 14 offering me a position as a trainee in your
Industrial Relations Department. I was hoping you would reach such a decision
after my visit to your office on March 12.

Although I am definitely interested in your offer, I must postpone a decision
until I have completed my secondary interviews with two other firms. My job
search has narrowed down to three promising possibilities, and I need to compare and evaluate the three offers in order to make the right decision for myself and for each of the companies.

My last two interviews are scheduled for March 27 and April 2. By the tenth of
April I intend to make my decision, and will contact you about that time. In the
meantime, I appreciate all your consideration, and assure you that I like your
offer and am very interested in your company.

Very truly yours,

Bruce Horowitz

Bruce Horowitz

Mellon Hall, R–56
Indiana University
Bloomington, IN 47401

May 5, 1990

Mr. Robert O. Forsythe
Principal
North High School
26 Meridian Street
Columbus, OH 43211

Dear Mr. Forsythe:

It was a pleasure to receive your letter of April 30 with the encouragement of joining your Mathematics faculty after I graduate from Indiana University on June 5, 1990.

As you know from my previous letters and visit, I am definitely interested in this offer. However, I have arranged to have my final interviews with two other high schools in Columbus on June 7 and 9. I'm sure you will understand the need to keep these appointments before reaching a decision.

During the week of June 12–17 I will contact you to ascertain which specific courses I am to teach, and which student activities you wish to have me serve as faculty advisor. At that time I also hope to reach a definite decision.

In the meantime, I am very appreciative of your consideration, and the offer to join your teaching faculty.

Very truly yours,

Nancy R. Brennan

Nancy R. Brennan

Fairview Apts. #48
Ames, IA 50011

February 25, 1990

Mr. D. Laurence Duvall
Supervisor, Personnel
Inland Steel Company
30 West Monroe Street
Chicago, IL 60603

Dear Mr. Duvall:

Thank you very much for the offer in your letter of February 23, 1990 to join Inland's Management Training Program. I am definitely interested in your offer, but need more time to reach a decision.

Two of your competitors have invited me to their places of business for secondary interviews following their visits to our campus. Because I do not like to miss classes or get behind on my assignments, I had arranged to make these visits during our school spring vacation period, March 7–12, 1990.

Since my interesting visit to your office during the Christmas break, I have been wondering about two questions. Do all trainees have the same curricula and length of assignments? Do they have any choice in which location they can begin their careers with Inland?

As soon as I complete my secondary interviews with the two other companies that interest me, and get information on the above questions, I should be able to notify you of my decision. In the meantime, I appreciate your continued interest in my application.

Very truly yours,

Roberto Mendes

Roberto Mendes

Simpson Hall, B-20
Rice University
Houston, TX 77251

April 10, 1990

Professor Thomas P. Dunn
Chairman, Biology Department
The Ohio State University
McPherson Hall
Columbus, OH 43210

Dear Professor Dunn:

My visit to your department last month was very interesting and informative, and I was delighted to receive your letter admitting me to your graduate program effective September 7, 1990.

Although I am definitely interested in joining your program, I need some more information before reaching a decision. At your convenience would you have someone send me the data requested in the following questions?

1. Does OSU have a separate housing facility for graduate students? If not, is there a university source to help me find an apartment near the campus?

2. You mentioned the possibility of financial assistance. Do I need to apply separately for such aid? If so, may I ask someone on your staff to send me the necessary forms?

3. I am especially interested in a teaching assistant position for undergraduate courses and lab work, or in a research assistant position during my graduate training. Do you have such positions available? If not, is there any work on projects that are funded by grants?

Your interest in and consideration of my application are really appreciated. I shall look forward to your reply on the above questions to help me decide which university to join.

Sincerely,

Susan Chin

Susan Chin

P.S. After graduation next month, I plan to stay at the above address through June.

Examples of Acceptance Letters

McGregor Hall, A–23
Boston University
Boston, MA 02215

April 15, 1990

Ms. Barbara D. Graham
Beth Israel Hospital
330 Brookline Avenue
Boston, MA 02215

Dear Ms. Graham:

Having completed my interviews, I found it very difficult to make a decision on which job offer to accept to begin my nursing career. Three of my offers seemed outstanding, and my evaluation took more time than I realized.

I am happy to accept your job offer as a General Nurse at a starting salary of $26,000 per year, effective June 1, 1990. The condensed course you offer to prepare for the state licensing exam should be of great assistance to help begin my professional career.

Per your instructions, I will report to your Personnel Office on June 1, 1990 and will arrange to have my credentials sent to them by our college's Career Planning and Placement Office.

I am looking forward with pleasure to becoming a part of your staff in a few weeks.

Very truly yours,

LaVerne Washington

LaVerne Washington

North Dormitory, R-12
State University
Laramie, WY 82071

April 9, 1990

Mr. Joseph J. Smith
Industrial Relations Manager
ABC Manufacturing Company
1906 North Michigan Avenue
Chicago, IL 60604

Dear Mr. Smith:

In my letter of March 19 I mentioned that my interviews would be completed on
April 2, and then I hoped to make a decision by the tenth of April.

Each of my three offers looks very promising, and each offers a career in the
Industrial Relations field. Making the necessary comparisons and evaluations
has been an agonizing experience, but I think I have reached the right decision.

It is a pleasure to accept your job offer of a Trainee in your Industrial Relations Department at a beginning salary of $25,000 per year. If it meets with
your approval, I would like to take a vacation and find housing during the two
weeks after graduation on May 20. Before starting work on your payroll on June
7, I will come to your medical unit for a physical exam.

I am anxious to begin my industrial relations career, and am looking forward
eagerly and enthusiastically to becoming a part of your staff.

Very truly yours,

Bruce Horowitz

Bruce Horowitz

2930 Maynard Avenue
Columbus, OH 43211

June 17, 1990

Mr. Robert O. Forsythe
Principal
North High School
26 Meridian Street
Columbus, OH 43211

Dear Mr. Forsythe:

Our discussion this past Tuesday clarified the last two questions I had regarding your teaching position, and I have completed my job search.

I am happy to accept your offer for a position as Teacher in the Mathematics Department at North High School with a starting salary of $18,000 per year on a nine-month basis. Since algebra is my favorite subject, I am happy to have the opportunity to teach it.

During the summer session starting June 27, I will be teaching two classes of Algebra I, and will get more familiar with the equipment in the department. The first week of August, I will see our department chairperson to get my teaching schedule for the fall semester.

I am looking forward with enthusiasm to becoming a part of North High School's teaching staff.

Very truly yours,

Nancy R. Brennan

Nancy R. Brennan

Fairview Apts. #48
Ames, IA 50011

March 17, 1990

Mr. D. Laurence Duvall
Supervisor, Personnel
Inland Steel Company
30 West Monroe Street
Chicago, IL 60603

Dear Mr. Duvall:

Having completed my other interviews, I am confident that the opportunity offered in your Management Training Program comes closest to my job and career
objectives.

Therefore I am happy to accept your kind offer to become a member of your 1990
Management Training Program at a starting salary of $30,000 per year. In accor-
dance with the statements in your letter of Febuary 28, I would like to start in
your East Chicago plant on June 20, 1990 (two weeks after graduation).

Since I am not well acquainted with that city, I would appreciate receiving
housing assistance from your Personnel Office. Would you have your secretary
send me the name and address of the personnel contact in East Chicago?

I am looking forward with pleasure and anticipation to making my career with
Inland Steel Company.

Very truly yours,

Roberto Mendes

Roberto Mendes

Simpson Hall, B-20
Rice University
Houston, TX 77251

June 15, 1990

Professor Thomas P. Dunn
Chairman, Biology Department
The Ohio State University
McPherson Hall
Columbus, OH 43210

Dear Professor Dunn:

Your letter of June 10 really brightened my day! I am pleased to accept your offer as a Teaching Assistant for three quarters of the school year 1990-91, at a stipend of $3,000. Your generous action in waiving the tuition is also greatly appreciated.

With the above financial arrangements, I will not need any further aid for the coming school year.

Thank you for sending me the application forms for graduate housing on the campus. I have completed and sent the forms to Mr. Howard S. Jones, the Housing Director for Graduate Student Housing. If I could be assigned to one of the one-bedroom apartments on the campus, it would certainly help.

I shall report to your office on Tuesday, September 6, 1990 to obtain your instructions for conducting the two laboratory sessions per week as part of my Teaching Assistant duties. The challenge of graduate work and getting teaching experience makes me eager to join your department.

Sincerely,

Susan Chin

Susan Chin

P.S. During July and August I can be reached at my cousin's address, which is c/o Linda Morris, 1224 West 10th Street, Dayton, Ohio 45402, telephone (513) 555-8234.

Examples of Rejection Letters

McGregor Hall, A-23
Boston University
Boston, MA 02215

April 15, 1990

Ms. Barbara D. Graham
Director of Nursing
Beth Israel Hospital
330 Brookline Avenue
Boston, MA 02215

Dear Ms. Graham:

The booklet containing information on your benefit package, and your letter of
March 28, were very helpful in supplementing the data on a nursing career at
your hospital which I had obtained previously.

Among the job offers I received, I agonized over the decision to choose and accept one. Although I was and still am very interested in Beth Israel, at this
time I regret to inform you that I accepted the offer from the Brigham and
Women's Hospital.

I was very impressed with your courtesy and the professional treatment of applicants, and have encouraged several of my nursing classmates to apply for a
position at your hospital.

Thank you for all the time you gave me, and for your consideration of my qualifications.

Very truly yours,

LaVerne Washington

LaVerne Washington

North Dormitory, R-12
State University
Laramie, WY 82071

April 9, 1990

Mr. Joseph J. Smith
Industrial Relations Manager
ABC Manufacturing Company
1906 North Michigan Avenue
Chicago, IL 60604

Dear Mr. Smith:

In my letter of March 19 I mentioned that my interviews would be completed on April 2, and that I hoped to make a decision by the tenth of April.

The secondary interviews I had on March 27 and April 2 both resulted in job offers that are very tempting. After discussing all three offers with family and faculty—I wish I could accept each one—they all seem very promising for a career in the field of Industrial Relations.

Regretfully, I must decline your kind offer because it seems that a similar opportunity with Ideal Manufacturing Company matches my interests and qualifications better at this stage in my career.

Because I was so favorably impressed with your company's philosophy and employee programs, I have encouraged fellow classmates who are in our Personnel Club to apply for positions in your company. I really enjoyed talking with so many of your people, and sincerely appreciate all of your kindness and consideration.

Very truly yours,

Bruce Horowitz

Bruce Horowitz

Mellon Hall, R-56
Indiana University
Bloomington, IN 47401

June 17, 1990

Mr. Robert O. Forsythe
Principal
North High School
26 Meridian Street
Columbus, OH 43211

Dear Mr. Forsythe:

In my letter of May 5, I promised to contact you regarding your kind offer to join the teaching faculty in your Mathematics Department.

Last week I completed my interviews at two other high schools in Columbus, and was very impressed with their offers. At this time the position at South High School seems to be more relevant for my career and personal plans. Therefore, I must decline your offer.

Because I liked the people I met at North High School, and think your Mathematics Department is excellent, I had a hard time reaching this decision. Your thoughtfulness and consideration are very much appreciated.

Very truly yours,

Nancy R. Brennan

Nancy R. Brennan

Fairview Apts. #48
Ames, IA 50011

March 17, 1990

Mr. D. Laurence Duvall
Supervisor, Personnel
Inland Steel Company
30 West Monroe Street
Chicago, IL 60603

Dear Mr. Duvall:

In my letter of February 25 I mentioned that I had two more secondary interviews to conduct before reaching a decision on job offers. During our spring
vacation March 7–12, I completed my job search and have reached a decision.

I regret to inform you that I must decline your kind offer to join your Management Training Program. All three of my offers appeared to be excellent from a
long–range career viewpoint, and I really deliberated carefully before making a decision. At this time it seems that the opportunity with National Steel
Company fits my needs and ambitions more closely than your company's.

The consideration you gave me, and the courtesy and cooperation of all the people I met at Inland Steel, were very much appreciated.

Very truly yours,

Roberto Mendes

Roberto Mendes

Simpson Hall, B–20
Rice University
Houston, TX 77251

June 15, 1990

Professor Thomas P. Dunn
Chairman, Biology Department
The Ohio State University
McPherson Hall
Columbus, OH 43210

Dear Professor Dunn:

The past few months have been hectic, requiring the completion of my B.A. degree and the application to a number of graduate schools. Fortunately, I have been admitted to three universities for graduate work, and have been pondering the offers before making the right decision.

Regretfully I must decline your kind offer for a Teaching Assistant position, and admission to your graduate program in biochemistry. I decided to go to Stanford University for my Master's degree, and hope you will reconsider my application in the future for your Ph.D. program.

Thank you for your thoughtfulness and consideration. In a couple of years I hope we can discuss my plans for a Ph.D. program at The Ohio State Unversity.

Sincerely,

Susin Chin

Susan Chin

PART FOUR

Developing Your Career

PART IV CONCENTRATES on the first fifteen years after graduation from college. Career planning does not stop with the decision to accept an offer for employment or the completion of a bachelor's or master's degree. The typical college graduate completes the first degree at twenty-two years of age. The first fifteen years after graduation are crucial in implementing career aspirations, but it takes planning and execution to make the dreams and development become a reality.

Chapter 13 covers your first year out of college, which can move in a direction that leads to nowhere, or on a career path that could lead you to real growth in your chosen career.

Chapter 14 gives insights and suggestions for those who want their own business or profession.

Chapter 15 provides information and suggestions to help you develop and maintain a career so that you can reach your desired professional or management level.

chapter thirteen

The First Year on the Job

In a talk to college seniors, Mr. William A. Delaney, president of Analysis & Computer Systems, Inc., stated:

> Look upon the first job as the first step up the ladder; don't hold out for some perfect job that you think you will stay with all through your career. You should have a personal career plan—be yourself, or you become a carbon copy. It is small wonder that people without a career plan seem to drift up dead-end channels; they blame economics, the recession, society, and anything but themselves.

Before graduating, you should visit the career center at school and ask for a copy of the leaflet, "You're on the Job...Now What?" distributed by the College Placement Council. As a new employee, you can benefit immensely from the suggestions given in this pamphlet to ease the transition from college to the first job.

Many students dread leaving the comfort and security of a college campus to enter "the real world," and they are quite naive about what to expect on the first career job. Even if they have located the job of their dreams, they still face the reality of moving to another location, finding housing, figuring the best transportation to work, learning to handle income and pay expenses, establishing a credit reputation, learning the protocol of their employer, and adjusting to the cultural, religious, and leisure opportunities of their new environment.

If your career decision takes you to a large city like New York, Chicago, or Los Angeles, it's best to develop a strong network of people to give you satisfaction and a greater chance at happiness. Roommates and fellow workers are ideal sources of meeting people. Recent graduates from your college, professional groups that you joined as an undergraduate, religious organizations, all can provide instant introductions. Lunching with co-workers, volunteering to work with humanitarian or political organizations, and participating in your employer's social, educational, and recreational activities all provide opportunities to make friends and contacts that will enhance your life and your career.

As you begin the work that influences your future career, try to get the maximum usable experience from early career jobs. Your future depends on your job performance and your ability to impress people favorably. Their appraisal will include how you fit into the culture of the organization as well as what you actually accomplished.

Three Important Career Influences

In all types of organizations, the new employee has to be aware of three basic career influences: the immediate supervisor, fellow employees, and the organization. The first few months on the job constitute the breaking in period, and the impression you make during this period can enhance or jeopardize your future employment in the organization. You can't expect to pick up the necessary knowledge about how to behave from the classroom; it must come from on-the-job training. Here's how to make a favorable impression on these three important influences on your career.

The Supervisor

Your immediate supervisor is the key person who can help launch you either into a successful career with the organization or into oblivion. Therefore, it is imperative that you develop a rapport with your supervisor by learning as quickly as possible what he or she wants and expects from you, how he or she wants it done, whom to go to for advice, what are the deadlines, and so forth.

Start by asking your supervisor to draw an organization chart so you can see the big picture—where your department fits into the total company, agency, or organization. Then ask him or her to give you another chart that shows your department in more detail so you will see where your boss and you fit into the organizational structure, and what other levels exist. It is important to learn the lines of authority and responsibility as quickly as possible, and to work within the organization's chain of command. An organization chart will help you learn the formal lines of communication in the organization.

All supervisors want employees who are willing to learn and who work hard to get the job done. They want people who are compatible, reasonably cheerful, fit the teamwork structure within the department, and show interest in the work of the department and of the company, agency, or organization. New employees should be careful to show respect and loyalty for their supervisors by not going over their heads to ask questions or solicit explanations for policy or procedural matters. When assignments or instructions are not clear, you should ask for clarifying instructions such as:

"I'm not sure what you want. Would you mind giving me more detail?"

"If I understand you correctly, you want . . ."

"Where can I get advice or reference data for this assignment?"

"Just to make sure I'm on the right track, I understand you want . . ."

"If I run into any problem, to whom can I go for assistance?"

In classrooms, especially in business courses, college students are taught to look at problems from management's viewpoint. Students think in terms of general concepts and rational principles to solve problems, with an emotional neutrality and an eye on economic results. On the first job, the college graduate soon discovers that supervisors want workers to get the job done, and all the advanced management training and concepts learned in college may have to be put on hold. In the real world, you will find supervisors and fellow workers who resist change or innovation.

People's feelings and organizational customs should be considered in making decisions.

Although there are numerous references to advise and assist new employees in becoming assimilated into an organization, the key items to please most bosses can be summarized as follows:

Show a friendly and courteous attitude, but do not be too familiar. Show interest and enthusiasm in your work.

Learn the names, job functions, and personalities of employees with whom you will be working.

Get assignments done on time. Supervisors want results, not excuses.

Learn and follow the basic rules and customs of the work place, and establish yourself as a responsible worker.

Be as cheerful as possible, even when older employees tend to dump undesirable tasks upon you.

Be honest. Since everybody makes mistakes, you should not be afraid to own up to yours.

Volunteer for committee and other assignments.

Accept criticism and suggestions on your work gracefully. They are meant to help you grow professionally.

Be a good team worker. Do what is necessary (all those piddly details and unglamourous but needed tasks) to achieve the objective of the assignment.

We advise recent college graduates to schedule a talk with their new boss so as to find out his or her goals for the year. What are the priorities? What possible strategies or actions are needed to implement those goals? Which persons can be approached for assistance or further information? Such a talk will enable you to learn your job more quickly, develop an effective work technique, and understand how your work will be evaluated. Once you know what needs to be done and which tasks are most urgent, you can concentrate on performing the assignments with the highest priority and thus begin to develop a favorable working relationship with your boss. "Work hard and make your boss look good" is sound advice.

Fellow Employees

Since there are practically no jobs left for hermits, you should learn how to get along with fellow workers. Concentrate on observing the people and processes around you. Note how people dress, how they keep their offices or work places, what schedules they arrange and observe, and their general behavior patterns. Although the organizational charts give the official chain of command (the formal communication channels of authority and responsibility), fellow employees are most helpful in learning the unofficial channels. Learn who can break through the bureaucratic red tape found in all organizations. The informal, unofficial communication channels are usually more effective in getting things done.

Substituting for fellow workers during lunch hours, covering their positions during breaks in work, and going out of your way to help employees and superiors, will generate warm feelings and help develop your reputation as a good team worker. By participating in employee activities (softball, racquetball, Ping-Pong, and other lunch and after-work sports), you will more readily get accepted by others. By contributing to committee work and showing a willingness (even volunteering) to help fellow employees and supervisors meet urgent deadlines, you can demonstrate interest in the well-being of your colleagues and organization. Co-workers usually have a wait-and-see attitude toward new employees, and suspend judgment until they see what recent graduates can do and how they go about doing it.

A cheerful disposition and an interest in your fellow workers will make the job more fun than work. Developing close working relationships could lead to lasting friendships, and begin the important process of networking. Career counselors repeatedly tell their students or clients that careers are made or broken by their ability to work effectively with other people. In selecting employees for managerial consideration, we often hear the evaluation, "He is quite competent, but his attitude and inability to work with others damage his chances for promotion to more responsible positions."

If you want to develop favorable relationships with fellow employees, you should not comment negatively on the work of predecessors or current colleagues. Ideas and questions should be presented tactfully, with due respect for experienced workers. A good policy to follow is to never say a bad word about anybody, and to show consideration for the feelings of others by respecting their turf, realizing that all employees have their own little empires to worry about.

The Organization

Although pioneers, entrepreneurs, and heroes are lauded for their independence and aggressive tactics, the real world today demands teamwork for the success of any organization. The Boston Celtics and Los Angeles Lakers illustrate the importance of teamwork by their unselfish contributions to each other's skills in winning the professional world basketball championship for several years. Our space program in landing men on the moon is probably the best example of teamwork in utilizing different skills and talents to achieve an objective. Every organization needs people with long-range vision to plan for the next five or more years, as well as people who can work together effectively to accomplish short-term goals.

New employees need to learn and follow internal rules and practices, and adapt to the environment. You are expected to learn and know both the written and the unwritten rules and customs. Are coffee breaks allowed, and if so, for how long? Are lunches eaten at desks, in the cafeteria, or out of the building? Are beards, mustaches, and exotic jewelry tolerated or frowned upon? Does management want clean desks and working areas at the end of working days, or does it tolerate stacks of papers left on top of desks? Is overtime expected, or does everyone pack up five minutes before the official end of the day or shift?

What about office politics? Some people interpret this term to mean nasty tactics, talking behind your back, back stabbing, and playing dirty games. If this is your definition, then obviously it is better to refrain from office politics. Although it is possible to ignore politics in the office, it is not possible to escape it. Office politics need not necessarily imply devious, underhanded behavior. The term can simply mean employees getting along with each other, working together to get a job done, or trying to get ahead.

You should not ignore personalities and loyalties in offices, or try to put yourself above politics. Instead of compromising your integrity, it is better to take a realistic approach and acknowledge that office politics exist and affect everyone. Try using positive ways to influence people and get what you want, such as getting to know your co-workers personally, greeting them cordially every morning, staying on congenial terms with everyone, not aligning yourself with any one group, offering to help the people you work with, and otherwise showing your concern for the good of your department and organization.

Since politics is never a substitute for doing one's job well, new employees are urged to avoid gossip because it is virtually impossible to keep a secret from your co-workers. Grapevine gossip may create problems of lowered productivity, violations of business confidentiality, squabbles that spill over into work time, and it can damage your credibility and reputation.

To learn about your new job duties, office procedures, and office politics, it is wise to cultivate or find a mentor. This could be your supervisor, an older employee who is knowledgeable and effective, or a friend who is there for you when disappointment and frustrations occur. New jobs throw you into a different culture that has its own language and customs. Mentors are good role models as they are usually five to ten years ahead of you, solid citizens in the organization, and generally satisfied with their jobs and with their lives. In selecting a person whom you trust and respect, you can cultivate him or her to become a mentor by watching how he or she gets things done, acts in meetings, sets priorities, and responds to problems. Ask for advice whenever you run into problems, frustrations, or have questions. It is human nature to want to help younger people, and few persons can resist the role of being a valued mentor. A word of caution, however. Don't become a nuisance by taking up too much of your mentor's time!

Training Programs

In the navy it is common practice to have young officers take a shakedown cruise to learn the details of their jobs and abilities. You should consider the training period as your "shakedown cruise," a springboard to launch your career.

The first week on the job will involve some paperwork to get you signed up for the employer's insurance and health programs, and obtain pertinent data for the telephone directory. In most organizations you will also get more reading materials than you expect. If there is a formal training program, be ready to go at full speed right from the first day. You may get the feeling of one of our graduates who said, "trying to absorb what they throw at you in this training course is like trying to get a drink out of a fire hose."

The training during the first year on the job may be hard work, often boring and routine, but essential to help you learn the business as quickly as possible. You will be learning from people who are not professional teachers, who are not always well organized, and who often do not present information in easily understood terms. When you start on that first job after college, you will have to reach out and ask a lot of questions, because very little may be handed to you.

Smaller and nonprofit organizations usually let the supervisor handle the orientation and training. Typically, the newly hired employee gets on-the-job training, learning a little each day, and doing whatever assignments are given by the supervisor.

Larger organizations usually have an orientation program for new employees, similar to the freshman orientation concept of many colleges, before job training starts. A good example is the orientation program at Exxon USA for newly hired college graduates:

> During a day-and-a-half session at corporate headquarters, new hires from all over the country are given an overview of all company units and operations with the idea of communicating a sense of the company's mission, traditions, values, and goals. A final session with the company president covers a broad range of issues and concerns, not only about company matters but also about career development and the challenges of balancing family and career commitments.[1]

Another example is The May Department Stores Company. As stated in the corporate recruiting brochure, this firm has four structured career support programs to facilitate constructive feedback during the first year of employment: Initial Orientation Program, Executive Sponsorship Program, Formalized Feedback Plan, and Performance Appraisal Process.

> Initial Orientation Program—to develop your understanding of May, its mission, culture and priorities, and to facilitate the transition from campus to the work environment.

Types of Training Programs

When you complete the orientation, your job training begins. There are three major types of training programs: on-the-job, formal classroom, and rotational. Sometimes a department or an organization will use these methods individually, or in combina-

---

[1]*Spotlight*, College Placement Council, June 2, 1986.

tion. All are designed to make the newly hired college graduates productive as soon as possible.

On-the-Job

This training is the simplest and most used method. The immediate supervisor is responsible for planning the day-to-day assignments, checking your work, and providing the necessary instructions and criticisms. If the supervisor is a well-organized person, the training will proceed in logical stages. Your initial assignments will be relatively simple and noncontroversial, then gradually they will increase to more and more complex and different tasks and projects. If you make a mistake, you probably will be given the benefit of the doubt by your supervisor and fellow workers, and get appropriate criticism and instructions. If your supervisor is not a well-organized person, you will probably feel disoriented, jumping from one crisis to another without learning the why or wherefore of your actions.

Formal Classroom

This training is most used by many large organizations, and is similar to the experience in college, with reading assignments, classroom schedules, discussions, and tests. This method of training is especially useful when integrating a large number of college graduates each year, and providing them with background information in a short time. In addition to the classroom experience, this method may include lectures, seminars, visual aids, field trips, and reference materials to acquaint you with the employer's industry, organization, services or products, its administrative structure, and personnel and general policies.

Rotational

This training involves being assigned to different departments for specific periods of time, with assignments designed to provide a firsthand feel for each department, its function, and its personnel. Instead of merely reading material about the function of that department or observing the work going on, the new employees actually work on the specific tasks and functions. By performing day-to-day duties, the new employee can get a better appreciation of the work, function, and environment of that department. The authors were favorably impressed with the practices of one large industrial corporation that required management trainees to recruit at colleges so that they would know how difficult it was to attract top talent, thus generating more cooperation with colleges and their company recruiters on future hires when the graduates reached management positions.

As a graduate just beginning your career, don't expect your employer to cram all the necessary knowledge into you. You must assume a major portion of the responsibility for your own training. In addition to the formal training you receive at your employer's instigation, look around for supplementary sources of the information you will find essential and useful in your career.

Since all training programs are developed to meet the employer's needs, there is no typical program for college graduates. Following are several examples of employer training programs to give you some idea of what to expect on the first job.

Examples of Training Programs

Arthur Andersen & Co.—Guidelines for Your Professional Development

Years 1-2	You will develop basic audit, business, and communications skills as well as in-depth knowledge of the tools of your profession.
Years 2-5	You will gain supervisory responsibility as you continue to expand your technical skills. You will learn to direct the work flow for others and for yourself as you learn to delegate authority.
Years 5-10	You will manage and guide staff involved in several client engagements. You will plan and control the work flow of others and you will assist in business development and preparation of new business proposals.
Years 10-	You will have overall executive responsibility for client engagements and the opportunity to demonstrate specialized skills. You will work to assure excellent client services and, in so doing, you will develop new business for the practice and for the firm.

Bank Of New England—Management Development Program

This inter-divisional, operations management program is designed to prepare a cadre of individuals for eventual placement in line management positions in operating groups throughout the Bank.

The increasing complexity and competitiveness of the commercial banking industry and rapid growth of the Bank of New England makes it imperative that our future managers receive thorough cross-training, both through a series of specific work assignments and through periodic classroom instruction, in a number of critical disciplines central to the successful administration of all of our operating units.

Management Development Program participants, therefore, are assigned to four job rotations in each of the following areas: a. Information Systems (9 months); b. Finance or Audit (9 months); c. Operations (1 year); d. Personnel (6 months). Operations areas include: Trust Operations, Securities Processing, Mutual Funds and Securities Operations, Loan Operations and Treasury Operations. The assignment to an operating area will be supervisory in nature. Many of these assignments will be located in Charlestown, Massachusetts (approximately 10 minutes from the Boston headquarters) where our newly expanded Operations Center is located. Following the successful completion of the four work assignments and the academic components of the program, the incumbent will be placed out of the program and into a supervisory or managerial position in any one of the areas listed above. The specific assignment ideally will reflect the needs and interests of both the individual and those of the organization.

General Electric Co.—Financial Management Program

For more than sixty years the Financial Management Program (FMP) has been the main entry point for business administration and liberal arts graduates into General Electric's finance organization. It also provides a strong foundation for those aspiring to a general management position.

The FMP lasts two and a half years and involves structured courses, professional seminars, rotational work assignments, effective mentorships and other key elements to enable you to sharpen analytical skills, develop practical work experience, and gain valuable knowledge of GE business practices.

Program assignments are approximately six months in duration and provide significant decision-making responsibility and exposure to management. Assignments are in five areas of accounting and finance: Accounting Operations, Cost Accounting and Analysis, Operations Analysis, Financial Planning and Auditing, and Information Systems. After the Program, your interests and demonstrated performance will be key factors considered during career planning, along with the business needs of the Company.

Beyond the first post-program position, advancement depends upon performance. A comprehensive record of employees' experience, interests and potential is maintained by the Corporate Financial Management Operation as part of an in-house inventory of candidates used to fill financial management positions within GE, anywhere in the world.

The May Department Stores Company—Executive Training Program

The program is structured; learning is guided to ensure executive trainee success.

There are both merchandising and stores experiences. You will be given a total overview of the business, see the big picture and understand how the organization functions as a team.

Both classroom seminars and in-store assignments are incorporated into the program:

Classroom work is pragmatic, focusing on both skills and behaviors needed for success. Classes are taught by the subject experts, including senior management of the company.

You will be placed in position assignments with executives who are not only good at their jobs, but are good teachers.

Placement in your first position assignment follows completion of the Executive Training Program. You will be placed knowing that you are ready to assume the responsibility and have all of the skills needed to be successful.

Ford College Graduate Program

At Ford Motor Company, the transition from student "to professional" is made easier through the Ford College Graduate Program. This program is designed to help the new employee contribute to Ford's success as quickly as possible while building a base of experience for future professional growth.

At Ford, supervisors, managers, and personnel representatives develop individual assignment plans based on the employee's job interests and skill level, as well as the needs of the organization.

Each FCG (as they are classified at Ford) is typically scheduled for assignments in different functions in the area they have been assigned. Each assignment is planned for a specific duration but may vary in length under certain circumstances. Employee progress is evaluated periodically to ensure that the rotation plan continues to meet developmental needs.

The role of the supervisor is perhaps the single most important element in the College Graduate Program at Ford. The supervisor is responsible for providing assignments that challenge and test the new employee's potential, broaden his or her experience base and, in general, facilitate an understanding of a function's interrelationship to the overall objectives of the organization.

At the conclusion of the College Graduate Program, the employee will be assigned to a position based upon the employee's performance in certain areas and the needs of the organization. This does not mean an end to rotational assignments but will be the beginning of a diversified career in the mainstream of his or her given profession.

The Turner Corporation Training Program

MOD I Basically provides technical training for our professional staff.

Contract Types	Sub-Relations	Basic Communications
Job Set-up I	Contracts I	Written Communications
Job Set-up II	Contracts II	Accounting
Teamwork	Cost	QA/QC
Line & Grade	Scheduling I	Mechanical/Electrical
Safety	Scheduling II	Systems I
Estimating	Effective Listening	

MOD II Focuses on management/supervision and higher technical training.

Effective Communications/Linking	Leading Job Meetings
Delegation	Performance Evaluation &
Motivation	Counsel
Dealing with Conflict	Essentials of Management
Problem Analysis	Effective Negotiations
Time Management	Mechanical/Electrical
Productivity	Systems II

MOD III Course content varies on a necessary needs basis and is attended by senior key staff (management, department heads, etc.).

Leadership Skills
Project Management Skills
Human Relations Skills
Building Financial Excellence
Project Development—The Owner's Point of View

MOD IV Collegiate training for senior executive personnel.

Harvard
Dartmouth
Stanford
Texas A&M
Michigan

General Mills, Inc.—Consumer Foods Sales Division

The Consumer Foods Sales Division of General Mills, Inc. is committed to providing Field Sales Representatives with the training necessary to sell our products in the most effective and efficient manner.

During the first 45 days of employment, Sales Representatives receive a combination of on-the-job training and audio/video training. All activities during this initial 45 days are coordinated by the District Sales Manager or Trainer.

The program is titled "G-Powered Selling." The program consists of 10 sessions, which address topics that are essential for the sales profession. Each of the following sessions is self administered.

Session Number	TITLE
1	Overview & Introduction to "G-Powered Selling" (Both Audio and Video Tape Available)
2	Consumer Foods Selling Today
3	Understanding Differences
4	Selling Distribution in Your Stores
5	Promotions and Suggested Order Selling
6	Answering Objections and Closing the Sale
7	Economics of the Grocery Industry
8	Setting and Achieving Your Retail Call Objectives
9	Implementing Your Retail Coverage Plan
10	Planning Your Time

During the initial 45 days of employment, Sales Representatives will learn a great deal about the products that General Mills, Inc. makes and sells. New recruits will also spend time working with experienced sales professionals. This on-the-job training helps introduce new sales professionals to the guidelines and procedures utilized by the Consumer Foods Sales Division.

Self-Evaluation

After the first three or six months, it is wise to take a reading, a self-evaluation, to judge your progress to date. A periodic review of performance should be common practice. After all, the Internal Revenue Service forces all of us to make an annual financial review, with tax returns constituting the report. Business and industrial firms publish quarterly and annual reports regarding their progress. And annual reports are very common for colleges, government agencies, and nonprofit organizations to summarize their activities and progress.

Since the first job after college literally begins your career, you should be the first person to realize that it is up to you to take the initiative in appraising your own progress. There is an adage that states, "The person who knows *how* will always have a job; the person who knows *why* will generally be the supervisor." The training you receive during the first year of employment will provide the know-how, but it is up to you to educate yourself so that you will know why tasks are performed.

Depending on the kind of training you are receiving, you should take time to think about your experiences during the first few months on the job and write down your assignments and what you learned from each one. If you understand why you were given each assignment, you have started to educate yourself properly for career purposes. In college, you received feedback on your performance through examinations and grades. In your first job you may become discouraged because you often receive no feedback from your boss or trainer. Therefore, it is imperative that you form the habit of taking an inventory of your progress periodically, and thus develop ammunition to discuss your status, progress, and future with your boss.

Review your notes from the initial stages of your training (as in college, it is wise to take notes of data and comments given by your supervisor or trainer) to refresh your memory on what should be learned, and then judge how well you have mastered the training. What have you learned from your assignments? What problems have you encountered with the work, resources, and people within and without the organization? What changes or improvements can you suggest in the procedures or in the tasks assigned to trainees? Next write a report of your accomplishments during this period of work.

Once you have completed your self-evaluation, schedule a talk with your supervisor. Start with the report you just completed by reciting your training assignments and what you learned or accomplished on each one, then ask the supervisor what else should you be learning, and what suggestions or assignments he or she could give you for the next six months or the next phase of your training. Find out the supervisor's priorities so you can plan your time more effectively. After this is done, ask your supervisor directly for an honest evaluation of your work to date, so that you can continue to learn and contribute more to the work of that department.

This will not only give you more confidence in what you are doing, but may also impress your supervisor with your willingness to learn and become an active member of the team. Furthermore, it will bring out any weak spots in your work and give you time to correct them before your reputation is affected.

Near the end of your first year of employment, you should start a similar self-evaluation. Go one step further this time by comparing the duties and responsibilities in your job description or in the statements made at the beginning of your employment, with your actual assignments. Then note not only your accomplishments but also the shortcomings of your first year's training and employment. Once you have obtained the results of your own evaluation, schedule another talk with your supervisor. Some organizations have a policy calling for a systematic review of each employee's work, called a performance appraisal, at stated intervals. If your employer does not have such a policy, the above procedure will help make sure you do not get lost in the shuffle. By taking such initiative you ensure that you are not "sent to Siberia," i.e., put on some assignment where management forgets about you.

A few years ago, an able and promising graduate came into the career center to discuss her employment status after three years of work. Her major complaint was that she was not learning any more on this job, and she wondered what she could do about it. Her career advisor suggested the self-evaluation approach described above, and then advised her to schedule a meeting with her boss. One of the comments made by the career advisor was that companies sometimes assign employees "to Siberia" to ascertain whether they have enough common sense to recognize such a status, and to determine whether they have the initiative to do something about it. You can imagine this woman's reaction when her boss said, "I've been wondering when you would bring up this problem. You should have learned all we expected from this assignment six months ago."

By developing the habit of making a self-evaluation at least once a year, and keeping a written record of all results, you can develop a continuous portfolio of your employment, which will be very useful whenever you need to compile a resume to change jobs or careers. Furthermore, such an evaluation will become a necessity when you want a salary increase or a promotion.

Salary Increases and Promotions

Although these terms are often used synonymously in our society, college graduates should know the difference. A salary increase could result from several reasons:

Merit—given for outstanding job performance, or work beyond the call of duty, such as an emergency.

Cost of living—given for the increased cost of living.

Seniority—given to long-term employees and based on length of service.

General raise—given to all employees to enable the employer to meet the competition for applicants.

Promotion—usually given for increased duties and responsibilities.

Policy—given at stated intervals, such as the completion of training, obtaining a professional designation like CPA, C.L.U., passing the bar or nursing exam, or obtaining certification.

A promotion could also take other forms, such as being given a private office, granted a company car, given an expense account, qualification for discounts on merchandise purchases, a reserved parking space, a choice of work days or shifts, stock purchases, or qualification for medical or retirement plans. Such promotions indicate you have been accepted!

There is no mystical formula for promotion. In most organizations, supervisors and managers generally sit down in an office and talk about the employees that are to be considered for promotion. Each employee slowly builds up a reputation, good or bad; if good, a promotion or at least a salary increase is usually given. If your reputation and performance have not come up to expectations, you probably will stay right where you are. If this continues, you will create a dead-end job for yourself; the fault will be yours, not that of your employer.

Several studies have shown that character traits are far more important for getting promotions than are skills or knowledge. These traits include attitude, willingness to work hard, carelessness, laziness, noncooperation, honesty, ambition, and initiative. Practically all of these character traits are under your own control and can be corrected or even eliminated. The real work of the world is not done by people who are always watching the clock.

In a restaurant in northern Indiana there is a sign on the wall that reads: "Quit your bellyaching; someday you will be the boss and work 16 hours a day and have all the worries." The ability and willingness to accept responsibility and work hard are still the surest way to get promotions, and they will largely determine your career progress. By submitting your ideas in the form of suggestions to your supervisor, you remind him or her that you are alert; such initiative over a period of time is sure to be noticed and rewarded. Most supervisors are just as anxious to discover efficient and productive employees as you are to demonstrate your talents and get recognition for your efforts.

Because salary increases are usually equated with success and the employer's satisfaction with your work, they are eagerly anticipated. Some employers (like schools, government agencies, and nonprofit organizations) typically make salary increases on a once-a-year basis. In most business organizations there is a salary increase upon the completion of the training program or after one year's service. Future salary increases in all organizations depend upon your performance and the employer's policies.

chapter fourteen

Should You Be an Entrepreneur?

In 1974, Steven Jobs was designing video games for the ATARI Company, while his friend Steve Wozniak was a designer at the Hewlett-Packard Company. Working in a garage after-hours, Wozniak built a small, easy-to-use computer in 1976, and Steve Jobs envisioned a tremendous need and market for such a machine, which he named Apple. Together these friends raised $3,000, then got additional financial backers, and by 1985 the company had sales of a billion-and-a-half dollars. Their Apple II and Macintosh machines pioneered the personal computer industry.

By 1988 both men left the Apple Company. Wozniak is currently forming a company that would make remote-controlled toys and devices for operating TV's, VCR's, and other household appliances. Jobs is chairman of a company trying to build work stations, the computer industry's hottest new business. His new machine, called the NeXT Computer System, is expected to transform the entire process of education and learning.

Few entrepreneurs have the spectacular success of these two men, but many individuals fantasize about being their own boss, running their own business, and having complete independence to work as they please. For most people, such thoughts are day-dreams and mere fantasies, but the success of others merits serious consideration in career planning.

Technically, the word "entrepreneur" means one who or-ganizes, manages, and assumes the risks of a business enterprise. In our everyday vocabulary we also use this word to refer to someone managing a small business, regardless of whether he or she actually started it. In addition, many professionals in private practice, like doctors, lawyers, and consultants, are independent entrepreneurs.

People who keep their eyes and ears open for new ideas, a better way to do things, or are constantly thinking about unful-filled needs, are the type that become entrepreneurs. They take action to satisfy a need, such as saving time or money, appealing to individuals' physical or mental well-being, or providing a service or product that is needed. A current trend is that of women choosing dual careers as mothers and job-holders, or setting up shop in their homes where they can determine their own working hours.

Periodically you read about entrepreneurs who found unique markets in the cosmetics field, in sports memorabilia, and in magazine publishing. Two very popular and successful entrepre-neurial ventures in New England were Steve's Ice Cream and Cape Cod Potato Chips. Both made sure there was a *demand* for their products, then spent the time and energy to develop their respec-tive businesses. The computer software business has many exam-ples of entrepreneurs who started small companies, and had several grow into large companies. In the biotechnology field, companies like Genentech, Immulogic, and Genetics Institute were developed by entrepreneurs who sensed a need. The Reebok athletic footwear has become a household word.

Organization of an Enterprise

In planning a sports tournament, a political campaign, a market-ing effort, or your own business, the key ingredient is proper organization. To be your own boss you generally need to purchase a franchise, establish your own business, or buy a company from its current owner. A franchise enables you to work with a large organization, rather than for a company. The fast food business contains numerous examples of franchising—McDonald's, Burger King, Arby's, Wendy's, Dunkin' Donuts, and so forth. Other examples of franchising include gasoline stations, automotive dealers, soft drink bottlers, convenience stores, and personal and business services.

Franchising has several advantages. You generally get a proven business format; a way of selling goods or providing services that is likely to succeed in any area. Most franchisors also offer training programs, as well as managerial and financial expertise that reduce many of the risks associated with a new business. Thus people without business education or experience can learn to organize their franchise. They learn how to hire and fire personnel, how to train people, how to take advantage of quantity discounts and lower prices through the franchisor's centralized purchasing, how to establish an effective accounting system, and how to develop and maintain a clientele.

As the franchisee, you own the territorial property, and can sell the franchise if you no longer wish to operate it. The franchisor organization helps you by providing the location and building design, the company's trade name and logo, and a package of supportive services such as advertising, promotion, and marketing research. However, you have to generate your own sales, hire and train your own employees, keep your own records, pay your own taxes, pay an initial franchise fee and a royalty (usually a percentage of sales), and otherwise meet all the responsibilities of running your own business. You should ask the franchisor what its future plans are, and what sites are available so your territory will be protected from competition by the same franchisor.

The International Franchise Association reports that franchised outlets account annually for one-third of all retail sales in the United States. In 1987, these sales were approximately $591 billion, which was a six percent increase over the preceding year. The number of outlets was projected to rise seven percent in 1988 to 498,000. And by year's end, franchised operations were expected to provide seven million jobs across the country.

According to U.S. Department of Commerce figures, 90% of franchise operations are successful, while only 16% of self-owned businesses succeed in today's market. Among the hottest franchise opportunities is the temporary service industry. Roy Cannon, president of TRC Temporary Services, said: To operate a successful franchise, you have to understand the type of industry, the market climate,

Figure 14-1. Before Purchasing a Franchise

1. Take a complete inventory of your abilities, values, finances, and career plans. Unless you are good at making decisions, are willing to take risks and make things happen, and really *want* to be your own boss, a franchise may not be the best thing for you.

2. Read and study articles and books on franchising, availabe in most libraries, from the Small Business Administration, and from the U.S. Government Printing Office in Washington, DC 20302. *The Franchise Opportunities Handbook* is published annually by the U.S. Dept. of Commerce; it describes more than 1,400 companies that offer franchises.

3. Write to the Bureau of Consumer Protection in the Federal Trade Commission, Washington, DC 20580, to obtain a copy of their *Rules and Guide for Franchising Business Opportunities.*

4. Shop around for franchises and compare them with other business opportunities. Study the disclosure document and proposed contract carefully.

5. Talk to current franchisees to see what their experience has been. Be sure to ask about the disadvantages, problems, and whether their experience matches the disclosure document. This will enable you to carefully calculate the risks.

6. To ascertain whether the earnings claims are exaggerated, ask the franchisor to show you and your accountant the audited financial statements. Make sure you understand the basis for a seller's earnings claims.

7. Discuss your plans, resources, and the franchisor's contract with your attorney, accountant, and insurance advisor. You should understand the terms of the contract, especially the costs and responsibilities expected of you and the franchisor, and get promises in writing.

8. If married, do you and your spouse work well together? Are your talents complementary? Write to the National Association of Entrepreneurial Couples, P.O. Box 3238, Dept. O., Eugene, OR 97403-3238, for their newsletter and information on various seminars and conferences.

9. Resist pressure to purchase before you complete a thorough investigation.

and how to manage people. Support from the home office and training are also important.[1]

Instead of jumping too quickly into a franchise opportunity, you would be prudent first to consider the suggestions in figure 14-1.

---

[1]*Spotlight,* College Placement Council, November 17, 1986.

Start Your Own Business

An alternative to a franchise is to organize your own business, perhaps starting on a part-time basis operating out of your home. Have an attorney check for zoning problems and local rules and regulations. In evolving your own business, you typically start with an idea or a need for a product or service. Then you try it out on your friends and neighbors. If the reaction is satisfactory, you get the necessary encouragement to develop your idea into a business. Initially you have to do everything yourself—getting telephone service, advertising or otherwise getting orders, filling the orders and collecting the money, keeping records, filing tax returns, and sweeping the floor. If you are married, you may persuade your spouse to give you a hand with the business.

In a typical husband and wife business, the man often does the bulk of the outside work in getting sales orders, delivering them, collecting payment, and ordering and storing necessary inventories and supplies. The woman will do the inside work, such as keeping necessary records, making deposits to the bank, and paying the bills. The duties can and often are transferred between spouses, depending on circumstances as well as talents, likes, and dislikes.

As the business grows, it generally becomes necessary to hire additional help. If the owner does not like to solicit orders, he or she would first hire someone to do the sales work while he or she handles the production, operating, and financial responsibilities. As the business continues to grow, the owner would probably seek a partner or hire someone to complement his or her own talents, or someone to take care of the production work or other duties that he or she did not particularly like to do. The first hired employees often become supervisors and then managers of departments as the business grows and develops.

In establishing your own business, you have to decide whether to organize it as a corporation, a partnership, or a single proprietorship. Learn the advantages and disadvantages of each form of structure by discussing your plans with an attorney and an accountant. Then decide what kind of an organization is best for you.

An alternative to setting up your own business is to buy an existing business. Owners may wish to retire but have no family members to take over their business, so they seek a buyer. If interested in buying, you should watch the business opportunities section in local newspapers, discuss your interest with The Small

Business Administration staff, or work through one of the business brokers listed in the yellow pages.

Personal Attributes Needed

Being your own boss is not the ideal role for everyone. You should examine your own talents, ambitions, and motivation to ascertain whether becoming an entrepreneur is the right career for you.

Motivation

Are you a self-starter, or do you operate better when someone tells you what to do, how to do it, and when to do it? Do you have the personal drive and a high-energy level to work between sixty and eighty hours a week, perhaps seven days a week, to give the business everything you've got? Are you used to setting goals for yourself, and have the perseverance to achieve them? It's easy to manage a business when everything goes right, but managing failures requires higher motivation. One of the hardest tasks in developing a business or profession is to motivate yourself to go out and get customers, orders, or clients.

Creativity

In your varied activities and employment to date, have you been making suggestions for improvements, initiated programs or events, or assumed a leadership role in organizations to which you belonged? If your behavior pattern to date has been that of a follower, you may not have the talent to generate ideas to become an entrepreneur. In addition, you must have some knowledge of marketing, and definite selling skills in order to attract clients, customers, employees, and finances.

Willingness to Work Hard

Most individuals work for a wage or a salary, and try to carry out the duties that have been assigned to them. Very few persons are willing to work overtime or on Saturdays or Sundays unless they get extra compensation. Organizing and managing your own business or running a franchise requires a great deal of self-discipline and responsibility along with lots of overtime work, often to the detriment of your social and family life.

Taking Risks

One of the foremost requirements for anyone desiring to have his or her own business is the willingness to take risks. It takes guts to invest your time and money in uncharted waters knowing that you may lose everything you have accumulated to date. Most people are not very good at gambling; they prefer the security of a steady income. Some factors are beyond an individual's control—farmers facing a drought, owners handling products that become obsolete, deaths of key people, markets that dry up from competition, or having the principal business move out of the area.

Capital (Financing)

Since our economy revolves around money, if you contemplate becoming an entrepreneur you should first make sure you have the necessary funds or other financial resources. In developing a new business, it is usually necessary to take any profits and re-invest them into the business to make it grow. Generally speaking, it requires at least two years' capital to ensure launching a successful business. The Small Business Administration (SBA) advises prospective entrepreneurs to plan on providing from 25 to 30 percent cash as an initial investment, for any loan amount requested.

For larger enterprises such as Genentech, Immulogic, and Genetics Institute mentioned previously, financing is usually sought from venture capital firms, from partnerships with universities, or from the sale of stock. If a stock issue is planned to raise capital, it may be necessary to obtain money to tide over a firm until the stock is offered. This is commonly referred to as "bridge financing." Small entrepreneurs usually pool their savings, and raise additional funds by taking a proposed budget of expected income and expenses to banks, insurance companies, the SBA office, and other possible financial sources.

Enthusiasm

Unless you personally believe in what you are doing, and enjoy doing it, it is very difficult if not impossible to persuade others to accept your leadership. Your self-confidence and your ability to communicate will be very important in obtaining financial support, in motivating the people around you, and in developing the kind of teamwork and spirit that are so necessary to accomplish the tasks needed to make a business successful.

Flexibility and Resiliency

These traits are often referred to as the ability to bounce back from failure. One of the important reasons why coaches and many parents encourage their students or children to participate in athletics is to help them develop the flexibility and resiliency to accept defeat, learn from their failures, and profit from their experiences. Successful entrepreneurs have these personal attributes, as evidenced by the numerous examples of businesspersons who have accumulated fortunes, lost them, then started other ventures.

Decision Making

Entrepreneurs need the ability to make decisions and live with the consequences. In compiling your inventory of strengths and weaknesses, it is helpful to write down at least five ideas you had, how you implemented them, and what were the results of your efforts. The process of creating and implementing ideas, and evaluating the results of your decisions, will help determine whether you are the type to be a successful entrepreneur and are willing to take full responsibility for your own life and career. Many small business owners get into major difficulties because they refuse to acknowledge what is happening to their business until it is too late.

One of the most effective entrepreneurs in our time was Georges F. Doriot, the primary influence in developing this country's first publicly traded venture capital company, American Research & Development. Doriot believed that people work hardest out of loyalty to an idea and to their associates, and that a creative man merely has ideas whereas a resourceful man makes them practical. He told his students at the Harvard Business School, "If you want to be a success in business, you must love your product." He suggested, "that an MBA degree should only be valid for fifteen years but it could be extended if the holders would give evidence that they have used their education no less effectively and constructively to help others in every way they could."

Entrepreneurial Problems

As in all careers, there are a number of problems in becoming an entrepreneur that you should consider.

Competition

If you get a good idea and are successful in developing it into a business, a larger company may want to buy you out or set up a department to compete with you. In central Ohio, a small company manufactured saws for carpenters. The entrepreneur emphasized quality and slowly built up a growing demand for his product. A buyer from Sears Roebuck gave him a small order, found a great demand for the saws, ordered a much bigger quantity, and again a larger quantity. Soon the resources of the company were unable to satisfy the huge orders, so it sold out to Sears.

Skills Needed

Until recently, anyone who wanted to own and run his or her own business could do so with little education, training, or experience. By relying on common sense, one could manage a company "by the seat of the pants" theory, facing problems and making decisions on the basis of what seemed practical at that moment. With the growing complexity of business, increases in governmental regulations, growing consumer knowledge, increasing insurance premiums and malpractice suits, and the dependence on machines and computers, many more skills are now needed.

Many people refer to the present as the computer age because of the increasing need to compile all types of information quickly to facilitate wise decision making. Very few people have skills in all fields, so it is necessary to supplement your own talents by hiring or contracting with others who are specialists in advertising, accounting, taxes, finances, marketing, production, or law. Running a business today requires many different types of analyses, such as making market research studies to segment markets on which to focus your advertising and sales efforts. Sometimes pride makes small business owners reluctant to seek advice and assistance, and often contributes to their failure to analyze problems and trends properly.

A critical skill required of entrepreneurs is that of negotiating. Whether dealing with labor unions, suppliers, or customers, the art of negotiation is not developed in classrooms or by reading books. It is best to ask someone who has done such negotiating to share some of his or her negotiating experience with you on problems in your business. As Jack Falvey states in *What's Next? Career Strategies After 35*: "The golden rule of business applies. Those who have the gold make the rules."

Employees

Probably the most frequently stated complaint by owners is "you can't get dependable help these days." Unfortunately, too many workers are more interested in a paycheck than they are in producing a quality product, or providing a superior service. Too many employees do not utilize their working time efficiently, and care little whether customers approve or disapprove of their work. The automobile industry's problems with quality and increasing costs have resulted in Japan's success in dominating our automobile markets. In a typical family business the lack of interest and application by employees results in the owner working overtime, getting more complaints from customers, and acquiring ulcers from worries. Americans look disdainfully on menial jobs, as evidenced by the perpetual "Help Wanted" signs in retail stores, restaurants, fast food establishments, and others.

Becoming a Workaholic

One of the major problems of entrepreneurs is that they are hard workers and expect a similar output from employees. They have so much drive and energy that they have to be involved in several projects simultaneously to satisfy their need for meeting challenges. Their motto is "time is money," so they demand maximum utilization of time on the part of their employees. They tend to be driven people, and have a difficult time relaxing. Their work becomes an obsession, requiring more and more of their time and energy, until they become workaholics. It plays havoc with their families, and too few realize the need for a balanced life. A small business owner is often so busy with daily operations that he or she doesn't have time to do any long-range planning.

Faith in Suppliers

A requirement of all small business owners and franchisees is that they have faith in themselves and also in their suppliers or franchisors. Those buying a franchise should check with other franchisees in nearby areas to ask two key questions: "Is your operation profitable?" and "Are the franchisor and other suppliers delivering on promises for training, supplies, and so on?" Small businesses often have to depend on a single supplier, and do not have the assurance of dealing with several suppliers for key items.

Growing Too Fast

A key problem for entrepreneurs is the danger of growing too fast. Although it is very encouraging to see steady growth, there comes a time when you cannot do all the work yourself. Trying to keep up with the work load first involves lots of overtime, and eventually the decision to hire employees to help out. Until new employees become productive, there is a great danger of a noticeable deterioration in the quality of service rendered or not filling the customers' orders on time. This could result in a loss of business or clients.

Preparing to Become an Entrepreneur

Students who think that someday they may want to be in business for themselves can take relevant courses in college to prepare themselves. Courses in marketing, accounting, law, finance, and management are recommended. Obtaining an MBA degree is especially helpful. Some knowledge of contracts, real estate, leasing, taxes, personnel management, and marketing is needed. If you are contemplating the manufacture of some product, then take courses in production management, operations management, time/motion study, and computers.

If you have graduated, seminars and workshops are conducted at major universities and in metropolitan centers for special fields and industries. You can get information from organizations like The Center for Entrepreneurship and Innovation, which was established in 1986 at Indiana University. Its aims are to create new businesses and encourage innovative ideas within existing businesses. Plans for the Center include research, workshops, and service programs.

The courses offered in the evening by many colleges and universities will help provide the background needed to understand what you are getting into. However, remember that studying a venture and performing it are two different things. The more hands-on, directly related experience you have, the better you will become.

Probably the most practical way to prepare to become an entrepreneur is to take a job with a company in the industry in which you are interested. Within three to five years you can learn how things work, the problems in that industry, how your firm handles them, the most effective methods of getting business or clients, how to satisfy customers, the best locations and real estate flexibility, and most importantly, whether you *like* that business. In other words, learn the business at someone else's expense.

A student was interested in owning a hardware store some day. In college he took a business course, and upon graduation accepted a job with Sears, Roebuck & Company. Upon completing their training program, he asked to be assigned to the hardware department. By asking a lot of questions and paying particular attention to details, he kept getting promotions until he became the manager of the department. Eventually he realized, "if I can make money for Sears, I can make it for myself. Why should I work so hard for someone else?" At this point he bought a hardware store from a man who was retiring, and became an entrepreneur in his own right.

Rewards for Risk Taking

There is an old adage that states, "the greater the risk, the greater the reward." For most entrepreneurs who become successful, there seem to be four major incentives for them to accept the risks.

Satisfaction of Work

Taking an idea, developing it, and making it work brings the utmost satisfaction and fulfillment to individuals. Meeting the challenges and solving the problems in establishing and managing a business venture massages the ego and builds self-confidence, along with the satisfaction of stating "I did it my way," and the good feeling that comes with providing a needed product or service.

Earn More Money

If the business is successful, and keeps growing, there is great potential for financial rewards. By astute management an individual can parlay an idea into a small company, keep developing it, and cause it to grow or else sell it at a profit to a larger company. A worker with a steady job can accumulate savings arithmetically, but an entrepreneur can build a fortune geometrically.

Create Jobs for Others

Successful entrepreneurs perform a vital service to their community because their initiative and perseverance create jobs for others. Our country has shifted from a manufacturing to a service economy. Thus, new opportunities for employment come from entrepreneurs who start a business that is initially small, but keeps adding employees as it grows. As a result, the entrepreneur performs a valuable service as a citizen, and gains prestige and stature in the community.

Learning from Mistakes

The old adage, "experience is the best teacher," certainly applies to entrepreneurs. Relying on your own judgment has a satisfaction of its own, especially when your decisions prove to be the right ones. Even failures help individuals learn. In fact, we usually learn faster from adverse experiences, and retain such memories longer.

Getting Started

Assuming you are anxious to start a business, there are a number of ways that you can go about it. Begin by working nights and weekends for yourself, out of your own home or basement.

1. Make up a circular announcing your product or service, get it duplicated, and hand deliver it to stores and houses in your surrounding community. Put copies under windshield wipers of parked cars in the street or in parking lots; on bulletin boards of churches, schools, and communities; or stand on busy intersections and hand them out to passersby like politicians do.

2. Put an ad in your daily or weekly newspaper, or in appropriate magazines or journals, announcing your new service or prod-

uct, and solicit inquiries and orders. Be sure you have someone available or an answering machine to take and give prospective customers accurate information.

3. Visit your local chamber of commerce and the nearest office of the local small business association or the trade association in that industry, to ask for advice and assistance. From these sources you can obtain helpful information on sites, regulations, taxes, financial sources, and marketing ideas. Your zeal in persuading them that you are a prospective future member will facilitate getting the kind of information you need for that community and industry.

4. After you have done the preparation work, consult with a lawyer to set up your business legally, with an accountant to establish a recordkeeping system and get advice on taxes, with your daily or weekly newspaper manager to discuss advertising rates and get ideas on effective promotion, and with a realtor to discuss a site for your business (after it grows large enough) unless the franchisor provides this service.

5. Visit the faculty and administrator of the Small Business Program at a nearby university. You may be able to work out a project to get free consulting service, since professors like to assign their students to real-life problems. Most faculty are willing to give advice for free up to a point, then they expect to get paid for their knowledge and advice.

6. Compile a pro forma budget statement by estimating your expenses and income for a two-year period. Take this budget plan with you and discuss it with several bankers and other lending institutions until you get the financial backing you need. If insufficient, go to venture capital firms in the nearest city to get financial assistance, or use the equity in your home to finance your business.

7. Visit the Small Business Administration office in the nearest metropolitan city. The SBA is the federal agency created to encourage and assist small business. Through a national network of 110 offices across the country, the SBA publishes and distributes pamphlets covering hundreds of business-related subjects from retailing to research, and sponsors seminars and classes. This agency provides financial assistance in the form of loans, advance payments, and business development expenses. Although dealing with the SBA can be time consuming and often frustrating, as is

the case in dealing with many government bureaus, the entrepreneur cannot afford to pass up this resource to get started in his or her own business.

8. Graduate students, especially MBA's, and other prospective entrepreneurs should explore opportunities for developing a business from one of the patents of companies that do a lot of research work, like DuPont, General Electric, or Monsanto. They have many patents "sitting on the shelf" and will finance up to forty-nine percent to help an entrepreneur develop a patent into a useful and productive business. Usually a separate department of the company handles all work related to establishing a business with one of their patents.

9. Other sources: Future entrepreneurs can also receive ideas from *VENTURE* magazine, and by competing for new business ventures by writing to organizations such as the ICIBY Contest Clearinghouse, 110 East 59th Street, Suite 1200, New York, NY 10022. Most newspaper classified ads in larger cities generally advertise for franchises in the "Business Opportunities" section. The federal government has several helpful publications, such as "Starting and Managing a Business from Your Home" ($1.75), and "Financial Management: How to Make a Go of Your Business" ($2.50). These can be ordered from the Consumer Information Center, Dept. 54, Pueblo, CO 81009.

The best time to try to go into business for yourself is between the ages of thirty to thirty-five when you have had some time to learn the business, but you are young enough to have the energy, confidence, and resiliency needed to bounce back if you don't make it.

chapter fifteen

Your Career Timetable and Development

At the end of the first year of work, you should take the time to make a systematic inventory and appraisal of the past year's experience. Develop this habit annually and you will continue to be the driver of your own career. At graduation you heard the term "commencement," which literally means you are starting on your life's work. By reviewing your work experience at least once a year, you will be able to know where you've been, where you are now, and where you want to go, thus navigating your career in the direction you wish it to take.

In professional sports, the rookie season is used to determine whether the star college player is worth keeping and developing. In other fields, a similar evaluation is made, sometimes informally and not mentioned to the employee, and sometimes through a formal evaluation process. In counseling thousands of recent graduates in a variety of industries, we found that it is best to evaluate your own performance first, then schedule a talk with your supervisor. It is not enough to do your own job, you must understand it and know how it relates to other employees and to other departments in your organization. A knowledge of what other departments do and how they operate will not only make you a better and more efficient employee, but also increases your opportunities for promotion.

Start your inventory by comparing your learning and experience during the first year with the statements given during your initial and secondary interviews. This will enable you to determine your progress or lack of growth. Your discussion with your supervisor should bring out whether your personal evaluation is correct and whether you missed any key points during the first year. It also will help identify your weak spots and what additional learning or experience you need to acquire. With the help of your boss, plan a program of corrective action so that you will not only correct any bad habits, but also fill in the gaps of your needed experience. Try for a variety of work assignments to improve your view of the organization and your chances for future promotional possibilities, and to make the job more interesting.

The Second-Year Malaise

Sometime during the second year of employment, college graduates generally get a feeling of anxiety and dissatisfaction with their jobs. In college they got used to a semester or a quarterly cycle of peaks and valleys with regular feedback via exams and course grades to ascertain how they were doing. Because many organizations expect you to do your job but provide little information on how well you are doing, it becomes very frustrating to the point that you may consider making a change.

The second-year malaise can be charted, as indicated in figure 15-1. From points A to B, the new employee is excited by the new job, has a high morale, and finds the environment quite stimulating. From points B to C, the glamour and stimulation of employment wear off and doubts and dissatisfaction begin to appear. Employees sometimes get a burned-out feeling, especially if their first year of employment was fast-paced and exciting. They begin to lose motivation, start to get bored, become uneasy and apprehensive about their job and career advancement, and their anxieties result in an attitude of malaise. Unfortunately, many persons change jobs when they experience this period, and then they have to go through the same emotional cycle with the next job. From points C to D, a recovery period, the employee finds that the additional experience solves many of the dissatisfactions, anxiety, and problems in the B to C period, and his or her perspective is improved considerably.

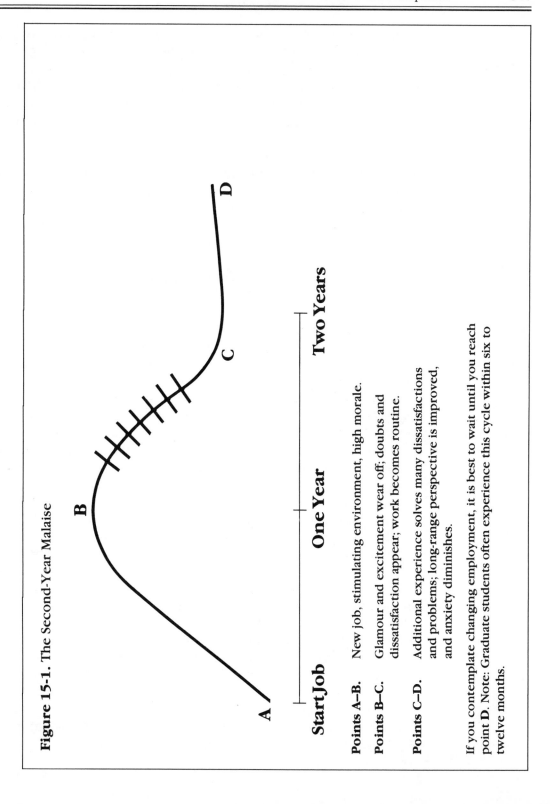

Figure 15-1. The Second-Year Malaise

StartJob   **One Year**   **Two Years**

Points A–B. New job, stimulating environment, high morale.

Points B–C. Glamour and excitement wear off; doubts and dissatisfaction appear; work becomes routine.

Points C–D. Additional experience solves many dissatisfactions and problems; long-range perspective is improved, and anxiety diminishes.

If you contemplate changing employment, it is best to wait until you reach point D. Note: Graduate students often experience this cycle within six to twelve months.

There are several lessons to be learned from this chart. First of all, develop patience! Your career development starts seriously at point D. If you quit during the B to C period, you generally face the same emotional cycle all over again on the next job. Unlike college, promotions are not on a fixed time schedule in the real world. Future employers question whether the early leavers left of their own accord, or whether they were fired or requested to leave. If you complete the two-year cycle, future employers rarely question the reason for leaving your job. Career counselors are unanimous in advising young workers against job-hopping the moment they run into difficulties at work.

If you did not plan a career timetable during your senior year, this should be one of your major accomplishments during the second year of employment. The research you did on your occupational field should have included interviews with executives in that line of work; this information will provide you with the time normally required to advance to each higher level of responsibility. By putting such data in chart form, you create a timetable that will provide checkpoints (landmarks) for your career development, serving the same purpose as a roadmap when driving a car on a trip. At the end of your second year of employment, you should know all the primary products or services of your employer, how your job and department fit into the rest of the organization, the chain of command and the best means of communication, how your work performance is evaluated and rewarded, and what is needed to reach the next checkpoint on your career timetable.

Figure 15-2 illustrates a career timetable for a college graduate interested in marketing. The career development plans of our five hypothetical graduates are illustrated at the end of this chapter. Putting your career development plans in writing provides tangible and reachable objectives toward your career goals, helps you make periodic comparisons and career appraisals, and facilitates taking corrective action when your career is not bringing you personal satisfaction.

Women will probably want to add another aspect to their career timetable because many will take time out from a career for family purposes. Figure 15-3 demonstrates alternative routes for flexibility and practicality. The dotted line shows a woman dropping out of the labor market to start a family, and returning to full-time work when her youngsters go to school. She may probably take a refresher course in her field from a continuing education program, and then renew her career or begin another one.

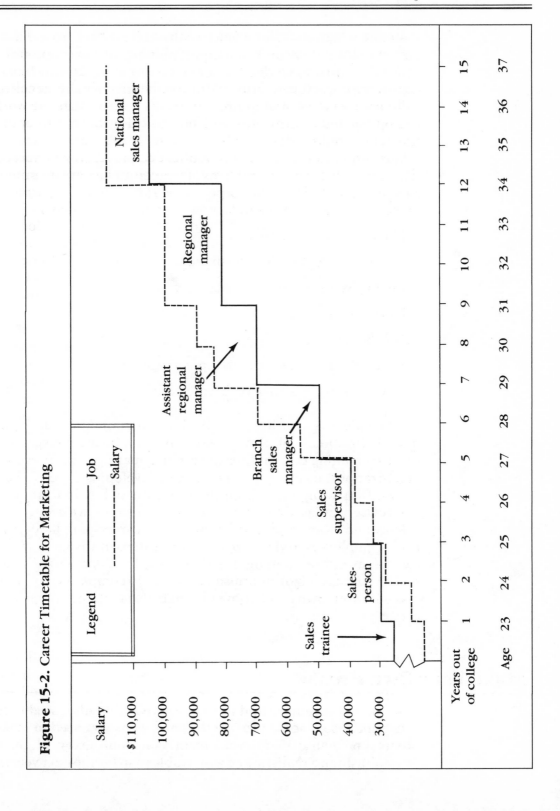

Figure 15-2. Career Timetable for Marketing

A more recent trend for women with a college background is to take maternity leave for two months, plus accrued vacation time, and then return to work either on a part-time or full-time basis depending on factors such as health, availability of baby-sitters or child-care services, and job requirements. For women choosing this option and returning to work on a full-time basis, the career timetable would be the same as the example in figure 15-3.

More and more articles and publications are being produced that concentrate on the problems of women advancing into management, especially in the corporate world. Examples contained in recent publications include topics similar to the following:

Making it in a man's world.

Earning more than your husband.

Dealing with on-the-job sexual harassment.

Having it all.

Breaking the glass ceiling.

Encountering roadblocks to top management.

Handling the crunch of corporate politics.

All employees aspiring to vertical or horizontal advancement must keep abreast of current developments in their respective fields by reading current literature, participating in professional organizations, meeting with peers, and developing effective networks. Borrowing ideas from these sources will help formulate and revise a career time chart as changes occur or are needed.

More and more employers are providing career-path ladders to enable employees to visualize the various steps in advancing their careers, as indicated in figures 15-4, 15-5, 15-6, and 15-7. As you make your annual job appraisal, it is wise to compare your progress with your own career timetable and also with the employer's career-path diagram.

Make Your Own Breaks

Your annual inventory and the corrective action discussed with your supervisor should provide the basic steps you need to make progress on your career development. Plan your next goal. Start by establishing a realistic and achievable plan for the next year. A

Figure 15-3. Career Timetable for a Woman Dropping Out of the Job Market Temporarily

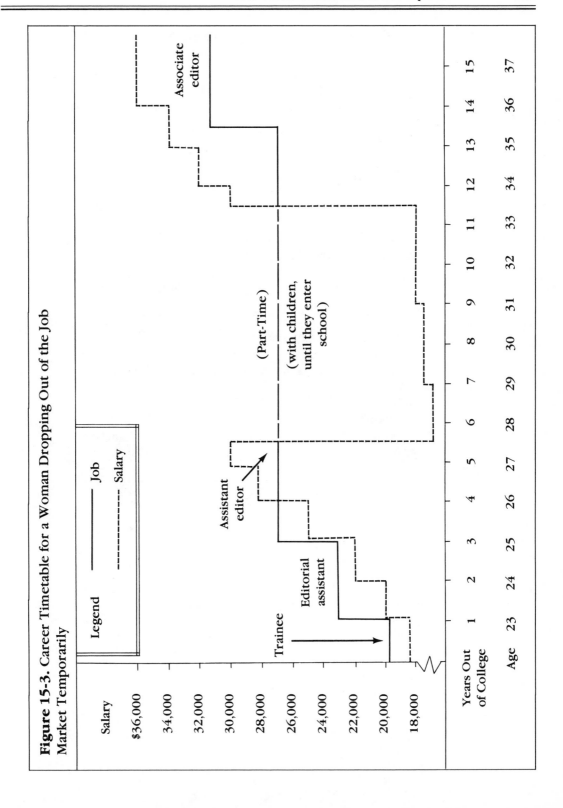

Figure 15-4. Career-Path Ladders for Accountants (The Turner Corporation)

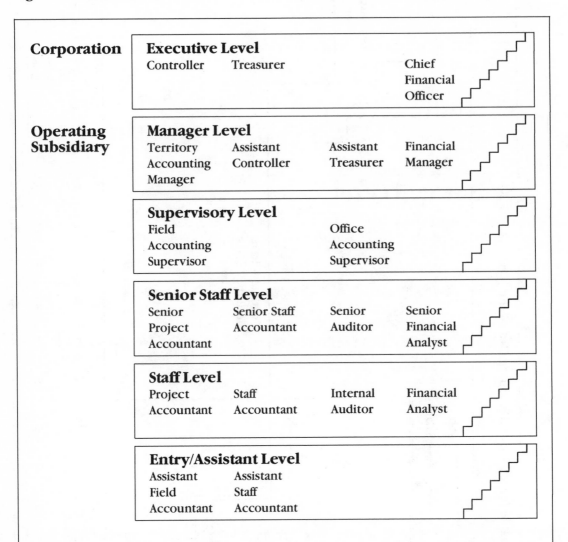

Corporation

Executive Level
Controller   Treasurer   Chief
                                     Financial
                                     Officer

Operating Subsidiary

Manager Level
Territory   Assistant   Assistant   Financial
Accounting   Controller   Treasurer   Manager
Manager

Supervisory Level
Field   Office
Accounting   Accounting
Supervisor   Supervisor

Senior Staff Level
Senior   Senior Staff   Senior   Senior
Project   Accountant   Auditor   Financial
Accountant   Analyst

Staff Level
Project   Staff   Internal   Financial
Accountant   Accountant   Auditor   Analyst

Entry/Assistant Level
Assistant   Assistant
Field   Staff
Accountant   Accountant

Turner prides itself on the competence, dedication and integrity of its people. We maintain a permanent staff of employees who have grown within the company from entry-level assignment to advanced executive level management positions. As a college graduate, your career path will begin in a field or office capacity with specific duties and responsibilities. Individual initiative and performance play a major part in your career advancement as well as defining your specific areas of interest at each level. Turner offers an opportunity for a rewarding career combining technical knowledge, management expertise, and leadership.

Source: The Turner Corporation

Figure 15-5. Career-Path Ladders for Engineers (The Turner Corporation)

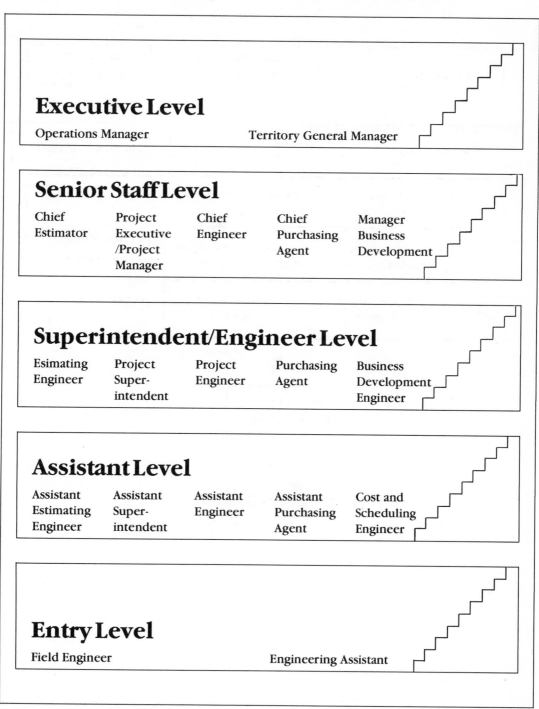

Executive Level

Operations Manager   Territory General Manager

Senior Staff Level

| Chief Estimator | Project Executive /Project Manager | Chief Engineer | Chief Purchasing Agent | Manager Business Development |

Superintendent/Engineer Level

| Esimating Engineer | Project Super- intendent | Project Engineer | Purchasing Agent | Business Development Engineer |

Assistant Level

| Assistant Estimating Engineer | Assistant Super- intendent | Assistant Engineer | Assistant Purchasing Agent | Cost and Scheduling Engineer |

Entry Level

Field Engineer   Engineering Assistant

Source: The Turner Corporation

Figure 15-6. Career-Path Diagram—Raytheon Company

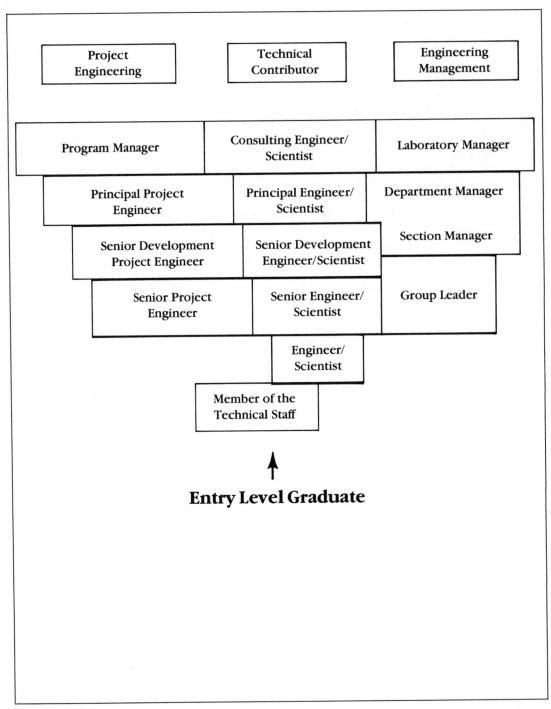

Figure 15-7. General Mills—Consumer Foods Sales Division

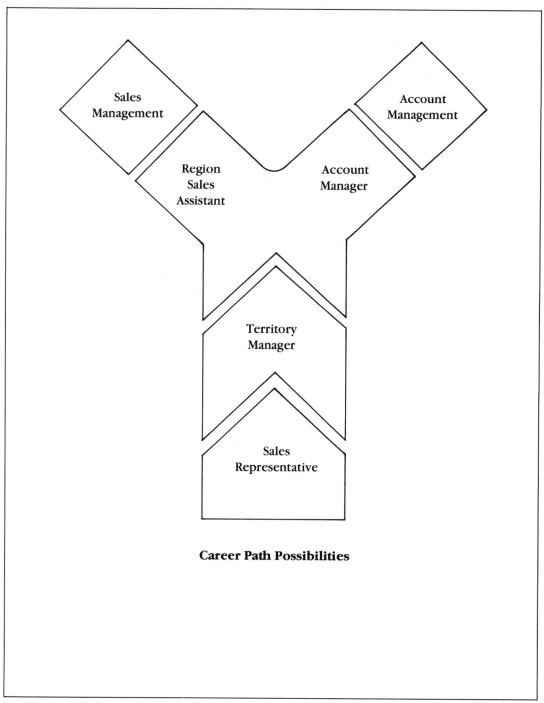

Career Path Possibilities

Source: General Mills, Inc.

goal helps motivate people because it is something you want. By setting a year's time schedule, you have a short-range objective that is practical and can be achieved. This type of planning will enable you to know where you are going, help you to make things happen, and help you develop the habit of controlling your own career. The principle of making your own breaks could be illustrated by the following examples.

Example 1
Suppose your boss, in the annual evaluation of your work, stated that you need to improve your ability to communicate. Since this involves your ability to speak effectively as well as to write concisely and clearly, you should explore the communication courses offered by nearby universities or colleges, read books on this subject, join groups like The Toastmaster's Club, and take advantage of in-house training sessions. Because all supervisory positions require some degree of written communication, you might benefit from a business writing, report writing, or similar course.

Example 2
Suppose you are a liberal arts graduate and started working in a bank. To better understand the functions of our monetary system, you should take some economic, finance, and accounting courses. Accounting is considered the language of business, economics provides the theoretical basis for our financial system, and finance gives you the technical vocabulary and tools to utilize in all types of organizations.

Example 3
Your major in college was sociology, and your first job is with the state welfare department. Your first goal is to become a professional social worker. Along with the training given by your department, it would be wise to join the National Association of Social Workers; consider graduate school, either part-time while working or full-time in a couple of years; ask to be assigned to a variety of cases; attend workshops and seminars outside your department; and cultivate contacts with community groups and leaders.

In the latest edition of his book, *Career Planning Today*, C. Randall Powell includes "Forty Action Ideas for Advancement" (see figure 15-8). These suggestions can be applied to all fields of endeavor since they constitute practical and achievable ideas to make your own breaks. Within two years of employment you find

Figure 15-8. Forty Action Ideas for Advancement*

Seek additional responsibilities.
Complete assignments immediately.
Make suggestions instead of critical reviews.
Solve problems instead of just identifying them.
Praise others for good work.

Develop new skills through training.
Seek assignments that offer exposure to managers.
Search for the reason behind each assignment.
Look at problems from a management viewpoint.
Do not underestimate your social responsibilities.

Nurture personal friendships in your peer group.
Ask for certain work assignments.
Study the normal promotional channels.
Develop your personal life outside the organization.
Make professional contacts outside the organization.

Seek line, not staff, responsibilities.
Be patient for rewards, but go after challenges.
Beware of "assistant to" titles. Watch go-fers.
Avoid internal politics and cliques.
Show your enthusiasm for the organization.

Discuss ideas, never people.
Advertise your abilities by superior performances.
Keep records of your work to show later.
Work on your public speaking skills.
Talk to subordinates as friends. They make you.

Never allow pressures to compromise quality.
Maintain personal and organizational ethics.
Make a written appraisal each year for your review.
Ask your superiors for advice about your career.
No negative criticism does not equal positive praise.

Rate your supervisors' potential for promotions.
Get help if an assignment is over your head.
Accept criticism and ask for it. Use it to improve.
Rethink your plans if the pressure bothers you.
Be prepared to relocate if promotion merits it.

Maintain organizational loyalty and advertise it.
Learn to delegate authority.
Accept blame for poor work of subordinates.
Expect two- to three-year plateaus in promotion.
Watch for earnings ceilings.

*Powell, C. Randall. *Career Planning Today*, HIRE ME! edition, 1990.

that some of the best ideas are summarily and undiplomatically rejected, that reports and suggestions may be adopted slowly and reluctantly (if at all), and that such frustrations require the patience of Job, the persuasiveness of Dale Carnegie, and the tact of a diplomat. Speaking of tact, it is well to remember the advice of one boss who counseled a recent college graduate on the need for improving her tactfulness. This boss advised the graduate to "develop your tact to such an extent that when you tell a worker to go to hell, he will actually look forward to making the trip."

One of the best ways to make your own breaks is to learn how to complete staff work, a concept borrowed from the military that can be applied to practically all situations. As stated in the *Army and Navy Journal:*

> "Completed staff work" is the study of a problem, and presentation of a solution (to a superior) in such form that all that remains to be done on his part is to indicate his approval or disapproval of the completed action. It is your duty to work out the details, no matter how perplexing they may be . . . so that the product should be presented to the superior in finished form.

A good example of the completed staff-work doctrine is the illustration given to explain pay differentials in a company house organ entitled, "Why is George Worth $2,200 per Month?" Here is the little story, slightly condensed and updated in salaries, but still providing a significant moral:

> Three brothers went to work for the same company on the same day, and at the same salary. A year later, one was getting $800 a month, the second $1,000, and the third $2,200. Their father felt this was unfair and went to his sons' boss to find out why.

> "I'll let *them* explain why," said the boss. He then called each son in turn, and gave him this assignment: "I understand the Oceanic has just docked. I want you to go down to the pier and get an inventory of her cargo."

> Jim, the lowest paid got the story and returned in three minutes. "She carries 2,000 seal skins," he said. "I got that from the first mate over the phone."

> Frank, the $1,000 man, took an hour. He came back with a list showing 2,000 seal skins, 500 beaver and 1,100 mink pelts.

> George, the $2,200 man, didn't return for three hours. "The Oceanic carries 2,000 seal skins," he began. "They can be had at $10 each, so I took a two-day option and wired a prospect in St. Louis. I think

he'll buy at \$15 if that's OK with you. I found 500 beaver pelts aboard: I've learned through a phone call we can sell them at a \$1,000 profit if you agree. There are also 1,100 mink pelts aboard, but they're of poor quality, so I didn't try to do anything with them."[1]

The father learned that Jim did not do as he was told, that Frank did only what he was told to do, and that George did completed staff work by showing initiative and exercising good judgment. Every employee can find ample opportunities to do more than is required, thereby developing a favorable reputation for dependability, possible advancement in pay, and in time, promotion to more responsible positions.

Gaining Visibility and Mobility

Another way of making your own breaks is to deliberately plan to gain better visibility and mobility. The two major ways to accomplish these are to explore the *internal* (within your own organization), and then the *external* (outside your organization) possibilities. Many people are too quick to change jobs and employers without adequately exploring the opportunities within their own organization. Or, they lack patience to await developments that are in the planning stages.

While on a consulting assignment with a major insurance company, one of the authors learned about the firm's plans to expand on a national basis. An alumnus who was on that company's payroll, came into the career center and said he was in a dead-end job and wanted to leave. Because the expansion plans were received on a confidential basis, they could not be revealed to the alumnus. However, the alumnus was counseled to wait six more months before making a definite decision. About five months later the alumnus came back and said, "I'm glad I took your advice. Our company is going to expand on a national basis, and I got promoted to a level that I did not anticipate for another five years."

---

[1]Adapted from *Embee Chips*, the employee magazine of the New Britain Machine Company.

Internal

There are several ways to gain visibility and mobility, including participating in employee and company activities. Some organizations sponsor glee clubs, drama groups, athletic teams, cultural events, speakers on various topics, and seminars for new products or services or procedures. Such participation not only adds to the fun of working (just like extracurricular activities did in college), but also enables you to make contact with interesting people. Some of these contacts could be very useful for networking purposes whenever you are seeking another job or another employer, or for promotional purposes.

The KVP Company in Kalamazoo, Michigan displays a sign that should be a reminder to all college graduates:

> Little Minds Discuss People
>
> Average Minds Discuss Events
>
> Great Minds Discuss Ideas

Your dependable attendance and thorough work assignments will be the best internal methods to impress your boss favorably, along with your flexibility and compatibility. Volunteering for committee work is another method of getting people to recognize you and your abilities. The real work of any organization is done through committees. Therefore, it is important for aspiring employees to become noticed; their suggestions, questions, and other work on committees will bring recognition very quickly.

Upon graduating from college, Ray Miller started his career with a manufacturing company. Near the end of the company's training program, Ray volunteered to be a solicitor for the firm's annual United Way Drive. A few months later he volunteered to serve on a Creative Ideas Committee, then played on the company's softball team during the summer months. The next fall he served as a team captain on the United Way Drive, continued his committee and softball activities, and volunteered to represent his department in a collaborative program with his community's school system.

In all these activities Ray made a special effort to learn and remember the names of all the people he met, and to learn something of their jobs and families. He was elected treasurer of the company's Employee Association, and thus had an official reason for visiting and talking to many executives. His ability to meet and work with action-oriented employees and executives, and benefit from their advice, experience, and contacts facilitated his rapid promotion in the company.

Obviously recent college graduates should take advantage of any training programs, especially if they have any ambition to get into management positions later. Since there is always a shortage of qualified people who are willing to assume more responsibility and are able to make good decisions, most organizations show interest in employees who aspire to leadership and management-level positions, and provide various programs to train them. By seeking and participating in such training programs, recent graduates automatically come to the attention of executives who make decisions on promotions.

Through the above internal methods you should be able to develop several mentors. As Dr. Rosabeth Kanter, in her article, "Upward Bound," advises women who aspire to executive positions: "Successful people have a multitude of backers and sponsors who provide a multitude of functions for them, ranging from information sharing to offering career advice to fighting for them in meetings to the reflected status of appearing to be close to someone who is important. But anyone who ties her career to a single manager in an organization will be running some grave risks."

Another method of increasing visibility and mobility within the organization is to seek a transfer to another job within your own department, or to another department. Sometimes it is necessary to move within the organization to take advantage of more advancement possibilities. Figure 15-9 illustrates this concept for transferring internally to be in a more favorable position for further advancement.

Since the first year of employment in any organization is one of training and apprenticeship, in most cases thoughts of promotion are not given priority. During the second year of employment, you will start thinking of alternative pathways to higher-level positions, and strategies to get there. If you started in department B, (figure 15-9) you can continue working upward to the top of your job classification, then seek a lateral transfer to another department to gain a different skill or experience. Sometimes you can get a promotion as indicated from department B to D. More often you can effect a lateral transfer to get into a department that has more rungs on its promotional ladder. For example, if you realize there is only oe more level in department B, your ambition alone should force you to contemplate a transfer to another department (such as A, C, or E), which has more opportunities for advancement.

Figure 15-9. Alternative Pathways to Promotion

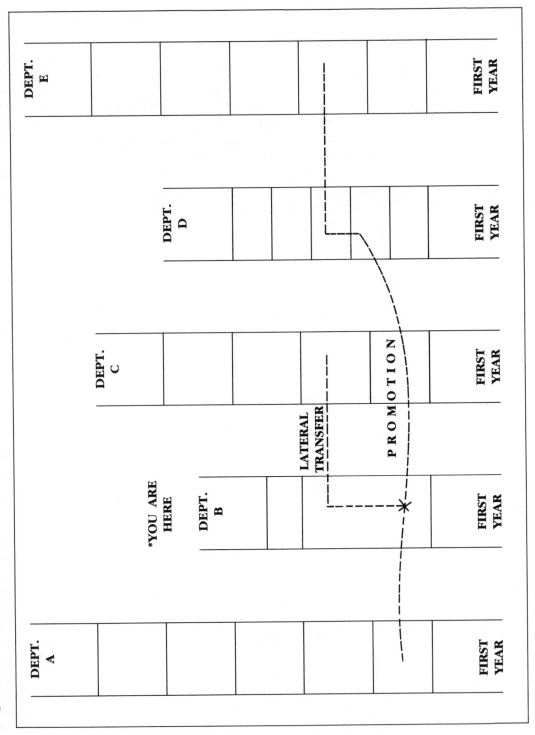

The "three-position philosophy" is very useful within organizations, and helpful when you need to change employment. Briefly stated, you try to do your own job as capably as possible, at the same time you try to develop an employee at a lower level to be able to do your job, and you also try to learn the job at the next level above you. This philosophy will make you a more valued employee, will facilitate promotion to a higher-level position, and make it easier to change jobs or employers because you have trained your replacement to take over your responsibilities.

By utilizing all these suggestions for internal contacts, you should be able to develop such a favorable reputation that the jobs within your organization will come seeking you!

External

If you find that all internal contacts and your present work do not utilize your energies and talents or satisfy your interests and desires, then seek activities outside your organization. Some organizations prefer that you devote your talents and energies to the job, and hold off on external activities until you have made considerable progress up the promotional ladder. One of the first such activities you should consider is the professional organization in your field. Join some of its committees and work your way up into leadership roles. This activity is especially helpful for those who prefer to develop professionally (horizontally instead of vertically). A similar suggestion is to join the local alumni club from your college, which is always appreciative of former students who are willing to work on committees and assume officer responsibilities. These two sources can be the most productive when you are networking for another position.

Another source for gaining visibility and mobility is volunteer work in your community. People who volunteer for community projects often find they get a lot more back than they put in. They feel better, get more out of life, make themselves more interesting, use different skills, find new friends, and often develop interests that follow them into retirement, making even those years more rewarding and fun. In our society we are experiencing more leisure time, but just having it does not necessarily guarantee happiness and a rewarding life.

Community volunteer work enables us to become more interesting as we meet different kinds of people, make new friends, and develop a new facet to our personalities. All community activities need people who can contribute their talents—from workers to executives—to make life in their community more enjoyable for all citizens. Probably the greatest reason for volunteer work is the fact that it brings out the best in people. When individuals work together and help each other voluntarily—in scouting, the community fund (United Way), working in hospitals, teaching, helping the elderly, or collectively fighting off raging spring floods or summer forest fires—they feel a warm satisfaction, a closer friendlier spirit toward each other for having worked together in this way, and a definite sense of fulfillment. In addition, they are making their own community a better place to live.

Another form of community activity is service to the church of your preference. Such organizations need people with initiative who can see things that need to be done, and have the willingness and energy to do them or get a group together that can get it done. Self-starters can gain valuable experience organizing and running activities, as well as getting the satisfaction from contributing to a good and worthy cause. As one executive stated after he had done many things for people: "I made an important discovery. Anything that makes one glow with pleasure is beyond money calculation in this world where there is altogether too much grubbing and too little glowing."

For recent college graduates another source for gaining mobility and visibility is to join the Junior Chamber of Commerce. Their activities enable you to contribute your talents on many projects that benefit the community, help you make contact (and often friends) with important and influential leaders in a great variety of businesses and agencies, and serve as an excellent training ground to test your ideas and ability to get things done.

In helping out or in running community activities on a volunteer basis, you get to practice your talents and develop your skills. If you get any kind of publicity or awards for such activities, your employer is sure to take notice when seeking promotable employees. For most people, however, doing volunteer work in the community has its own internal reward.

Wherever you are working, you should continue your education, but not just to retool your mind or to learn the latest techniques for job purposes. As Morton Hunt points out, "adult learning increases our self-esteem, public recognition, and gives us the pleasure of the new knowledge itself." Intellectual skills get rusty if we don't use our minds by thinking of something new. Emotional benefits from adult learning help us think better of ourselves. It gives us a greater self-reliance, a sense of being in charge of our lives, and gives increased meaning to life, mostly because we experience growth when we learn.

Continuous education takes many forms; many communities provide college courses or individual seminars or workshops on specific topics. Many companies provide advanced education, like the Management Educational Institute of the Arthur D. Little Company in Cambridge, Massachusetts. Some people prefer self-study via magazine articles or books; others learn from colleagues and friends, particularly about hobbies or recreational pursuits. For tough problems affecting careers (marital discord, alcohol, drugs, medical), therapy groups under professional guidance may be most helpful.

By utilizing the internal and external suggestions given here, you can assume the necessary responsibility to be in control of your career development. There are dead-end jobs, and there are dead-end people. Since changes affect all of our lives, only the people who prepare themselves and remain flexible find themselves growing in their jobs, accepting new responsibilities, gaining promotions, and coping with the changing world.

Occupational Hierarchies

To understand the basic tenets of promotion, you should review the echolons of jobs, the occupational hierarchy, in your organization. Although the number of job echolons and titles will vary, the traditional concept is very characteristic of many organizations. Management studies generally use two types of occupational hierarchies. The most influential is the pyramidal model used in larger organizations (see figure 15-10); the other type is used for professionally trained employees (see figure 15-13). For individuals aspiring to management-level positions, they should have a career timetable or else they will find themselves bypassed for important positions.

Occupational Hierarchy A (traditional)

Figure 15-10 depicts the five echelons of job levels in larger organizations. Note the importance of age in illustrating the promotional upward levels of jobs; major job changes usually come in five-year internals. This concept is a guide—the actual speed of promotions will depend on the size of your organization, its poli-

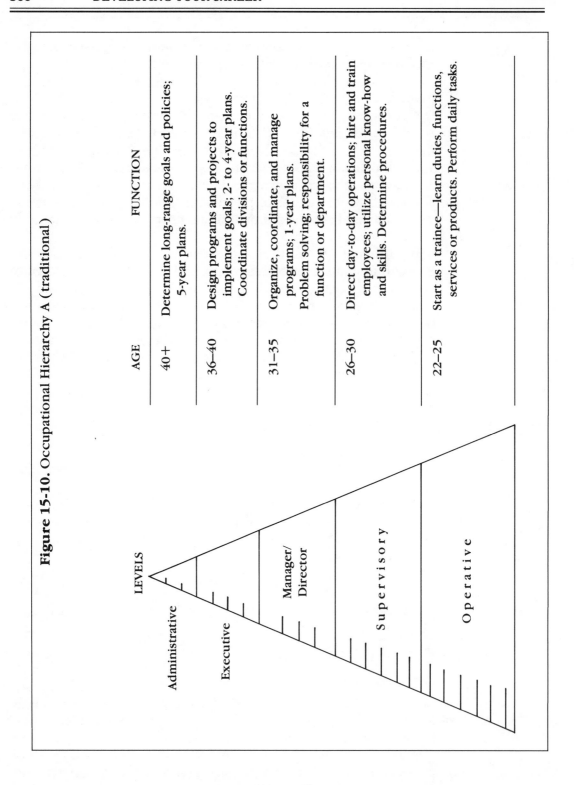

Figure 15-10. Occupational Hierarchy A (traditional)

LEVELS	AGE	FUNCTION
Administrative	40+	Determine long-range goals and policies; 5-year plans.
Executive	36–40	Design programs and projects to implement goals; 2- to 4-year plans. Coordinate divisions or functions.
Manager/Director	31–35	Organize, coordinate, and manage programs; 1-year plans. Problem solving; responsibility for a function or department.
Supervisory	26–30	Direct day-to-day operations; hire and train employees; utilize personal know-how and skills. Determine procedures.
Operative	22–25	Start as a trainee—learn duties, functions, services or products. Perform daily tasks.

cies, the practices in that type of industry and area, the economy, and the performance of the individual employee.

Operative
Typically you will start your career at age 22 as a trainee in the operative echelon. With one to three years of experience you are expected to have the personal know-how and skill to perform the duties thoroughly, know the function of the department and how it relates to other departments, know the services or products of your organization and industry, and be familiar with the day-to-day tasks that keep the organization going.

Supervisory
Employees who have established a good reputation for efficiency and production, and have mastered the skills required on the job in the department are considered for the supervisory echelon. Between the ages of 26–30, you should acquire experience being in charge of a unit, with responsibility for day-to-day operations. In addition to personal know-how and skills, this level requires the training of other employees and following up to make sure they are doing the job right, evaluating their progress, designing operating procedures or improvements, and making periodic reports to higher management. As you prove capable of handling one unit, your responsibilities may be gradually increased with authority for a larger unit, or for several units. One of the interesting experiences at this level is to learn how much easier it is to do a task yourself as compared to getting someone else to do it.

Manager/Director
With effective career planning, you should reach the manager/director level between the ages of 31–35. At this level you may have responsibility for a particular function, or for a department. The work typically involves carrying out the policies established by executives, usually through one-year objectives for budgetary, personnel, and other purposes. Other duties include coordinating the work of several units; initiating and developing policies, projects, and procedures; developing new programs; making decisions on recommendations or problems brought up by supervisors; and reporting operating results to higher levels. This level is especially important in deciding who will be considered for executive and top administrative jobs.

Edmond F. Wright, former chairman of the board of Wright-Porter, Inc., a pioneer in the executive recruiting and development field, provided some useful advice on management levels. Figure 15-11 shows his hourglass and wineglass concepts of the opportunities available in organizations, and the job structure in different-sized companies. In the hourglass figure, there is a surplus of people who have abilities at the lower occupational levels, and a great number of opportunities above the managerial level because of the shortage of capable people. Once a person develops a reputation as an effective manager and squeezes through the bottleneck of the hourglass, then opportunities open up quickly and various organizations would come seeking him or her (a typical function of executive recruiting firms).

In most organizations, the results accomplished on the manager/director level determine whether you will be considered for higher-level positions. Two of the major factors are (1) the ability to get results, and (2) the ability to provide effective leadership. In his wineglass example, Wright points out that in small organizations an employee gets minimum training, then broader and more varied assignments, although there are fewer echelons of jobs. In medium-sized organizations it takes a while to work up the functional "stem." Then one's reputation for ability and initiative opens up a breadth of opportunities. In large corporations, the college graduate goes through a training period, then works in one functional area (the stem of the wine glass) through the manager/director level. After that, assuming a demonstrated ability to get results, the number of opportunities for the executive and top management administrative positions increase rapidly.

Executive

From a career planning viewpoint an individual should reach the executive echelon of jobs between the ages of 36–40. On this level, one has to plan two- to four-year goals to implement the long-range plans and policies determined by the top administration. This involves coordinating several functions or departments; deciding which programs will affect established policies and plans; organizing new or abolishing old departments; controlling the results of major organizational units; deciding major personnel problems and policies; establishing motivational programs to provide the right environment for creativity and productivity; and providing leadership to keep the company on course.

Administrative

Persons who have planned their career and utilized the various strategies available should reach the top management level of an

Figure 15-11. Wright's Hourglass and Wineglass Examples

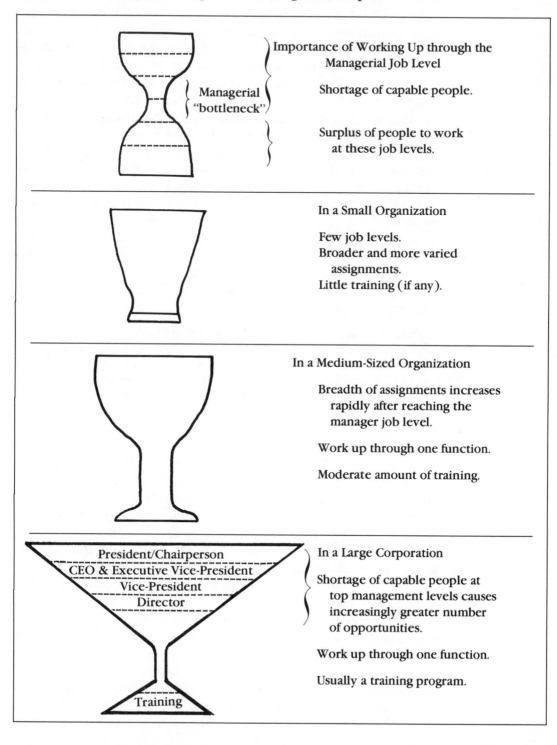

Importance of Working Up through the
Managerial Job Level

Managerial "bottleneck"

Shortage of capable people.

Surplus of people to work
at these job levels.

In a Small Organization

Few job levels.
Broader and more varied
assignments.
Little training (if any).

In a Medium-Sized Organization

Breadth of assignments increases
rapidly after reaching the
manager job level.

Work up through one function.

Moderate amount of training.

President/Chairperson
CEO & Executive Vice-President
Vice-President
Director

Training

In a Large Corporation

Shortage of capable people at
top management levels causes
increasingly greater number
of opportunities.

Work up through one function.

Usually a training program.

organization around the age of 40 or over, depending on the size of the organization. At this level, responsibilities include charting the direction or course to be followed for long-range purposes (usually five years); determining broad major personnel, financial, and functional policies; and reporting cumulative results achieved as well as needs and problems to boards of trustees or directors, stockholders, or legislatures. Research studies indicate that the typical age when persons become presidents of medium and large corporations is between 45 and 55.

As Beverly Kaye in her 1982 book, *Up Is Not the Only Way*, states, "our recruitment programs and cultural norms promote ladder-climbing as the one true career path. However, many individuals can and will find happiness in lateral movements within their organization, or movement among organizations." Although the occupational hierarchy described above is traditional in America, horizontal moves will probably become traditional in the future. According to former Executive Director of the College Placement Council Jesse M. Smith, in "Editorial," *Journal of Career Planning and Employment:*

> Organizations are becoming flatter or more horizontal in appearance as management levels are eliminated. Our society is heavily geared to promotion as a measure of success and achievement. As we move from a product society of the past to a service/information society, and experience the changing infrastructure, individuals will be forced to take more control of their own careers.

Smith's concept received further emphasis from Professor Shoshana Zuboff, associate professor at the Harvard Business School, when she stated in, *In the Age of the Smart Machine: The Future of Work and Power:* "The corporate hierarchy is dead, killed off by computers." The impact of computers and the increasing information technology makes work much more complex, causing many organizations to redesign their structure to emphasize the analysis, interpretation, and the integration of data. Further changes are undoubtedly forthcoming in our concepts of corporate responsibilities.

Professor William J. Horne of Boston College uses the chart originally developed by Keith Davis (see figure 15-12) to show his graduate students and persons attending executive seminars, how responsibilities change throughout the forty-plus working years. In the first few years after graduating from college a person can expect to spend about fifty percent of his or her time on "technical work" (utilizing the skills and abilities to get the work done);

Figure 15-12. Change in Responsibilities

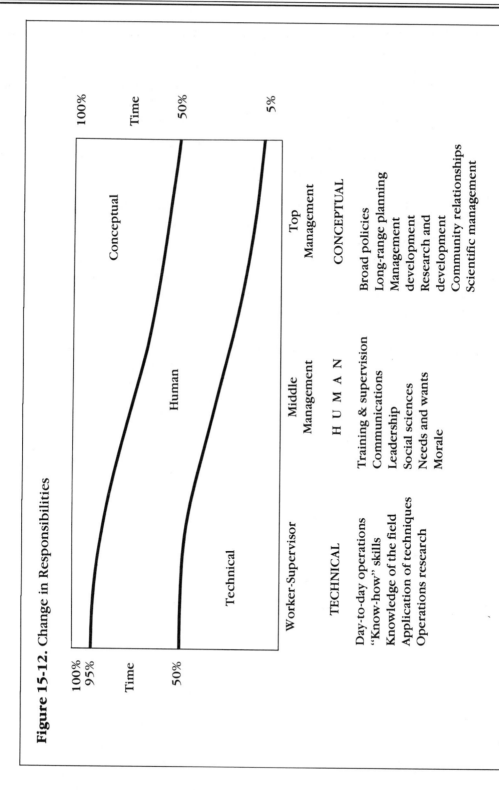

Source: Adapted from Keith Davis and John W. Newstrom, *Human Behavior at Work.* 1989.

forty-five percent of the time on human relationships (getting along and communicating with fellow workers and supervisors); and five percent on conceptual work (creative work like generating ideas). With upward progress, the emphasis shifts to more and more conceptual and human work—creating policies and programs, generating ideas, clarifying policies and procedures, developing motivational programs, and spending more time on people problems as compared to technical work.

Career planning can be summarized by decades and phases as follows:

The *twenties* are molding years, when you form those habits that will direct your career. You finish college training, start on a career, and may get married, and eventually buy a home. With few roots and responsibilities, this is the time to take chances and move around to get breadth of experience. If the job does not turn out well, get another job (or two or three) during the first decade of your working life.

The *thirties* are crucial to career development, being the period when you can make your greatest advancement and become a professional or get into management. You generally know what you can do, and you should work and study to gain more depth of experience in those areas of greatest use to you. This decade offers the greatest opportunities for career development as well as for personal and family growth.

The *forties* should see you at the peak of your profession and career, able to capitalize on your knowledge and experience and provide effective leadership. As one executive stated: "These are the years of vision, when a person finishes his or her castles in the air, and knows the value of his or her dreams."

The *fifties* should see the continuation of a successful career, with greater influence or clout on what should be done and how it should be done, and a maturing family providing personal satisfaction.

The *sixties* enable us to broaden our perspective considerably so as to appraise how our organization fits into society, determine which changes in direction and policies are needed (if any), spend more time on developing our successors, and provide more leadership in community activities.

One of the biggest responsibilities for all persons in management is to provide the type of environment that will encourage and enable employees to grow and be innovative so as to utilize their creative talents and bring them fulfillment. Since changes make employees uncomfortable, it is necessary to set high standards, expect peak performance, and affirm the individual's worth. If you aspire to top management in any organization, you must learn to be a self-starter and a self-manager.

Liberal arts graduates usually start their careers more slowly than do business or engineering graduates. However, they catch up in ten to twelve years and then move more quickly into middle and senior management positions. As cited earlier, the human and conceptual skills become more and more important as your career develops. Liberal arts training helps individuals appreciate and understand people and see overall relationships and ethical concerns. It also provides motivation for assuming leadership responsibilities.

As Dr. Charles Garfield stated: "Peak performers are made, not born. They learned the necessary skills to achieve success. All were mission-driven, challenge-driven individuals." In 1986, two men gave ample proof of this statement. One example was the nonstop, record-breaking solo trip around the world by Dodge Morgan (the first American to do so) who said: "Determination, dedication, and desire are necessary to realize your dream." Another example was the statement by Larry Bird when he received his third *Most Valuable Player* award in professional basketball: "The number one thing is *desire* to do the things you have to do . . . working at basketball is something I like to do." From the above three statements, people who are seeking security should realize that the only true security in any job or profession is based on one's ability (skill), productivity (performance), and flexibility in coping with change.

Occupational Hierarchy B

In some fields the normal occupational hierarchy includes four distinct stages. College graduates with professional training can apply their technical training immediately, and they don't stay in a trainee (apprentice) status very long. Figure 15-13 applies to such fields as engineering, advertising, medicine, law, media reporting, public accounting, nursing, and teaching. Many of these fields have professional practitioners who literally run their own business, which they call "their practice." Practitioners judge their growth and success by the increase in number of clients; the increase in billings; the number and volume of projects obtained; the expansion to statewide, regional, national, or international basis; the increase in sales or profits (if an entrepreneur); and

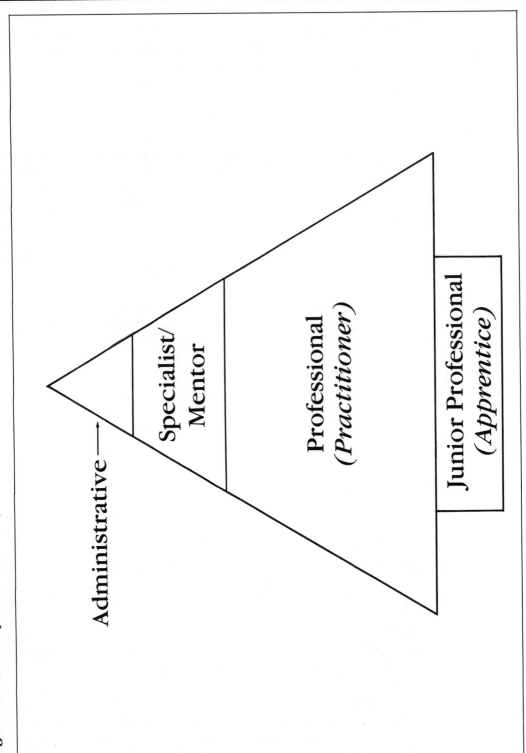

Figure 15-13. Occupational Hierarchy B

similar yardsticks. Personal growth or development depends much more on skill, competence, and reputation, rather than on age, and advancement is often horizontal more than vertical. In smaller organizations, practitioners often stress the psychic income as being more important than the paycheck.

Junior Professional

For the first year or two after college, the professionally trained graduate usually works under the supervision of an experienced professional in the field, similar to an apprenticeship. The initial assignments are relatively simple, with specific directions given regarding the objective: where to find resources, how to approach the task, what to look for, which activities require the greatest attention, what kind of report or result is expected, and who to see for background, assistance, or verification purposes. He or she needs to prove competence and future potential, and learn to give priority to the most crucial elements of the assignment. For career development purposes, it helps the young professional to find a good mentor.

Professional

At this occupational level a person is expected to demonstrate competence by handling almost any assignment, doing a thorough job, and obtaining the desired results. In many cases graduates spend the rest of their professional career at this occupational level, expanding on a horizontal basis instead of through vertical promotions. Thus the nature, variety, and responsibility of projects or assignments are increased, and there is less and less supervision given (if in a large organization). Employees rely more and more on their own initiative, technical competence, and know-how to get the job done. They need to gain confidence in their own judgment, and develop their own ideas and standards of performance.

Specialist/Mentor

As individuals learn more and more about a specific field, they become specialists and/or mentors. As an authority in that field, they handle only the most difficult cases or assignments, and are consulted by other professionals, clients, and individuals who wish to get an expert's advice or assistance. In this occupational classification, the professional is often called a consultant or project manager, and deals with individuals outside the organization to obtain contracts, resources, or project funds. Within the organization, mentors have a direct influence in guiding and developing employees' talents and careers.

At this level, the professional has to learn to take care of others, and finds "that he or she needs interpersonal skills in setting objectives, delegating, supervising, and coordinating . . . and now has responsibilities downward as well as upward. One has to conceive, sell, and direct a program."

Administrative

In all organizations some individuals remove themselves from day-to-day operations and transactions so they can concentrate on where the organization should be going instead of where it is at the moment. In this occupational level, people formulate broad policies, initiate programs and ideas, determine or approve job levels and pay scales, determine what products are to be produced or what services are to be provided, and chart a course to shape the future and the direction in which the firm is to go.

In our working vocabulary we usually refer to people in this occupational level as being in top management. This job level requires people who can bring resources, money, and talent into the organization, and who can represent the firm to the public and in key relationships outside the organization. Through the selection and development of key people, top management has a direct influence on the goals and effectiveness of the organization.

For individuals moving into this occupational level, they need to broaden their perspectives and lengthen their time horizons. Executives must learn to think about the needs of the organization beyond the time period during which they will be personally affected and to make long-range plans for the next five to ten years.

College graduates usually relate to both forms of occupational hierarchies. In academia they got used to four professional job levels: instructor, assistant professor, associate professor, and professor. They also experienced contact with various levels of administration from functional heads of service departments to deans and vice-presidents.

If you are going to a law firm, expect to serve an apprenticeship before you are acknowledged as a professional practitioner. Then go on to specialize in tax, labor, patents, or other legal fields. If you are anticipating a career in social work, know that you will have to begin as a caseworker before advancing to a social work professional. After medical school, doctors know they have to work first as interns in a hospital, then as resident physicians, and progress to practitioners before becoming specialists in surgery, orthopedics, internal medicine, allergies, cardiology, and so forth. Engineers start as junior engineers and then go on to become professional chemical, civil, electrical, industrial, mechanical or consulting engineers. Or, they go into management. In public accounting, college graduates start as junior accountants, go on to senior accountants, then principal or managerial accountants, or move to specialties, such as tax, estate planning, financial services, or management advisory services, and finally become partners.

Some professional organizations eliminate the job classification nonmenclature and use the simple I, II, III, or more, designated job levels. For example, most reporters have similar duties and responsibilities, so the grade levels (in Roman numerals) reflect their experience, skill, capability and resourcefulness, and the amount of independence or supervision given.

Obviously the age level for the different echelons of jobs will depend on the size of the organization, the practices in that industry and area (what is the competition doing), the national and local economy, internal policies on promotion, and of course the initiative, ambition, and performance of the individual.

Should You Change Jobs or Careers?

Warning Signs

Numerous signals or warning signs indicate that it may be time to consider looking for a new job or career. Today, Americans want not only a paycheck, but also fulfillment in their careers. More and more people need the satisfaction of achievement, rewards for their efforts, advancement possibilities, and recognition that what they are doing is really important, necessary, and a service to society.

If your boss and co-workers ignore you, and you are not getting your share of raises, promotions, or other recognition, then you have likely been frozen out. Sometimes you find that you have nothing to do, or have so many tasks that you cannot possibly do any of them well. Sometimes you may get no feedback, or get a poor job evaluation. All of these factors can contribute to various symptoms that are like flashing red lights on the job or career.

You have to be careful not to blame all of your problems on the job. The problems may be rooted elsewhere. Maybe the job dissatisfaction is just a smokescreen because it is easier to complain about work than to be honest with yourself and admit that the problem may be caused by your marriage, your role as a parent, your relationship with relatives, the fact that the job is really too big for you, or other personal reasons Staying with a job that no longer fits your needs and talents can be very stress-producing. Be alert for a number of telltale signs that indicate when it is time to consider looking for a new job or career. Probably the first symptom is reluctance or a dread of going to work, followed by a prevailing sense of ennui, which can lead to a feeling of depression. Such a mental state could easily lead to warning signals like sleeplessness, back pains, upset stomach, trouble at home, and a loss of self-respect, self-confidence, or identity.

To Stay or Change Employment

Suppose you have been in charge of your own career and have applied most of the suggestions given in this book and other references, yet you are not getting promotions or satisfaction. What then? Should you change employers, or try to stay where you are and hope for the best? Sooner or later every individual has to face the big question—should I stay with this employer, or seek a job elsewhere? You should sense when it is time to change. If part of the problem is you, perhaps there is something you can do to help remedy the situation. In any event, you would be wise to first examine some warning signs and compare the advantages and disadvantages of staying with your present employer or changing. Figures 15-14 and 15-15 cite some reasons for staying with or for changing jobs.

In an interesting article written primarily for women, Elizabeth Keiffer states, "A variety of circumstances push women into new fields, but these are the most common reasons they cite:

1. Economic necessity. Nearly two-thirds of all working women are single, separated, divorced, or widowed, or are married to men who earn less than $10,000 a year.

2. Changing marriage patterns. An increasing number of unmarried women face the likelihood of remaining single and look to their jobs for financial support and emotional fulfillment.

3. Shrinking markets. In some traditional women's fields—such as the apparel and textile industries—jobs are simply disappearing.

4. Plateauing. Many women are finding that they cannot get beyond a certain level in their careers; they have to move sideways to advance.

Figure 15-14. Reasons for Staying on the Present Job

Although each individual must appraise his or her own desires and satisfactions, there are a number of resons to warrant staying with your present employer.

1. If the organization has a strong promotion-from-within policy, you have excellent chances for advancement.

2. If the organization has strength, stability, and growth, you will probably have a good future there.

3. If you are trying to escape problems, stay. There is an old saying, "it's better to deal with the devil you know than with one you don't know."

4. If you have been getting salary increases and/or other evidence of appreciation of your work, it is obvious that your superiors are pleased and will likely promote you when the opportunity becomes available.

5. If you are restless, remember that several studies conclude that those who remained with the same employer for ten years are earning more than those who change several jobs. Be patient!

6. If you want to avoid the label of being a job-hopper, since this has a negative connotation.

7. If you like the benefits package of your present employer, stay. It may take time to qualify for similar benefits with another employer, and you may find that another employer does not have as good a program of hospitalization and life insurance, athletic facilities or employee activity programs, profit-sharing plan (in business organizations), educational assistance, and so forth, as your present employer has.

8. If you want to capitalize on your knowlekge and experience, you will probably get recognition quicker where people know you, as compared with developing a favorable reputation with another employer.

9. If you are happy with your co-workers and the working environment.

5. Burnout. This occurs particularly for women in human-services jobs such as teachers, nurses, and social workers who feel they are always giving, without receiving the recognition and money they deserve.

6. Relocation. When their husbands are transferred to a new area, many working wives are unable to find work in their former occupations."[2]

---

[2]Keiffer, Elizabeth. "Bored? Burned Out? Underpaid? Switch Careers." In *Woman's Day*, 1987.

Figure 15-15. Reasons for Changing Jobs

For the great majority of college graduates, the first job after graduation is merely a stepping-stone to greater opportunities. Some of the more pertinent reasons for changing jobs and organizations include:

1. If you need to relocate because of health or family problems, or because the commute to work through heavy traffic becomes too nerve-wracking.

2. If you need to diversify your experience to facilitate your professional growth. More and more people are experimenting with different careers.

3. If you need a bigger challenge than your present job or future jobs on that payroll may offer. Frustration affects motivation; if you can't go any further in your organization, try something new or different.

4. If you need to improve your acceptance. For example, joining the faculty where you received your degree(s) will often result in being treated as a student with little recognition for your ideas or suggestions. A liberal arts graduate in a public accounting firm may get the feeling he or she is a second-class employee. Another working environment may be more conducive for you to develop your initiative and career.

5. If your organization is weak and you can see the handwriting on the wall for a reduction in force.

6. If you are offered an attractive new job in another organization with a healthy increase in compensation and an interesting challenge.

7. If you have reached the ceiling for the salary range in your present job and for its responsibilities, and there are too many able young people ahead of you, or too few additional rungs up the promotional ladder.

8. If you are willing to pay the price of moving, starting anew to make friends and meet new co-workers, developing a favorable reputation in a new environment, and playing a greater role in your organization and in society.

9. If your boss is unreasonable in loading you down with more and more tasks and responsibilities without increasing compensation, or expects you to work so much overtime it affects your personal/family life.

10. If you need work that has more meaning for you and would help you utilize more of your talents, thus satisfying your need for fulfillment and self-identity.

Ms. Keiffer goes on to state that it's time to consider switching to a new career when:

You can't live on your salary.

The job you have offers no satisfaction.

You want more challenge, responsibility or recognition than your work allows.

You feel exploited, either emotionally or financially.

You're hopelessly stuck on a plateau.

A field that has long intrigued you is opening up to women.

Word of Warning

One word of warning is appropriate for anyone contemplating a change in jobs or careers; beware of the "greener grass" problem. When people get tempting job offers, the experience is similar to looking at the grass on the other side of the fence. It looks better and greener, but as we get closer to the field, we see that it is full of weeds. It is wise to look carefully and investigate fully before leaping into a new job environment. Talk with the person who left the job you're seeking to find out what kind of environment you can expect in the new job. Some people are always looking around, and thus never develop a reputation for stability or loyalty.

As we get older, we get more concerned with retirement benefits. "People who change jobs frequently lose retirement earning power each time a job switch is made. The value of many small pensions never equals the value of one large pension reflecting a full career in a single pensioned covered job. As a result ... employees may lose up to 50% of their retirement benefits through job changes."[3]

If and when you decide to make a change in either job or career, start planning a job campaign as described in the preceding chapters. A main difference in future job searches will be the emphasis on the experience you have gained, and the achievements you have accomplished. In researching the job market, the value and extent of your network will be much more important because such contacts will be of more assistance now than they were when you were graduating from college. Construct a timetable for your new career so that you can readily recognize landmarks to appraise your progress (or lack thereof) in the future.

Whenever you make a job or career change, be prepared to experience some depression in the first few months and some second-guessing thoughts about whether you made the right decision to change.

---

[3]Reprinted with permission of the *AARP News Bulletin*, Sept. 1987.

Concluding Remarks

In the United States we have more freedom of choice than other countries enjoy. Individuals are relatively free to do what they want, to work in any type of job or industry or location, to change jobs and/or careers, and to adopt any life-style they wish. Every citizen has many alternatives, a choice that is denied to most people throughout the world. Planning the various steps in your career will enable you to take advantage of the many opportunities for self-improvement, and make all those choices meaningful to you.

This book has emphasized the importance of career planning. It has provided concepts, principles, strategies, and descriptions of resources to enable you to understand how to build and develop a vocational life, a career. Applying these principles and utilizing this knowledge should enable you to make better use of your talents, find out what works best for you, help you cope with change, progress in your career in such a way that you will achieve your personal goals in life, and gain fulfillment and satisfaction.

Most people know that a successful financial plan must be both personalized and current, then constantly updated to reflect changes in tax laws, the market, the economy, and personal circumstances. To be successful, your career plan also requries a personalized approach with constant updating to reflect changes in legislation, in the job market, and in personal circumstances. With attention to career planning, you will be able to have the flexibility and the peace of mind to cope with life's ongoing cycle of never-ending changes.

But remember, *you* must be the driver!

Examples of Career Timetables

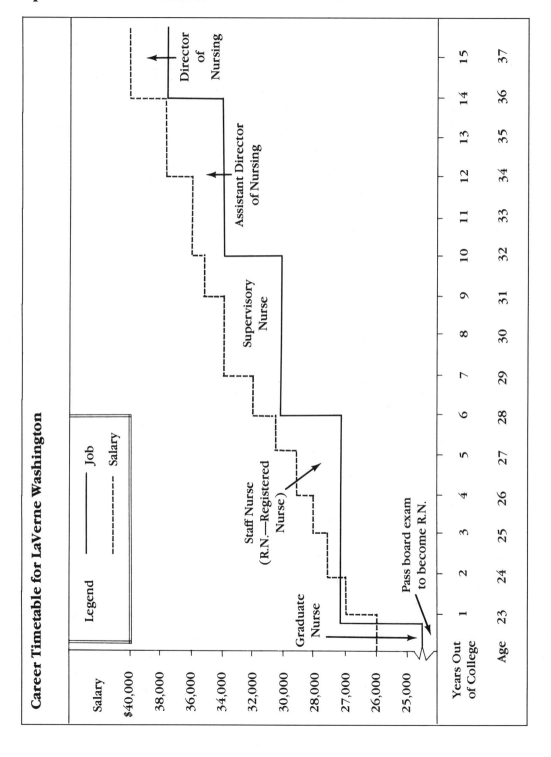

Career Timetable for LaVerne Washington

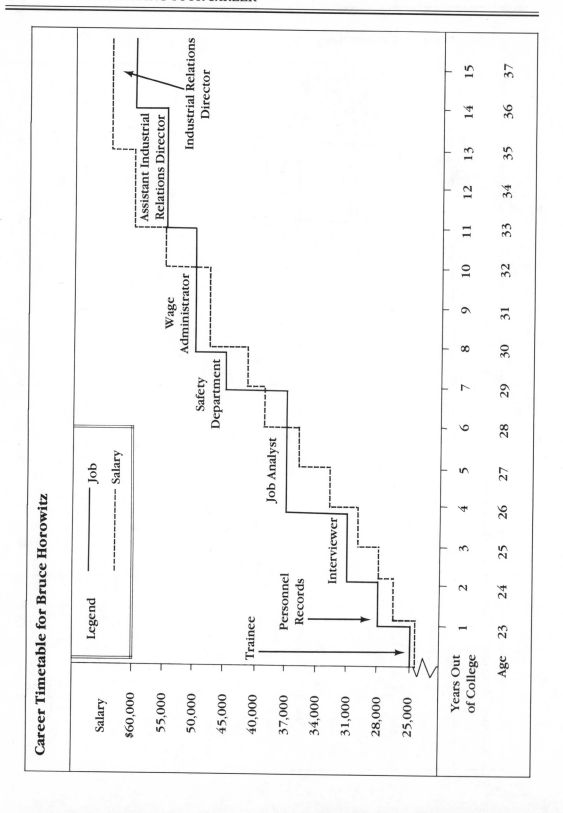

Career Timetable for Bruce Horowitz

Legend
——— Job
- - - - - Salary

Salary

$60,000
55,000
50,000
45,000
40,000
37,000
34,000
31,000
28,000
25,000

Years Out of College: 1 2 3 4 5 6 7 8 9 10 11 12 13 14 15
Age: 23 24 25 26 27 28 29 30 31 32 33 34 35 36 37

Trainee
Personnel Records
Interviewer
Job Analyst
Safety Department
Wage Administrator
Assistant Industrial Relations Director
Industrial Relations Director

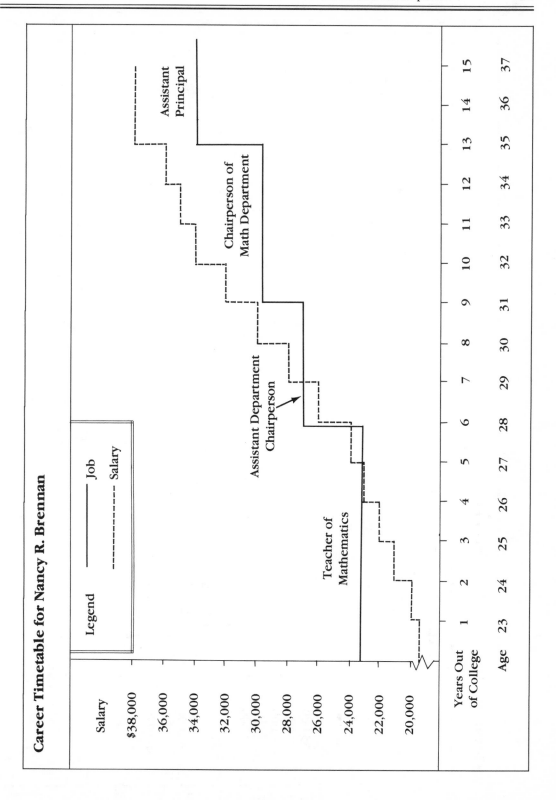

Career Timetable for Nancy R. Brennan

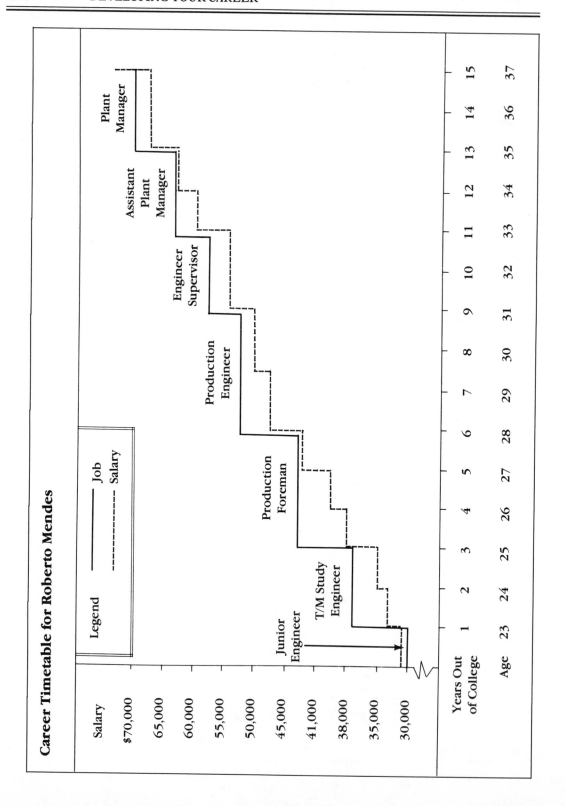

Career Timetable for Roberto Mendes

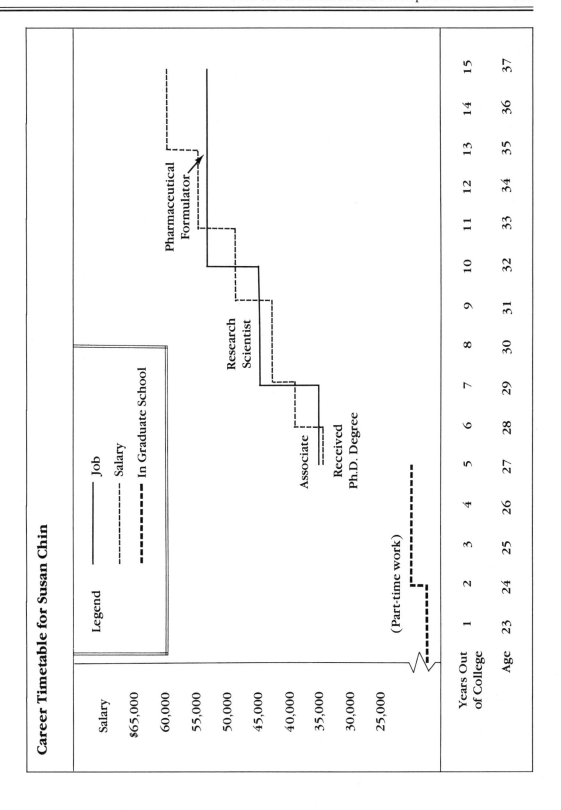

Career Timetable for Susan Chin

Appendix A
Theories of Career
Planning

As Assistant Dean C. Randall Powell of Indiana University's Business Placement Office states, in *Career Planning Today*, 2nd edition, vocational theories are important because "they help us understand the *how* and *why* of certain life sequences that assist in the selection of appropriate occupational endeavors. A theory shows a systematic relationship between certain variables and helps define relevancy. A theory helps you understand why you make certain career decisions."

Theories can be based on research to show a systematic relationship used to predict facts or a course of action, such as was done by our scientists and engineers to put a man on the moon. They also can be based on empirical experience to support a proposed course of action, such as the counseling given by practitioners in college career centers. To date, the formulation of vocational theories has been dominated by psychologists, but professionals in the college career planning and placement field are providing pragmatic applications of their own theories. This section features three theories by practitioners in the college career planning and placement field, and the excerpts from some of the major psychologists' thinking on occupational choice. Understanding these can help you better utilize career counseling and make better occupational choices.

The Roadmap Theory

This theory was initiated and developed at Boston College to help students realize how their experience in planning a vacation can benefit them when planning a career. In classroom and personal counseling sessions, we found this theory is easily understood by students, and it adds a little fun and anticipation to their career planning efforts.

The *Roadmap Theory* states that career planning is a step-by-step process that invites you to discover your talents and interests, to ascertain where to use them, and to plan the years after college to both fulfill your personal life and make a valuable contribution to society.

To achieve most objectives in life, you have to follow certain processes or procedures. Students usually remember the multi-step process they went through to get their driver's license. First comes a driver's education course and study of the driver's manual. Then comes success on a written test that leads to a learner's permit. This is just the beginning, however.

Next comes practice with an experienced driver; and the tiresome hassling with parents or friends for additional driving experience. Then there is the memorization and practice of the rules of the road involving side streets, expressways, and parallel parking between cars that seem to leave too little room.

After your confidence reaches a certain level, there is the road test with an official inspector. The words, "you passed," bring much elation, but even that is not the last step. You still have to return for your official, multicolored, plastic-coated license bearing your picture.

All of these steps took you weeks or months just to get your driver's license and the accompanying satisfaction of having done it (primarily) on your own. Planning a career is a similar step-by-step process, but it generally takes and warrants much more of your time.

Let's look at career planning another way, by comparing it to planning and taking a cross-country vacation. Few people would jump into their cars and start driving. It would be much wiser to first select a destination, then get the car checked over to avoid any breakdowns that might spoil the trip. You would need to estimate how much cash to take, or make sure you have widely accepted credit cards. Making motel reservations or contacting friends for anticipated stops would facilitate the journey and avoid many frustrations.

Your chosen destination and the time of the year will help you anticipate the weather and potential activities that will dictate whether to pack sleeping bags, skis, bathing suits, hiking shoes, tennis rackets, or golf clubs. Let's assume you have chosen San Francisco as your destination, and you will drive from Boston and back. You would have several options in your vacation travel planning, but let's assume that you decide to take the northern route. Perhaps there is rainy weather as you leave Boston, head across Massachusetts, and get on the New York Turnpike. By the time you reach Syracuse, fatigue makes you decide to check into a motel for the night and start out again in the morning. Such a change in your first day's destination does not alter your vacation plan—only your time schedule.

The next day you're back on the Turnpike and heading for Buffalo. As you get closer to that city you notice many signs for Niagara Falls. Since you always wanted to see them, you take a detour. By the time you get back on the Turnpike to Buffalo, an extra half day or more has passed. Such a detour would affect your time schedule, but not your long-range vacation plan.

You continue west toward Cleveland and remember a friend at The Ohio State University whom you have not seen for some time. You decide on another detour—driving to Columbus, visiting your friend, and looking over that giant Big Ten university.

The next morning you check over the car, review the map to get back on a major highway, and start for Chicago. The day following you would start for Minneapolis, continue for the next few days to Denver, and eventually arrive at San Francisco. You will have traveled the approximate route that you had planned, made some changes, probably encountered some delays en route, but made some detours that actually enriched the trip.

If it is helpful to plan for a trip, how much more important is it to plan for your life—to anticipate your career needs! Let's apply this vacation plan to your vocation, your career. Now is the time to plan, during your college years. Start packing!

Have you identified the threads of personal interest that run through your life? Have you evaluated your strong points, your skills, your abilities, what you do well, enjoy the most? Are you beginning to get a good idea of *who* you are, *why* you are in college, and *what* life-style you desire? Have you realistically looked at your future needs for income, status, independence, and location? Have you begun to research different possible career paths?

When you've started to get a feel for the direction in which you wish to go, check on the degree credentials you might need and which department's courses will give you these credentials. What part-time and summer job experiences will be useful to such a career? What extracurricular activities would help prepare you for your career? What skills need to be sharpened—communications, academic, social? Start planning now, so that when you graduate you are packed and ready to go.

The first job you take after graduating from college is like the road from Boston to Syracuse. Maybe you run into rough weather—the job isn't what you thought it would be, you don't like your supervisor, or you don't like all the travel that is required. While you feel all this to be delaying the development of your career plan, it would not be wise to quit too soon, so you survive this troublesome period and continue working on job #1.

As you reach another landmark in your plan, you decide that you need another kind of work experience and take a detour on your career highway by taking job #2 (similar to the Niagara Falls detour). You then start back on your career plan with job #3.

At a certain point in your work you may decide that you want or need some graduate training, so you take another detour to study for a master's degree. (This would be similar to taking the detour from Cleveland to Columbus on the vacation trip). Once you get the master's degree, it would be a good idea to reassess your career needs and desires before looking for job #4. At this time it may be more practical to start on a different career highway going in another direction, or you may decide to return to your original plan by taking job #4 (going to Chicago in our vacation example trip).

Over a period of years, job #5 will bring you to the equivalent of Minneapolis, job #6 to Denver, and so forth. Periodically, you should take inventory to see if you are on the right career road, changing jobs or careers until you reach your career objective (your destination—San Francisco in our vacation trip example).

The important thing to remember, whether we are talking about a cross-country vacation trip or your personal career plan, is that *you are the driver!* As the driver, you determine how enjoyable and satisfying the trip can be. It is the same with jobs and careers. You can utilize various jobs to pick up different skills or experiences, take time out to earn a graduate or professional degree, change careers, and take in the sights as you go along.

This theory also empasizes the fact that the trip itself may be the goal, rather than the destination, so enjoy today's and tomorrow's steps along the way. Not all people want to advance to the top management position in an organization. Jack Falvey, in his recent film, *What Have You Done for Yourself Lately?*, "challenges viewers to develop within their current jobs rather than seeking to leave them behind—to seek professionalism as a career goal, not just advancement." In his film he shows viewers that "personal fulfillment in a job is as valid an objective as career advancement, that it's OK to like your job, and that staying in a position does not mean stagnation."

Over the forty-plus years between college graduation and retirement, you can make your career go the way you want it to. Remember, you are in the driver's seat!

The Economic Theory

Parents are especially interested in this theory as the basis for planning a career. Students who work their way through college or earn a significant portion of college expenses are also very interested in this career theory, which is founded upon the high cost of a college education, and a desire to get an appropriate return—to capitalize on the investment. Of all the motivation behind higher education, its expected economic value is probably the most obvious to Americans.

Cost of College

Parents and students are especially aware of the constantly increasing cost of a college education. At present the average cost per year ranges from around $5,000 in some small public colleges, to around $15,000 in private colleges. In the New England area, especially among the Ivy League colleges, the costs are even greater, going up to $20,000 per year.

In its Annual Survey of Colleges, the College Board estimates the cost of tuition, room and board, books and fees generally increases from five to eight percent each year. College administrators find that this inflation rate is usually one and one-half percent higher than the Consumer Price Index (CPI) because schools are labor-intensive institutions and spend more on salaries in proportion to other expenses.

A specific example of the inflationary cost of a college education is indicated by one school's history. In 1959, the annual tuition was $800, and room and board and other school expenses were $1,350, for a total cost per year of $2,150 or over four years, of $8,600. During the 1988-89 school year, the annual undergraduate tuition was $10,760, room and board averaged $3,030, books and other expenses $2,380, for a total package of $16,170 per year, or $64,680 for four years. At this private institution, which is *not* included in the most expensive schools, the cost over the past thirty years has increased seven and a half times!

The above costs reflect only direct expenses; to figure the true cost of a college education, it is necessary to also include the "opportunity costs," what individuals would earn if they were not attending college. Assuming a young person would work forty hours a week at a minimum wage of $3.50 per hour, a gross income of $140 per week, or $7,280 per year, would be earned. A more accurate picture of total costs (assuming an average of $12,000 for direct expenses) would include the following:

Figure A-1. Total Costs of College

Costs	Average
Direct Costs	$12,000
Wages lost per year	+ 7,280
Annual cost of college	19,280
Four years in college	x 4
Total cost of a college education	$77,120

The above figures reflect the approximate average current costs throughout the country. Obviously a college education is very expensive and therefore deserves considerable thought and attention. The financial burden emphasized in the above figures plus inflation factors, add credence to the economic theory desiring an adequate return on such a sizable investment.

Competition

In addition to the constantly increasing cost of college, another factor emphasizing the economic theory is the growing competition as indicated in the number of degrees that are granted annually in the United States, and in the changing work force. As indicated in figure A-2, the number of bachelor's degrees granted annually is almost 1,000,000 per year. In 1950, three times as many men received bachelor's degrees as did women (328,841 to 103,217), but in 1986 women surged ahead with 501,900 as compared to men's 485,923 degrees.

One of the most interesting results of competition is signified by the increasing percentage of degrees granted for graduate work. Earlier, a person could assume that the education he or she received in youth would serve well all of his or her life. However, because of the explosion of knowledge, which once required centuries to double but now doubles every ten years or less, people have found it necessary to devote more and more time and money to education.

As indicated in figure A-2, the increasing numbers and percentage of graduate degrees granted reflect the competition in the last

Figure A-2. Number of College Degrees Granted in the U.S.A.

Year	Bachelor's	First Professional*	Master's	Doctor's	All Degrees
1920	48,622	- - - - - - - -	4,279	615	53,516
1930	122,484	- - - - - - - -	14,969	2,299	139,752
1940	186,500	- - - - - - - -	26,731	3,290	216,521
1950	432,068	- - - - - - - -	58,183	6,420	496,671
1960	392,440	- - - - - - - -	74,435	9,829	476,704
1970	792,316	34,918	208,291	29,866	1,065,391
1980	929,417	70,131	298,081	32,615	1,330,244
1986	987,823	73,910	288,567	33,653	1,383,953

*(Until 1970, the first professional degrees were included with the bachelor's degree numbers.)

Source: *Digest of Educational Statistics*, 1987. Center for Statistics, U.S. Department of Education, Table 116, p. 141.

three decades. In 1950, the total number of graduate degrees granted came to 13.0 percent of all college degrees granted; in 1986, the graduate degrees granted were 28.6 percent of all college degrees granted. With the growing emphasis on technology, the trend toward graduate degrees seems to be inevitable.

The competition from graduate degree holders is only one of the increasing number of factors affecting the careers of college graduates. From a national viewpoint, the reflections of the College Placement Council's Executive Director Warren Kauffman are worth noting. In a recent editorial he noted that one of the latest phrases to join the list of overused words in our profession's lexicon is "job turbulence." Since so many people in today's working world leave or change jobs, either voluntarily or involuntarily, individuals find that job turbulence places a premium on flexibility and adaptability. Kauffman summarizes some of the phenomena that are currently important to college students and recent graduates, as well as employers and career advisors, as follows:

- Fewer 18- to 24-year-olds.

- More baby boomers with fewer opportunities as they move up the management ladder, leading to disenchantment and displacement.

- Minorities becoming majorities.

- More than half of jobs held by women.

- A mobile labor force with reduced job security—hence reduced organizational loyalty.

- Most people working for small employers.

- A significant number working part-time.

- A service economy with lower-paying jobs, resulting in the first generation with a lower standard of living than their parents.

- Twenty percent of college graduates having to settle for jobs not really requiring college degrees.[1]

---

[1]Kauffman, Warren E. "Perceptions." *Journal of Career Planning and Employment*, winter edition, 1988.

Income

The economic theory also emphasizes potential lifetime income, and its relation to education. Since a college degree is required for many high-paying jobs, it is no surprise that there are clear economic advantages in the attainment of post-secondary degrees. In addition to increasing earnings, a college education provides more security for employment purposes, as illustrated in figure A-3.

One of the most difficult decisions that students in college have to make, is the choice of a major. The perceived economic rewards that may accrue from a degree in the chosen field is an important factor to consider. Degrees in the fields of law and medicine are generally associated with some of the highest incomes. A comparison for several other fields of study is shown in figure A-4. In round numbers, a college graduate in most fields can expect to earn at least a million dollars during his or her working lifetime. Surely this amount is enough reason for serious thinking about a career plan!

If we multiply the annual salary figures in the CPC Salary Survey by 43 (the number of working years between graduation from college and traditional retirement at age 65), we can get a projected lifetime income for the selected fields of study as indicated in figure A-4. These figures are actually too low because inflation and salary raises will produce higher results.

Figure A-3. Unemployment Rates by Level of Education in U.S.

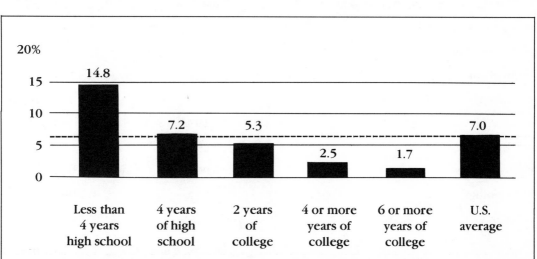

Source: "Educational Attainment of Workers," March 1987. U.S. Dept. of Labor, Bureau of Labor Statistics.

Figure A-4. Income for 1989 College Graduates, by Field of Study

Field of Study for Bachelor's Degree	Average Annual Offer	Projected for Lifetime (Minimum)
Accounting	$25,290	$1,087,470
Agribusiness	23,177	996,611
Biology	20,998	902,914
Business administration	22,274	957,782
Chemical engineering	32,949	1,416,807
Chemistry	26,698	1,148,014
Communications	20,761	892,723
Computer science	28,557	1,227,951
Economics and finance (including banking)	24,649	1,059,907
Electrical engineering	30,661	1,318,423
Elementary education	18,578	798,854
History	21,275	914,825
Information sciences and systems	26,853	1,154,679
Journalism	19,595	842,585
Management information systems	26,861	1,155,023
Marketing	22,523	968,849
Mathematics	26,789	1,151,927
Mechanical engineering	30,539	1,313,177
Nursing	24,789	1,065,927
Pharmacy	35,173	1,512,439
Physics	28,296	1,216,728
Psychology	19,061	819,623
Sociology	19,021	817,903
Average for above fields	$25,016	$1,075,686

Source: *CPC Salary Survey Report*, July 1989.

The Talent Theory

This theory is based on the story in St. Matthew's Gospel, chapter 25, verses 14-30, wherein the owner was going on a long journey and called his servants together. He gave five talents to one servant, two talents to another, and one talent to a third servant, with instructions to manage them well.

When he returned from his trip he called the servants in to give an account of their actions. The one who received five talents had gained five more, was commended by his master, and given a promotion. The servant receiving two talents had gained two more, was also commended by his master, and given a promotion. The third servant hid his one talent and returned it to his master, who was so disappointed with the results that he took the talent from the servant, gave it to the one who had ten talents, and reprimanded the third servant.

A modern-day application of the above story was given recently by Dr. Norman Vincent Peale, one of the most noted preachers of our century and author of *The Power of Positive Thinking, Power of the Plus Factor,* and many other publications. Dr. Peale encourages people to do the best they can with whatever talent they have, and to believe in themselves. By having faith in their abilities, people can realize their full potential.

From a career planning viewpoint, the above examples can be interpreted to accentuate the need for each of us to utilize whatever gifts or talents (the modern term is skills and abilities) we have, not only for our own good, but also for the benefit of others. For persons who are not motivated by money but who are altruistically inclined, this theory has great appeal. Psychologists tell us that most people use only fifty percent of their abilities; supervisors in all walks of life would undoubtedly appreciate a greater number of employees who would utilize more of their talents not only in performing their own jobs more efficiently, but also in helping other employees and in doing worthwhile deeds for their community.

Psychologists' Theories

A number of interesting vocational theories are provided by consulting psychologists. Every student who is serious about careers, and every person who contemplates a career as an advisor in the career planning and placement field, should at least be acquainted with the principal features of the theories promulgated by some of the better-known psychologists.

Parsons

In 1909, Frank Parsons propounded what is generally accepted as the oldest theory of vocational choice, commonly known as the trait-factor approach. This system assumes that a matching of an individual's abilities and interests with the world's vocational opportunities can solve the problem of vocational choice for that individual. This theory consists of three steps:

1. Understand self (your assets, liabilities, and preferences).

2. Acquire knowledge of jobs.

3. Match up the above two.

The simplicity and accuracy of the above theory is still very practical today, and provides a good foundation for understanding some of the more complex theories developed later.

Strong

In 1943, Dr. Edward Strong promulgated a theory that is based on the assumption that occupations involve work activities, that people employed in a certain occupation hold interests similar to other members of that occupation, but have interests different from workers in other occupations. His Strong Vocational Preference Test has been expanded and has incorporated other theories, especially Holland's hexagon, into the present Strong-Campbell Interest Inventory. This inventory gives information about one's interests in doing various things, and relates such data to the interests of people in a variety of careers. Because this test is so widely used in colleges to counsel students, more details are provided in chapter 6.

Ginzberg

In 1951, Dr. Eli Ginzberg and several colleagues at Columbia University proposed a theory of occupational choice which was defined as a process of development, or the self-concept theory.

This theory is based on the assumption that an individual is largely passive in the process of choosing a career, typically reacting to various events and forces and thus gravitating into an occupational field that becomes one's career.

This theory is based on three major concepts that form a person's vocational choice: process, irreversibility, and compromise.

Process
Because career development changes over various periods in one's lifetime, the process generally can be broken down into three periods:

Fantasy stage.   Youngsters before age eleven generally role-play what they wish to become as adults. They are often influenced by the models or attitudes of their parents, and by glamour or recognition of fields such as firefighters, astronauts, doctors, or teachers.

Tentative stage.   During the years of eleven to seventeen, individuals begin to develop some values, while additional interests emerge, evolving into making choices that frequently change. During this time, individuals begin to realize that there are some things they do better than others, and the problems of deciding on the type of work or career is influenced by the fact that certain activities have more value than other activities.

Realistic stage.   During the 18 to 22 years (typical of college students), individuals begin to realize that compromises have to be worked out between what they want and the opportunities available. They begin to integrate their interests, values, abilities, and competencies by selecting a specific major in college or a special field of graduate work.

Irreversibility
Because of crises, health and family problems, financial or other significant obstacles, the choice of an occupation often becomes irreversible in terms of expenditure of time and resources. Such pressures cause emotional, financial, and other realistic hindrances to making a change in careers.

Compromise

Within the realities of personal, family, and job problems, individuals tend to compromise their vocational choice. What usually happens is that they try to select a field of work that satisfies many of their interests, utilizes some of their abilities, provides satisfactory financial remuneration, and brings sufficient fulfillment of their personal goals and values.

Thus the individual tries to choose or is forced into an attempt to balance his or her abilities, skills, interests, and values against job and career alternatives as new information or experience is obtained. Although this theory allows for career changes, individuals obviously have to build on earlier experiences and career achievements, often resulting in compromises and trade-offs.

Others

In 1954, Anne Roe, Abraham Maslow, and their associates stated the theory that vocational choice is based on satisfying our basic needs such as self-approval, affection, mastery or achievement, creativity, economic security, independence, helping others, and status. Motivation is attributed to the intensity of needs—the greater the need, the more effort one puts into satisfying it.

Super

In 1957, Dr. Donald Super's book developed the theory that career choice is the end product of development over a long period of time—a process—and that value goals are crystalized many years prior to graduation. Thus choosing and developing a career is a synthesizing and evolutionary process, striving for compatibility between one's chosen occupation and a person's interests and needs. Super's theory segregates life into several stages:

1. *Growth*—typically the childhood years.

2. *Exploratory*—a floundering process going from fantasy, to tentative, to realistic attempts to develop and implement a self-concept, and activities that test the reality and transition from school to the working world.

3. *Establishment*—a period of modifying one's self-concept, getting started on a job that leads to a career, striving for achievements in one's chosen field so as to establish credibility and confirm the career choice.

4. *Maintenance*—activities preserving one's self-concept, advancing in the chosen career, and bringing a sense of being settled.

5. *Decline*—the years wherein individuals are nearing retirement, have to make adjustments for a new self, and think of what advice and experience they should pass on to the younger persons in their organization and family.

Holland

In 1959, Dr. John Holland first formulated his theory in a journal article. After some encouraging research he made a more systematic formulation of his theory in 1966 by writing a small book entitled, *Making Vocational Choices: A Theory of Careers.* Basically, the theory states that there is an interaction between personality and environment, and that people gravitate toward an environment that is congruent with their personal orientations. As Dr. Holland states: "We can characterize people by their resemblance to each of six personality types...and the environments in which people live can be characterized by their resemblance to six model environments: realistic, investigative, artistic, social, enterprising, and conventional."

Holland developed an instrument called the Self-Directed Search (1974), which helps individuals ascertain which people and environments would be most compatible and permit them to develop their abilities and careers. Holland's six personality and environment types are usually depicted in a hexagon:

Realistic
People in this category enjoy activities requiring physical strength or skill, aggressive action, and motor coordination. They prefer dealing with concrete, well-defined problems as opposed to abstract, intangible ones. Careers appealing to this type of person include engineers, farmers, forest rangers, mechanics, and production managers.

Investigative
People in this category are inclined to be analytical and inquisitive, tending toward careers and environments that require intellectual, independent, and "thinking" activities in such careers as physical and biological scientists, computer designers and programmers, mathematicians, college faculty, and writers of scientific articles or journals.

Artistic

This category includes people who are independent, creative, intuitive, imaginative, impulsive, and idealistic, and have a great need for original self-expression. Typical careers include artists, designers, musicians, actors, advertising staff, dancers, and architects.

Social

In this category are people who have verbal and interpersonal skills; are more susceptible to social, humanitarian, and religious influences; and prefer to deal with others by being friendly, helpful, and cooperative. Typical careers include workers in religion, social welfare, personnel, nursing, and recreation.

Enterprising

This group is characterized by people who possess leadership and speaking ability, and see the world in terms of power, status, setting of goals, managing an organization, and otherwise assuming responsibility. Typical career fields include owners and managers of a business, sales, consultants, lawyers, politicians, and diplomats.

Conventional

This group is characterized by the dominance of environmental demands that require law and order, and where goals, tasks, and values are sanctioned by custom and society. People have traits such as conforming, being orderly, efficient, practical, and self-controlled. Preferred careers include accountants, tax experts, office workers, librarians, bankers, business and economic professors, and supply officers.

Holland introduced a concept known as *self-knowledge*, which refers to, "The amount and accuracy of information an individual has about himself. It differs from self-evaluation, which refers to the worth the individual attributes to himself."

There are a number of other theories of vocational choice, all of which provide the concept needed for understanding the importance of early career planning. Most of the theories emphasize the developmental process, appreciating the compromises that have to be made, and acquiring as much occupational knowledge as possible in order to make a sound career decision.

For students, counselors, and others who may be interested in a comprehensive review and evaluation of research on vocational choice, development, and behavior, *Theories of Career Development* by Samuel H. Osipow is highly recommended.

Appendix B
Principles for
Professional Conduct

T he career planning, placement, and recruitment process is a vital, integral part of the total educational experience. Therefore, it is essential that those involved in the process be governed by a set of professional ethics. The College Placement Council is the nationally recognized professional society in this field. Periodically CPC has a committee review, study, and update the standards in our field. The following principles are intended to serve as current guides for professional conduct.

Principles for Career Planning

Career planning is an ongoing process that has become increasingly critical to an individual's success in attaining desired goals. The career planning function rests on a philosophical foundation consistent with the basic developmental theories of vocational choice and the free enterprise system.

Colleges and Universities

- Assist individuals in developing a career plan without exerting undue influence.

Career planning is an educational process dedicated to the student's self-realization and self-direction. The counselor should not impose personal values or biases, nor encourage decisions based on insufficient data. Any conflicts of interest should also be acknowledged and examined at once.

• Be knowledgeable in the career planning field.

Practitioners should possess: appropriate education; experience in career planning; counseling skills; the ability to deal effectively with students, faculty, administrators, and employers; and the capacity to teach and do research in the career planning field.

• Be well-versed in administering and evaluating assessment tools.

The career planning practitioner should: have an adequate understanding of the characteristics being measured to assure selection of the most effective testing tools; administer and interpret tests only within the range of the practitioner's professional knowledge; educate students so they understand the purpose and limitations of all test results; and keep all results confidential.

• Provide a comprehensive program that includes all pertinent campus resources without charge.

Career planning practitioners should identify, mobilize, educate, train, and coordinate the various personnel involved in the career planning process. These resource personnel should also abide by the same principles and practices set forth in this document.

The career planning function is an integral part of the education process and it is recommended that students should not be charged for professional services.

• Ensure confidentiality and accuracy of information.

Such data as referrals, records, and career information should only be disseminated in a professional, unbiased, and accurate manner with the consent of all parties involved.

• Encourage and follow nondiscriminatory practices.

Career planning practitioners should be prepared to provide competent assistance to all students regardless of background. This includes those who do not fit a majority pattern in terms of age, disability, socioeconomic status, or other irrelevant variables.

- Help fulfill the educational mission of the institution.

Career planning practitioners have a responsibility to offer assistance in establishing priorities of the college or university and reaching the institution's stated objectives. While their primary concern is the career planning needs of the individual student, counselors are ultimately accountable to the institution, and to that institution's educational mission.

Employers

- Provide accurate, unbiased information without charge.

In this way, employers can best serve students, and help them to make intelligent, informed decisions about which career path is right for them. Materials should be presented in an unbiased, ethical, and responsible manner, drawing generalizations beyond the employer's organizations whenever possible.

- Possess a thorough knowledge of the employer's organization and industry.

To be effective in their career planning involvement with students, employers should be well-versed in the career opportunities available in their field. Employers should also demonstrate how academic preparation can be applied to the "world of work."

- Become involved in the career planning process.

Employers should be responsible for becoming a part of the process. To accomplish this they should: develop campus contacts with faculty and student groups; expose the college community to their organization through tours, career days, on-campus speakers, research projects; alert career planning and placement offices and faculty to employment trends which have curricular implications; and develop cooperative education programs and other experiential work that would enable students to gain experience in their chosen fields.

All the above activities should be coordinated through the career planning offices and should have no "strings" attached.

- Honor the policies and procedures of individual institutions.

Employers should not expect preferential treatment from career planning personnel, and should abide by the institution's rules and administrative practices. Any deviation from normal could seriously impugn the integrity of both the employer and the institution.

Students/Clients

- Take responsibility for their own actions in the career planning process.

Students/clients should acknowledge responsibility for their actions when involved in experiential opportunities and their own career decisions. They should also take the initiative to involve themselves in the career planning process.

- Present accurate personal information.

Falsifying data is not only unethical, but might also hamper the overall self-assessment, career exploration, and decision-making process.

- Honor the principles and procedures of the institution.

Students/clients should be sure to notify the career planning office of any related activities undertaken independently.

Principles for Placement/Recruitment

As the placing of students has taken on greater importance over the years, the influence of placement practitioners has increased proportionately. This elevation in status has thrust upon the profession certain responsibilities relating to ethics and principles of conduct.

Colleges and Universities

- Establish and monitor practices which ensure the fair and accurate representation of students and the institution in the recruitment process.

Placement practitioners should also encourage such accuracy in other offices of the institution as well. Examples of unethical practices are: condoning misrepresentation of information on student resumes; knowingly permitting students to continue the interviewing process after notification that they have accepted an offer; knowingly permitting students to utilize the interview process strictly for practice or for purposes other than those acceptable to the recruiting organization; knowingly permitting students to interview with recruiting organizations for which they would be ineligible for hire.

• Provide the placement office's professional services to students without charge.

The placement function is an integral part of the education process, and the institution's support of such services is a necessity. Although rising costs stretch academic budgets, it is recommended that students should not be charged for routine services. However, charging students fees for services they would ordinarily pay for, such as copying and mailing, is acceptable, as long as the charges are based on actual production and postage costs.

• Make the placement facilities and support services available to employing organizations without charge.

On-campus recruiters offer a wide variety of career opportunities, which encourage and support the students' decision-making process. Charging for routine services may adversely affect the working relationship between recruiting and placement practitioners, and might encourage recruiters to pressure placement offices for services not in the best interest of students or the institution.

Fees charged for special services, such as job fairs, etc., should not exceed costs. Soliciting funds for special projects is also considered acceptable.

• Promote and follow nondiscriminatory practices.

Students' rights should not be infringed upon by unethical or illegal dissemination of information. No information covered by federal or state laws should be disclosed to any organization without the student's written consent. Organizations should also be advised that student information cannot be disclosed to another party without additional written consent.

- Protect the candidate's freedom of choice in selecting a career or position from undue influence by faculty, administrators, and/or recruiters.

When assisting students in examining career options, practitioners should not impose personal values or biases on candidates, nor encourage decisions based on insufficient data.

- Inform students of obligations they will incur, both financial and otherwise, when utilizing the services of agencies or other organizations performing recruiting services for a fee.

Where policy permits such organizations to interview students on campus, placement practitioners should require an advance copy of their contracts and a description of all fees and services. Students should be told to read this information and be aware of all its provisions before signing any contract.

Employers

- Be responsible for the ethical and legal conduct of the organization's representatives throughout the recruiting process.

Questions that are illegal, discriminatory, or unrelated to the selection process should not be asked, nor should candidates' opinions of other candidates be solicited. Sharing of candidate information with other organizations without prior written approval of the student is unethical.

- Assume responsibility for all representations made by authorized representatives.

Honor all commitments made, and respond to candidates in the time frame mutually agreed to. An authorized representative should not misrepresent a position being offered. All offers should be confirmed in writing and copies should be sent to the appropriate placement office.

Reimbursements for travel expenses associated with an authorized plant visit should be equitable and prompt. The organization should not impose undue hardships on the candidate when planning the visit.

- Utilize only qualified, informed interviewers to represent the organization.

Selection and training of recruiters is a key aspect of the college recruiting process. Recruiters should be well prepared to conduct effective interviews.

- Respect the legal obligations of placement offices, and request only those services or information that legally can be provided.

Only valid criteria should be used as screening devices. Recruiters also should not disclose confidential information to students, such as information obtained from the student's references.

- Honor the policies and procedures of individual institutions.

Recruiters should not expect preferential services from placement personnel and should abide by the institution's rules and administrative practices. Examples of unacceptable practices by recruiters are: failing to honor commitments; arriving late and/or leaving early; failing to adhere to the interview schedules established; failing to notify the placement office of changes far enough in advance to avoid undue hardship on the office or candidates involved.

- Refrain from any practice that adversely affects the interviewing and decision-making processess.

It is in the best interest of candidates, colleges, and employers that the consideration of careers and the selection of opportunities be based on an understanding of all relevant facts. The open and free selection of opportunities is a basic principle of the placement and recruitment field, and all recruiting practices should support this principle.

Recruiters should not subject candidates to undue or excessive pressure to accept offers. The time frame for decision making should be mutually agreed upon by both parties. It is incumbent upon both parties to keep each other informed of their status.

Special inducements, such as offering or soliciting gifts to gain favor in student referrals to extract preferential treatment, adversely affect the recruitment and decision-making process, and are considered unethical. However, contributions for legitimate projects are acceptable, so long as no special consideration is expected in return.

All commitments, oral or written, should be honored by all parties. Recruiters should refrain from making any unauthorized commitments during the interviewing process.

Organizations should be prepared to honor all offers extended. Any inference that only the first acceptances received will be honored is unethical.

• Make a full and accurate presentation of all relevant information during the recruiting process.

Misrepresentation of any aspect of employment is unethical. Recruiters should notify students and the placement office in advance whether they are interviewing for anticipated hiring purposes or to maintain an image or presence on campus.

• Advise the placement office of all recruiting-related activities not conducted through that office.

Organizations should not recruit through student associations or academic departments without the support and/or knowledge of the placement office. This practice tends to undermine the placement function, reducing its effectiveness as a recruiting service to students and its support to the recruiting organization.

• Honor an employment offer that is accepted as a contractual agreement.

Employers should not withdraw accepted job offers, but should honor all such commitments.

In the event of severe economic changes or other conditions requiring exceptions to this principle, the organization should initiate discussions with the affected placement office at the earliest possible time. Further, the organization should pursue a course of action for affected candidates which is fair and equitable.

All offers to students should be confirmed in writing. Organizations should notify placement offices of all offers when extended to students of their institutions and job acceptances as received.

Candidates

• Honor the institution's policies and procedures.

Candidates and student groups should coordinate with the placement office any activities involving organizations that will recruit on campus.

• Prepare for the recruiting process and accurately present qualifications and interests.

Candidates are responsible for reading the organization's recruiting materials and completing required forms prior to the interview.

Falsifying data, such as GPA, date of graduation, major/minor, institutions attended, and eligibility to work in the United States, is not only unethical but may be grounds for dismissal if the candidate begins employment with the organization.

- Sign up for interviews only when genuinely interested in the position for which the organization is interviewing.

Interviewing for practice takes advantage of recruiters and limits interviewing opportunities for other students who may be sincerely interested in the opportunities being offered by the organizations.

- Adhere to the interview schedules.

If the candidates must cancel, they should notify the placement office well in advance so that other students may have an opportunity to interview.

An invitation for a plant/office visit should be acknowledged promptly, regardless of the student's decision; it should only be accepted when the candidate has a sincere interest in that employer. If a scheduled plant/office visit needs to be changed or cancelled, the candidate should notify the organization far enough in advance to alleviate any undue hardship or expense.

- Notify organizations of the acceptance or rejection of offers by the earliest possible time and no later than the time mutually agreed upon.

Candidates should expect offers to be confirmed in writing. Likewise, candidates should respond in writing to offers with acceptances or refusals as soon as they make their decisions, regardless of the deadline date. If candidates have legitimate reasons for extended consideration of offers, they should contact employers whose offers they are considering to establish mutually satisfactory decision dates. Candidates are expected to respond to all organizations whose offers they have received.

- Honor an accepted offer as a contractual agreement. Withdraw from the interviewing process and notify the placement office, as well as other organizations with offers pending.

Continuing to interview after accepting an offer, or reneging on accepted offers, is unethical. If a candidate encounters problems after accepting an offer, the circumstances should be discussed with a placement official and the organization which tendered the offer.

- Expect reimbursement of expenses incurred during plant/office visits for only those expenditures pertinent to the trip.

Candidates should discuss expected costs with the organization's recruiter. Information should be clarified in advance, including class or mode of travel, entertainment, automobile rental, lodging, accommodations, and food arrangements. If other organizations are visited on the same trip, the candidate should inform the organizations involved and prorate the costs.

Recommended Problem-Solving Procedures

Questionable practices or problems involving recruiters, college and university personnel, or candidates should be addressed as follows:

- Discuss the incident with all affected parties as quickly as possible to determine the specifics of the situation and explore alternative courses of action.

- Attempt to resolve the incident among the affected parties.

- Refer unresolved concerns to the supervisors of the involved parties or other appropriate officials.

- Obtain additional information on resolution procedures from the appropriate regional association and/or the College Placement Council, Inc.

Conclusion

Adherence to these principles will facilitate a mutually satisfying relationship among colleges and universities, employers, and candidates. The recruitment process should be fair and equitable to all, with large and small organizations having equal access to candidates, and candidates having the maximum exposure to opportunities available.

References

AARP News Bulletin (September 1987): 8.

ACCRA Cost of Living Index, 4th quarter, 1987.

Akin, James N. "Average Salary Reports for Teachers." *ASCUS Research Report* (1989): supplement.

Akin, James N. "Relative Demand by Teaching Area." *ASCUS Annual* (1989): 8.

Austin, William. "Opportunities in Franchising." *Occupational Outlook Quarterly* (Fall 1986): 18.

Baum, Laurie. "The Fine Art of Job Satisfaction." *Career Vision* (April 1989): 75.

Boettcher, Richard E. Statement in *PERI–Newsletter,* Public Employees Retirees, January–February 1986.

Bolles, Richard N. *What Color Is Your Parachute?* Berkeley: Ten Speed Press, 1976.

Brown, Newell. "Are You an Occupational Ignoramus?" Bethlehem, PA: The College Placement Council. Leaflet.

Calvert, Robert and John E. Steele. *Planning Your Career,* "Advantages of Large and of Small Employers." New York: McGraw-Hill Book Co., 1963.

Chaffee, John. "Outstanding New Englander Ken Curtis: Foreign Trade Begins with Canada," *Connection,* (Spring/Summer, 1987), p. 18.

Davis, Keith and John W. Newstrom. *Human Behavior at Work,* 8th ed. New York: McGraw-Hill Company, 1989.

Delaney, William A. "Your First Job After College." In a talk to Boston College seniors.

Dennis, Donn L. "Why College Recruiting?" *Journal of Career Planning and Employment* (Fall 1985): 42.

Dictionary of Occupational Titles. U.S. Department of Labor, 1977.

Doriot, Georges F. From a booklet distributed at his memorial service in Boston on September 22, 1987.

Dorsey, Anne M. "How To Create a Winning Ad Campaign for the Career Center." *Journal of Career Planning and Employment* (Winter 1986): 40.

Dreyfus, Lee S. In a speech at the Eastern College Personnel Officers annual conference. Reprinted in *ECHO,* fall 1985.

Eckberg, Arthur R. "Stalking the Elusive Job." *CPC Annual* 1 (1984–85): 13.

Embee Chips. Employee magazine of the New Britain Machine Company.

Emerson, Dorothy May. *Myers-Briggs Type Indicator* (MBTI), rev. ed. Austin, TX: Luzader & Company Original Communications, 1982.

Encyclopedia of Associations, 23d ed. Detroit: Gale Research Inc., 1989. Three volumes.

Encyclopedia of Careers and Vocational Guidance, 6th ed. Chicago: J.G. Publishing Company, 1984. Volumes 1 and 2.

Falvey, Jack. *What Have You Done for Yourself Lately?* Watertown, MA: EFM Films.

Falvey, Jack. *What's Next? Career Strategies After 35.* Charlotte, VT: Williamson Publishing Company, 1987.

Figler, Howard E. *The Complete Job-Search Handbook.* New York: Holt, Rinehart and Winston, 1979.

Figler, Howard E. *PATH: A Career Workbook for Liberal Arts Students.* Cranston, RI: The Carroll Press, 1979.

Fountain, Melvin. "Matching Yourself with the World of Work." *Occupational Outlook Quarterly* (Fall 1986): 6–7.

Garfield, Charles. In his keynote speech before the CPC National Meeting, Nashville, May 1986.

Graduating Engineer. New York: McGraw-Hill Publications Company, 1986.

Groennings, Sven. "New England in a World Economy." *Connection* (Winter–Spring 1987): 5–9.

Holland, John L. *Making Vocational Choices: A Theory of Careers.* Englewood Cliffs, NJ: Prentice-Hall, Inc., 1973.

Jobst, Katherine. *1987 Internships.* Cincinnati: Writers Digest Books.

Kaplan, Rochelle K. "When an Employer Says Yes, . . . And Then Says No." *Journal of Career Planning and Employment* (Winter 1986): 48–54.

Kaplan Test Preparation Program. Stanley H. Kaplan Educational Center, Ltd.

Kauffman, Warren E. "Perceptions." *Journal of Career Planning and Employment* (Winter 1988) 3 and 6.

Kaye, Beverly. *Up Is Not the Only Way.* San Diego: University Associates, 1982.

Keiffer, Elizabeth. "Bored? Burned Out? Underpaid? Switch Careers." *Woman's Day* (September 1, 1987): 68.

Kilby, Jan E. and B.J. Bryant. "The Academic Job Search for Graduate Students in Education." *ASCUS Annual* (1981): 11–13.

Kotter, John P., Victor A. Faux, and Charles C. McArthur. *Self-Assessment and Career Development.* Englewood Cliffs, NJ: Prentice-Hall, 1978.

Krasna, Jodi C. *The Official Guide to MBA Programs.* Princeton, NJ: Educational Testing Service, 1988–90 ed.

Litt, Benjamin. "Life-Work Planning for the Individual in a Changing World." *Journal of College Placement* (Winter 1984): 58.

Longcope, Kay. "A Lab for Detecting Hidden Aptitudes." *The Boston Globe*, September 19, 1985, pp. 73–74.

Maine, University of. "Workshop Schedules." *Placement Manual* (1986–87): 4–5.

Marland, Sidney P. *Career Education.* U.S. Department of Health, Education, and Welfare. Publication No. (OE) 73-00501, pp. 1–2.

Massachusetts, University of. *Placement Manual* (Fall 1986): 7.

Menninger, Walter. In his speech before the annual meeting of the Midwest College Placement Association.

Monan, J. Donald S. J. In his annual message to parents during Freshman Parents Weekend, Boston College.

National Association of Entrepreneurial Couples. P.O. Box 3238, Eugene, OR.

National Directory of Personnel Consultants. Alexandria, VA: National Association of Personnel Consultants, 1987.

Occupational Outlook for College Graduates, 1980–81 ed. U.S. Department of Labor, Bureau of Labor Statistics, Bulletin 2076, p.iii.

Occupational Outlook Handbook, 1988–89. U.S. Department of Labor, Bureau of Labor Statistics.

Osipow, Samuel H. *Theories of Career Development.* New York: Meredith Corporation, 1973.

Powell, C. Randall. "Career Planning Theory Sets the Foundation." *Career Planning Today.* Dubuque, IA: Kendall/Hunt Publishing Company, 1990.

Powell, C. Randall. "Forty Action Ideas for Advancement."

Powell, C. Randall. "Infosearch Interviewing."

Reich, Charles A. *The Greening of America.* New York: Random House, Inc., 1970.

Rosovsky, Henry. "Undergraduate Education: Defining the Issues." *Dean's Report 1975–76.* Harvard University.

Ryan, Bob. "A Short-Order Rook." *The Boston Globe*, December 11, 1985, pp. 89 and 93.

Shingleton, John D. "The Economics of the Job Market." *CPC Annual* 1 (1989–90): 15–20.

Shingleton, John D. "Estimating Job Demand by Field of Study in 1989–90." *CPC Annual* 1 (1989–90): 17.

Shingleton, John D. "Sources of New College Hires." *CPC Annual* 1 (1989–90): 20.

Shingleton, John D. and Robert Bao. *College to Career: Finding Yourself in the Job Market*. New York: McGraw-Hill Book Company, 1977.

Sinnott, Patricia A. "A New Image for the Federal Government." *Journal of Career Planning and Employment* (Winter 1988): 28–31.

Smith, Jesse M. "Editorial." *Journal of Career Planning and Employment* (Winter 1986).

The Standard Industrial Classification Manual (S.I.C.). U.S. Office of Management and Budget, 1987.

Standard & Poor's Register of Corporations, Directors, and Executives. New York: McGraw-Hill Publications Company, 1989.

Stanton, Michael. "Playing for a Living: The Dream Comes True for Very Few." *Occupational Outlook Quarterly* (Spring 1987): 2–15.

Strong-Campbell Interest Inventory. Stanford, CA: Stanford University Press.

Tackett, Anna A. "Using Your Career Planning and Placement Office." *ASCUS Annual* (1983): 2–3.

Toffler, Alvin. *Future Shock*. New York: Bantam Books, Inc., 1970.

Trask, William F. "Stall Letters." *Placement Manual*. Worcester, MA: Worcester Polytechnic Institute, 1986.

Welch, Mary Scott. "Networking: The Great Way for Women to Get Ahead." New York: Harcourt Brace Jovanovich, 1980. As quoted in "Making the Best Connections," by Martha Osmun, *Business World Women*, 1982.

Westvaco Career Opportunities. College recruiting brochure, New York.

Wood, Orrin G. Jr. "Approaching the Hidden Job Market," in *Your Hidden Assets*. Homewood, IL: Dow Jones-Irwin, 1982.

Wright, Edmond F. "Wine Glass Examples of Management Levels." In a talk to alumni of Harvard Business School.

Wright, John W. *The American Almanac of Jobs and Salaries*, 1987–88. New York: Avon Books, pp. 683–686.

Zuboff, Shoshana. *In the Age of the Smart Machine: The Future of Work and Power*. New York: Basic Books, 1988.

Index